TRAVELER

the
mediterranean

TRAVELER

the
mediterranean
ports of call & beyond

by Tim Jepson &
the National Geographic Travel Team

National Geographic
Washington, D.C.

CONTENTS

TRAVELING WITH EYES OPEN 6

CHARTING YOUR TRIP 8

■ **History & Culture** 12
The Mediterranean Today 14   Mediterranean History 18
Feature: Food & Drink 22   Arts & Culture 24

■ **Coastal Spain** 28
Barcelona 32   Málaga & Granada 49   Valencia 57   Balearic Islands 59

■ **French Riviera & Provence** 64
Marseille & Provence 68   Cannes & St.-Tropez 76   Nice & Around 78
Monaco 84

■ **Italian Riviera & Tuscany** 86
Genoa & the Coast 90   Florence 94   Pisa 112   Lucca 114
Siena 116   San Gimignano 118

■ **Rome & Naples** 120
Rome 124   Bay of Naples 144   Capri 152   Amalfi Coast 156

■ **Sicily, Malta, & Puglia** 158
Sicily 162   Malta 170   Puglia 174

■ **Venice & the Adriatic** 178
Venice 182   Split 206   Dubrovnik 208   More Ports to Visit
on the Adriatic 216

■ **Athens & the Islands** 218
Athens 222   The Peloponnesus 236   The Islands 240   Crete 244

■ **Turkey** 248
Istanbul 252   Ephesus 268

TRAVELWISE 272
Restaurants 274   Shopping 304   Cruise Lines 307
Language Guide 308

INDEX 311   **CREDITS** 318

Pages 2–3: The view from Mount Srđ overlooks Dubrovnik and its walled Old Town.
Opposite: Architectural gems such as the ornate bridge over Carrer del Bisbe Irurita pepper
the narrow stone lanes of Barcelona's Barri Gòtic, the historic Gothic Quarter.

TRAVELING WITH EYES OPEN

Alert travelers go with a purpose and leave with a benefit. If you travel responsibly, you can help support wildlife conservation, historic preservation, and cultural enrichment in the places you visit. You can enrich your own travel experience as well.

To be a geo-savvy traveler:

- Recognize that your presence has an impact on the places you visit.

- Spend your time and money in ways that sustain local character. (Besides, it's more interesting that way.)

- Value the destination's natural and cultural heritage.

- Respect the local customs and traditions.

- Express appreciation to local people about things you find interesting and unique to the place: its nature and scenery, music and food, historic villages and buildings.

- Vote with your wallet: Support the people who support the place, patronizing businesses that make an effort to celebrate and protect what's special there. Seek out shops, local restaurants, inns, and tour operators who love their home—who love taking care of it and showing it off. Avoid businesses that detract from the character of the place.

- Enrich yourself, taking home memories and stories to tell, knowing that you have contributed to the preservation and enhancement of the destination.

That is the type of travel now called geotourism, defined as "tourism that sustains or enhances the geographical character of a place—its environment, culture, aesthetics, heritage, and the well-being of its residents." To learn more, visit National Geographic's Center for Sustainable Destinations at *nationalgeographic.com/travel/sustainable.*

TRAVELER

the
mediterranean

ABOUT THE AUTHOR

Based in London, **Tim Jepson** has been a passionate and lifelong devotee of Italy and a regular visitor by both land and sea to the beautiful Mediterranean coast. He has written some 15 books on the countries around the Mediterranean, as well as many articles for the *Daily Telegraph, Vogue, Condé Nast Traveller,* and other publications. For National Geographic he has written the following guides in the National Geographic Traveler series: *Italy, Florence & Tuscany, Naples & Southern Italy, Piedmont & Northwest Italy,* and *Sicily.* He is also the co-author of the *National Geographic London Book of Lists.*

Charting Your Trip

Try to invent a region to be seen from the sea, and it's unlikely you'd come up with anything better than the shores of the northern Mediterranean. No other region in the world offers the wealth of art, culture, history, food, and landscape found here. This in turn obviously makes it a superb area to visit by boat, either traveling on your own or on a chartered vessel or, more likely, aboard a cruise ship. As a result, planning, more than usual, is an essential part of your trip.

Where to Visit

The clue is in the name: "Mediterranean," from the Latin *mediterraneus,* meaning "between lands" or "in the middle of the earth"—for this is effectively a vast inland sea bounded by the continents of Europe, Asia, and Africa. Numerous countries ring its shores and countless islands dot its waters. Individual countries, even individual cities, are places you could visit any number of times, with the scope for sightseeing and excursions almost limitless.

This guide focuses on the northern coast of the Mediterranean, stretching from the British territory of Gibraltar—where the Strait of Gibraltar, just 8.7 miles (14 km) across, provides the Mediterranean's only western access by sea—to Turkey. It covers Spain's eastern coast, then heads east along the French Riviera, circles around Italy, runs down the Adriatic coastlines of Slovenia and Croatia to Greece, and cruises over to Istanbul and the west coast of Turkey.

Along the way it touches on the islands of **Mallorca** (Majorca), **Menorca** (Minorca), **Eivissa** (Ibiza), **Sicily, Malta, Corfu, Crete,** as well as a couple of smaller Greek islands.

Cities & Regions

Along these coasts are ports of call with myriad charms and attractions—**Valencia, Barcelona, Nice, Genoa, Palermo, Dubrovnik, Athens, Istanbul,** to name a few— as well as easy access to outstanding inland cities and sights. Thus **Málaga** in Spain is convenient for **Granada** and its stunning Alhambra; in France,

Olive oil characterizes the cuisine of nearly all the Mediterranean countries.

Marseille for **Provence** and the towns of **Arles, Aix-en-Provence,** and **Avignon,** and **Nice** for **Cannes, St.-Tropez,** and **Monte-Carlo; Livorno,** in Italy, for the Tuscan jewels of **Florence, Siena, Lucca, Pisa,** and **San Gimignano; Civitavecchia** for **Rome; Naples** for **Capri, Pompeii,** and the **Amalfi Coast;** and **Kuşadası,** Turkey, for the Roman ruins at Ephesus.

Exploring Beyond a Port of Call: From each port of call, you can easily see much of the region by car or train, as major roads and railroads closely follow the coasts of Spain, France, Italy, Greece, and Turkey.

Cars are a liability in most cities, but railroads are excellent ways to get around, with many high-speed options in Spain (renfe.com), France (sncf.com), and Italy (trenitalia.com), and rail lines that take you to stations at the heart of the cities you want to see. Railroads also often offer quick and convenient ways of reaching inland destinations, such as Florence from Livorno or Avignon from Marseille.

Cruising the Mediterranean

Given the northern Mediterranean's attractions, it's no wonder that this is the world's second most popular multicountry cruising destination after the Caribbean. The fact that it is also a compact region means that cruising is a great way to see a lot in a short time—you can be in one city for breakfast, another for lunch, and yet another for dinner.

At the same time, be careful that cruises don't become whirlwind tours, with a day or less visiting cities in which you could happily spend a fortnight such as Rome or Venice. This is particularly true on seven-day cruises, so look for cruises

NOT TO BE MISSED:

Barcelona's Barri Gòtic quarter and La Sagrada Família **36-37 & 44-45**

Granada's Alhambra **50-54**

Cannes's glitzy promenade, La Croisette **76**

Piazza del Duomo, the religious heart of Florence **96-100**

Vestiges of ancient Rome **125-132**

Naples's Museo Archeologico Nazionale and Pompeii **145-146 & 149-151**

A trip down the Canal Grande in Venice **182-184**

Diocletian's Palace, Split **206-207**

A stroll along Dubrovnik's medieval walls **210-211**

The Acropolis, Athens **222-226**

Istanbul's Topkapı Palace, Hagia Sophia, and Blue Mosque **252-260**

Best Time to Visit

The main Mediterranean vacation season runs from May to October, with peaks in July and August (when many Europeans vacation, too), but many of the most celebrated cities, especially in Italy, are busy almost year-round. Avoid July and August if possible, when the crowds and high temperatures (86°-90°F/30°-32°C, or higher the farther south you go) across most of the region make sightseeing unpleasant. Off-season visits have the advantages of less busy cities, lower prices, and kinder temperatures for sightseeing: Rain can be an issue in spring (March-April), but fall (Sept.-Oct.) tends to be dry with mild weather.

Online Information

Official city and regional tourism websites, along with transit sites, are given in the text, but as a starting point visit the official sites of individual countries: **Spain,** *spain .info;* **France,** *franceguide.com;* **Italy,** *italia.it;* **Malta,** *visitmalta.com;* **Slovenia,** *slovenia.info;* **Croatia,** *croatia.hr;* **Greece,** *visitgreece .gr;* and **Turkey,** *goturkey.com.*

that overnight in key ports, allowing you a little more time on land, or choose longer voyages if you want more time sightseeing or relaxing on board or at sea.

The region's popularity can also be a problem. Most cities visited by cruises are also cities visited by many other travelers: Venice, for example, is busy at the best of times; when a big cruise ship pulls in, things can become very busy indeed (see sidebar p. 9).

Cruise Itineraries: The Mediterranean's popularity means there is a huge choice of cruises and itineraries, so you usually can find a trip that combines your preferred ports of call. All the major cruise companies offer itineraries to the region (see Travelwise p. 307).

On the whole, shorter (seven-day) and mid-length itineraries divide between the western Mediterranean (Gibraltar and Spain, including the Balearic Islands, the south of France, and down Italy's west coast) and the eastern Mediterranean (Italy's Adriatic coast and Venice, Slovenia, the Croatian coast, Greece and its islands, and Istanbul and the west Turkish coast).

The division is blurred around Italy, where "western" cruises that run from Genoa and/or Civitavecchia (Rome) to Venice may visit Sicily as well as Bari (Italy), Malta, Corfu (Greece), and the Croatian ports of Dubrovnik and Split.

Which Ship?: Once you have decided between different areas of the Mediterranean, you will still be confronted by a vast choice of ships and itineraries. When trying to choose a trip, identify the main cities you want to see, but also look at an itinerary's lesser known ports and let those help shape your decision.

Larger ships will have more onboard facilities and diversions, a consideration on longer cruises or if you're traveling with children; they may also offer a wider and more unusual selection of excursions. In addition, as they tend to visit the region's key cities, they may also be better for a first-time Mediterranean cruise.

Shore Excursions

Even travelers unfamiliar with European cities should feel confident about organizing their own sightseeing in cities where ships dock close to the center. For the sake of a short walk, or a cheap transit ticket, you will save money on cruise excursions. Beware, though: Research and book reputable local operators before you travel. Save time using cruise or shore-based excursions where cities, regional attractions, and other themed excursions are some distance from the port. At the end of each major sight in this book you'll find a "NEED TO KNOW" detailing, among other things, port logistics, suggestions on how much time to allocate to big-city highlights, and how to set out beyond the port of call. With all excursions, bear in mind the need to be back at your ship in time for departure.

Warm azure waters and beautiful scenery draw beachgoers to Greece's shores.

But note that bigger ships (1,600 passengers and up) can only dock at the biggest (and busiest) ports and cities, or at smaller ports where a lot of time will be lost to security checks and tendering to shore.

Cruises aboard smaller ships are usually more expensive, but they often offer more unusual or intimate destinations. This is especially true in Italy, where you might stop in Sorrento (as opposed to Naples), Portofino (instead of Genoa), or Bari (for visits to Puglia). Smaller ships also visit more intimate French Riviera, Balkan, and Balearic Island ports.

Planning Your Trip

If you are flying in and out of the Mediterranean for your trip, especially if it's a cruise, consider booking extra nights in your start and/or finish cities. Many cruises depart from or conclude in Barcelona, Venice, and Civitavecchia (Rome), three standout cities, so it makes sense to add a day or two to give them at least some of the time they deserve.

Many cruise companies offer air-hotel packages for these extra days. These can be more expensive than booking the components yourself, but there is likely to be more support on the ground, useful if you are unfamiliar with the cities in question.

If you intend to sightsee independently, be sure to go online to book sights that offer or require timed-entry tickets. If you don't, you will endure long lines year-round, especially in Granada (for the Alhambra), Florence (entry to the Galleria degli Uffizi and Galleria dell'Accademia for Michelangelo's "David"), and for several sights in Rome.

If you intend to do a lot of sightseeing, also visit official city tourist websites for details of money-saving transit and multisight entry passes. ∎

History &
Culture

The Mediterranean Today   14–17

Mediterranean History   18–21

Feature: Food & Drink   22–23

Arts & Culture   24–27

**Inside Istanbul's sixth-century Hagia Sophia,
first a basilica, then a mosque, now a museum**

The Mediterranean Today

The powerful strands of geography, history, and culture across thousands of years have ensured not only that the destinies of countries around the Mediterranean have been tightly interwoven, but also that the past continues to exert a profound effect on many aspects of the region in the present day.

The Mediterranean throws up many conundrums. How could it be otherwise in an area with so much history and so many peoples and nations? For most visitors, the biggest conundrum lies in the fact that we come to see the region's past but are obliged to deal with its present.

Near Sorrento, a departure point for a road tour around Italy's dramatic Amalfi Coast

The glories of the past, of ancient Greece and Rome, of history's most resonant names and places, and the artistic wonders of some of the greatest cities on Earth is why many come to the Mediterranean, and a grasp of the region's history will help you make the most of a visit.

A Region of Regions

A visit to Spain or Italy is never simply a visit to a single country, for in the Mediterranean there are differences between people who live only an hour apart—for example, Florentines see themselves as different from their nearest neighbors, the Sienese—never mind in different countries.

Similarly powerful regional identities are repeated across the Mediterranean, a result of long ethnic, cultural, and historical encounters. Florence and Siena, for instance, are cities that were at each other's throats for several centuries in the Middle Ages, while Italians are a relatively recent phenomenon, citizens of a country that was only created in 1861. Long enough ago, you would think, to be of little contemporary relevance. Not so.

Yet even in a region as diverse as the Mediterranean . . . you'll find that shared past experiences have profoundly shaped modern sensibilities.

A country like Croatia has what appears to be an even more recent history, created in 1991 after the collapse of Communism in the West. Yet this was an ethnically and administratively coherent kingdom as long ago as the tenth century. As a result, a country that you might expect to be unsure of its identity is actually one whose culture, language, religion, and more are all deeply ingrained.

At its most benign, as in Florence and Siena, the Mediterranean's regional differences amount to little more than vocal support for the local soccer team. But at the other extreme are the separatist ambitions of the PKK—Turkey's Kurdistan Workers Party—or the violent nationalist divisions that brought Croatia itself into being after the breakup of Yugoslavia.

Somewhere in the middle is a semiautonomous region like Catalunya (Catalonia), in Spain, where, after years of being marginalized by the state, many inhabitants now champion their regional roots, proud Catalans as much as, or more so than, proud Spaniards.

The People

Yet even in a region as diverse as the Mediterranean, from English-speaking Gibraltar, with its British postboxes and warm beer, to Istanbul, with its mosques and Oriental bazaars, you'll find that shared past experiences have profoundly shaped modern sensibilities.

One of these is poverty. In the Mediterranean, the vast proportion of people belonged to impoverished agricultural communities until a generation or so ago. Most were shackled to harsh southern Mediterranean landscapes—olives, vines, and sun-drilled mountains—and tied to ways of life and dreams of emigration that remained unchanged for centuries.

Such ways of life invariably implied more traditional customs and habits, which is why a more conservative outlook often prevails today in the "Latin" south of the Mediterranean—Greece, southern Spain, and southern Italy. Here, at least on the surface, you will generally find a more male-dominated society and greater adherence to family, religion, and sober dress.

But beware generalizations. Some 97 percent of Greeks profess themselves Orthodox Christians, and virtually the same proportion of Italians are baptized and declare themselves Catholics. Yet fewer than 10 percent of Italians regularly attend Mass, and divorce, birth control, and abortion have all been freely available in Italy since the 1970s. Many people in the Mediterranean are shaped by their past, but they are far from being constrained by it.

The Lure of the City

Many rural Mediterranean communities are often poor and becoming poorer. One reason is the drift to urban areas and the huge increase in the population of the region's cities. In Italy this rural exodus largely took place in the 1950s and before, with Rome almost doubling in population to around 2.7 million in the 50 years after World War II. In Turkey it is happening now: In 1965 Istanbul was home to 2 million people; in 1990 there were 7.6 million inhabitants; and today the figure is a staggering 12.5 million.

People on the Move

You will come across busy and polyglot cities such as Istanbul swollen by a drift from the land time and again as you tour the Mediterranean, just as much as the rural areas—Tuscany, Andalusia, and Provence—that depopulation has helped transform into idyllic areas for a visit (see sidebar this page). But the northern Mediterranean is also seeing the movement of peoples from elsewhere: refugees and economic migrants from North Africa and the Middle East.

On the surface, these cities may appear little different from cities at home, with all the usual pluses and problems of any metropolis. But in some Mediterranean cities immigration and rapid growth are putting pressure on the indigenous and incoming populations alike.

European Union

European unification has been tried before, but it was a long time ago—and it didn't end well. For centuries, the Roman Empire extended across much of the region covered by this book. In the third century A.D., the same Roman bronze *sestertius* coin could be used to buy a loaf of bread in southern Spain, Athens, or Rome. Today, a euro or two will do the same job across much of the same area.

Many Europeans argue about whether the European Union (EU) should have been, or was ever intended only to be, a free-trade area and economic union, or whether its founding members took a longer view that always envisaged a federal body of ever greater social, financial, legal, and political union. Whatever its origins

Neapolitan children enjoy an alfresco snack. Much of life in southern Italy takes place on the street.

or future, the EU's present fortunes are mixed, especially in the southern Mediterranean. Deep-rooted economic and cultural disparities between the generally more prosperous north and poorer southern member states along with the economic convulsions of 2008 have resulted in calamity in Greece. Spain, too, and to a lesser degree, Italy, have also been affected, with social tensions and high youth and other unemployment resulting from austerity and budget-cutting measures.

Most visitors will remain unaware of such problems, however. And in places such as Nice and Monte-Carlo, among others, visitors will find it hard to imagine that hardship is or ever could be an issue.

One Way of Life

Recent economic events, and the tensions inherent in integration across the Mediterranean, only serve to underline the limits that exist when trying to draw broad similarities across the region. This is because the Mediterranean is what it has always been: rich in parts, poor in parts, and—inevitably—as often divided as unified by all that it shares and holds in common.

But for visitors and locals alike, there's something that transcends the differences of past and present. Let's call it the Mediterranean lifestyle. It may be many things, and it may manifest itself slightly differently depending where you are, but most of us recognize it, and most of us come to this most blessed of regions to indulge in it.

We visit the Mediterranean for its rich past, but when do we do it? When the weather is warm and we can turn our faces sunward. And once we've seen the ruins, admired the frescoes, or completed the guided tour, what do we do? We kill a little time in what the Italians call *il dolce far niente,* or sweet doing of nothing: a coffee, an ice cream, a stroll around town; a glass of wine; a long lunch, a siesta; an aperitif, dinner under the stars, a walk around the people-filled streets on a balmy evening.

Perhaps this is how you should look at the Mediterranean. Not so much a place, or a product of its past, or a patchwork of similarities and differences, but as something much more simple: as a way of life—and a very pleasant one at that. ∎

Mediterranean History

Mediterranean history has a vague and distant beginning, but "Europe" began to take shape from 10,000 to 2000 B.C., when groups of hunter-gatherers wandering present-day Greece, Turkey, and the Iberian, Italian, and Balkan peninsulas first settled into permanent pastoral communities.

Some of these communities became increasingly sophisticated, especially on the isle of Crete and in other parts of Greece, which saw the emergence of Cycladic and Minoan cultures from around 3200 B.C. and Mycenaean culture from 1600 B.C.

The centuries from about 1300 to 800 B.C. saw the first villages on the seven hills that would become Rome, along with the growth of advanced city-states across Greece—notably Athens—and the subsequent dissemination of Greek civilization as Greek colonies were established in southern Italy and the wider Mediterranean.

In the third and fourth centuries A.D., the Roman Empire was increasingly divided between east and west.

Greece prospered until the rise of Rome after 500 B.C. and the creation of the Roman Empire, which would embrace and influence most of the Mediterranean basin for more than 1,000 years.

In the third and fourth centuries A.D., the Roman Empire was increasingly divided between east and west, with Rome the capital of the western empire and Constantinople (modern Istanbul) the capital of the eastern territories. This division would have far-reaching consequences.

After Rome

After the final collapse of the western Roman Empire in the fifth century, much of Iberia, Italy, and parts of the Balkans fell to the so-called barbarians from northern Europe, notably the Visigoths (ca 409–711) in Spain and the Lombards (568–774) in Italy.

Another northern European people, the Franks, shaped Italian and wider history when their leader, Charlemagne (742–814), a Christian, bequeathed the lands he had conquered in central Italy to the papacy. These lands were the germ of the Papal States, which would survive until 1861–1870 and provide the papacy with a source of temporal wealth that would underpin its religious influence across Italy, France, Spain, and beyond.

At the same time, the former eastern Roman, or Byzantine, Empire, which had survived the western Roman

Empire's fall, became the focus, among other things, for Orthodox Christianity. This empire and its successors endured as the dominant political, religious, and cultural power across much of Greece, Turkey, and the Balkans until the 15th century.

Muslim Mediterranean

The rise of Islam after the seventh century informed another of the great forces that would shape much of the region, most notably present-day Spain, where Islamic rulers (the Moors, of Arab and Berber descent, who invaded from North Africa) held sway in the south of the country from 711 to 1492. Here they greatly influenced art, culture—even food—until they were expelled by the increasingly unified Christian kingdoms of northern Spain.

Islam was also predominant in much of the Middle East, leading to the Crusades, the attempt between the 11th and 13th centuries by Christian European armies to retake Jerusalem and the Holy Land. Malta, Rhodes, and elsewhere, still bear the stamp of these crusading "Knights."

Roman emperor Caesar Augustus founded the city of Zaragoza, Spain, in 24 B.C.

Venice & Florence

The Arabs were also in Sicily from 831 to 1072 where, as in Spain, they had a profound affect on the island. However, the history of the rest of Italy in this period and beyond is one of the most fragmented of any in the Mediterranean.

By around the 12th and 13th centuries sophisticated city-states prevailed in central and northern Italy, and their power would be felt well beyond their borders. This was especially true of Venice, whose maritime prowess and trade with the Orient saw it take control of much of the Balkan coast, Corfu, and beyond for centuries. It was also true of Florence, one of the largest cities of its age, which grew rich on textiles and banking, and which in the 15th century would be one of the motors of the great artistic flowering known as the Renaissance (see p. 27).

Ottoman Empire

In 1453 the Byzantine Empire in the eastern Mediterranean, with Constantinople at its head, fell to the Ottomans, the most powerful of the Muslim forces that had been harrying it since the seventh century. The new Ottoman Empire would effectively survive until after World War I. At its height, notably under Süleyman the Magnificent (1494–1566), it was one of the world's most formidable powers. It ruled modern-day Greece, Turkey, the Balkans, much of North Africa, most of Hungary, and large areas of the Middle East. In 1529—famously—it even threatened the gates of Vienna.

Spain

Just as the arrival of the Muslim Ottomans heralded a long period of hegemony in the eastern Mediterranean (see sidebar this page), so the expulsion of the Muslim Moors in 1492 marked the start of a generally more unified rule in Spain. Control fell first to the Habsburgs (from 1516 to 1700), who had Swiss origins but eventually—through marriage and military might—became an imperial and dynastic superpower that also controlled some or all of Austria and central Europe as well as parts of Italy and the Balkans, on and off, until World War I.

Spain's fortunes were also transformed after 1492 by Christopher Columbus's landing in the New World, and by the subsequent flow of wealth from the country's new central and southern America colonies. Venice, for one, along with much of the eastern Mediterranean, would suffer after the opening up of the New World, partly in the face of Ottoman expansion and partly because Europe's attention and trade turned west, away from the Orient.

After 1700 a branch of the Bourbons, a dynasty with French origins, ruled Spain, as well as France itself and much of southern Italy. They would remain in power in Spain, with the occasional break, until 1931.

Revolution

Bourbon rule was less secure in Italy, which, with the Balkans and the rest of the western Mediterranean, became increasingly caught up in the power struggles of the great emerging powers of Britain, France, and the Austro-Hungarian (Habsburg) Empire.

This was especially true during the Napoleonic Wars, when the French emperor Napoleon Bonaparte (1769–1821), who emerged in the chaos following the French Revolution of the 1790s, would conquer all of Spain, most of Italy, much of present-day Croatia, and large areas of central Europe.

After the fall of Napoleon, treaties restored much of the previous status quo, but ultimately could do little to rein in the liberal and revolutionary forces unleashed by Napoleon and the French Revolution. Nationalist and revolutionary fervor spread to Greece, for example, where there was a war of independence against the Ottomans in 1821; and to the great patchwork of states, cities, and kingdoms that made up Italy, which was eventually unified in 1861 after defeats for the Austrians, Bourbons, and others.

Two World Wars & Beyond

Long-standing nationalist and imperial resentments and alignments burst forth again in World War I, the aftermath of which greatly transformed much of the eastern Mediterranean. Spain remained neutral, and Italy and southern France were little altered, but the defeat of Austria-Hungary and the Ottomans saw profound changes in Greece, the Balkans, and the Near East, notably the emergence of the modern Turkish state.

During World War II the entire region, save Spain, was at the center of the battles for Europe, Africa, and the Middle East. Even the region's smallest countries were deeply affected; Malta, for example, suffered a grievous siege.

Even 50 years after the war, the unravelling of Communist Eastern Europe and the resurfacing of ancient resentments saw war in the Balkans during the 1990s. Thousands of lives were lost and great historic cities such as Dubrovnik were damaged before the conflict was resolved. "New" countries such as Slovenia and Croatia would emerge from the chaos.

Croatia's admittance to the European Union (EU) in 2013—as its 28th member state—might suggest that at last some of the Mediterranean was shaking off its historical shackles, and that in the EU the region was achieving a hegemony it has lacked since the height of the Roman Empire.

Not quite. Some of the old political, social, and religious uncertainties remain. Just ask the Turks. They applied to join the European Union in 1987. They're still waiting. ∎

World War II air raid damage in Valletta, Malta

Food & Drink

Eating is one of the major pleasures of visiting the Mediterranean. Countless regional specialties complement the superb French, Italian, Turkish, and other national cuisines, along with common culinary elements bequeathed by the region's shared seas, climate, and history.

Sicilian cheeses round out the offerings at Catania's well-known Pescheria fish market.

Simple things link the food and drink of much of the Mediterranean. This is a region that is mostly warm and dry, for example, but has just enough rainfall—at the right time of the year, and to the right degree—to provide perfect growing conditions for all manner of plants, trees, fruits, and vegetables.

Take the olive, whose oil is the bedrock of the region's cooking: A native of Turkey, the tree spread across the Mediterranean over countless millennia and is perfectly adapted to often parched (and occasionally frosty) conditions. Or the grape, another regional staple, prolific within certain climatic limits and worked to produce wines in almost infinite variety across much of the region.

Elsewhere, climate occasionally produces something out of the ordinary. Most of the hotter and drier climes of the south, for example, produce oranges, lemons, eggplants, almonds, peppers, peaches, melons, and more. Warm-water seas also produce a variety and abundance of fish and seafood.

A Culinary Patchwork

Other exotic ingredients have taken hold as a result of the Mediterranean's complex history. Where, for example, would Italian and other cuisines be without the foods of the New World, largely introduced in the 16th century by the Spanish? No cocoa or vanilla for ice cream, for a start; no tomatoes for pizzas, salads, and sauces; and no potatoes, maize, zucchinis, avocados, bell peppers, chilies, or sunflower oil.

History also accounted for the influence of the Arabs, who controlled Sicily and much of Spain for several centuries. Along the way they introduced innovative culinary and agricultural practices, as well as rice, citrus fruits, couscous, cane sugar, cinnamon, and saffron, along with ice cream and sorbets, supposedly first made in Sicily from the snow found year round on Mount Etna.

It was the Arabs, too, who encouraged a sweet tooth in the southern Mediterranean, with the introduction, among other things, of marzipan and Sicily's *cassata* dessert (candied fruit, almond paste, sponge cake, and sweetened ricotta cheese). Latterly, immigration from North Africa to places such as Sicily, Malta, Marseille, and elsewhere has reinvigorated the many Arab strands already present in southern Mediterranean cooking.

Last but not least, Africa also provided the earliest coffee beans—how the Mediterranean would function (or not) without caffeine is hard to imagine.

Similar historical legacies are repeated across the Mediterranean. On many Croatian menus, for example, pasta sits alongside goulash, a result of the region's domination by Venice and then its assimilation into the Austro-Hungarian Empire.

In Istanbul geography means that cooking might draw on the dishes of the nearby Black Sea—with dishes such as corn bread or *hamsi pilavı* (anchovy pilaf)—as well as the wide range of now commonplace ingredients that were indigenous to Anatolia: chickpeas, wheat, broad beans, walnuts, apples—even yogurt.

A sampling of meze dishes, including *dolmadhes* and roasted eggplant, at an Athens taverna

But just as there are many similarities in Mediterranean food—and these include a tendency toward the simple dishes of the region's poor, peasant societies of the past—there are also many differences, not least the dramatic regional differences within the same country.

Simple Pleasures

This variety, of course, and the sense of discovery it entails, only adds to the enjoyment of eating out. Yet when all is said and done, it's perhaps the eating out itself that counts for most when it comes to Mediterranean food. Eating in Rome, Barcelona, or Istanbul is more a social experience than a gastronomic one, so while fine dining is invariably available, more often than not eating out means an informal Italian trattoria, a homey Greek taverna, a bustling Spanish tapas bar, or a no-nonsense Croatian *konoba* (a cozy, relaxed restaurant).

When you find yourself in one of these, ideally it will be outdoors and involve supper under the stars on a balmy evening or a long lunch on the harbor of a tiny fishing village: places and occasions, in short, where the simple pleasures of conversation and conviviality are every bit as important as the food itself.

Arts & Culture

Culture in the Mediterranean has been shaped by individual genius but above all by the great religions and civilizations that overlapped across the region for centuries. Almost any city you visit will boast great artistic and architectural treasures, but innumerable smaller towns are also graced by the enchanting work of more local writers, poets, painters, and composers.

Some of the northern Mediterranean's earliest surviving artifacts date from the Cycladic and Minoan cultures of Crete and Greece's Aegean islands: vases, bowls, and sculptures of the human form from the Neolithic period, more than 6,000 years ago. Other ancient remnants across the region include the rock art of southeast Spain and southwest France—which may be up to 35,000 years old—and the work of the Phoenicians and the 3,000-year-old stone megaliths of the Balearic Islands.

The rise of mainland Mycenaean cultures meant that Greece remained the cradle of artistic endeavor through the late Bronze Age (around 1600–1050 B.C.). Trade and the movement of peoples then introduced this Mycenaean art into the Iberian Peninsula, but especially to Italy, where first Villanovan and then Etruscan art flourished: distinctive painted vases, large works in bronze, and exquisite gold and other jewelry.

> **For the most part the Romans adopted and refined the art of the Greeks and Etruscans.**

Greece

Greece continued to dominate the region during the golden age of Greek civilization around 500 B.C. This was especially true in the fields of sculpture and architecture, underlined by the building of the Parthenon, completed in 438 B.C.

Again, the spread of Greek influence beyond Greece led to the dissemination of this later Greek art and architecture into southern France—Marseille, for example, was a Greek colony—and to Italy, especially Sicily and Campania, where the great Greek temples and theaters of Agrigento, Taormina, and elsewhere still stand.

The Romans

Roman art and architecture would also be widely disseminated, from Spain to Turkey and beyond, something illustrated by the surviving temple columns of Barcino (Roman Barcelona); Diocletian's Palace in Split, Croatia; the many monuments of Italy itself; and the ruins of Ephesus in western Turkey.

For the most part the Romans adopted and refined the art of the Greeks and Etruscans. They copied Greek statues and adopted their predecessors' love of mosaics and painted motifs. In architecture, by contrast, the Romans were innovators, making use of arches and new materials such as concrete to build on a gigantic

One of four statues symbolizing knowledge, wisdom, valor, and intelligence that adorn the A.D. 135 Library of Celsus in Ephesus, Turkey

scale. While their temples still looked to Greece, their theaters moved away from the Greek model—arenas cut into the landscape, as in Taormina, Sicily (see p. 164) or Epidavros (see sidebar p. 237) in Greece—to the freestanding amphitheaters of the Colosseo in Rome (see pp. 129–131) and the Arènes d'Arles (see p. 71).

Greece and Rome's legacy would prevail for centuries, notably in the Romanesque style of architecture, which was based on the arches and floor plans of Roman basilicas and would inform church and other buildings across the region until at least the 13th century.

A 12th-century Byzantine mosaic depicting Jesus Christ, in the Hagia Sophia, Istanbul

Islamic & Byzantine Art

The fall of Rome in the late fifth century A.D. left an artistic void that was filled differently across the region. The Arabs of North Africa moved into Sicily and much of Spain, resulting in a proliferation of Islamic motifs and styles that persisted long after their power had waned. The greatest legacy of this period, and the degree to which later styles would adapt elements of Islamic art, can be seen in Granada, Spain's Alhambra (see pp. 50–54) and the Palazzo dei Normanni in Palermo, Sicily (see p. 166).

Elsewhere in Spain and Italy from about 600, but also in Greece and Croatia, invaders from the north, the so-called barbarians (the Visigoths, Franks, Lombards, and others), introduced their own art, though little except some of their stone carving has survived.

At the same time, two other powerful artistic movements were taking hold: Christian art and the closely linked Byzantine art. The latter, born of the decision to divide the old Roman Empire into two, with one capital in Rome, the other in Constantinople (now Istanbul), had both eastern and Roman roots, so it developed along distinctive lines, emerging as a hybrid of classical and more ornate Oriental styles that found its greatest expression in icons and mosaics.

The Byzantine influence was extensive and extended: It was and is found in Greece, Turkey, and much of Italy, especially in Venice, where the Basilica di San Marco (see pp. 185–189) is one of the world's greatest architectural and decorative hybrids.

But the former Byzantine Empire, along with its art, was prey to another powerful newcomer. Whereas the Arabs in Spain and Sicily had eventually been supplanted, in the eastern Mediterranean it was the Arabs themselves who did the supplanting, when they took Constantinople in 1453. In artistic terms, the result was the same as in Spain: a mingling of Muslim and existing styles that resulted in Istanbul's wealth of wonderfully mixed medieval art and architecture.

The Art of Frescoing

Frescoes—mural paintings—can be seen all over Italy, but perhaps those of the Cappella Sistina (see pp. 142–143) are the most famous. They take their name from *fresco*, or fresh, because they were painted on wet, or "fresh," plaster—a technique popular during the Renaissance period. When pigments are painted onto wet plaster—a mixture of lime, water, and fine sand—a chemical reaction occurs as the plaster dries. The resulting calcium carbonate crystallizes around the sand and pigment particles, fixing them and leaving them resistant to action by water. However, the technique restricted the range of pigments, and thus colors, that the artists could use. Pigments were also difficult to mix, unlike oil paints, making it hard to achieve depth of tone or subtlety of shade, and artists could only work on areas small enough to complete before the plaster dried. Stripping off the plaster and starting again was the only way to rectify mistakes.

From Gothic to Baroque

In the meantime, new architectural styles were being developed in northern Europe, especially the Gothic (in France, around the 12th century), a more ornate approach, that superseded the simpler Romanesque style, and began to be imported to the areas around the Mediterranean. Gothic in turn was superseded by the Renaissance. The Renaissance was an extended period of increasing artistic sophistication (especially in frescoes; see sidebar this page) nurtured by greater prosperity, greater civic and social sophistication, and a renewed interest in the art and culture of the classical world. Florence and other Italian cities in the 15th century were at its heart, but its influence spread to Spain, France, Croatia, and elsewhere. In the 16th century came the baroque, a still more lavish and exuberant style also found in art and sculpture. The latter style was informed partly by the demands of the Counter-Reformation—one of the ways the Catholic Church attempted to turn the tide of Protestantism was through the splendor of its churches—and partly by the vast wealth flowing into Spain from the New World in the 16th and 17th centuries.

Music & Other Art Forms

Away from art and architecture, the Mediterranean boasts a multitude of music: flamenco in southern Spain, Provençal folk song in the south of France, the sound of the bouzouki in Greece, the Arab-influenced *arabesk* in Istanbul, and so on. And although the language barrier precludes most visitors from enjoying Mediterranean literature, theater, or cinema, these art forms, like music, reveal many styles and individuals that reflect but also often transcend national boundaries.

The modern age has also been marked by increasingly singular artists, freed of the conventions of more recent pan-Mediterranean artistic and architectural styles such as mannerism, rococo, and art nouveau. So you can be sure of discovering work that you often won't find anywhere else: the art of Paul Cézanne (1839–1906) in the south of France, say; the work of Antoni Gaudí (1852–1926) in Barcelona; or the genius of Pablo Picasso (1881–1973) in Málaga and beyond. ∎

Four gateways to the Mediterranean that encapsulate the region's rich blend of history, art, food, and culture

Coastal Spain

Introduction & Map   30-31

Barcelona   32-48

Barri Gòtic Walk   36-37

A Walk Down La Rambla   40-41

Feature: Gaudí & *Modernisme*   46-47

Need to Know: Barcelona   48

Málaga & Granada   49-55

Need to Know: Málaga   55

Feature: Gibraltar   56

Valencia   57-58

Need to Know: Valencia   58

Balearic Islands   59-63

Need to Know: Mallorca, Eivissa, & Menorca   63

Restaurants   274-278

Cap de Formentor, the northernmost point on the Balearic isle of Mallorca

Coastal Spain

The cultural and historical legacy of Spain—from Roman to Moorish and beyond—sets the tone for almost any Mediterranean odyssey, underlining the broad influences that have shaped and colored this most complex of regions. At the same time, the distinct identities of cities such as Barcelona, which is passionately attached to its regional roots, or the particular heritage of Granada, emphasize the individuality of certain destinations, providing a powerful lure for millions of visitors.

Catalan architect Ricardo Bofill's W Hotel, a contemporary addition to Barcelona's skyline

Barcelona

For decades Barcelona, the country's second city after Madrid, languished, deliberately marginalized under Fascist dictator Francisco Franco (1892–1972), who feared the separatist inclinations of a city and region—Catalunya, or Catalonia—that have always been fiercely independent.

All that changed when Barcelona hosted the 1992 Olympic Games, a catalyst for urban renewal and an event that brought world attention. Today, the city is one of the Mediterranean's most popular ports of call for cruise ships, being ideally suited to a short visit. There's more than enough to see and do for days, but if time is short you can still discover much of what the city has to offer.

Barcelona's historic district of small streets and old buildings, the Barri Gòtic (Gothic Quarter), is smaller than you might

expect, but it is still worth exploring, especially when combined with the adjoining La Ribera (home to an outstanding museum devoted to artist Pablo Picasso) and Ciutat Vella quarters. And architecture enthusiasts must see some of the works by Catalan architect Antoni Gaudí, notably La Sagrada Família, a still unfinished Catholic church, and one of the city's highlights.

Málaga & Granada

The port city of Málaga, like Barcelona, has recently strived to reinvent itself. Long seen as little more than the gateway to the big beach resorts of the neighboring Costa del Sol, it now has a revamped waterfront and—in its Museo Picasso (the artist was born in the city)—a cultural attraction of the first rank.

If your time in Málaga is short, it takes an effort of will not to pass over the city altogether in favor of an excursion to Granada, a city 80 miles (128 km) northeast, and the Alhambra, a sublime Moorish and Renaissance fortress and palace complex. The single most visited sight in Spain, it's deserving of its fame, but it can be crowded and you'll need to plan and book the compulsory timed entry for parts of the complex well ahead of your visit. West of Málaga, British-held Gibraltar also appeals, it's famed rock guarding the western entrance to the Mediterranean Sea.

Valencia

Valencia, the third in the triumvirate of major ports on Spain's Mediterranean coast, has made attempts at reinvention and regeneration, too. Unlike its rivals, however, it lacks the big-hitting sights that might bring it to wider international attention, but it has plenty of sights to keep you busy on a short visit (such as the Ciudad de las Artes y las Ciencias, a futuristic cultural center) as well as the wide range of other activities that make visiting almost any Spanish town or city a pleasure, not least a balmy climate made for outdoor living, vibrant streets and colorful markets, an energetic nightlife, and the chance to sample

superb tapas, fish, and other delicacies at almost every turn.

Balearic Islands

The same applies to Spain's Balearic Islands—Mallorca, Menorca, and Eivissa—but on a more intimate scale. Perfectly sited between Italy, Spain, and the south of France, these are some of the most visited isles in the Mediterranean (1.75 million cruise passengers annually, against 640,000 for Málaga and 390,000 for Valencia). It's easy to see why, for they have delightful scenery, a thriving cultural and artistic life, and plenty of points of historical interest. ■

Barcelona

Catalunya's vibrant capital is among the front-runners of Spanish business, theater, cuisine, and design while Catalan identity is constantly expressed. The city is also a tantalizing mix of different neighborhoods, each one with its own distinct flair. Its heritage ranges from Roman ruins to state-of-the-art contemporary architecture, with a good dose of Gothic and *modernisme* (Catalan art nouveau) mixed in.

NEED TO KNOW p. 48

Barcelona

△ 31 E4

Visitor Information

✉ Plaça de Catalunya 16 bis, Ciutat Vella

☎ 932 853 834

🚇 Metro: L1, L3

✉ Visitor information points at Terminals A, B, C, D, & World Trade Center (Terminals N & S)

☎ 932 853 834

🕐 Opening hours correspond to cruise ship arrivals

barcelonaturisme.com

Catedral (La Seu)

△ Map p. 33

✉ Plaça de la Seu, Barri Gòtic

☎ 933 428 262

💲 Cathedral: free, but $$ 1 p.m.– 5 p.m. (includes entry to choir, chapter house, & rooftop); choir: $; chapter house museum: $; rooftop: $

🚇 Metro: Jaume I

catedralbcn.org

Public transportation, notably the metro, is very user friendly. Restaurants are of high quality. And the surrounding hills and sea give a clear sense of the layout of this culturally rich city.

Barri Gòtic

Start your visit in the Barri Gòtic (Gothic Quarter), where the cathedral, palaces, and museums all echo the zenith of Catalan trading prowess.

Catedral (La Seu): The imposing facade and spires of Barcelona's cathedral—which is also known as La Seu—may look Gothic, but they actually date from the 19th century, when they were added to the existing 14th- and 15th-century structure, built atop a site formerly occupied by a Romanesque church, a mosque, and a Roman basilica. The original 1408 designs were used, which ensured overall visual harmony.

Penetrate the interior and you are in a lofty single nave, a vast space broken midway by an elaborate choir. This, in turn, fronts stairs leading down to the **crypt**. Here, in a low-vaulted chamber beneath the main altar, stands the carved marble sarcophagus of Santa Eulàlia, a

locally born virgin martyr who was executed by the Romans in the fourth century and who then became Barcelona's patron saint. From the sunken steps you have a magnificent view of the soaring vaulted ceiling supported by ribbed columns.

The **choir** is among the cathedral's many masterpieces, with a white marble screen that depicts Santa Eulàlia's life and encloses beautifully carved Renaissance choir stalls. These were later decorated with the coats of arms of European kings.

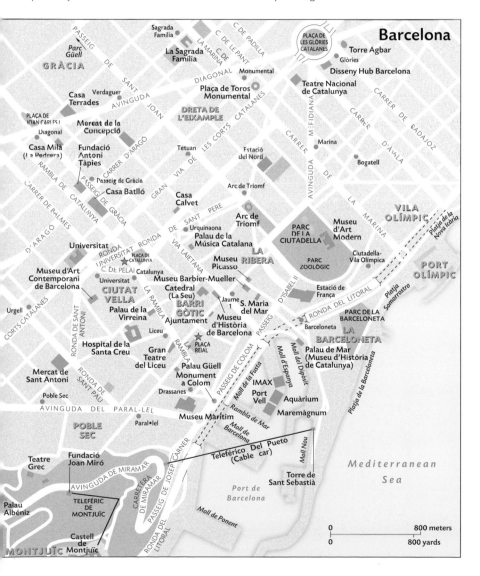

No fewer than 29 side chapels line the nave and apse, nearly all of them containing an altarpiece or sculpture of interest. On your immediate right as you enter the main doors is the large **Capella del Santissim Sagrament,** whose 16th-century crucifix with its twisted Christ is alleged to have adorned the prow of Don Juan of Austria's flagship during the Battle of Lepanto (1571). In the opposite corner a side chapel contains

Dancing the *Sardana*

The *sardana* is the traditional dance of Catalunya. One of the best places to see it is during spontaneous performances by groups that gather outside Barcelona's Catedral. Noon on Sunday or early summer Saturday evenings are best. A simple and precise dance, it features musicians (the *cobla*)—led by brass, tambourine, and distinctive *flaviol*, or flute—and dancers (often strangers), usually in normal attire and from all walks of life, who move in a circle and hold hands with raised arms. Steps are precise and meticulous. As the dance progresses, the circle can become bigger, breaking into smaller circles until five or more groups are moving in unison.

a huge marble font (1433) and a historic plaque recording the baptism of six Carib Indians brought back by Christopher Columbus in 1493.

At the back of the cathedral, the first side chapel to the left of the altar holds the alabaster tomb of Ramon d'Escales, Count of Barcelona, sculpted by Antoni Canet in 1409. Farther around the ambulatory,

Chapel VI contains a lovely 1390 painting of St. Gabriel on 18 panels, by Lluís Borrassà. Between these is the **Capella de Sant Benet,** dedicated to the Benedictine Order, which is celebrated by an altarpiece (1452) painted by Bernat Martorell. This corner of the apse also gives access to the elevator for the rooftop. Look for two modest coffins attached to the transept wall that belong to Ramon Berenguer I (Count of Barcelona) and his wife.

Another surprise lies in store in the Gothic **cloister** (1498), which you can also enter directly from Carrer del Bistre through the Porta de Santa Eulàlia: A gaggle of geese roams among a palm tree, potted plants, and a fountain mounted with a statue of Sant Jordi (St. George), Catalunya's patron saint. Huge vaulted chapels line the cloister, each dedicated to a saint, and the **chapter house** has a small museum. The font in the lobby was salvaged from the original Romanesque cathedral.

La Ribera & El Born

If you enjoyed the Barri Gòtic, then the neighboring La Ribera district, which extends east of Via Laietana, should prove even more fascinating. **Carrer de Montcada,** with wall-to-wall art galleries, craft shops, Gothic palaces, and museums (in particular, the acclaimed Museu Picasso), slices northwest through here to reach the funky El Born district. Both districts offer history and gastronomy.

La Ribera has been a residential quarter since medieval times. Any detour down its shady side streets takes you beneath balconies festooned with laundry, past neighborhood bars and Chinese-owned shops. The entire port area used to look like this before it was transformed for the Olympic Games. Since then, designers and restaurateurs have made it one of Barcelona's hippest neighborhoods, especially around lively Passeig del Born.

Museu Picasso: This museum on Carrer de Montcada may not have the world's finest or most comprehensive collection of Picassos, but it certainly has the most illuminating. The richest sections here cover Picasso's early years, his "Las Meninas" series, and his last burst of creativity, expressed in engravings. All this and more is displayed in the neighboring Gothic palaces of **Berenguer de Aguilar** and **Barón de Castellet.**

The collection moves chronologically through Pablo Picasso's life (1881-1973). Sketches he produced as a ten-year-old prodigy show the artist's lively imagination and academic prowess. Skillful portraits and oil landscapes of A Coruña, painted when his family moved there from Málaga, demonstrate his early application and humor (look for his self-portrait in a wig, 1897). These are followed by stylistic experiments, much influenced by a visit to Paris in 1900.

The Museu Picasso in La Ribera celebrates the ever changing work of the great artist.

After a room devoted to his **Blue Period** (1901-1904), the collection leaps to 1917, when Picasso's artistic freedom was in full flower, then to his **"Las Meninas" series** (1957). These 57 oils, inspired by Diego Velázquez's 1656 painting "Las Meninas," are astounding in their deconstructed abandon. The last rooms on this floor display landscapes of Cannes and ceramics made at Mougins.

Upstairs is Picasso's twilight masterpiece, **"Suite 156"** (1969-1972), a series of engravings that was the culmination of both his cultural inspirations and strong erotic impulses.

Santa Maria del Mar: At the end of Carrer de Montcada you

(continued on p. 38)

Museu Picasso

- Map p. 33
- Carrer de Montcada 15-23, La Ribera
- ☎ 932 563 000
- Closed Mon.
- Permanent collection: $$$; temporary exhibition: $$; combined ticket: $$$$
- Metro: Jaume 1, Line 4

www.museupicasso .bcn.cat

Santa Maria del Mar

- Map p. 33
- Plaça de Santa Maria del Mar 1, La Ribera
- ☎ 933 102 390

Barri Gòtic Walk

This walk takes you through the evocative narrow alleyways of Barcelona's oldest quarter—Barri Gòtic (Gothic Quarter)—passing major monuments, such as the cathedral and a medieval palace, while offering vivid insights into the daily life of the city.

Leave **Plaça Reial** by the street in the northeast corner, Carrer del Vidre, and then cross Carrer de Ferran to walk up the alley of Carrer d'en Quintana. Turn right onto Boqueria and immediately left to emerge in Plaça del Pi. In front of you is the apse of **Santa Maria del Pi ❶** and its 177-foot

---

NOT TO BE MISSED:

Catedral (La Seu) • Museu d'Història de Barcelona • Museu Frederic Marès

---

Barcelona's Catedral (Cathedral) is commonly referred to as La Seu, a reference to its position as the seat of the diocese.

(54 m) octagonal tower. Walk around the church to the main plaza, backed by ornately decorated 18th-century houses, and admire the huge rose window. Turn into narrow, tile-studded **Carrer de Petritxol,** then right onto Carrer Portaferrissa. Walk straight into **Plaça Nova,** where the cathedral looms behind the Casa de l'Ardiaca (Archdeacon's House).

Turn right here, past remains of the Roman wall, onto Carrer del Bisbe, where ahead of you is a surprising neo-Gothic **covered bridge** (1929) linking the medieval Casa dels Canonges (Canons' Residence) to the Palau de la Generalitat (Parliament Building). Turn right again onto Carrer de Montjuïc del Bisbe to see the baroque church of **Sant Felip Neri ❷** in a delightful little square. On the corner is the **Museu del Calçat** (Shoe Museum; *tel 933 014 533, closed Mon. & p.m.*), a must for shoe fanatics.

Returning to Carrer del Bisbe, enter the **Catedral (La Seu) ❸** (see pp. 32–34) through the cloister doorway. Leaving via the cathedral's main door, turn right past the **Museu Diocesà** (*tel 933 152 213, closed Sun. p.m., Mon., & holidays*) to walk beside a monumental section of the **Roman wall** and sections of the medieval royal palace that lead to impressive **Plaça Ramon Berenguer el Gran,** named after the Catalan ruler who is honored by an equestrian statue. Turn right off the main avenue, Via Laietana, onto

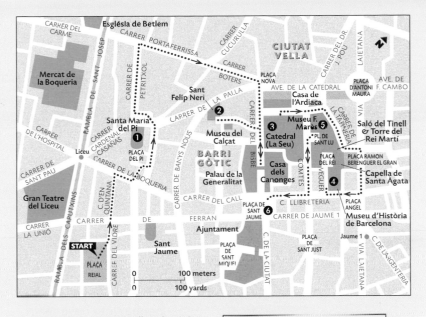

Carrer Llibreterla, past a candlemakers' shop
dating from 1761.

Two Must-See Museums

Turn right again onto Carrer del Veguer,
where you reach the **Museu d'Història
de Barcelona ❹** (MUHBA; *Plaça del Rei,
Barri Gòtic, tel 933 562 122, museuhistoria
.bcn.cat, closed Mon. & holidays, $$*). Made
up of and housed in the complex of build-
ings that make up the **Palau Reial Major,**
the Gothic-Renaissance palace used by
Catalan viceroys, this museum relates the
history of Barcelona and overlooks the
evocative 14th- to 16th-century **Plaça del
Rei.** Of paramount interest is the exten-
sive subterranean section showing Roman
foundation walls and water channels.
Aboveground, don't miss the lovely 14th-
century **Capella de Santa Àgata** and, at
the back of the square, the vast ceremony
hall, **Saló del Tinell,** a majestic construc-
tion of semicircular arches. Adjoining it is
the five-story **Torre del Rei Martí:** Climb
this former watchtower for fine views of
the entire Barri Gòtic.

> 🅰 Also see area map pp. 32–33
> ▶ Plaça Reial
> 🕐 1–2 hours (without visits)
> ↔ 1.25 miles (2 km)
> ▶ Plaça de Sant Jaume

Now walk around the outside of the
palace to the back of the cathedral and turn
right to reach Plaça de Sant Lu. In front is
the renovated **Museu Frederic Marès ❺**
*(tel 932 563 500, museumares.bcn.cat, closed
Mon., $).* This exceptional collection has
Spanish sculpture from pre-Roman times to
the 19th century. The "Collector's Cabinet"
displays thousands of curios assembled by
Frederic Marès (1893–1991).

Return to Carrer Llibreteria and turn
right to reach the administrative heart of
Barcelona, the **Plaça de Sant Jaume ❻.**
On the right is the **Palau de la Generalitat,**
home to the Catalan government, and on the
left the **Ajuntament** (City Hall; *tel 934 027
000, closed Mon.-Sat.*). Guided tours show
the remarkable Saló de Cent and Saló de
Cròniques, and Catalan artworks.

Palau de la Música Catalana

- Map p. 33
- Carrer Palau de la Música 4-6, El Born
- 932 957 200
- Guided tours: $$$$$

palaumusica.org

Museu Marítim

- Map p. 33
- Avda. de les Drassanes, The Waterfront
- 933 429 920
- $$
- Metro: Drassanes, Line 3

mmb.cat

cannot miss the popular Gothic church of Santa Maria del Mar, founded by local sailors in the 14th century to rival the extravagance of the bourgeois cathedral and known as the People's Cathedral. It has perfect proportions and a lovely 15th-century **rose window** above the western portal. An incongruous modern window (1997) at the other end celebrates the 1992 Olympics.

El Born: Just north of Santa Maria del Mar is the **Passeig del Born,** a square once used for jousting at the center of a delightful medieval merchants' quarter, El Born. Today this area forms a maze of enticing fashion and design shops, as well as lively tapas bars and affordable young restaurants. Gourmet stores, art galleries, and more upscale restaurants are booming. Finally, by following Via Laietana northwest, you reach the landmark modernisme building, **Palau de la Música Catalana,** a concert hall designed by Lluís Domènech i Montaner in 1908. Guided tours are offered daily.

The Waterfront

In the 1990s the port area was transformed from a grimy, neglected quarter into a glossy new window on culture and gastronomy, the harbor now bristling with marinas, leisure facilities, state-of-the-art museums, restaurants, and plenty of viewing points. The main artery in this area is **La Rambla** (see pp. 40–41), a long avenue stretching from Plaça

de Catalunya to the statue of Christopher Columbus by the harbor. Alongside the new is the illustrious old, nearly all of it connected with the city's maritime history. Not least, 4 miles (7 km) of golden sand run from here to Parc del Fòrum (Forum Park).

INSIDER TIP:

Barcelona's waterfront is a great place for a stroll and to fantasize about the lifestyles of the rich and famous while ogling boats big enough to have their own helicopter.

—ZACHARY BRISSON
National Geographic contributor

The symbolic **Monument a Colom** (Columbus Monument; *tel 933 025 224*) makes a good starting point. Take the elevator (*$*) up this 160-foot (50 m) iron column to join the statue of Christopher Columbus surveying the harbor. In front is the mooring for trimarans (*Las Golondrinas, tel 934 423 106*) that tour the harbor to the Port Olímpic.

Just to the left of the trimarans is a boardwalk, **Rambla de Mar,** that cuts across part of the harbor. It leads from the Monument a Colom to **Port Vell** and the **Moll d'Espanya** (Jetty of Spain), devoted to entertainment. Here the Maremàgnum mall and cinema complex jostle with the **IMAX theater** (tel 932 251 111, imax portvell.com) and the **Aquàrium** (tel 932 217 474, aquariumbcn .com, $$$$).

Looking northwest from atop the statue, you look down on some of the world's largest **medieval shipyards,** a unique complex of 13th-century vaulted halls built around a central courtyard large enough to contain galleons. Luckily for Barcelona they were saved from demolition and in their refurbished form make a fitting background for the **Museu Marítim,** where model ships, paintings, figureheads, navigational instruments, maps, and charts illustrate Barcelona's maritime history. Exhibits also give a wider picture of the evolution of seafaring, ending with submarines before you are plunged into an aquatic virtual reality show. The restaurant overlooks orange trees in the sunken courtyard.

La Barceloneta & Port Olímpic: The 18th-century grid of streets at the northern end of the harbor, known as La Barceloneta, was traditionally the sailors' quarter. Here, the 1900 Palau de Mar, the former main warehouses of the Barceloneta wharf, was also successfully converted into a museum. The **Museu d'Història de Catalunya** offers a lively chronological survey of Catalan history using interactive exhibits, information panels, charts, audiovisuals, photos, reconstructions, and

models. Texts are in Catalan, but you can borrow a translation brochure at the ticket desk. The most interesting section is on Floor 2, showing man's origins in Catalunya, the Iberians, and the Romans. It also covers the short Moorish occupation, medieval times, and the Habsburg Empire. Don't miss Floor 4, where the café opens onto a terrace with fabulous port views.

To the south of La Barceloneta looms the rusty **Torre de Sant Sebastià,** from where you can catch a **Teleféric cable car** (tel 934 304 716, telefericode barcelona.com, $$$$), with heart-stopping views over the harbor, to Montjuïc (see pp. 42–43). Seafood restaurants abound, and sandy beaches stretch northward. Two highrises tower over Port Olímpic. One houses the avant-garde Hotel Arts, fronted by a giant metallic fish designed by Frank Gehry.

The beaches end at the junction with lengthy Avinguda Diagonal, now graced (continued on p. 42)

A statue of Christopher Columbus overlooks Barcelona's harbor.

Museu d'Història de Catalunya

- Map p. 33
- Palau de Mar, Plaça de Pau Vila 3, The Waterfront
- 932 254 700
- Closed Sun.– Mon. & p.m. holidays
- $$
- Metro: Barceloneta, Line 4

mhcat.cat

A Walk Down La Rambla

Soak up Barcelona's varied 21st-century spirit by exploring the animated Rambla—each section has its own name—and its side streets. These harbor a wealth of historical and contemporary interest in an inspirational mix of styles, as well as endless street theater.

Walk down La Rambla to set your eyes—and feet—on mosaics designed by Joan Miró.

NOT TO BE MISSED:

Museu d'Art Contemporani de Barcelona • Mercat de la Boqueria • Palau Güell • Plaça Reial

With your back to the modern fountain **"Homenatge a Francesc Macià"** ❶ on the southwest corner of Plaça de Catalunya, cross to the central pedestrian walkway of **La Rambla.** This immediately gives you a taste of Barcelona's most famous avenue, with sidewalk cafés, street performers, flower sellers, and people strolling. At the sign pointing to Anteneu, cross to the left and take a sharp left onto the pedestrianized Carrer de Santa Anna. At No. 32, walk into the courtyard where the charming Romanesque church of **Santa Ana** ❷ (*tel 933 01 35 76, open a.m. & 6 p.m.– 8 p.m., closed Sun. p.m.*) now stands jammed between 19th- and 20th-century buildings.

Retrace your steps to La Rambla. Cross to the other side, noting the ornate pharmacy, and walk down Carrer d'Elisabets. This street crosses the Plaça del Bonsuccés before reaching a junction at Carrer dels Àngels. Immediately visible on your right are the contemporary forms of the **Museu d'Art Contemporani de Barcelona** ❸ (MACBA;

Plaça dels Àngels 1, Raval, tel 934 120 810, macba.es, closed Sun. p.m. & Tues., $$$), a stone, glass, and metal-plated building designed by Richard Meier that opened in 1995. The permanent collection starts in the late 1940s with artists such as Jean Dubuffet, Alexander Calder, and Marcel Broodthaers, and ends with contemporaries such as Christian Boltanski, Rosemary Trockel, Richard Long, and Jaume Plensa. The museum has inspired a rash of art and design-related shops in the surrounding streets of El Raval.

From here, turn right down tree-lined Carrer dels Àngels until you come to Carrer del Carme. Opposite stands the massive Gothic-style **Hospital de la Santa Creu,** which currently houses the **Biblioteca de Catalunya** ❹ (*tel 933 170 778*). It is worth walking around to **Carrer de l'Hospital 56** to enter the courtyard and Gothic patio.

Continue across the pretty little square named for Alexander Fleming (the Scottish bacteriologist who discovered penicillin) and return to La Rambla via Carrer del Carme. On your left is the rusticated baroque facade of the **Església de Betlem** (*Carrer del Carme 2, Raval*). The interior of the church dates from a 1930s renovation after a fire and is of little interest. Turn right onto the lively **Rambla de Sant Josep,** monopolized by a **bird market,** where caged parrots squawk beneath the chestnut trees.

Rambla de Sant Josep to Plaça Reial

On the right is the imposing 1778 **Palau de la Virreina** ❺ *(La Rambla 99, Raval, tel 933 161 000, lavirreina.bcn.cat, closed Mon.)*, whose baroque and rococo interior now hosts photography exhibitions. Next comes the cornucopian **Mercat de la Boqueria** (also called Mercat de Sant Josep; *closed Sun.*), where foodstuffs are sold beneath a soaring wrought-iron and glass roof. Flower stands on La Rambla partly conceal a **Joan Miró design** on the sidewalk as it widens into Plaça de la Boqueria. Look, too, at **No. 77,** its facade decorated in art nouveau mosaics. Almost opposite is a kitsch example of the 1920s chinoiserie craze that bristles with dragons and parasols.

On the right stands the **Gran Teatre del Liceu** ❻, Barcelona's most prestigious theater. After the Hotel Oriente turn right onto Carrer Nou de la Rambla to see Gaudí's extraordinary **Palau Güell** ❼ *(Carrer Nou de la Rambla 3, Raval, tel 934 725 775, palauguell.cat, closed Mon. $$$$, guided visits only)*, an apartment building built 1885–1890. Back on La Rambla you pass the curved facade of Barcelona's oldest theater, **Teatre Principal** (1847), opposite which stands a statue of the founder of modern Catalan theater, Frederic Soler.

The 17th-century **Convento de Santa Mònica** hides behind the nondescript facade of a cultural center. Cross over and walk back up La Rambla to No. 42 and enter a covered passageway. This leads to the elegant **Plaça Reial** ❽, where overpriced cafés overlook palm trees and lampposts designed by Gaudí.

🅰	Also see area map pp. 32-33
►	Plaça de Catalunya
🕐	1-2 hours (without visits)
↔	1.75 miles (2.8 km)
►	Plaça Reial

Museu Blau

- 🅰 Map p. 32
- ✉ Plaça Leonardo da Vinci 4-5, Poblenou
- ☎ 932 566 002
- 🕐 Closed Mon.
- 💲 $$
- 🚇 Metro: Maresme-Fòrum, Line 4

museuciencies.cat

by the Fòrum, which houses the **Museu Blau,** an innovative museum of natural sciences.

Montjuïc

Hilltop Montjuïc ("mount of the Jews") is an essential destination for its culture, gardens, and panoramic views. The bucolic setting of the 1929 Barcelona World's Fair, the area was revitalized in 1992, when the

Calatrava's telecommunications tower crowns Montjuïc.

Fundació Joan Miró

- 🅰 Map p. 33
- ✉ Parc de Montjuïc, Montjuïc
- ☎ 934 439 470
- 🕐 Closed Sun.-Mon.
- 💲 $$$
- 🚇 Cable car or bus: 55 & 150

fundaciomiro-bcn.org

stadium was remodeled for the Olympics. More of Barcelona's 40-odd museums—including one dedicated to Joan Miró—can be found here. Montjuïc is easily accessible from the city below, and easy to get around (see sidebar p. 43).

Fundació Joan Miró: Near the funicular terminus is the

Fundació Joan Miró, set up by Catalan artist Joan Miró (1893–1983) in 1971 to conserve his work and promote contemporary art. It remains popular thanks to excellent temporary exhibitions and a lovely setting overlooking the city. Josep Luis Sert's architecture creates luminous free-flowing spaces with changing vistas. The permanent collection is concentrated on the upper floor, leaving most of the ground floor for temporary exhibitions.

On the ground floor don't miss Alexander Calder's spellbinding **"Mercury Fountain,"** commissioned by the Spanish government for the 1937 Exposition Internationale des Arts et Techniques dans la Vie Moderne, held in Paris. Beside this are wonderful, playful Miró sculptures and a large room showing his early work from the 1930s and '40s, with the **"Constellations"** series. Upstairs is the main body of work from the 1950s to '60s. The last, equally revealing section comprises works donated by friends, from Henry Moore to Henri Matisse. Look for Arnold Newman's 1979 photograph of Miró, which spells out the intense humanity of this man.

You can also venture out onto a rooftop area to see other installations and take in views over the city.

Museu Nacional d'Art de Catalunya: The **Palau Nacional** was Spain's national pavilion at the 1929 World's Fair. This extravagant building

now houses the world's largest collection of Romanesque art, an equally impressive Gothic section, the Cambó collection of Renaissance and baroque paintings, a large section on Catalan art, and a recently added section of the Thyssen-Bornemisza Collection.

The **Romanesque section** is largely composed of beautifully remounted church interiors salvaged from remote churches in the Pyrenees. Also look for the late 12th-century **altar frontals,** notably those from Avià and Ballarga.

The **Gothic section,** dazzling with gilt and altar paintings, includes a row of life-size saints by Pere Llobet (ca 1387). Look for the fine double portrait of John the Baptist and St. Stephen from Santa Maria de Puigcerdà (1445–1453), the room devoted to Bernat Martorell, and Jaume Huguet's magnificent paintings.

Other Montjuïc Sites: At the base of the wide steps to the Palau Nacional, beside the 1929 **Font Màgica** (Magic Fountain), stands the serene **Pavelló Mies van der Rohe** (*Avda. Francesc Ferrer i Guàrdia 7, Montjuïc, tel 934 234 016, miesbcn.com, $*)—the eponymous pavilion designed by the modernist architect for the 1929 World's Fair. The inner pool comes to life with a copy of Georg Kolbe's sculpture "Morning." Inside are examples of Mies's famous Barcelona chair.

Heading west along Avenida Francesc Ferrer i Guàrdia, you'll find a beautifully restored art

nouveau factory that is now a showcase for the contemporary art collection of **CaixaForum** (*Avda. Francesc Ferrer i Guàrdia 6–8, Montjuïc, tel 934 768 600, obrasocial.lacaixa.es, $*)—a bank foundation—and a popular venue for concerts and talks.

Farther west is the **Poble Espanyol** (*Avda. Francesc i Guàrdia 13, Montjuïc, tel 935 086 300 or 933 257 866, poble-espanyol .com, closed Mon., $$$$*), an architectural museum of regional Spanish styles in the form of a village. Inside are dozens of craft shops, bars, restaurants, and a flamenco *tablao,* a floorboard where the dance is performed.

Eixample

To the northwest of Montjuïc lies the district of Eixample. Most of Barcelona's art nouveau monuments are here,

---

Mobile on Montjuïc

Getting to and around Montjuïc can take some time. Decide on where you want to start, as this will influence how you get into the area in the first place.

The nearest metro stops are Espanya, Paral•lel, and Poble Sec. With map in hand you can walk from these and follow paths up the hill. A funicular operates between the Paral•lel metro stop and Montjuïc, where it links with the Teleféric de Montjuïc cable car (*telefericdemontjuic.cat, $$$$*) to take you as high as the Castell de Montjuïc.

The Bus Turístic (*barcelonabusturistic .cat)* runs three hop-on, hop-off circuits in single-deck, open-top buses around the central part of the city. The red line runs from the waterfront to the Teleféric de Montjuïc.

Museu Nacional d'Art de Catalunya

- 🅐 Map p. 32
- ✉ Palau Nacional, Parc de Montjuïc, Montjuïc
- ☎ 936 220 360
- 🕐 Closed Mon. & p.m. both Sun. & holidays
- 💲 $$$ (free Sat. after 3 p.m.)
- 🚇 Metro: Espanya, Lines 1 & 3 Bus: 13, 55, & 150

mnac.cat

La Sagrada Família

- **A** Map p. 33
- **✉** Carrer de Mallorca 401, Eixample
- **☎** 932 073 031
- **$** $$$
- **🚇** Metro: Sagrada Família, Lines 2 & 5

sagradafamilia.cat

standing beside designer shops and restaurants. Here, too, is where you will find the unmistakable spires of the still-to-be-finished Sagrada Família cathedral, Antoni Gaudí's masterwork.

La Sagrada Família: The unorthodox Sagrada Família is a must-see. The cathedral's steeples, surrounded by cranes and a builders' site below, have become the emblem of Barcelona's individualism. The story behind the ambitious structure is of an architect's total, and ultimately tragic, dedication to his greatest work.

Nativity facade, La Sagrada Família

Begun by Francisco de Paula del Villar in 1882, this building was taken over by Gaudí a year later. He planned to create a church in the form of the Latin cross, with four towering spires over each of the three facades to represent the 12 Apostles and a central cluster of five more to symbolize Christ and the Evangelists. Much of the structural inspiration came from trees, leading to branching columns.

The architect intended this neo-Gothic church to synthesize his deepening sense of spirituality, developed in mystical theories of symbolic structure while he lived as a virtual recluse during the latter part of his life. His work on the church became so obsessional that when funds were low Gaudí even sold his possessions and begged money from friends.

On his death in 1926, just one spire, the **crypt,** the **apsidal walls,** and the **Nativity facade,** on the east side, had been completed. Since then, work has continued sporadically, fraught by personality clashes, controversy, and, above all, a total absence of plans, as was Gaudí's modus operandi. Work continued under Domènec Sugrañes until 1938, and in 1936, during the Civil War, much of the workshop and models were destroyed. Since 1984 the work has been under Jordi Bonet i Armengol.

In 1986 the **Passion facade** (on the west side) was commissioned from Josep Maria Subirachs—who added yet another thorny aesthetic issue with his

INSIDER TIP:

Don't miss La Sagrada Família's Nativity facade. Its riot of ornamentation—with more than 40 animal species depicted—highlights Gaudí's love of the natural world.

—MARY STEPHANOS
National Geographic contributor

stiff, stylized sculptures—and 2010 brought the completion of the roof over the apse and the transept, forming the base of the central tower. Brave the crowds at the tower elevator on each facade for stunning views (timed entry tickets).

Gaudí is buried in the crypt, and a small museum relates the complexities of the cathedral's history and Gaudí's role.

Casa Milà: Far more successful as a Gaudí memorial is Casa Milà—familiarly known as La Pedrera—in the heart of Eixample. This innovative apartment block was built in 1906–1912, defying all architectural norms. An apartment is set up to re-create the bourgeois life of the early 20th century, and on the top floor is the Espai Gaudí, an interactive display of Gaudí's designs and models. This gives access to the extraordinary roof terrace crowned with organically shaped ventilation shafts. Caixa, the dynamic

Catalan bank that runs the space, organizes high-profile art exhibitions on the first floor (the adjoining gift shop and snack bar are excellent, too).

Other Gaudí designs in the neighborhood are **Casa Batlló** (1906) at Passeig de Gràcia 43, **Casa Calvet** (1899) at Casp 48, the **Torre de Bellesguard** (1909) at Bellesguard 16–20, and **Casa Vicens** (1888) at Carolines 24.

The Rest of the City

Monestir de Santa Maria de Pedralbes: On the flank of the Collserola hills, west of Eixample, drift back to medieval times at the Monestir de Santa Maria de Pedralbes. The walled Gothic convent was founded in 1326 by the widowed fourth wife of Jaume II, Elisenda de Montcada, who spent her last 37 years living here. Her companions were Clarissa nuns whose tiny cells surround a beautiful three-story cloister. A small chapel, **Capella de Sant Miquel,** is faced in exquisite frescoes (1346) painted by Ferrer Bassa, a follower of Giotto. The former dormitory, kitchen, pharmacy, and church give fascinating insight into the cloistered life. In 1983 the community moved to an adjoining building, opening this Gothic jewel to the public.

Palau Reial de Pedralbes: Originally a farm, the Palau Reial de Pedralbes was bought by Eusebi Güell (a patron of (continued on p. 48)

Casa Milà
- 🅰 Map p. 33
- ✉ Carrer de Provença 261–265, Eixample
- ☎ 934 845 900
- 🕐 Closed Mon.
- 💲 $$$$
- 🚇 Metro: Diagonal, Lines 3 & 5

lapedrera.com

Monestir de Santa Maria de Pedralbes
- 🅰 Map p. 32
- ✉ Baixada del Monestir 9, Pedralbes
- ☎ 932 563 434
- 🕐 Closed Mon. year-round & p.m. Tues.–Fri. & holidays Oct.–March
- 💲 $
- 🚇 Metro: Maria Cristina, Line 3

bcn.cat/monestir pedralbes

Palau Reial de Pedralbes
- 🅰 Map p. 32
- ✉ Avda. Diagonal 686, Pedralbes
- ☎ 932 563 465
- 🕐 Closed Mon.
- 💲 $
- 🚇 Metro: Palau Reial, Line 3

Gaudí & *Modernisme*

The barriers of Spain's artistic conservatism were shattered in the early 20th century when Antoni Gaudí (1852–1926) and others, including Lluís Domènech i Montaner and his son Pere Domènech, turned architectural tradition on its head. Their organically inspired structures, extensive use of decorative brickwork, and design "follies" were Spain's answer to art nouveau.

The Catalan version of art nouveau, *modernisme*, became the most extreme form and Gaudí its most controversial and intuitively brilliant protagonist. Through his complete dedication to organic forms, he revolutionized architecture in Catalunya.

Gaudí originated from Reus, near Tarragona, where he showed a fascination with natural forms found in zoology, botany, and anatomy. This, combined with a taste for craft techniques inherited from his father (a coppersmith), became the unifying thread running through his work. For Gaudí, structure was inseparable from form, color, and texture, a holistic approach inspired by the arts and crafts movement. He transformed these ideas into reality with the aid of architectural training and an enlightened backer.

Gaudí's Influence & Approach

Gaudí's early designs in the 1880s incorporated Mudejar and Gothic influences, using ornamental brickwork, ceramic tiling, parabolic arches, turrets, and domes. By the 1900s he had developed his inimitable, curvilinear style in ambitious, groundbreaking **Parc Güell** in Barcelona. Conceived as a housing estate for the wealthy (only a couple houses were actually built within the Gaudí-landscaped grounds), this project was financed by Eusebi Güell, a local industrialist who became his faithful patron. Free-flowing, organic form and extensive use of fragmented ceramic tiles became the hallmarks of Gaudí's complex, playful style.

Other examples in Barcelona are the 1906 **Casa Batlló** (*Passeig de Gràcia 43, Eixample*), nicknamed the "house of the emaciated tibia," and the 1912 **Casa Milà** (see p. 45), where chimney pots and access staircases on the roof were transformed into colorful, surrealistic sculptures. This rooftop fantasyland is still a popular meeting place for Barcelona's art-oriented youth.

Paeans to Pioneering Design

As of 2013 Barcelona at last had a spectacular design center to reflect the city's pioneering role in the world of decorative arts. The new building, **Disseny Hub** (*Plaça de les Glòries Catalanes 37–38, Poblenou, tel 932 566 700 or 932 566 713, dhub-bcn.cat, Metro: Glòries & Line 1*), was designed by MBM of Barcelona to utilize underground space beneath a striking parallel-piped section projecting above the street. Inside, three major collections are combined: the Museu Textil i d'Indumentària (fashion design), the Museu de les Arts Decoratives (product design), and the Gabinet de les Arts Gràfiques (graphic design).

Soaring behind this new structure is Jean Nouvel's unmissable **Torre Agbar** (2005), the 466-foot-high (142 m) headquarters of Barcelona's municipal water company. Its glittering outer skin, allegedly inspired by architect Antoni Gaudí, is spectacular when illuminated at night (*Fri.–Sun.*).

Fantastical and twisted towers top Gaudí's sinuous Casa Milà, an apartment building.

Gaudí's approach to construction was equally unorthodox: He never used plans, instead depending on sketches, elevations, and models. This deliberate nonrationality may have predated the surrealists but later produced insurmountable difficulties in completing Gaudí's last project, Barcelona's **Sagrada Família** cathedral (see pp. 44–45), after his death.

Death of an Eccentric Genius

Gaudí's life came to an end in a tragic yet fittingly unconventional way: He was knocked over by a tram in 1926, and his appearance was so tramplike that nobody recognized him. Since then his star has risen, and the still incomplete Sagrada Família has become the architectural symbol of Barcelona.

Parc de la Ciutadella

Map p. 33

Metro: Ciutadella-Vila Olímpica, Arc de Triomf, Barceloneta, Line 4

Gaudí) in 1882 and remodeled by architect Joan Martorell i Montells into an incongruous-looking palace together with a neo-Gothic chapel. Gaudí later contributed to the work and partially designed the magnificent gardens with fountains, a pergola, and Mediterranean plants.

After the estate was donated to the royal family in 1918, the palace was again remodeled, bringing lavish interior decoration that zigzags crazily from Louis XIV to art nouveau. In 1932 it became a decorative arts museum, now part of the Disseny Hub Barcelona (see sidebar p. 46).

Parc de la Ciutadella: Barcelona's largest park lies east of La Ribera on the site of the 1888 World's Fair. Between the paths, lawns, and ponds stand buildings from that period: the **Umbracle** (tropical greenhouse), the **Hivernacle** (winter greenhouse), and the **Castell dels Tres Dragons** (designed as an elaborate restaurant by Lluís Domènech i Montaner), all now sections of the **Museu de Ciencies Naturals** (museuciencies.cat). The neoclassical **Museu Martorell** (1878) was Barcelona's first custom-built museum and is also part of the natural sciences network. ■

NEED TO KNOW

Port Logistics: Barcelona

Most large ships dock at **Port Vell** (portde barcelona.cat), at one of four terminals (A, B, C, & D) at Muelle Adosado (Moll Adossat in Catalan). The nearest is a 20-minute walk from the Monument a Colom, close to the southern end of La Rambla, the main street through the city.

There is a visitor center near the monument and a departure point for the city's main hop-on, hop-off sightseeing bus, **Bus Turístic** (barcelonabusturistic .cat). The Drassanes metro station is nearby: It is two stops (or a 30-minute gentle uphill walk along La Rambla) to Plaça de Catalunya, the heart of the city.

Otherwise, take a taxi or the regular T3 shuttle, also known as the **Portbús** (every 20 min., $) that links all the terminals to the Monument a Colom, but be prepared for lines at busy times. Smaller

ships dock at the **World Trade Center,** which has three terminals, N, S, and E (North, South, and East).

Barcelona Highlights

You can spend your entire port of call time at any one of these destinations, but here are some suggested times to help with your planning. Note, these do not allow for travel time to and from and/or waiting in line:

• Museu Picasso: 1 hour
• Barri Gòtic (including Catedral/La Seu) & walk down La Rambla: 4 hours
• La Sagrada Família: 1 hour
• Casa Milà: 1 hour

The city's main sights are too widely spread to see on foot; use taxis or the metro (tmb.cat). To avoid lines, book tickets for the Museu Picasso and Sagrada Família in advance. Visit barcelonaturisme .com for details on time-saving passes.

Málaga & Granada

Picasso is the buzzword in Málaga, a port that once attracted Phoenicians, Romans, and Moors but today lures art lovers who flock to its museums, restaurants, tapas bars, and beaches. Mountain-backed Granada is the key excursion from the city, home to the Alhambra palace, Spain's most visited sight, along with a wide range of historic and other attractions.

Málaga

Much of Málaga's attraction lies in its breezy walking areas, from the **Paseo Marítimo** beside the town beach to the luxuriant gardens of the **Paseo del Parque** leading to the leafy **Alameda.** Just north of the gardens is the Moorish **Alcazaba,** with towers and walls enclosing the former palace. Running north from the Alameda is the shopping street, Marqués de Larios, which ends at the **Plaza de la Constitución.** The web of pedestrian streets on both sides bristles with restaurants, bars, and shops. Three blocks west of Marqués de Larios, the **Mercado de Atarazanas** has wonderful fresh produce.

The view from Gibralfaro, a hill near Málaga's waterfront and the site of a 14th-century Moorish fortification

Inside the must-see **cathedral** *(Calle Molina Lario 9, Málaga, tel 952 215 917 or 952 220 345, closed holidays, $$)* cupolas crown the three naves, with spectacular choir stalls, while in the rear **gardens** the church of **El Sagrario** has a magnificent altarpiece and an ornate Isabelline-Gothic portal.

Museo Picasso & Around:

This homage to the town's native son, Pablo Picasso (1881-1973), is housed in a beautifully renovated Renaissance mansion, the Palacio de Buenavista, in the heart of Málaga's historic center, a couple minutes' walk from the cathedral. The collection stems from Picasso's daughter-in-law, Christine Ruiz Picasso, and the artist's grandson, Bernard, who together donated 155 works, as well as 89 long-term loans. The result is an electrifying display, hung chronologically. **Casa Natal de Picasso** *(Plaza de la Merced 15, tel 952 926 060, fundacionpicasso.es, closed Tues. Nov.-March, $)*, Picasso's charming childhood home, is a five-minute walk away.

Art-lovers may also want to visit the Palacio de Villalón,

NEED TO KNOW p. 55

Málaga
- 31 B2

Visitor Information
- Plaza de la Marina 11, Málaga
- 951 926 020

malagaturismo.com
malaga.eu

Museo Picasso
- Palacio de Buenavista, Calle San Agustín 8, Málaga
- 952 127 600 or 952 443 377
- Closed Mon.
- $$

museopicasso
malaga.org

CAC

- ✉ Calle Alemania, Málaga
- ☎ 952 120 055
- 🕐 Closed Mon.

cacmalaga.org

Granada

- ◭ 31 B2

Visitor Information

- ✉ Oficina de Turismo, Plaza del Carmen, Granada
- ☎ 902 405 045
- 🕐 Closed Sun. p.m.

granadatur.com
turgranada.es

Alhambra

- ◭ Map p. 51
- ✉ Av. de los Alixares, Granada
- ☎ 902 441 221; reservations online at alhambra-patronato.es or at ticket master.es
- 🕐 Open for night visits 10 p.m.–11:30 p.m. Tues.–Sat. March–Oct. & 8 p.m.–9:30 p.m. Fri.–Sat. Nov.–Feb.
- 💲 $$$$

alhambra-patronato.es
alhambra.org

converted to house the **Museo Carmen Thyssen** (*Plaza Carmen Thyssen, Málaga, tel 952 303 131, carmenthyssenmalaga.org, closed Mon., $*); it's a five-minute walk west of the Museo Picasso. Some greats (Francisco de Zurbarán, Juan Gris, Joaquín Sorolla) hang among the 230 paintings from the baroness's collection. Málaga's contemporary art space is the **CAC** (Centro de Arte Contemporáneo), a dynamic exhibition center with a fine permanent collection and a lively program of cutting-edge exhibitions; it's just a few minutes' walk north of the port.

Granada

All visitors to Granada will want to see the Alhambra, but you should not overlook the rest of this beautiful city. Focus on three areas: the hilltop Alhambra; the steep, rambling lanes of the Albaicín opposite (sprinkled with restaurants and fine views); and the "new" town below, with specialty shops, graceful avenues, and a sprinkling of historical musts.

The Moors ruled Granada from 731 to 1492, longer than any other Muslim city in Spain, a period largely of splendor, wealth, and poetry. Arts and sciences flourished in an era of brilliance and religious tolerance that drew together thinkers from Europe, North Africa, and the Middle East. The era gave rise to the magnificent buildings of the Alhambra, but Granada continued to flourish in the

Renaissance and beyond, with the cathedral and monastery of San Jerónimo, and later the monastery of La Cartuja. Today, this is a sophisticated, vibrant, city, redolent of the past but not buried in it.

Alhambra: Visible from all over the city, the Alhambra reigns in splendor, its crenellated towers and walls rising above a cloud of greenery. The color of the walls, built from a mixture of red earth and stone, gave the Alhambra its name, derived from the Arabic word for "red." The walls once enclosed a self-contained town with 4 gateways, 23 towers, 7 palaces, workers'

INSIDER TIP:

Granada is one of the best cities in Spain for free tapas. Visit a bar, order a drink, and then wait and see what they bring you.

—YUKO AOYAMA
National Geographic grantee

houses, workshops, baths, a madrassa (Islamic school), and mosques. Many of these have disappeared, but the surviving palaces continue to exert their magic.

The Alhambra's immense popularity means that in peak season you have to dodge large guided tours. For the Palacios Nazaríes you have to reserve

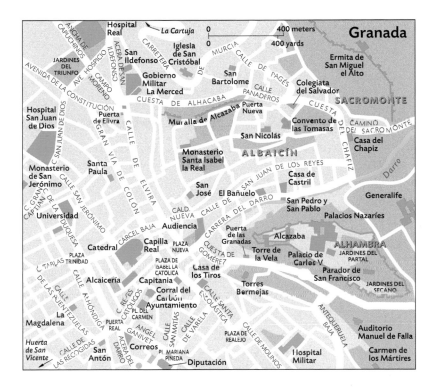

a visit (if you can, try for late in the afternoon when crowds have thinned), but you can soak up the atmosphere of the rest of the Alhambra for as long as you want.

Walk up the steep incline of **Cuesta de Gomérez,** through shady pines to the Puerta de la Justicia, or ride in a minibus from the Plaza Nueva. You can also approach from the Darro river-bank up **Cuesta del Rey Chico,** where a steep path leads to the main entrance.

The military fortress of the **Alcazaba** (the oldest part) is a good place to start your tour. Climb to the roof of the **Torre de la Vela** for a fantastic panoramic view of the entire site, and of

the rest of Granada, the Sierra Nevada, and the endless *vega* (plain) to the west. Dating from the ninth century, the Alcazaba was Granada's first major Moorish structure, though the front two towers were built four centuries later. A garden on the southern side provides a meditative oasis.

The **Palacios Nazaríes** (Nazrid, or Nasrid, Palaces) complex was built for Yusuf I and Mohammed V in the 1300s, and its two patios, intricately carved stucco ceilings, friezes, capitals and archways, geo-metric mosaics, fountains, and infinite perspectives constitute the ultimate flowering of Moor-ish style in Spain.

From the beautifully tiled **Mexuar** (Council Chamber) you enter the Patio del Cuarto Dorado, then the overwhelming **Salón de los Embajadores** (Hall of Ambassadors). Its domed marquetry ceiling is said to consist of more than 8,000 polygonal pieces of cedar. Look at the beautiful *muqarnas* (honeycomb stuccowork used in ceiling, archways, and domes), then admire the wonderful views from the windows. Outside, the **Patio de los Arrayanes** (Court of Myrtles) presents one of the Alhambra's finest perspectives.

From here, a passage leads to the **Sala de los Mozárabes,** an anteroom that opens onto the **Patio de los Leones** (Court of Lions). This rhythmical, colonnaded courtyard is divided into four sections, in traditional Islamic style, accentuating the trickling fountain and water channels, symbols of the four rivers of life. You have to imagine this patio planted with cypresses, palms, orange trees,

Alhambra

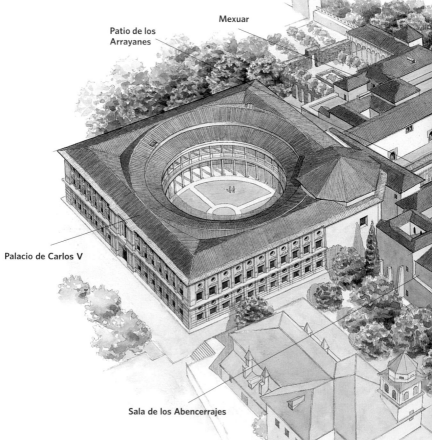

Mexuar

Patio de los Arrayanes

Palacio de Carlos V

Sala de los Abencerrajes

pomegranates, and flowers. Twelve stone lions hold the fountain basin, whose rim is carved with a poem—one of many inscribed in the Alhambra's surfaces—that extols the beauty of the court, the garden, and the play of water.

Around the patio are three halls, each one a jewel of delicate craftwork. In the most breathtaking, the **Sala de las Dos Hermanas** (Hall of the Two Sisters; to the left as you enter the patio), the domed octagonal

Generalife

Built on a higher level than the Alhambra, the Generalife is a delightful summer palace that celebrates the outdoors. An oblong pool edged by fountain jets, the **Patio de la Acequia,** is its heart; terraced gardens, pergolas, bowers, and cypress trees provide shade in summer. Don't miss the **Mirador de la Sultana** viewpoint at the very top.

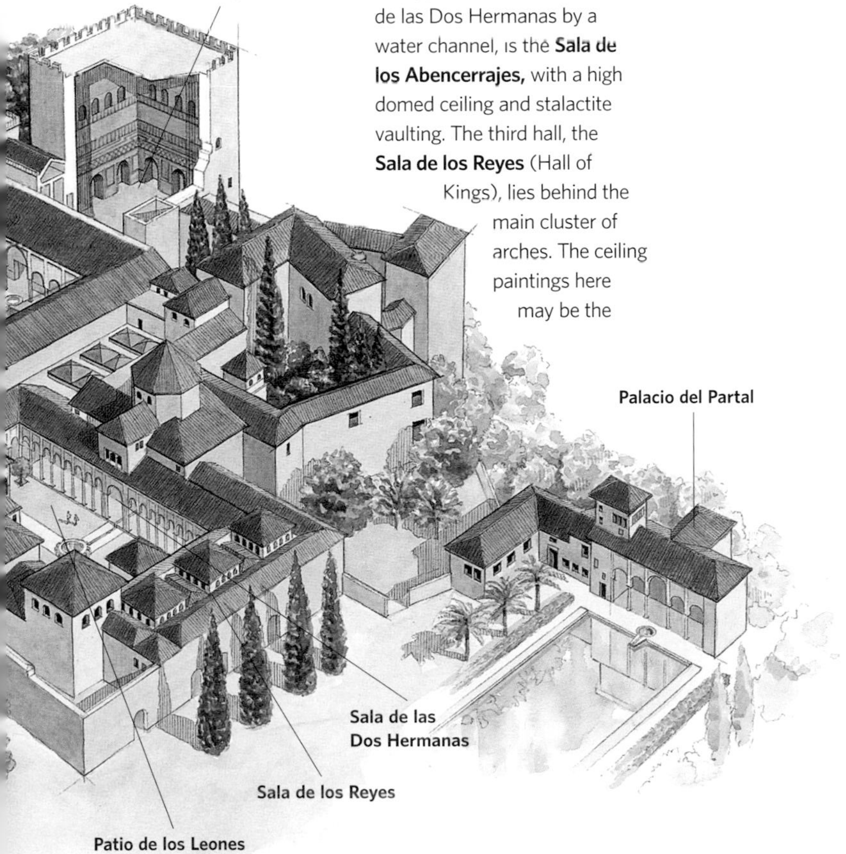

ceiling has finely worked muqarnas resembling stalactites, lit by natural light filtered through the windows just below.

Opposite, linked to the Sala de las Dos Hermanas by a water channel, is the **Sala de los Abencerrajes,** with a high domed ceiling and stalactite vaulting. The third hall, the **Sala de los Reyes** (Hall of Kings), lies behind the main cluster of arches. The ceiling paintings here may be the

Salón de los Embajadores

Palacio del Partal

Sala de las Dos Hermanas

Sala de los Reyes

Patio de los Leones

Lower level of the Renaissance Palacio de Carlos V located in Granada's Alhambra

Catedral de Granada

- ⚑ Map p. 51
- ✉ Gran Vía de Colón 5, Granada
- ☎ 958 222 959
- ⏱ Closed 1:30 p.m.–4 p.m. & Sun. until 4 p.m.
- 💲 $

work of Christian painters commissioned by Mohammed V. North of the Sala de las Dos Hermanas, another hall leads to the **Mirador de Daraxa,** overlooking a lovely garden patio.

Outside the main palace, you come to the **Palacio del Partal,** probably the first part of the complex to be built. Its arched gallery leads to the Torre de las Damas (Ladies' Tower) and through the different levels of the **gardens** to the **Generalife** (see sidebar p. 53).

A late addition to the Alhambra, the **Palacio de Carlos V** is one of Spain's most spectacular Renaissance buildings, designed by Pedro Machuca, a disciple of Michelangelo, with a stunning, vast circular courtyard (representing the Universal Empire, or the globe) that is unlike anything else in the complex. However, Carlos V used it only for ceremonial functions, preferring to live with his family in the more

congenial Moorish palaces. Inside this palace are the dull **Museo de Bellas Artes** (tel 958 575 450, closed Mon.) and better **Museo de la Alhambra** (tel 958 027 929, alhambra-patronato .es, closed Mon.), with beautiful Hispano-Muslim ceramics, carved screens, and fragments of sculpted stucco.

Downtown Granada: The Gran Vía de Colón is the main artery through downtown Granada, whose focus is the Plaza de Isabel la Católica. This square is dominated by the grandiose **Catedral,** its main building a Renaissance masterpiece, begun in 1528, with a facade recalling a three-arched triumphal arch completed in 1667.

The cathedral's highlight, however, is the earlier **Capilla Real** (Calle Oficios 3, Granada, tel 958 229 239, capillarealgranada .com, closed 1:30 p.m.–3:30 p.m., $), the Royal Chapel commissioned by Spain's Catholic monarchs to house their tombs; it is on the cathedral's southern flank and entered through the **Lonja** (the old Stock Exchange). The superb funerary monuments of Fernando and Isabel are by the Florentine sculptor Domenico Fancelli (1469–1519). Bartolomé Ordóñez (ca 1485–1520) was responsible for those of their daughter Juana ("the Mad") and her husband Felipe. The monuments lie beneath a soaring rib-vaulted ceiling, but the lead coffins are actually in the crypt below.

The **sacristy museum** contains chalices, processional crosses, reliquaries, the crown and scepter of Isabel herself, Fernando's sword, and banners carried during the 1492 conquest of Granada. Here, too, is Isabel's impressive collection of Flemish and Italian paintings, including works by Memling, van der Weyden, and Botticelli.

The cathedral was built on the site of the Great Mosque, a remnant of which stands opposite the Capilla Real. Another relic of this period, tucked away behind Calle de los Reyes Católicos, is the **Corral del Carbón** *(Calle Mariana Pineda, Granada, tel 958 221 118 or 958 225 990),* a sober courtyard building that once functioned as a storehouse and merchants' inn. Between this edifice and the cathedral lies the old Arab souk, the **Alcaicería,** rebuilt following a fire and now full of overpriced souvenirs.

South of the cathedral, a succession of animated squares and shopping streets offer visitors a break from sightseeing in the form of tapas bars and restaurants.

West of the cathedral, follow Calle San Jerónimo to the 16th-century **Monasterio de San Jerónimo,** a jewel of Spanish Renaissance architecture with a wonderful two-tiered cloister, the work of Diego de Siloé, architect of the cathedral. Nuns still live here: You can buy their cakes and jams at the entrance, and occasionally hear them singing.

La Cartuja: If time allows, take a bus from along Gran Vía de Colón to La Cartuja, a Carthusian monastery and Granada's greatest baroque monument, which stands on the outskirts of town, about 2 miles (3.2 km) from the city center. The Carthusians lived austerely but ornamented lavishly: Gold leaf, mirrors, stuccowork, marble, Venetian glass, mural paintings, marquetry, and a profusion of sculpted cherubim, flowers, and vines set the tone—and that's just in the **sanctuary** (1704–1720), rivaled only by the later **sacristy.** Recover from this visual assault in the peaceful **cloisters.** ∎

Monasterio de San Jerónimo
 Map p. 51
✉ Calle Rector López Argüeta 9, Granada
☎ 958 279 337

La Cartuja
Map p. 51
✉ Paseo de la Cartuja 49, Granada
☎ 958 161 932
🕐 Closed 1 p.m.– 3 p.m. (4 p.m. in summer)
🚌 Bus: 15

NEED TO KNOW

Port Logistics: Málaga

Málaga's attractive and state-of-the art **cruise terminal** *(puertomalaga.com)* lies immediately south of the city center— the Museu Picasso is a 10-minute walk from the waterfront—with shuttle buses connecting the port and terminal areas.

Taxis offer the quickest transfer to the bus station, and buses, not trains, provide the fastest public transit connections to Granada, 80 miles (128 km) northeast of Málaga *(departures roughly hourly; fastest journey time 90 min.; buy tickets online at* alsa.es*).*

Gibraltar

Navigating the narrow strait from the Atlantic into the Mediterranean, there could be no more imposing an introduction to the sea and lands that lie ahead than Gibraltar, one of the Pillars of Hercules in ancient myth and for centuries one of the world's most important strategic strongholds. A British territory since 1713—and bitterly disputed by Spain ever since—it is a little piece of the Mother Country on a foreign shore, complete with red mailboxes, pubs, double-decker buses, and more.

The Rock of Gibraltar stands sentinel at the entrance to the Mediterranean Sea.

Grown prosperous on the back of offshore finance and gambling, among other things, Gibraltar (for visitor information consult gibraltarinfo.gi) is a favored port of call for many cruise ships, which have a dedicated terminal within the port (gibraltarport .com). It offers a compact and readily explored town center (easily reached on foot or by taxi; the latter should be booked at busy times), as well as a medley of out-of-town sights, also easily reached. If time is short, consider one of the excursions offered by Gibraltar Rock Tours (gibraltar tours.org) from the terminal.

In town life revolves around **Main Street,** with the period buildings of Library Street, the cathedral, and interesting **Gibraltar Museum** (18–20 Bomb House Ln., tel 200 74 289, gibmuseum.gi, closed Sat. p.m.–Sun., $) at its southern end and **Casemates Square,** the Rock's social hub, at its northern limit.

Out of town to the south, and up the rocky monolith itself, is a cluster of sights entered on a single ticket at the **Upper Rock Nature Reserve** ($$$$), best reached by cable car from the southern end of Main Street. As well as superb views, it offers

INSIDER TIP:

Scale the Mediterranean Steps (E side of Gibraltar Rock) to O'Hara's Battery—an artillery battery at the rock's highest point—and on a clear day you can see over the Mediterranean to Morocco 14 miles (22.5 km) away.

—CHRISTEL CHERQAOUI
National Geographic Books
promotions director

access to **St. Michael's Cave,** the largest of 150 caves on the rock; the **Great Siege Tunnels,** part of Gibraltar's staggering defensive system, in this case created in 1779 to defend against the Spanish (the nearby World War II tunnels are less interesting); and the **Apes' Den,** home to so-called Barbary apes (actually monkeys, despite their name), famous for the legend that as long as they remain on Gibraltar, so the territory will remain British.

Valencia

Valencia's Renaissance and baroque buildings testify to its long and often prosperous history, but this is a city that, while retaining its traditions, has reinvented itself over the last 15 years through dazzling new architecture and museums and a sophisticated new seaside quarter.

Valencia's history embraces the Greeks, Carthaginians, Romans, and, in A.D. 714, the Arabs. El Cid conquered the city in 1094, but the Moors retook it and ruled until King Jaime I of Aragón's conquest in 1238. This marked the start of a golden age when Valencia became one of the Mediterranean's strongest powers.

The city's historic sights are close to one another. Start with the Gothic **Catedral** (*Plaza de la Reina, tel 963 918 127*) and climb **El Miguelete,** its octagonal bell tower, for sweeping views. The cathedral's main sight is the **Capilla del Santo Cáliz** (Chapel of the Holy Grail), a Flamboyant Gothic chapel with a superb alabaster altarpiece that enshrines a marvel, a first-century agate goblet said to be the one used by Christ at the Last Supper.

In front of the cathedral you can't miss the baroque bell tower of **Santa Catalina.** A block northeast is the beautiful 13th- and 14th-century **Almudín** (*Plaza San Luis Bertrán 1, tel 963 525 478, closed Sun. p.m.–Mon.*), the city's former granary, now used for art exhibitions. Outside, a large archaeological site contains Roman and Moorish ruins.

A couple blocks north of the cathedral is the **Palacio de Benicarló** (*Plaza San Lorenzo 4*),

a striking Gothic structure of two arcaded stories, now the seat of the Valencian parliament.

For Valencia's greatest vision of excess, head south a few blocks past the cathedral to visit the **Palacio del Marqués de Dos Aguas,** a wedding

Valencia
🅰 31 D3
Visitor Information
✉ Plaza del Ayuntamiento
☎ 963 524 908
🕐 Closed Sun. p.m.
turisvalencia.es

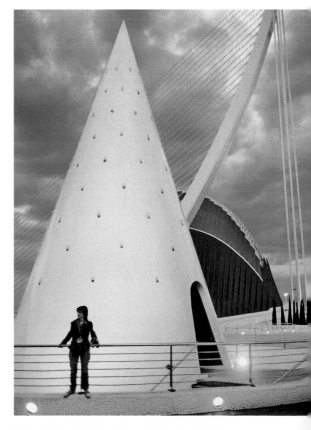

Valencia's Ciudad de las Artes y las Ciencias includes a museum, IMAX theater, and aquarium.

Palacio del Marqués de Dos Aguas

✉ Calle Poeta Querol 2

☎ 963 516 392

⊕ Closed Sun. p.m.–Mon., 2 p.m.–4 p.m. daily, & holidays

$ $

mnceramica.mcu.es

Lonja de la Seda

✉ Plaza del Mercado

☎ 963 525 478

⊕ Closed Sun. p.m.–Mon.

$ $ (free Sat.–Sun. & holidays)

Ciudad de las Artes y las Ciencias

✉ Av. Autopista de El Saler

☎ 902 100 031

$ $$

cac.es

cake of a building with one of Spain's most ornate domestic facades. The building dates from the 15th century but was heavily restructured in 1740. Don't miss the cupola painting by Hipólito Rovira (1693–1765), the Chinoiserie Room, the inlaid ivory and ebony furniture of the Smoking Room, or the marquis's bedroom with carved marble bath. On the top floor, the **Museo Nacional de Cerámica** gives an excellent overview of the development of Spanish ceramics, including six superb Picasso works and contemporary pieces.

Farther south still, Valencia's palatial railway station, the **Estación del Norte** (Calle de Xàtiva 24), is an artistic treasure of a different sort—a fine example of the use of illustrative azulejos (tiles) and decorative woodwork that dates from 1910–1917, the creative period that also produced the **Mercado Central** (Central Market) on Plaza Ciudad de Brujas, worth a morning visit to see the incredible wealth of produce.

Nearby stands the 15th-century **Lonja de la Seda** (Silk Exchange), an exceptional

Flamboyant Gothic building commissioned by the city's wealthy silk merchants; it is a UNESCO World Heritage site. Take the stairs from the patio to the upper floor to admire a masterfully carved and gilded ceiling recovered from the old town hall.

To the southeast, heading back toward the harbor, is the futuristic and highly recommended **Ciudad de las Artes y las Ciencias** (City of Arts and Sciences), much loved by locals. Completed in 2003, the four components of this ambitious cultural complex are the Hemisféric, showing IMAX films; the Science Museum; the Palace of the Arts, where concerts and opera are staged; and finally the Oceanogràfic—Europe's largest seaquarium, a universe of lakes and islands complete with an "underwater" restaurant.

If you have time to spare, while away a couple hours on **Playa de la Malvarrosa,** the popular beach north of the marina. It is home to some of the city's best paella restaurants, joined by tapas bars in the atmospheric old fishermen's quarter, **El Cabañal.** ■

NEED TO KNOW

Port Logistics: Valencia

Valencia's **cruise terminal** (valenciaport.com) is 2.5 miles (4 km) from the city center, although at busy times ships may dock farther away; a visitor information office (tel 963 674 606) is open here during cruise ship stopovers. The walk to the city is pleasant, but you can also take the shuttle or a taxi. Visit turisvalencia.es or valenciatouristcard.com for details of tourist passes that cover the shuttle and transit fares and offer discounts at sights.

Balearic Islands

This jewel-like cluster of islands scattered over the Mediterranean azure draws visitors from across Europe. Mallorca (Majorca), in particular, has been pulling in the package crowds since the 1960s, while mellow Menorca (Minorca) is favored by quieter travelers and Eivissa (Ibiza) can now boast of being one of Europe's summer nightlife capitals.

Turquoise waters surround Mallorca, the largest of the Balearic Islands.

The Balearics are not just about sun and sea; the isles have great beauty, and (especially Mallorca) a rich history set against idyllic, rural interiors. Carthaginians, Romans, Vandals, Moors, French, and British were all attracted to these shores strategically located on Mediterranean trade routes, and they left contrasting historical imprints on the various islands.

Mallorca is the largest isle—and the most developed—and the one with the most varied landscapes and history. Palma, the capital, is cosmopolitan and sophisticated. The island boasts extraordinary beauty and unique points of historical interest, not least its megalithic structures, also a feature of Menorca.

Artists have left major legacies, especially on Mallorca, while military history is explored at length in Menorca, and Eivissa has an excellent archaeological museum. A mild climate also makes for wonderful hiking and cycling year-round. Swimming and other water sports are popular from May to October, and sailing and scuba diving are widely available. Golf is another major attraction.

NEED TO KNOW p. 63

Balearic Islands
31 D3–E3

Along Passeig del Born, Palma de Mallorca

Palma de Mallorca

⚑ 31 E3

Visitor Information

✉ Port, Recinte Estación Marítima 2, Palma

☎ 608 173 307

infomallorca.net
illesbalears.es

La Seu

✉ Plaça Almoïna, Palma

☎ 902 022 445

🕐 Closed Sat p.m.–Sun.

💲 $$

catedraldemallorca.info

Baños Árabes

✉ Carrer Serra 7, Palma

☎ 971 721 549

Museu Es Baluard

✉ Plaça Porta de Santa Catalina 10, Palma

☎ 971 90 82 00

🕐 Closed Mon. Oct.–May

💲 $$

esbaluard.org

Mallorca (Majorca)

Mallorca's highlights are charming Palma de Mallorca; sights along the northwestern coast; large cave complexes; and the Alfàbia gardens.

Palma de Mallorca: More

than half of Mallorca's 700,000 people live in the Balearics' attractive, upbeat capital. Waterfront palm trees, marinas, and elegant 18th-century mansions create a grand backdrop, while tree-lined **Passeig del Born,** the social center of the old town, hums with life. Palma was founded by the Romans in 123 B.C., captured by the Moors in A.D. 903, and entered the Catalan net in 1229.

Dominating the port is the **Almudaina** (*Carrer del Palau Reial, Palma, tel 971 214 134, closed Sat. p.m.–Sun.*), the Moorish citadel. It acquired Gothic extensions as the palace of Jaume II, and it is still an official royal residence. You reach it by steps from the breezy **Parc de la Mar,**

an elongated lake. Sunset views from here are often sublime.

Opposite stands the massive Gothic cathedral, **La Seu,** a city highlight begun in 1230. The ornate southern portal, the Portada del Mirador, gives fine sea views. Vast proportions continue in the sober nave overlooked by rose windows (1912) designed by Antoni Gaudí. One chapel contains an installation (2007) by Miguel Barceló. Kings Jaume II and Jaume III are buried in the lovely Mudejar chapel of La Trinitat.

Just behind La Seu are the tenth-century **Baños Árabes** (Arab Baths), Palma's only complete relic of Moorish presence. From here, northward, extends a network of more than 150 patios, the heart of old Palma, also epitomized by a Roman arch and the **Calle Platería.**

Northwest of the center, the **Fundació Pilar i Joan Miró** (*Carrer de Saridakis 29, Palma, tel 971 701 420, miro.palmade mallorca.es, closed Sun. after 3 p.m. & Mon., $$*) was set up by the artist and his wife to preserve his studios, where he worked from 1956 until his death in 1983. Some of his art is displayed here; you can see more of it at the **Museu Fundación Juan March** (*Carrer de Sant Miquel 11, Palma, tel 971 713 515, march.es, closed Sat. p.m.–Sun.*) alongside other Spanish greats such as Picasso, Juan Gris, and Dalí, plus the sculptor Eduardo Chillida. The stunningly designed **Museu Es Baluard** also has a fine collection of international contemporary art.

Northwestern Mallorca: If time permits, don't miss the island's dramatic northern coastline. Even when glowering clouds blanket the granite sierra, the mountain villages and rocky cliffs are spectacular.

Just inland from the picturesque **Port d'Andratx,** a fishing harbor and summer yacht haven, is **Andratx,** 10 miles (16 km) west of Palma, dominated by a fort. From here a road leads down to **Sant Elm,** where boat tours take you past the island nature reserve of **Sa Dragonera.**

INSIDER TIP:

A tour of the Cuevas del Drach includes a boat ride across Lago Martel, the largest subterranean lake in the world.

—FIONA DUNLOP
National Geographic author

Next, stop at the Carthusian **monastery of Valldemossa,** 11 miles (18 km) north of Palma. The nearby beautiful hilltop village of **Deiá,** discovered decades ago by writers and artists, makes a bucolic stop. It can be crowded, but is still a lovely spot for a leisurely lunch.

Just over 5 miles (9 km) away, northeast, the market town of **Sóller** is connected by tram with a burgeoning resort in the bay below. Boat tours travel along the magnificent coast, or you can get here from Palma (18 miles/27 km) on a quaint old railway *(trendesoller.com)*.

Make the detour from Sóller through the hills to see the palm trees, oleanders, and bougainvillea of the lush **Jardines de Alfàbia,** 9 miles (13 km) from Sóller and 19 miles (30 km) north of Palma.

The Rest of Mallorca: Key targets farther from Palma include **Pollença,** a town where strong artisan traditions vie with gastronomy; **Bahía de Pollença,** a much developed area but with a pretty port; and **Capdepera,** a striking hill town with sweeping views. **Artà,** too, rises in medieval fortified splendor from a high rock crowned by the church of Sant Salvador. Both Capdepera and Artà have megalithic settlements on their outskirts.

Mallorcan scenic drama returns in the island's 800 limestone caves, notably the magnificent **Cuevas de Artà** and the mile-long (1.6 km) chambers of the **Cuevas del Drach.** In southeastern Mallorca, **Felanitx** is an important ceramics center with a road that switchbacks up through pine trees to the gloriously sited Santuari de Sant Salvador.

The coastline to the east is a succession of stunning creeks of transparent water edged with white sand, with wooded hills rising above. **Cala Figuera** still has the atmosphere of a fishing village, but tops in beauty goes to **Cala Mondragó,** a nature reserve.

Valldemossa monastery

- ✉ Plaça de Cartoixa, Valldemossa
- ☎ 971 612 106
- 🕐 Closed Sun. p.m.–Mon.
- 💲 $$$

Sóller

Visitor Information

- ✉ Plaça d'Espanya 15
- ☎ 971 638 008
- ajsoller.net/turisme

Jardines de Alfàbia

- ✉ Carretera Palma-Sóller km 17
- ☎ 971 613 123
- 🕐 Closed Sun. year-round & Sat. p.m. Nov.–March
- 💲 $$
- jardinesdealfabia.com

Cuevas de Artà

- ✉ Via de las Vuevas, Canyamel
- ☎ 971 841 293
- 💲 $$$$
- cuevasdearta.com

Cuevas del Drach

- ✉ Carretera Cuevas, Porto Cristo
- ☎ 971 820 753
- 🕐 4–7 tours daily
- 💲 $$$$

Eivissa (Ibiza)

🅰 31 D3

Visitor Information

✉ La Cúria, Plaça de la Catedral, Eivissa Town

☎ 971 399 232

🕐 Closed p.m.

eivissa.es

Museu Arqueológic d'Eivissa

✉ Plaça de la Catedral 3, Eivissa Town

☎ 971 301 231

🕐 Closed Mon. & p.m. daily Oct.–March, & 2 p.m.–6 p.m. daily April–Sept.

Madina Yabisa-La Cúria

✉ Carrer Major 2, Eivissa Town

☎ 971 392 390

🕐 Closed Mon. & p.m. both Sat. & Sun.

💲 $

Eivissa (Ibiza)

Eivissa (Ibiza's name in Catalan) is hot in temperature and mood. Hip young people flock here for the nightlife. If clubs and street fashion are not your scene, then avoid July and August, or spend time on one of the island's trendy beaches.

Menorcan Megaliths

Menorca's ancient stone monuments can be divided into three categories: *talaiots* (conical stone mounds, rising to 25 feet/7.6 m); *taules* (enormous T-shaped structures thought to have been temples), and *navetes* (resembling upturned hulls of boats). They were either graves or altars, but their sheer number and scale have inspired countless esoteric theories. The Torre d'en Gaumés is the largest prehistoric settlement in the Balearics, with three talaiots surrounded by a defensive wall, pillared naves, and a *taula*. Nearby is a dolmenic burial chamber, Ses Roques Llises.

Eivissa Town: The old capital of Eivissa sits on a promontory dominating the harbor and defined by the silhouette of the cathedral and Renaissance walls encircling the **Dalt Vila** (Old Town), a UNESCO World Heritage site. Spectacular 16th-century ramparts, steep stone steps, and elegant mansions bespeak its history, in contrast with the bars, restaurants, and boutiques that line the streets of the "new town" below.

Enter the Old Town through the **Portal de ses Taules,** the ancient main gate, flanked by headless Roman-era statues of Juno and an anonymous, armless male. The **Catedral** (cathedral) stands on a site occupied by religious buildings since the times of the Phoenicians: It dates from the 13th century, but it was largely remodeled half a century later.

To get an idea of the island's ancient past, look at the Carthaginian and other artifacts at the **Museu Arqueológic d'Eivissa,** located beside the cathedral. Behind the cathedral, the **Madina Yabisa-La Cúria** is full of slick audiovisual displays devoted to Eivissa's period under Arab domination.

If you have time, take an excursion to the interior of the island to take in the scenery and examples of the traditional rural house, a composition of white-washed cubes around a central, communal room, with verandas for storing crops. Beside these North African–looking houses are simple, fortified churches where inhabitants would shelter from pirate attacks.

Beaches: Some of Eivissa's 56 beaches and their transparent warm waters remain unspoiled. Both sandy and rocky **Cala Salada,** near Sant Antoni, is one of the more tranquil beaches in the developed area. (Sant Antoni is the capital of Eivissa's clubbing culture.) Less accessible Sant Joan to the northeast has **Calad'en Serra** and **S'Illot des Renclí** along its vertiginous coastline. This wilder end of the island is a haven from the crowds. Santa Eulària des Riu is a booming high-rise resort. Head south to the nature reserve of **Ses Salines** to find surprising landscapes, extensive salt flats, and endless water sports.

Menorca (Minorca)

Long outshone by Mallorca and Eivissa, this peaceful, 271-square-mile (702 sq km) island is gaining in popularity. A history of occupation by a series of invaders has given it a distinctive flavor and gastronomy. North African couscous meets British desserts here, and the capital, Maó (Mahón), is the place where French mayonnaise was created.

Maó: Life in town revolves around the cafés, shops, and restaurants of the old town in the streets between **Plaça de s'Esplanada** and **Plaça d'Espanya.** Signs of sporadic British occupation from 1713 to 1802 are evident in older houses. In the town of Es Castell, 2 miles (3 km) away, the well-preserved **Fort Marlborough** gives you a picture of the period.

Far more memorable are the 500 **megaliths** from the second millennium B.C. dotted over the island (see sidebar opposite).

Two sites are outstanding: the settlement of **Trepucó** with its 16-foot-high (4.9 m) taula, just outside Maó, and the **Naveta des Tudons,** 3 miles (5 km) east of **Ciutadella,** the delightfully scenic former capital. In the last see the fine

historic buildings on Carrer del Seminari. One old house, **Palau Salort** *(Carrer Major des Born),* is occasionally open to the public. Also visit the Gothic **Catedral** *(Plaça de la Catedral, Maó)* for its lovely carved choir stalls and note the bell tower, the converted minaret of the mosque that once stood on the site.

The **north coast** beaches are mainly red-ocher sand backed by windy heath. An exception is Pregonda, protected by rocky islets. Finer sand lines the **south coast creeks** attracting the majority of visitors, but you can still find solitude at **Son Saura, Cala Mitjana** in the south, and **Platja d'en Tortuga** in the northeast. Tops for transparent turquoise is Cala Macarella in the far southwest. ■

Menorca (Minorca)

🗺 31 E3

Visitor Information

✉ Maó Port: Moll de Llevant 2, Maó

☎ 971 355 952

✉ Maó Old Town: Plaça Constitució 22, Maó

☎ 971 363 790

menorca.es

Ciutadella

Visitor Information

✉ Plaça des Born, Ciutadella

☎ 971 484 155

NEED TO KNOW

Port Logistics: Mallorca

Visit *portsdebalears.com* for details of ports across the Balearic Islands. In Mallorca, most ships dock close enough to the city's old quarter that you can walk from the ship, though at busy times boats may moor 5 miles (8 km) away in the city's industrial zone.

Port Logistics: Eivissa

Cruise ships dock at the **Eivissa town pier,** a simple walk to the Dalt Vila: There is a small visitor center *(closed Sun.)* on the harbor at Avinguda de les Andanes.

Port Logistics: Menorca

Cruise ships dock at **Maó's commercial port,** a short but steep walk to the town's old quarter.

The lovely countryside of Provence and the historic and glamorous towns of Nice, Cannes, St.-Tropez, Arles, Aix, and Avignon

French Riviera & Provence

Introduction & Map   66-67

Marseille & Provence   68-75

A Stroll Around Vieil Aix   72-73

Need to Know: Marseille   75

Cannes & St.-Tropez   76-77

Need to Know: Cannes   77

Nice & Around   78-83

Walk: Exploring Vieux Nice by Foot   80-81

Need to Know: Nice   83

Monaco   84-85

Need to Know: Monaco   85

Restaurants   278-282

Nice's beaches bloom with colorful umbrellas and bathing beauties in summer.

French Riviera & Provence

The French Riviera—or Côte d'Azur (Azure Coast)—is France's southern jewel. Clear blue waters and sublime coastal landscapes provide a setting for towns and cities that are a byword for glamour and wealth—Nice, Cannes, St.-Tropez, Monte-Carlo—stylish vacation playgrounds full of mega-yachts, casinos, luxury hotels, nightclubs, and superb restaurants. Edgier cities such as Marseille lie nearby, and in the region's hinterland the beautiful pastoral countryside of Provence plays host to the fine historic towns of Arles, Avignon, and Aix-en-Provence.

Atmospheric villages dot Provence.

Marseille & Provence

Marseille is southern France's largest city and the country's largest port. It has a busy, no-nonsense air and gritty, workaday edge, but it has tidied up its waterfront and added polish to its museums and monuments. You could easily spend a day or so here, but on a short visit it makes sense to visit one of a trio of interior towns nearby—Arles, Avignon, or Aix-en-Provence—and leave any remaining time for a quick taste of Marseille.

Visiting these towns gives you a glimpse of Provence, the geographical region north of the French Riviera, renowned for its pastoral beauty, all vineyards, olives groves, lavender fields, and rolling hills. Provence is very much part of the warm south, sheltered and cut off from the rest of France by the Alps and Massif Central. In the east, above Nice, the mountains drop almost to the sea, while in the west the great arc of the Rhône Delta closes the region in a sweep of beaches and lagoons.

Historically, the south of France bears many Roman traces, but it was the 19th and early 20th centuries, when the world's wealthy elite came south for the balmy winter climate, accompanied by artists drawn to Provence's light and color, that most shaped this region. The legacy of this creative spirit lives on in the area's many fine museums and galleries. More recently, celebrities

French Riviera

The sublime coastline continues to draw the visiting and residential elite, who hide themselves away, in the gleaming tower blocks of the tiny city-state of Monaco or in the vast houses or exclusive hotels of the idyllic Cap Ferrat peninsula, both east of Nice. Casual visitors can still get a taste of what makes this coast so celebrated, however. You might dip into the casino at Monte-Carlo, Monaco, for example, and walk around Nice's quaint historic quarter. Or stroll La Croisette at Cannes, walking in the red-carpet footsteps of the film stars who attend the town's famous annual film festival. Or admire the coast from a boat trip to St.-Tropez, and sample the quieter,

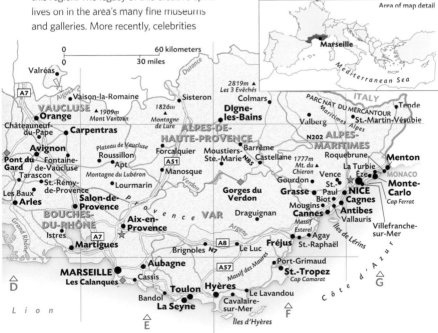

cemented the idea of the south of France as a chic and desirable place both to live and to take a vacation, either in the bucolic Provence region or along the sun-drenched Côte d'Azur.

old-world charms of smaller centers such as Villefranche-sur-Mer. And, of course, sample the superb food and wine that is an integral part of any visit to France, but especially of its sunny, southern shores. ∎

Marseille & Provence

France's oldest and largest port is tough, raffish, cosmopolitan, and undergoing a cultural renaissance, with revamped museums and tidied-up streets. It still has spice and edge, however, in marked contrast to the trio of easily reached historic towns—Arles, Aix-en-Provence, and Avignon—in its Provençal hinterland.

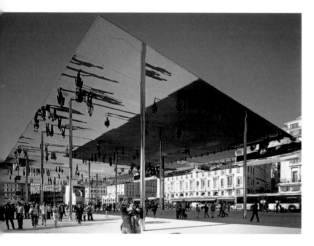

The Norman Foster–designed steel pavilion in Marseille's Vieux Port offers visitors a unique view of the harbor.

NEED TO KNOW p. 75

Marseille
A 67 E2
Visitor Information
✉ La Canebière 4
☎ 0826 500 500
marseille-tourisme.com

MuCEM
✉ Three sites: Fort St.-Jean (*Quai du Port 210*), Panier (*Parvis de l'Église St.-Laurent, Esplanade de la Tourette 16*), & J4 (*Esplanade du J4 1*)
☎ 04 8435 1313
🕑 Closed Tues.
$ $$$
mucem.org

Marseille

Founded by the Greeks in the seventh century B.C., Marseille remained independent of France until the 15th century, but was always France's gateway to the Middle East and North Africa, and always a cultural melting pot. Western magnates and Eastern potentates once met along **La Canebière,** the city's bustling main thoroughfare, which dead-ends at the Vieux Port.

The **Vieux Port** remains the city's focus, the old forts that once guarded its entrance now overlooking a fish market and some superb seafood restaurants. **Fort St.-Jean,** on

the port's north side, houses some exhibits of the **MuCEM** (Museum of the Civilizations of Europe and the Mediterranean), one of the city's newest museums (opened in 2013). The museum's sleek main building next door offers a dynamic overview of Roman, Greek, Phoenician, and other cultures across the centuries.

The hill-encompassing old quarter of **Le Panier,** stretching east from Fort St.-Jean and north of Vieux Port's Quai du Port, is the main focus of the city's drive for renewal. The Germans destroyed much of the area during World War II, but old streets (notably Rue du Panier, Rue du Petit-Puis, and Rue des Muettes) and a few historic buildings remain. The outstanding 17th-century hospice of **La Vieille Charité** (*Rue de la Charité 2, tel 04 9114 5880, closed Mon., $–$$*) is literally the quarter's crowning jewel. The former poorhouse now houses the **Musée d'Archéologie Mediterranéenne** (*tel 04 9114 5859, closed Mon., $$*)—its archaeological collections beautifully presented in a tomblike ambience—and other museums, but it is worth a visit for the restored building alone. It comprises a central courtyard surrounded on all four sides by arcaded buildings.

Nearby, the 19th-century **Cathédrale de la Major** (*Place de la Major, tel 04 9190 5287, closed Mon.*) dwarfs the 12th-century **Ancienne Major,** the original cathedral that was partially destroyed to make space for the new one. The **Musée des Docks Romains,** down by the port, displays Roman finds.

From here, head to the **ferry** (*below Hôtel de Ville, every 10 min.*) on nearby Quai du Port and ride over to the Vieux Port's south side, landing below the Bar de la Marine on the Quai de Rive Neuve. A few blocks west stands the fifth-century foundation of the **Basilique St.-Victor** (*Rue de l'Abbeye, Quai de Rive Neuve, tel 04 9611 2260, saintvictor.net*); be sure to venture into the eerie crypt (*$*) and catacombs.

South of St.-Victor is the 19th-century **Basilique Notre-Dame-de-la-Garde,** atop the Colline de la Garde, Marseille's highest point. A walkway extends around the neo-Byzantine-style basilica, providing a 360-degree panorama overlooking Marseille, the hills behind, and the islands offshore. Inside, gilded mosaics, murals, remarkable collections of ex-votos, and other works of art dazzle the eyes.

Musée des Docks Romains

✉ Place Vivaux 10
☎ 04 9191 2462
🕐 Closed Mon.
💲 $$

Basilique Notre-Dame-de-la-Garde

✉ Rue Fort du Sanctuaire–Parvis de la Basilique de Notre-Dame-de-la-Garde
☎ 04 9113 4080
notredamedelagarde.com

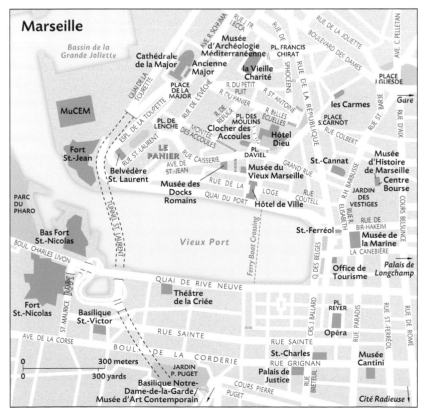

Marseille

Bassin de la Grande Joliette

QUAI DE LA TOURETTE

MuCEM

Fort St.-Jean

PARC DU PHARO

Bas Fort St.-Nicolas

BOUL. CHARLES LIVON

Fort St.-Nicolas

AVE. DE LA CORSE

Cathédrale de la Major

PLACE DE LA MAJOR

RUE DE L'ÉVÊCHÉ

PL. DE LENCHE

LE PANIER

Belvédère St. Laurent

RUE ST.-LAURENT

AVE. DE ST.-JEAN

ESPL. DE LA TOURETTE

TUNNEL ST. LAURENT

ST.-MAURICE

Basilique St.-Victor

Musée d'Archéologie Méditerranéenne

Ancienne Major

R. DU PETIT PUIT

R. DU PANIER

R. DE REFUGE

MONTÉE DES ACCOULES

RUE CAISSERIE

Musée des Docks Romains

QUAI DU PORT

Théâtre de la Criée

QUAI DE RIVE NEUVE

RUE SAINTE

BOUL. DE LA CORDERIE

JARDIN P. PUGET

Basilique Notre-Dame-de-la-Garde/ Musée d'Art Contemporain

la Vieille Charité

R. ST.-ANTOINE

R. BELLES ÉCUELLES

Clocher des Accoules

PL. DES MOULINS

PL. DAVIEL

Musée du Vieux Marseille

RUE DE LA LOGE

Hôtel de Ville

Vieux Port

Ferry Boat Crossing

RUE SAINTE

PL. FRANCIS CHIRAT

RUE DE LA RÉPUBLIQUE

les Carmes

PLACE S.CARNOT

RUE COLBERT

Hôtel Dieu

GRAND RUE

St.-Cannat

RUE COUTELLI

St.-Ferréol

Q. DES BELGES

PL. REYER

CRS. J. BALLARD

St.-Charles

RUE GRIGNAN

Palais de Justice

COURS PIERRE PUGET

RUE BRETEUIL

RUE DE LA JOLIETTE

BOULEVARD DES DAMES

AVE. C. PELLETAN

PLACE J. GUESDE

Gare

RUE ST.-BARBE

RUE D'AIX

R.H. BARBUSSE

JARDIN DES VESTIGES

RUE ELISABETH

RUE DE BIR-HAKEIM

Musée d'Histoire de Marseille

Centre Bourse

COURS BELSUNCE

Musée de la Marine

LA CANEBIÈRE

Office de Tourisme

Palais de Longchamp

Opéra

RUE PARADIS

RUE ST.-FERRÉOL

RUE DE ROME

Musée Cantini

Cité Radieuse

0 | 300 meters
0 | 300 yards

Aix-en-Provence

Aix-en-Provence

🗺 67 E3

Visitor Information

✉ Les Allées Provençales, Av. Giuseppe Verdi 300, Aix

☎ 04 4216 1161

🕐 Closed 1 p.m.– 2 p.m. Sun.

aixenprovence tourism.com

Aix-en-Provence

Only 17 miles (27 km) north of Marseille, Aix is an easy excursion by train, and though it has no "conventional" sightseeing treasures, it offers a perfect slice of provincial France and streets that are a pleasure to explore for their own sake: a chic and elegant city, with graceful boulevards, shady squares, and hundreds

Bouillabaisse

Bouillabaisse is a fish soup cum stew that you will find across much of Provence. It has its origins in Marseille, however, and in particular in a dish made by local fishermen from the poorer types of fish they were unable to sell. It is typically served with grilled slices of bread and a rouille—a sauce made from olive oil, garlic, saffron, and cayenne pepper. It comes in numerous versions, many of them pale imitations of the real thing. To be sure of eating something approaching the genuine article, look for signs proclaiming adherence to the Marseille Bouillabaise Charter, drawn up by local restaurateurs concerned at the debasement of the dish.

Cathédrale St.-Sauveur

✉ Place des Martyrs de la Résistance, Aix

☎ 04 4223 4565

---

of beautiful fountains. Ninety minutes would be enough to get a taste of the city, but you could easily linger longer.

At the heart of Aix lies the majestic **Cours Mirabeau,** the famous tree-shaded boulevard laid out on the site of the old ramparts, flanked by elegant 17th- and 18th-century houses and punctuated by numerous fountains. Take time to watch the world go by from the terrace of one of the cafés here, but beware the high prices.

To the north, **Vieil Aix** (see pp. 72–73) extends through a maze of squares, with Place d'Albertas and Place Richelme fine targets, along with Rue Aude, medieval Aix's main street. On Saturdays, when it is taken over by a market, this area is even more irresistible. Among its many buildings is the lovely Gothic **Cathédrale St.-Sauveur,** known for its 16th-century carved doors, the cool columns of its 5th-century Merovingian baptistery, and its Romanesque cloisters. Look for Nicolas Froment's exceptional 15th-century triptych, "The Burning Bush."

Cézanne & More: Aix's most famous son is the Postimpressionist artist Paul Cézanne. Eight of his works are on display at the **Musée Granet** (*Place St.-Jean-de-Malte, Aix, tel 04 4252 8832, closed Mon., $*), an art and archaeological museum located in the elegant **Quartier Mazarin,** south of Cours Mirabeau. You'll find statuary and objects found at the Oppidum d'Entremont (see p. 71) here, too. North of Old Town, the **Atelier Cézanne** (*Av. Paul Cézanne 9, Aix, tel 04 4221 0653, atelier-cezanne .com, closed 12 p.m.–2 p.m. & Sun. Dec.–Feb., $$*), where the artist worked from 1897 until he died in 1906, has been re-created just as he might have left it. West of the city center, the **Fondation Vasarely** (*Av. Marcel Pagnol 1, Aix, tel 04 4220 0109, fondationvasarely .fr, closed Mon. & 1 p.m.–2 p.m.,*

$$$), is an extraordinary museum designed by artist Victor Vasarely himself, with exterior walls that look like his paintings.

Outside Town: About 2 miles (3 km) north of Aix, in the direction of Puyricard, is the **Oppidum d'Entremont** (*closed Tues. year-round & Sat.–Sun. Oct.–May, entremont.culture .gouv.fr*), site of the original Gallic settlement of Aix. Excavations here have revealed fortifications and commercial and residential buildings.

West of Aix is the **Site Memorial Les Milles** (*Chemin de la Badesse 40, Aix, tel 04 4239 1711, campdesmilles.org, $$$*), a brick factory used as a concentration camp during World War II. Artists and intellectuals considered "undesirables" were imprisoned here, among them Max Ernst. Documents and photos tell the story; in the refectory are restored fragments of caricatures and murals created by the prisoners.

Arles

Enough remains of this great Roman city, 58 miles (93 km) northwest of Marseille, to convey a powerful sense of its long history. Nowhere is this more true than with the first-century **Arènes d'Arles** (*Rond-point des Arènes, Arles, tel 04 9049 3674, $$*). A large Roman amphitheater now used for bullfights and festival pageants, it was once the scene of gladiatorial combat. Measuring 446 feet by 351 feet (136 m

by 107 m) with two stories each made up of 60 arches, it could seat 25,000 spectators. As you walk around the lower arcade, look for the tunnels through which wild beasts charged into the arena.

Nearby is a slightly earlier **Théâtre Antique.** The great columns of the stage wall (formerly used to hang prisoners) today provide a backdrop for performances during the Arles Festival in late June and early July.

The town's Roman remains are rivaled by its medieval buildings, notably the **Église St.-Trophime** (*Place de la République, Arles, tel 04 9049 3353*), a masterpiece of Provençal

Romanesque famed for its glorious cloister and an elaborately carved 12th-century portal.

Not content with being a great "open-air museum," Arles has a number of exceptional indoor museums. The impressive *(continued on p. 74)*

Arles
A 67 D3
Visitor Information
✉ Boul. des Lices, Arles
☎ 04 9018 4120
🕐 Closed Sun. p.m.
arlestourisme.com

The 1860 Rotonde fountain on Place du General de Gaulle marks the western end of the stately Cours Mirabeau, Aix.

(continued on p. 74)

A Stroll Around Vieil Aix

This delightful promenade takes in some of Aix's most charming—and historic—streets in the jumbled labyrinth of its old town, Vieil Aix.

Cathédrale St.-Sauveur's two green-and-gold organ cases, facing each other, date from the 1740s.

Begin at **La Rotonde** ❶, the fountain on the former site of the city's main gate, at the foot of elegant **Cours Mirabeau** (see p. 70). Walk up the thoroughfare, admiring the cafés, *hôtels particuliers,* and fountains. Two of the largest town houses are No. 20, the 17th-century **Hôtel de Forbin,** and No. 28, the 18th-century **Hôtel du Chevalier Hancy.**

At the **Fontaine des Neuf Canons** ❷, take a left at Rue Nazareth and, at Rue Espariat, go right, past Rue Aude, to **Place d'Albertas** ❸, full of Parisian elegance. Rococo facades front three sides of this secluded square, and the base of the fountain dates from 1912.

Backtrack to Rue Aude and go right. At the junction, keep going straight, on Rue Maréchal Foch, to **Place de l'Hôtel de Ville,** which is dominated by the **Tour de l'Horloge.** The clock tower has two clock faces: a typical one and, below that, an astronomical clock from 1661. On the latter, four statues, each

NOT TO BE MISSED:

NOT TO BE MISSED:

Cours Mirabeau • Place de l'Hôtel de Ville • Cathédrale St.-Sauveur

representing a season, are shown in turn. The adjoining **Hôtel de Ville** ❹ (Town Hall), with its Italianate facade and sculptured wood doors, was built between 1655 and 1670 by Pierre Pavillon. On the square's south side, the **Ancienne Halle aux Grains** (former Wheat Exchange), built between 1759 and 1761, reflects the importance of wheat at the time. Topping the north facade is an allegorical pediment featuring the two important sources of water for farmers: the strong, steady Rhône, represented by a rough-looking man, and the temperamental, flood-prone Durance, symbolized by a woman half jumping out of the sculpture. On the square's south side is another square, **Place Richelme,** site of a daily fruit and vegetable market.

Beyond Place de l'Hôtel de Ville

Pass through the clock tower and proceed up Rue Gaston de Saporta. Just beyond the **Musée du Vieil Aix,** on the left, will be the **Hôtel de Châteaurenard ❺.** A splendid town house built in the mid-1600s by Pierre Pavillon, it's a cultural center now. Peek inside to see the trompe l'oeil on the staircase, the 1660 work of Bruxellois Jean Daret, appointed king's painter by Louis XIV. The images rotate around the central figure of Minerva, on the ceiling above, who represents nobility.

Just up Rue Gaston de Saporta, at No. 28 Place des Martyrs de la Résistance, is the **Palais de l'Archêvéché,** once the archbishops' residence, built between 1650 and 1730. It houses, among other museums, the **Musée des Tapisseries** (tel 04 4223 0991, closed Tues., 12:30 p.m.–1:30 p.m. year-round, & a.m. daily in winter, $), featuring a collection of Beauvais tapestries.

The walk ends up the street at the glorious **Cathédrale St.-Sauveur ❻** (see p. 70). The **Atelier Cézanne** (see p. 70) is just a half a mile farther, via Avenue Pasteur.

> 🅜 Also see area map pp. 66–67
> ► La Rotonde
> 🕒 1 hour (more with stops)
> ↔ Half mile (800 m)
> ► Cathédrale St.-Sauveur

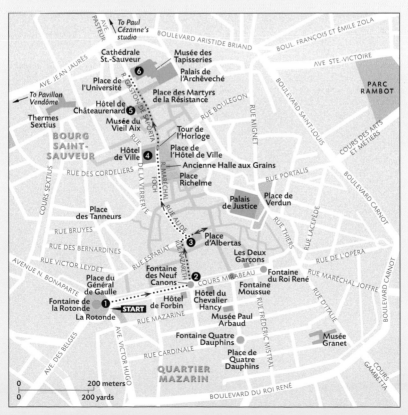

Musée Départemental Arles Antique

- ✉ Av. 1ére Division France Libre, Presqu'île du Cirque Romain, Arles
- ☎ 04 1331 5103
- ⏱ Closed Tues.
- 💲 $$$

arles-antique.cg13.fr

Museon Arlaten

- ✉ Rue de la République 29–31, Arles
- ☎ 04 1331 5199
- ⏱ Closed for renovation
- 💲 $

Musée Réattu

- ✉ Rue du Grand Prieuré 10, Arles
- ☎ 04 9049 3758
- ⏱ Closed Mon.
- 💲 $$

Avignon

- 🅐 67 D3

Visitor Information

- ✉ Cours Jean Jaurès 41, Avignon
- ☎ 04 3274 3274
- ⏱ Closed Sun. p.m. Nov.–March

avignon-tourisme.com

Palais des Papes

- ✉ Place du Palais, Avignon
- ☎ 04 3274 3274
- 💲 $$$$

palais-des-papes.com

Musée Départemental Arles Antique, on the riverbank, uses models of the city and individual buildings to help explain the evolution of Roman Arles. Farther east on the riverbank, head inland a couple blocks on Rue Anatole France to the ethnology museum, **Museon Arlaten.** Devoted to Provençal folklore, crafts, and costumes, it is expected to reopen by 2015 after a lengthy renovation. Farther east still, back toward the riverbank, is the excellent **Musée Réattu.** It features a collection of 16th- to 18th-century paintings, contemporary sculptures, and more, including 57 Picasso drawings donated by the artist, who loved the bullfights staged in Arles.

But the artist most closely associated with Arles is Vincent van Gogh. Here he fell in love with the south and its brilliant colors; here in 1888 he painted some of his best known works, including "Sunflowers"; and here, shortly afterward, he sliced off his earlobe in a fit of dementia. The **Espace van Gogh** (*Place Docteur Félix Rey, Arles, tel 04 9049 3939, closed Sun.–Mon.*), once the hospital where the artist was committed, is now an exhibition space and library with a garden planted to resemble a van Gogh painting. The **Fondation Vincent van Gogh** (*Rue du Docteur Fanton 35 ter, Arles, tel 04 9093 0808, fondation-vincentvangogh -arles.org, $$*), opposite the Arènes d'Arles, makes up for its lack of original van Gogh works with paintings inspired by him.

Avignon

Secure within its great walls, Avignon retains the grand self-assurance of its 14th-century heyday, when a series of popes lived here. These days the city is a thriving cultural center.

INSIDER TIP:

Fans of van Gogh: Follow the art trail [map at tourist office] around Arles with panels of his most famous artworks set up on the precise spots where he painted them.

—BARBARA A. NOE
National Geographic Travel Books senior editor

The coldly magnificent **Palais des Papes,** begun in 1334, dominates the historic city. Most of the interior of this great white edifice—it is actually two palaces—is empty after the depredations of the revolution, but six magnificent Gobelins tapestries and remarkable frescoes by Matteo Giovanetti reflect its former glory. The Chambre du Cerf, the study of Clement VI, has beautiful ceramic tiles and frescoes.

The lovely 14th-century **Petit Palais** (*tel 04 9086 4458, closed Tues. & 1 p.m.–2 p.m., $$*) opposite contains distinguished medieval painting and sculpture—an impressive introduction to the International Gothic style pioneered in Avignon by

14th-century Italian artists. Look for works by Simone Martine and a "Madonna and Child" by Botticelli.

Next to the palace are the **Cathédrale Notre-Dame-des-Doms** (*Place du Palais, Avignon, tel 04 9082 1221*) and, behind it, the lovely park of the **Rocher des Doms**. Below are the Rhône River and the celebrated remains of the Pont St.-Bénezet, usually known as the **Pont d'Avignon** (*Boul. du Rhône, Avignon, tel 04 3274 3274, www.avignon-pont.com, $*). The 12th-century bridge was partly swept away by the Rhône in the 17th century. Only four spans of the original 22 remain.

To the south are the narrow streets of the **Old Town,** one of the prettiest of which is **Rue des Teinturiers** (Street of Dyers), beside the Canal de Vaucluse. Here, until the 19th century, textile makers produced the Provençal patterned cottons known as *Indiennes,* inspired by Indian calicos brought back from the Crusades.

If you are interested in museums, search out the eclectic **Musée Calvet,** with displays of fine and decorative arts; the **Fondation Angladon-Dubrujeaud** (*Rue Laboureur 5, Avignon, tel 04 9082 2903, angladon.fr, closed a.m. & Mon. year round & Tues. Nov.–March, $$*), with the only van Gogh painting still in Provence, "Les Wagons de Chemin de Fer"; and the contemporary art of the **Collection Lambert.** ∎

Musée Calvet
- ✉ Hôtel Villeneuve-Martignan, Rue Joseph Vernet 65, Avignon
- ☎ 04 9016 0909
- ⏱ Closed Tues.
- 💲 $$

Collection Lambert
- ✉ Hôtel de Caumont, Rue Violette 5, Avignon
- ☎ 04 9016 5621
- ⏱ Closed Mon. Sept.–June
- 💲 $$$$ during exhibitions
- collectionlambert.fr

NEED TO KNOW

Port Logistics: Marseille

Most ships dock in the busy and unattractive port area 5 to 6 miles (8–10 km) north of the Vieux Port (Old Port), the heart of historic Marseille, and provide shuttles between the two points. Making your own way to the Vieux Port involves a 30-minute walk, then bus or subway. Some shuttles continue to the **Gare St.-Charles** railroad station (*sncf.com*), for trains to Aix-en-Provence, Arles, or Avignon.

Smaller ships dock within walking distance of the Vieux Port at La Joliette.

Sightseeing Tours

If your time is tight in Marseille, the **Train Touristique** (*petit-train-marseille.com, $$$*), a wheeled tourist train, runs 1–3 times hourly from the Vieux Port around the city's highlights in about an hour (the "Circuit 1" tour includes Notre-Dame-de-la-Garde). The hop-on, hop-off **Grand Tour** (*marseillelegrandtour.com, $$$$$*) buses follow a similar route.

Getting to Provence

Given a day in Marseille, the best plan is to take an excursion to either Aix, Arles, or Avignon—each needs at least a morning—and then return to Marseille to spend any remaining time. Up to 5 trains hourly run to Avignon (*quickest journey time is 27 min.; most services 60–90 min.*); up to 4 hourly to Arles (42–75 min.); and 1–4 hourly to Aix (33–44 min.). To reach the Gare St.-Charles from the Vieux Port, ride the metro (subway)—buy a ticket ($) at an automated machine—two stops to St.-Charles on "La Rose" service; alternatively, the station is a 20-minute walk.

Cannes & St.-Tropez

A perfect Riviera base and one of southern France's most glamorous cities, Cannes is big enough to have all the grand restaurants, beaches, and shopping you could ever want yet is small enough to walk around. St.-Tropez, meanwhile, has become one of the hot spots for which the Côte d'Azur is famous. It's an easygoing, albeit moneyed place of some charm, and its old quarter and yacht-filled harbor are pleasant to stroll, window-shopping and people-watching.

Crowds of well-heeled vacationers descend upon Cannes to soak up the sun on its warm beaches.

NEED TO KNOW p. 77

Cannes

🅰 67 F3

Visitor Information

✉ Palais des Festivals, Boul. de la Croisette 1

☎ 04 9299 8422

cannes.fr
cannes-destination.com

St.-Tropez

🅰 67 F2

Visitor Information

✉ Quai Jean Jaurès

☎ 08 9268 4828 or 04 9497 9272

🕐 Closed 12:30 p.m.–3 p.m.

ot-saint-tropez.com
saint-tropez.fr

Cannes

In the 1830s foreigners, following in the footsteps of Britain's lord chancellor, Lord Brougham, fell in love with the fishing village and surrounds of Cannes and built summer villas here. Cannes soon blossomed. Now Cannes is best known for the International Film Festival held every May. The action centers on **La Croisette,** lined with palm trees, grand boutiques, and world-famous hotels such as the Carlton (its terrace is favored by movie moguls for cocktails during the film festival).

The beach is wide, sandy, and mostly private: Cannes is chic and expensive and determined to stay that way. To the west of the new **Palais des Festivals,** the

main venue for the film festival, lies the yacht-filled harbor of the old port, also the scene of the morning flower market. The covered **Marché de Forville** (*Rue Louis Blanc 12, Cannes*), two blocks inland, is a must-see and offers a mouthwatering array of all the local delicacies: Most stalls close around 1 p.m., and Mondays are often devoted to a flea market.

From the market, little lanes lead up to the old town of **Le Suquet,** a charming alternative to the ostentatious pleasures of the seafront, with lots of restaurants to choose from. If you climb as far as the 12th-century **Tour du Masque** (*Rue du Mont Chevalier 9, Cannes*)—a tower built as a citadel; an iron mask

INSIDER TIP:

To best appreciate the coastal scenery en route from Cannes to St.-Tropez, take a boat rather than a train. The trips are popular, however, so reserve a few days ahead.

—TIM JEPSON
National Geographic author

hangs above the door—you will be rewarded by a splendid coastal view. Above Cannes the immodestly named and exclusive **Corniche du Paradis Terrestre** also offers spectacular views.

From Cannes, you can take a boat trip to the peaceful **Îles de Lérins,** visible across the bay. Boats depart from the Quai Laubeuf *(SW corner of Port de Cannes, trans-cote-azur.com, $$$$).* The monastery on the isle of St.-Honorat once controlled much of the coast; now the monks cultivate lavender and grapes. The island of Ste.-Marguerite is still forested. In the 17th century, the prison here held the Man in the Iron Mask.

St.-Tropez

Once just a tiny fishing village more easily reached by sea than land, St.-Tropez began attracting artists in the 1880s, beginning with writer Guy de Maupassant. Now celebrities moor their yachts or have villas here, attracting hordes of visitors. Rich bohemians rent restored village houses on the surrounding hills and spend their days on **Plage de Pampelonne** (the hippest by far) and other inviting beaches.

And yet the little town remains charming: Visit the market on **Place des Lices** in the morning, and in the evening head for the cafés around the harbor. The 16th-century citadel offers evocative views. The same panoramas translated into paint are on view in the harborside **Musée de l'Annonciade.** The old chapel of the Annunciation now houses the art collection given to St.-Tropez by Georges Grammont. Excellent examples of Postimpressionism include works by Seurat, Dufy, and Braque, many of whom were pilgrims to the quiet of old St.-Tropez.

At the eastern end of town, above the harbor, the **Citadelle** (Citadel) guarded the town. The hexagonal keep, built in the 16th century, has three towers and ramparts and houses a maritime museum, the **Musée de l'Histoire Maritime.** ∎

Musée de l'Annonciade

- ⊠ Quai St.-Raphael, Rue de l'Annonciade 2, Place Grammont, St.-Tropez
- ☎ 04 9417 8410
- 🕒 Closed Tues., 1 p.m.–2 p.m., & Nov.
- 💲 $$

Musée de l'Histoire Maritime

- ⊠ Montée de la Citadelle 1, St.-Tropez
- ☎ 04 9454 8414
- 🕒 Closed 12:30 p.m. 1:30 p.m. Oct.–March
- 💲 $

NOTE: Boats leave Cannes for St. Tropez daily at 10:15 a.m. July 7–Sept. 1, & on Tues., Thurs., & Sat.–Sun. May 30–July 7 & Sept. 3–Oct. 6; no service Oct. 6–May 30. The boat returns to Cannes for 5:45 p.m. *(trans-cote-azur.com, $$$$$, journey time 75 min. one way).*

NEED TO KNOW
Port Logistics: Cannes

Cruise ships tender to the west side of **Cannes port** *(riviera-ports.com),* an easy walk to La Croisette, Cannes's famous waterfront promenade. If you are taking an excursion to or from Nice (see pp. 78–79), trains run at least every 30 minutes *(journey time 30–40 min.).* Cannes's railroad station *(Place de la Gare)* is a 15-minute walk from the tender dock, but close to La Croisette and the city center.

Nice & Around

Combining a Provençal heart with a welcoming joie de vivre, and a wealth of museums, gardens, fountains, and palm trees, the wonderful city of Nice raises life alfresco to an art form. The small streets of Vieux Nice, the city's small historic core, are a delight to wander, as is the long seafront esplanade, the Promenade des Anglais, but you need to travel farther afield to see the Chagall museum, the city's most celebrated artistic treasure.

Café patrons soak in the atmosphere of Nice's Cours Saleya, a long street turned market square.

NEED TO KNOW p. 83

Nice

  67 G3

Visitor Information

✉ Promenade des Anglais 5, Nice

☎ 08 9270 7407

nicetourisme.com

Musée d'Art Moderne et d'Art Contemporain

✉ Places Yves Klein, Nice

☎ 04 9713 4201

🕐 Closed Mon.

💲 $$

mamac-nice.org

Nice

Once deliciously dangerous and seedy, **Vieux Nice** (Old Nice; see pp. 80–81) is now a fashionable enclave of bistros, nightclubs, and galleries. And its little stores remain the best places for food shopping. The outdoor market on **Cours Saleya,** the heart of Vieux Nice, is famous for its flowers and local produce.

The tiny squares and lovely chapels of Vieux Nice are dominated by the huge dim **Cathédrale Ste.-Réparate** (see p. 80), with its dome of glazed tiles, and closed to the east by the **Colline du Château** (see p. 81). Walk up the hill or take the elevator from the east end of Promenade des Anglais to the park to enjoy the waterfall, café, and views.

Vieux Nice ends in the north, away from the sea, close to Place Garibaldi and the long, narrow **Promenade du Paillon** park. The latter is the site of the striking glass-and-marble **Musée d'Art Moderne et d'Art Contemporain.** The collections here focus on French and American avant-garde art.

City Center: To the west of Vieux Nice stretches the 4-mile-long (7 km) **Promenade des Anglais,** lined with grand hotels as well as the beautiful gardens of the newly restored Palais Masséna. The latter, a splendid belle epoque villa, houses the **Musée d'Art et d'Histoire** (Rue de France 65, Nice, tel 04 9391 1919, closed Tues.). Through art and other exhibits, this museum details Nice's history from the end of the 18th century through the early 20th.

Beyond the river lies 19th-century Nice: dignified arcaded squares, Italianate apartment buildings, fashionable shops, and an array of art galleries. The **Musée International d'Art Naïf** (Château Ste.-Hélène, Av. de Fabron, Nice, tel 04 9371 7833, midan.org, closed Tues.), serving up a collection of international folk art, is housed in a pink château; and the **Musée des Beaux-Arts,** in an elegant neighborhood just to the east, displays works by Monet, Degas, and Sisley. North of here, on the other side of the A7, stands the ornate Russian Orthodox cathedral, **Cathédrale St.-Nicolas** (Boul. Tzaréwitch, Nice), populated with frescoes and icons.

Cimiez: Art treasures dot the wealthy Nice suburb of Cimiez, a cradle of hills to the north where you can see the remains of Nice's original Roman settlement. Among the fabulous collection at the **Musée National Marc Chagall** (Av. du Dr. Ménard, Nice, tel 04 9353 8720, closed Tues., $$$) are Chagall's "Biblical Message" canvases.

Farther up the hill, a 17th-century villa houses the **Musée Matisse** (Av. des Arènes de Cimiez 164, Nice, tel 04 9381 0808, musee-matisse-nice.org, closed Tues., $$), with Matisse's personal collection, including still lifes and sketches of Chapelle de la Rosaire, as well as the "Tempête à Nice."

Villefranche & Points East

Some 3.5 miles (6 km) east of Nice lies the small town of **Villefranche-sur-Mer,** a pleasant and easygoing place to explore. Here, narrow streets rush steeply down to the

INSIDER TIP:

Villefranche-sur-Mer's Port Darse harbors boats large and small. A beach and several cafés sit behind the harbor walls.

—AMY ALIPIO
National Geographic Traveler
magazine associate editor

deep natural harbor that has turned this small fishing village into an important naval port, lending it a more raffish flavor than most of this coast. Pretty, pastel-colored houses and lively cafés line the tiny harbor, overlooked by the **Chapelle St.-Pierre,** a beguiling little (continued on p. 82)

Musée des Beaux-Arts

 Av. des Baumettes 33, Nice

☎ 04 9215 2828

🕐 Closed Mon.

💲 $$

musee-beaux-arts-nice.org

Villefranche-sur-Mer

 67 G3

Visitor Information

✉ Jardin François Binon, Villefranche-sur-Mer

☎ 04 9301 7368

🕐 Closed Sun. & 12 p.m.–2 p.m. mid-Sept.–mid-June

villefranche-sur-mer.fr

Walk: Exploring Vieux Nice by Foot

In the shadow of Colline du Château (Castle Hill), Vieux Nice's tightly packed warren of lanes harbors centuries-old Italianate houses, baroque churches, lively cafés, tourist traps, food stalls, and an energetic marketplace. This is where the seafaring Greeks first settled in 350 B.C., and this is today the bustling Nice of the Niçois.

Begin at **Place Masséna ❶**, surrounded by red arcades and wander through the garden paths of the 19th-century **Jardins Albert 1er.** Next cross Boulevard Jean Jaurès and enter Vieux Nice on Rue de l'Opéra, turning left on Rue St.-François-de-Paule, which is a jumble of cafés and souvenir shops. Soon you see the neo-baroque **Théâtre Municipal** (*Rue St.-François-de-Paule 4–6, Nice, tel 04 9217 4000*) on the right, Nice's opera house rebuilt in the style of Paris's Opéra after a fire in 1881. The road soon widens into **Cours Saleya ❷**, a long plaza that fills with a flower market every morning but Monday, when antiques vendors take over. When there is no market, the space is crowded with café tables.

Midway, Place Pierre Gautier is overlooked by the huge **Palais des Ducs de Savoie** (Palace of the Dukes of Savoy), constructed in 1559 for the sovereign family. The building is now known as the Ancienne Préfecture. On the square's opposite side, the 1740 **Chapelle de la Miséricorde ❸** (*tel 04 9200 4190, hours vary*) boasts a beautiful and exuberant baroque interior.

Turn left on Rue de la Poissonnerie, where, at No. 8, you'll see the 1584 **Adam and Eve House,** named for the bas-relief above the door. At the corner of Rue de la Préfecture stands the **Église Notre-Dame de l'Annonciation,** dedicated to Ste.-Rita, the venerated patron saint of hopeless causes. Its staid exterior conceals an exquisitely baroque interior—a mélange of columns, marbles, gilding, and moldings. On the church's northern exterior wall is a

NOT TO BE MISSED:

Cours Saleya • Cathédrale Ste.-Réparate • Palais Lascaris • Colline du Château • Promenade des Anglais

haphazard display of artifacts dating back to Roman times.

Continue straight to Rue du Jésus, turning right to Place du Jésus and the **Église St.-Jacques ❹**, with its blue and yellow facade. Constructed between 1640 and 1690, this was Nice's first example of baroque work. The interior is filled with dozens of gilded cherubs and frescoes.

Follow Rue Droite to Rue Rossetti and turn left to the café-filled **Place Rossetti,** the Old Town's centerpiece. The baroque **Cathédrale Ste.-Réparate ❺** lords above, built between 1650 and 1680. It's named after the 14-year-old martyr and patron saint of Nice, who died in the 14th century in the Holy Land and was said to have been brought here in a flower-bedecked boat by angels. Another place of pilgrimage also stands on the square at No. 2: **Fenocchio,** master ice-cream maker (*fenocchio.fr*).

Backtrack on Rue Rossetti and turn left on Rue Droite. At No. 15, **Palais Lascaris ❻** (*tel 04 9362 7240, closed Tues., $$*) provides a glimpse into an aristocratic palace. Designed in baroque-Genoese style, it features frescoed rooms arranged around two small courtyards adorned with statues and busts.

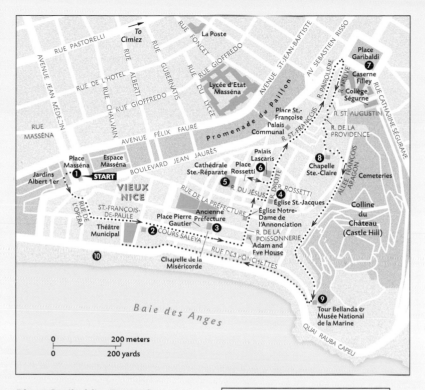

Place Garibaldi & Beyond

Proceed up Rue Droite to Rue St.-François. At Place St.-François stands the former **Palais Communal** (Town Hall) from the 16th and 17th centuries. Follow Rue Pairolière to busy **Place Garibaldi ❼**, and then take a quick right onto Rue Neuve. Here you enter into a quiet residential world of ruby and apricot houses, where laundry flaps out of open windows, opera wafts through the air, and, around lunch and suppertime, dinnerware clinks over the soft hum of voices.

Take a right on Ruelle St.-Augustin, alongside the church. Turn right on Rue St.-Augustin, then left on Rue de la Providence. You go up some stairs and climb a little hill to **Chapelle Ste.-Claire ❽**. Go up the stairs to the left (Montée Ménica Rondelly) to start the trek up **Colline du Château.** Several castles have stood on this outcrop, though

the only remains you'll see belong to the **Tour Bellanda ❾**, built in the 1800s after the last castle was destroyed; it holds the **Musée Naval** (Naval Museum; *tel 04 9380 4761, closed Mon.–Tues., $*). The old castle grounds are now woodsy gardens offering bay-and-city vistas, along with cafés, a waterfall, and two lovely old cemeteries.

Descend to **Quai des États-Unis,** edged with *ponchettes*—low white buildings once used by fishermen but now filled with restaurants and shops. From here you can join the crowds strolling along the **Promenade des Anglais ❿** (see p. 79).

- Also see area map p. 67
- Place Masséna
- 2 hours
- 3 miles (km)
- Promenade des Anglais

La Gravette, a sheltered bay beneath Antibes's ramparts

Cap Ferrat
🅐 67 G3

Villa Ephrussi de Rothschild
✉ Av. Ephrussi de Rothschild, St.-Jean-Cap-Ferrat
☎ 04 9301 3309
🕐 Closed until 2 p.m. Nov.–Feb.
💲 $$$$
villa-ephrussi.com

Beaulieu-sur-Mer
Visitor Information
✉ Place Georges Clemenceau, Beaulieu-sur-Mer
☎ 04 9301 0221
🕐 Closed Sun. p.m.
beaulieusurmer.fr

Villa Grecque Kérylos
✉ Impasse Gustave Eiffel, Beaulieu-sur-Mer
☎ 04 9301 0144
🕐 Closed a.m. Mon.–Fri. Nov.–mid-Feb.
💲 $$$
villa-kerylos.com

church decorated by Jean Cocteau in 1957.

Jutting out into the sea just beyond Villefranche, the **Cap Ferrat** peninsula is famously the preserve of the seriously rich, its natural beauty embellished by fabulous villas and luxuriant gardens. Do not miss the **Villa Ephrussi de Rothschild,** a pink-and-white villa with marble floors and Tiepolo ceilings, housing a superb decorative arts collection and surrounded by magnificent gardens.

At the peninsula's rocky end, the **Grand Hôtel du Cap-Ferrat** features among other luxuries a funicular railroad to the beach. The little fishing and yachting village of **St.-Jean-Cap-Ferrat** makes a picturesque place for lunch; relatively quiet **Plage des Fosses** leads to a path around the peninsula with fantastic views.

A couple of miles (3.5 km) farther east of Villefranche, sheltered **Beaulieu-sur-Mer** has some extremely grand hotels.

Its most bizarre and delightful offering is the remarkable **Villa Grecque Kérylos,** an authentic reproduction of an ancient Greek villa, in which the eccentric archaeologist Théodore Reinach lived in the manner of an Athenian citizen. One of his few concessions to the 20th century was glass in the windows.

Both Beaulieu-sur-Mer and Cap Ferrat can be reached via bus 81 from Villefranche (2 hourly, journey time 15 min., $); it departs from Avenue Foch, by the Jardin François Binon.

Antibes
West of Nice, across the Baie des Anges, the ancient town of Antibes sits at the base of its eponymous cape. A Greek settlement (Antipolis) that later became a frontier town (neighboring Nice was in Savoie), Antibes had its fortress and port reconstructed by Vauban in the 17th century.

Walk first along the **harbor and old port,** and then turn up Rue Aubernon, lined with places to eat and drink, and climb to the not-to-be-missed **Old Town,** a maze of narrow streets with one of the region's best daily markets (closed Mon. Sept.–May) and a great flea market twice a week.

On the ramparts, overlooking the sea, looms the 16th-century **Château Grimaldi** (Place Mariejol, Antibes). Here, Picasso was given a studio after World War II, and in gratitude he gave the town paintings, drawings, and ceramics of the period, including "La Joie de Vivre," "Night Fishing at Antibes," and the "Antipolis Suite." The château is now the revamped **Musée Picasso** (tel 04 9290 5420, closed 12 p.m.–2 p.m. mid-Sept.–mid-June & Mon., $$), and the works are beautifully displayed in the lustrous sea light pouring in through the windows. Paintings by Nicolas de Staël are also on show, along with works by artists of the school of Nice. The terrace garden provides the perfect setting for sculptures silhouetted against the sea.

The **Musée d'Archéologie** (Bastion St.-André, Av. Adm. de Grasse, Antibes, tel 04 9395 8598, closed Mon. & 12 p.m.–2 p.m., $), farther along the ramparts, presents Greek, Roman, and other finds in two huge barrel-vaulted chambers.

Cap d'Antibes is one of the most exclusive hideaways of the Côte d'Azur, its exotic belle epoque and modernist villas and fabulous hotels discreetly veiled by dense vegetation, through which paths lead to private beaches. But its eponymous town also has a surprisingly down-to-earth air, as seen on its free public beaches which, though mostly rocky, are unspoiled; try **Plage de la Salis**, on the eastern shore, or tiny **Plage de la Garoupe.** ∎

Antibes

▲ 67 F3

Visitor Information

⊠ Place du Général de Gaulle 11, Antibes

☎ 04 9723 1111

🕓 Closed 12 p.m.–2 p.m. Sept.–June

antibesjuanlespins.com

NEED TO KNOW

Port Logistics: Nice

Cruise ships dock at Terminals 1 and 2, in **Nice Port** (riviera-ports.com), east of the city center below the landmark hill, Colline du Château. Free shuttles (navettes) circle the port, connect the terminals, and run to the top of the port exit for the city.

Terminal 2 is nearer Vieux Nice (Old Town): Walk west, with the sea on your left, and you'll be there in 10 minutes. From Terminal 1 it's quicker to bear right on Rue Cassini to Place Garibaldi, a large square north of the port and the hill; from its bottom left corner take Boulevard Jean Jaurès, which bounds Vieux Nice on its northern edge: Turn left at any point to enter Vieux Nice's streets.

Trains to Villefranche-sur-Mer and Antibes leave from the **Gare SNCF** station. To reach it, take bus 30 from the top of the port, or from Place Garibaldi, take a tram marked for "Las Planas" to the Gare Thiers stop, a block from the rail station.

Getting to Villefranche & Points East or Antibes

Several trains per hour run from Nice to Villefranche (journey time 10 min.). However, some cruise ships also stop in Villefranche, tendering to a smart terminal at Port de la Santé, right in front of Villefranche's historic quarter.

Trains run at least every 30 minutes between Nice and Antibes (15–30 min.). Allow 5 hours round-trip, including transit, for the excursion from Nice. Turn right out of the **Gare d'Antibes** train station and seconds away is the stop for bus 14 (tel 04 8987 7200, envibus.fr, $), which runs every 20 minutes to the Gare Routière (for Old Town) and continues to Plage de la Salis. It is a 15- to 20-minute walk from the Gare Routière to the Old Town and port. A small tourist "train" runs around the main sights (tel 06 1577 6747, capdantibestour.com, April–Oct., $$$) if you want a quick tour.

Monaco

Smaller than New York's Central Park, the tiny independent city-state and tax haven of Monaco is a magnet for those in search of glamour. Visitors flock here for its glittering nightlife, luxurious hotels, and expensive restaurants. After his accession in 1949, Prince Rainier III transformed the principality, extending it vertically and horizontally with skyscrapers and landfill, and earning it the epithets "Hong Kong on the Mediterranean" and "Las Vegas *plage.*"

The fairy-tale principality of Monaco is the playground of the rich and famous

Monaco
🅰 67 G3
Visitor Information
✉ Boul. des Moulins 2A
☎ 377 9216 6116
visitmonaco.com

Palais Princier
✉ Place du Palais
☎ 377 9325 1831
🕐 Closed Nov.–March
💲 $$$

Today Monaco is tourist-filled, expensive, and Disneyesque in places, but it is also oddly irresistible.

Monaco-Ville

Also known as Vieille Ville (Old Town) or Le Rocher—the latter because it straddles a rocky plateau—the area of Monaco-Ville is an immaculate affair of elegant mansions, charming little squares and fountains, and souvenir stores.

The **Palais Princier,** seat of the ruling Grimaldi family, is packed with gorgeous furniture, paintings, and frescoes; it is open to visitors when the prince is away. The changing of the guard is a daily spectacle.

The great white 19th-century neo-Romanesque cathedral nearby contains the tomb of Princess Grace, perpetually strewn with roses. On the cliff is the **Musée Océanographique,** a world-class aquarium and museum with more than 2,500 specimens and numerous maritime displays.

West of Monaco-Ville, on the cliffs, rises the magnificently situated **Jardin Exotique**. The garden shelters a huge range of exotic plants, as well as prehistoric caves and an anthropological museum. Nearby is the Villa Paloma, one of two restored villas that houses the **Nouveau Musée National de Monaco,** dedicated to art and performance (the other villa, Villa Sauber, is in Monte-Carlo.)

Below Monaco-Ville is the marina of **Fontvieille,** with grand promenades for yacht-ogling, and the lovely **Roseraie Princesse Grace** (Av. des Guelfes), a 4,000-rosebush-strong garden in honor of the princess.

Monte-Carlo

Beyond the port is Monte-Carlo, with its celebrated **Casino de Monte-Carlo**

(Place du Casino, tel 377 9806 2121, montecarlosbm.com) and **Opéra** (opera.mc) inside. Neither should be missed, but note that there's a casino dress code for all to make sure visitors look the part: Jacket and tie are required for those gambling in the grander rear rooms, which open at 2 p.m. Designed by Charles Garnier, who was also responsible for the Opéra Garnier in Paris, the interiors retain their extravagant belle epoque glamour. Note, too, that there are fees ($$$–$$$$) to enter most of the casino's period gaming rooms, and you should bring your passport.

Outside, the palms and gardens and the wonderful terrace surrounding them afford beautiful views over the Mediterranean. If you don't want to bet, spend over the odds instead on a people-watching drink at a café in Place du Casino. ■

Musée Océano-graphique
- ⊠ Av. St.-Martin
- ☎ 377 9315 3600
- 💲 $$$$$
- oceano.mc

Jardin Exotique
- ⊠ Boul. du Jardin Exotique 62
- ☎ 377 9315 2980
- 💲 $$
- jardin-exotique.mc

Nouveau Musée National de Monaco
- ⊠ Villa Paloma, Boul. du Jardin Exotique 56
- ⊠ Villa Sauber, Av. Princesse Grace 17
- ☎ Villa Paloma: 377 9898 4860; Villa Sauber: 377 9898 9126
- 💲 $$
- nmnm.mc

NEED TO KNOW
Port Logistics: Monaco
Cruise ships dock at a terminal on **Promenade des Pêcheurs** below and south of Monaco-Ville. The newer town, Monaco-Carlo, with its skyscrapers and famous Casino, is opposite, on the north side of the harbor (known as La Condamine). On busy days ships may tender to the harbor.

A few minutes' walk from the terminal (bear left), the "Le Palais" elevator runs partway up to Monaco-Ville, where all the sights are within walking distance. From Monaco-Ville or the harbor

to Monte-Carlo is a 20- to 30-minute hilly walk; buses 1 and 2 (5-6 hourly, $) run to Monte-Carlo in 10 minutes from a stop near the cathedral; bus 2 stops at the railway station if you wish to take the train to Nice (journey time 20 min.) or elsewhere on the Riviera during your stopover. Allow half a day to explore Monaco-Ville and Monte-Carlo. If time is short, take the little **Azur Express** (monacotours.mc, $$$) tourist train that runs around all the main sights in both centers, leaving from in front of the Musée Océanographique.

Intoxicating coastal cities and landscapes and some of Italy's
finest artistic centers and loveliest pastoral countryside

Italian Riviera
& Tuscany

Introduction & Map   88-89

Genoa & the Coast   90-93

Need to Know: Genoa   93

Florence   94-111

Feature: Brunelleschi's Dome   98-99

Need to Know: Livorno   111

Pisa   112-113

Need to Know: Livorno to Pisa   113

Lucca   114-115

Need to Know: Livorno to Lucca   115

Siena   116-117

Need to Know: Livorno to Siena   117

San Gimignano   118-119

Need to Know: Livorno to San Gimignano   119

Restaurants   282-286

Manarola, one of the five Cinque Terre villages that are strung along the Ligurian coast.
Collectively, they are listed as a **UNESCO World Heritage site.**

Italian Riviera & Tuscany

Two great ports dominate Italy's northwest coast—Genoa (Genova) and Livorno. Between them lies a coastline beloved of writers and artists across the centuries and dotted with fishing villages, picturesque towns, and a medley of dramatic maritime landscapes. Genoa is the springboard for the best of this scenery—and worthy of exploration in its own right—while the more low-key Livorno is a base for trips to Florence (Firenze), Europe's greatest artistic capital, and the smaller Tuscan towns of Siena, Pisa, and Lucca.

Genoa & Around

Genoa has its attractions—not least its state-of-the-art aquarium, one of Italy's most visited sights—but the city is also a big, briny port with a gritty edge. So if your trip is going to take you to more noted Italian centers, it can

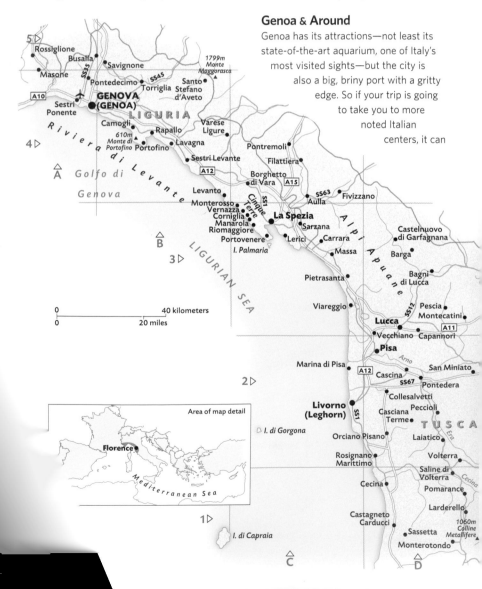

be worth skipping Genoa in favor of the villages and landscapes along the coast to the southeast.

The chic little resort of Portofino is closest, and is best approached by boat, thanks to the pretty coastline on all sides, though there's little to see or do in the village itself. A better option if you have a day to spare is the Cinque Terre, literally "Five Lands," a quintet of tiny, picturesque fishing villages perched under spectacular cliffs and terraced hillsides. Rail is the best approach, followed by a boat trip between the villages, but note that the region can be very busy.

Fabulous Florence & Other Tuscan Gems

Farther south, Livorno does its best to seduce visitors into spending time in its streets, but few will be able to resist the more persuasive call of Tuscany, Italy's most beautiful region, or the wide range of superb historic towns and cities that can be seen as excursions from a port whose attractions pale by comparison.

Florence is the obvious daylong destination for first-time visitors to Italy. Numerous companies offer fully guided or transportation-only tours to the

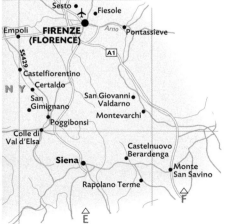

city, but rail links from Livorno make it an excursion that can be done under your own steam. Don't attempt to combine it with other excursions, however, as it takes around two hours to reach the city from Livorno.

Central Florence is not large and even in a short time you'll get a good taste of its sights and historic streets, although if you want to see Michelangelo's "David" or the paintings of the Uffizi gallery it is essential to book timed entry tickets to avoid spending the best part of your day in lines (see sidebar p. 111). Visiting any Italian town or city involves more than admiring art and churches, so leave an hour for gelato, coffee, and simply exploring Florence's many medieval corners

For those who have seen Florence, a full day in Siena is the next best excursion you could choose. The cross-country trip there by car takes time, but the pretty scenery en route makes the journey an attraction in itself. San Gimignano, famous for its medieval towers, is much smaller—you can see it in 90 minutes—and very crowded in summer, but it, too, lies in pretty countryside; organized excursions often pair it with another Tuscan town.

Pisa is the next town on most people's list, thanks to the Leaning Tower—where you must also book tickets (see pp. 112–113)—but the city was badly bombed in World War II (like Genoa and Livorno), and as a result much is modern. This said, the Tower and the sights around it, notably the Duomo and Baptistery, are exquisite, although you'll need no more than an hour for these and the same to explore the city's surviving historic core. Allow four hours in total from Livorno and back.

Pisa is also manageable by train or bus from Livorno, and given it only requires half a day, can and should be combined with Lucca, one of Italy's most charming towns, and far less crowded than Pisa, Siena, and Florence. ■

Genoa & the Coast

The fame of Liguria's Genoa (Genova) rests on the seafaring exploits of its mariners and the trading potential of Italy's premier port. Its historic core has a wealth of churches, palaces, and galleries, as well as the waterfront Acquario (Aquarium), one of Italy's most visited sights. The city is also a base for trips to Portofino and the Cinque Terre, highlights of the region's rugged and romantic coast.

A pair of 19th-century lions flank the early 14th-century striped facade of Genoa's San Lorenzo.

NEED TO KNOW p. 93

Genoa

🅰 88 A4

Visitor Information

✉ Via Garibaldi 12/r, Genoa

☎ 010 557 2903

visitgenoa.it
turismoinliguria.it
turismo.provincia .genova.it

Cattedrale di San Lorenzo

✉ Piazza San Lorenzo, Genoa

☎ 010 247 1831

🕐 Closed 12 p.m.– 3 p.m.

Genoa

Genoa, with its strategic position and fine harbor, rose to great power by the 14th century, its territories extended as far as Syria, North Africa, and the Crimea. Defeat by Venice in 1380 curtailed its maritime expansion, but within two centuries, banking and trade had restored its primacy. Among its most famous medieval names was Christopher Columbus (1451–1506), who was probably born in the city. Great dynastic families of the period enriched the city with palaces and works of art, a second golden age undermined by the eventual loss of colonies to Venice and the Ottomans and the increasing share of trade taken by other Mediterranean ports.

San Lorenzo & Around:
Start at the **Cattedrale di San Lorenzo.** Consecrated in 1118, the cathedral received countless embellishments over the centuries, creating a medley of styles inside and out. The baroque interior is offset by the **Cappella di San Giovanni,** a glorious Renaissance chapel (1450–1465) dedicated to St. John the Baptist, Genoa's patron saint. The chapel

contains a 13th-century French sarcophagus once said to have held the remains of the saint.

A few steps east is Piazza Matteotti, dominated by the gargantuan **Palazzo Ducale.** Built over several centuries as the erstwhile home of Genoa's ruling medieval doges, it now hosts exhibitions and other cultural events.

Just north of San Lorenzo stands **Piazza San Matteo,** a very pretty square. To the south, the church of **San Donato** has a lovely bell tower, doorway, and a

INSIDER TIP:

Ligurian pesto is the world's best—and that's not an overstatement. The basil that grows locally has a distinctive flavor. Order it in any decent restaurant in Genoa.

—JANE WOOLDRIDGE
National Geographic author

painting of the "Adoration of the Magi" by Joos van Cleve, while Gothic **Sant'Agostino** nearby is worth a look for its museum of frescoes, sculptures, and archaeological fragments.

Romanesque **Santa Maria di Castello** (*off Piazza Embriaci, Genoa*) owes its name to an earlier Roman *castrum* (castle) on the site. The church also has several frescoes and sculptures, but its most compelling treasures lie in the adjoining

Dominican convent, where the loggias of the second cloister feature captivating 15th-century frescoes.

Via Garibaldi: Via Garibaldi, several blocks north of San Lorenzo, is often called the most beautiful street in Italy. Laid out between 1551 and 1558, it was created for newly rich merchants eager to escape the cramped medieval quarter.

Today, their palaces still follow one another in a splendid parade: Palazzo Cambiaso (No. 1), Palazzo Parodi (No. 3), Palazzo Carrega-Cataldi (No. 4), Palazzo Doria (No. 6), and Palazzo Podestà (No. 7). **Palazzo Doria-Tursi** (No. 9) is now the town hall and home to a museum that includes letters by Christopher Columbus and a violin that belonged to the famous Genoa-born violinist Nicolò Paganini (1782–1840).

Another essential stop on the street is **Palazzo Bianco** at No. 11, home to paintings by high-profile Italian masters—Caravaggio, Veronese, and Filippino Lippi among them—as well as exceptional Dutch and Flemish works by Memling ("Christ Blessing"), van Cleve ("Madonna and Child"), and Jan Provost ("St. Peter").

Virtually opposite Palazzo Bianco lies **Palazzo Rosso** (No. 18), where you can admire similarly outstanding paintings: portraits by Anthony Van Dyck and paintings by Dürer, Veronese, Palma il Vecchio, and lesser Genoese artists.

Sant'Agostino
- Piazza Sarzano 35/r, Genoa
- 010 251 1263
- Closed Mon.
- $$

Palazzo Doria-Tursi, Palazzo Bianco, & Palazzo Rosso
- Palazzo Doria-Tursi: Via Garibaldi 9, Genoa
- Palazzo Bianco: Via Garibaldi 11, Genoa
- Palazzo Rosso: Via Garibaldi 18, Genoa
- 010 557 4972
- Closed Mon.
- Combined ticket for all three palaces: $$$

museidigenova.it

Portofino, the jewel of an already richly embellished coastline

Palazzo Spinola

- ✉ Piazza di Pellicceria 1, Genoa
- ☎ 010 270 5300
- 🕐 Closed Sun. a.m. & Mon.
- 💲 $

facebook.com/ palazzospinola

Acquario

- ✉ Ponte Spinola, Strada Aldo Moro, Genoa
- ☎ 010 23451
- 💲 $$$$$

acquariodigenova.it

Palazzo Reale

- ✉ Via Balbi 10, Genoa
- ☎ 010 271 0236
- 🕐 Closed Mon. & p.m. both Tues. & Wed.
- 💲 $$

palazzorealegenova
.beniculturali.it

Palazzo Spinola: A few blocks south of Via Garibaldi stands another art gallery, housed in the sumptuous Palazzo Spinola. The beautiful salons from the 17th and 18th centuries in which the exhibits are hung are almost as beguiling as the works of art. Genoese artists figure large but there are also paintings of wider renown, notably van Cleve's sublime triptych of the "Adoration of the Magi," Antonello da Messina's "Ecce Homo," Rubens's equestrian portrait of Giovanni Carlo Doria, and Van Dyck's "Portrait of Lady and Child."

Acquario: Set in the port area, where Renzo Piano, one of Europe's leading architects, transformed previously derelict swaths of waterfront in the early 1990s, is the Acquario, a state-of-the-art aquarium. Europe's second largest, it is based around 50 vast basins containing some 20,000 marine creatures. Here you can see dolphins, seals, sharks, and penguins, along with countless smaller fish and miscellaneous marine life.

North of the Acquario, if you have time, visit the sumptuous **Palazzo Reale,** with its host of sumptuous salons and chambers.

Portofino

Romantic and beautiful, the former fishing village of Portofino, roughly 20 miles (32 km) east of Genoa, is now one of Italy's most exclusive and expensive little resorts. If venturing here on your own from Genoa, take a train to Santa Margherita Ligure and then bus 82 or a taxi from the railway station.

When you tire of the yachts, the upscale stores, the summer crowds, the tangle of cobbled streets, the chic cafés, and the candlelit restaurants that make up the village, walk to the church of **San Giorgio** (Salita San Giorgio), home to the reputed relics of San Giorgio (St. George), brought from the Holy Land in the 12th century by homeward-bound crusaders. Then go past the old castle and follow the path to the lighthouse, a walk of about 2.5 miles (4 km). This is the most popular of many easy local trails that crisscross the promontory above the village, thanks to its glorious views. If you don't want to walk out to the lighthouse, and time allows, there are ferries and boat tours (*traghettiporto fino.it*) around the coast to the **Abbey of San Fruttuoso** and to the towns of **Rapallo** and **Sestri Levante** (4 hours), as well as dolphin- and whale-watching trips in the bay.

Cinque Terre

Most secrets are eventually discovered, and this, sadly, is true of the Cinque Terre (Five Lands), a quintet of tiny seafront villages that until recently were all but inaccessible by road and all but unknown to visitors. So far the villages' charms remain unspoiled, as does the allure of their surrounding countryside, a national park, which is a jumble of plunging cliffs and steeply terraced slopes covered in olives and vineyards.

The ideal way to see the region is to take a train to one of the villages—**Riomaggiore**

is the farthest from Genoa (*journey time about 1.5 hours*)—then board the scheduled ferry (*navigazionegolfodeipoeti.it*) that links four of the villages in just 40 minutes. See the coast, then disembark at one of the villages, explore, and catch the train back to Genoa.

None of the villages takes more than a few minutes to see, and none has any major sights. Instead, the attractions are intimate pebbly beaches, tiny coves, crisp white wines, romantic fish restaurants, and quaint huddles of pastel-colored houses.

Vernazza is the village to make for if time is tight, with **Manarola** a close second: The former's railroad station is moments from the tiny square on the seafront, which is lined with restaurants with plenty of outdoor tables. Like all the villages, it is linked to neighboring settlements and its scenic hinterland by a lattice of trails (*$$ day-use fee for the Cinque Terre coastal trail*). A short coast walk north of the village offers superlative views. ■

Portofino
 88 B4
Visitor Information
✉ Via Roma 35, Portofino
☎ 0185 269 024
portofinocoast.it
comune.portofino
.genova.it

Cinque Terre
 88 C3
Visitor Information
cinqueterre.it
turismoinliguria.it
parconazionale
5terre.it
www.ati5terre.it

Vernazza
 88 C3
Visitor Information
✉ Railway station, Vernazza
☎ 0187 812 533

Manarola
 88 C3
Visitor Information
✉ Railway station, Manarola
☎ 0187 760 511

NEED TO KNOW
Port Logistics: Genoa
Cruise ships dock at one of two terminals northwest of the city center: **Ponte Andrea Doria** and the larger **Ponte dei Mille**. The **Stazione Principe**, for train connections to Portofino and the Cinque Terre, is some 330 yards (300 m) from the latter.

If exploring on your own, take a taxi or bus shuttle to avoid the long walk to

the historic center. At the terminal exit at Piazza Caricamento, you'll find a visitor center (*tel 010 557 4200 or 010 557 4202 visitgenoa.it*) and the departure point for hour-long hop-on, hop-off city bus tour with **Genoa City Bus** (*tel 010 530 52 genoacitytour.com*) or **City Sightse Genova** (*tel 335 541 7825, www .city-sightseeing.it*). To book ci visit *guidegenova.com* or *gen*

Florence

In Florence (Firenze), Europe's premier artistic capital, Renaissance treasures fill a host of museums and churches, while the roll call of famous names from the city's past—Dante, Machiavelli, Michelangelo, and Galileo among them—are some of the most resonant of the medieval age. Much of the art, along with lively markets, fine shops, pretty piazzas, gardens, and picturesque streets, can easily be seen during a short visit.

Battistero di San Giovanni and Santa Maria del Fiore

NEED TO KNOW p. 111

Florence
 89 E2
Visitor Information
✉ Via Cavour 1r
☎ 055 290 832
🕙 Closed Sun.

Piazza San
Giovanni 1
5 288 496
d Sun. p.m.

lla

m.

Start a tour in the city's two main squares: Piazza del Duomo and Piazza della Signoria, the former home to the Duomo (cathedral), Battistero di San Giovanni, and Campanile; climb the Campanile or cathedral dome for great views. From the squares, tackle one or more of the city's key galleries: the Uffizi (paintings), Bargello (sculpture), and Museo Storico dell'Opera del Duomo (sculpture).

A short walk east from either square takes you to Santa Croce, the city's key church (see the second ranked Santa Maria Novella if you have time), followed by a choice of Florence's many one-off attractions: the Galleria dell'Accademia (for Michelangelo's "David"), the Palazzo Medici-Riccardi (home to a charming fresco cycle), and the Cappelle Medicee (sculptures by Michelangelo).

Be sure to cross the celebrated Ponte Vecchio and, if you have time to spare, explore the quieter Oltrarno district across the Arno River, where more artistic treasures can be found in the Palazzo Pitti and Cappella Brancacci.

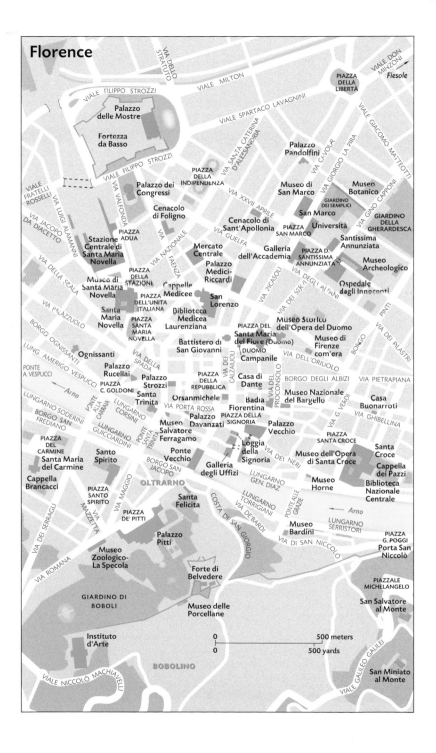

Florence

VIALE DELLO STRATUTO

VIALE FILIPPO STROZZI

VIALE MILTON

VIALE DON MINZONI

Fiesole

PIAZZA DELLA LIBERTÀ

Palazzo delle Mostre

Fortezza da Basso

VIALE FILIPPO STROZZI

VIALE SPARTACO LAVAGNINI

VIALE GIACOMO MATTEOTTI

VIA SANTA CATERINA D'ALESSANDRIA

VIA C.VOLTA

VIA GIORGIO LA PIRA

Palazzo Pandolfini

VIALE FRATELLI ROSSELLI

VIALE FILIPPO STROZZI

VIA VALFONDA

PIAZZA DELLA INDIPENDENZA

Palazzo dei Congressi

VIA XXVII APRILE

Museo di San Marco

GIARDINO DEI SEMPLICI

Museo Botanico

VIA GINO CAPPONI

VIA DELLA SCALA

VIA JACOPO DA DIACETO

VIA LUIGI ALAMANNI

PIAZZA ADUA

Cenacolo di Foligno

Cenacolo di Sant'Apollonia

PIAZZA SAN MARCO

San Marco

Università

GIARDINO DELLA GHERARDESCA

VIA NAZIONALE

VIA FAENZA

VIA GUELFA

VIA 27CASOLI

Santissima Annunziata

Museo Archeologico

Stazione Centrale di Santa Maria Novella

Mercato Centrale

Galleria dell'Accademia

PIAZZA D. SANTISSIMA ANNUNZIATA

PIAZZA DELLA STAZIONE

Palazzo Medici-Riccardi

VIA DEI SERVI

Ospedale degli Innocenti

PINTI

Musco di Santa Maria Novella

PIAZZA DELL'UNITA ITALIANA

Cappelle Medicee

San Lorenzo

VIA DEI PUCCI

PIAZZA SANTA MARIA NOVELLA

Santa Maria Novella

Biblioteca Medicea Laurenziana

Museo Storico dell'Opera del Duomo

VIA DEI PILASTRI

BORGO OGNISSANTI

LUNG. AMERIGO VESPUCCI

PONTE A. VESPUCCI

VIA PALAZZUOLO

Ognissanti

VIA DELLA SPADA

Battistero di San Giovanni

PIAZZA DEL DUOMO

Santa Maria del Fiore (Duomo)

Campanile

Museo di Firenze com'era

BORGO PINTI

VIA DEL CALZAIUOLI

Palazzo Rucellai

Palazzo Strozzi

PIAZZA DELLA REPUBBLICA

Casa di Dante

VIA DELL'ORIUOLO

Arno

PIAZZA C. GOLDONI

Santa Trinita

VIA PORTA ROSSA

Orsanmichele

Badia Fiorentina

BORGO DEGLI ALBIZI

VIA PIETRAPIANA

Museo Nazionale del Bargello

VIA G. VERDI

Casa Buonarroti

LUNGARNO SODERINI

BORGO SAN FREDIANO

PONTE ALLA CARRAIA

LUNGARNO CORSINI

LUNGARNO GUICCIARDINI

Palazzo Davanzati

PIAZZA DELLA SIGNORIA

VIA DEL PROCONSOLO

VIA GHIBELLINA

Museo Salvatore Ferragamo

PONTE SANTA TRINITA

Palazzo Vecchio

PIAZZA SANTA CROCE

PIAZZA DEL CARMINE

Santa Maria del Carmine

Cappella Brancacci

Santo Spirito

Ponte Vecchio

BORGO SAN JACOPO

Loggia della Signoria

Galleria degli Uffizi

VIA DEI NERI

Museo dell'Opera di Santa Croce

Museo Horne

Santa Croce

Cappella dei Pazzi

Biblioteca Nazionale Centrale

PIAZZA SANTO SPIRITO

VIA MAGGIO

VIA MAZZETTA

PIAZZA DE' PITTI

OLTRARNO

Santa Felicita

COSTA DI SAN GIORGIO

LUNGARNO GEN. DIAZ

LUNGARNO TORRIGIANI

PONTE ALLE GRAZIE

Arno

VIA DEI SERRAGLI

VIA ROMANA

Palazzo Pitti

Museo Zoologico-La Specola

Forte di Belvedere

VIA DI SAN NICCOLO'

Museo Bardini

LUNGARNO SERRISTORI

PIAZZA G. POGGI

Porta San Niccolò

GIARDINO DI BOBOLI

Museo delle Porcellane

PIAZZALE MICHELANGELO

San Salvatore al Monte

Instituto d'Arte

0   500 meters

0   500 yards

BOBOLINO

VIALE NICCOLÒ MACHIAVELLI

VIALE GALILEO GALILEI

San Miniato al Monte

Santa Maria del Fiore (Duomo), Battistero di San Giovanni, & Campanile

🅰 Map p. 95

✉ Piazza del Duomo

☎ 055 230 2855

🕐 Duomo: closed Sun. a.m. & some holidays Battistero: closed a.m. Mon.–Sat. & Sun. p.m.

💲 Duomo: free; combined ticket for Santa Reparata, Campanile, Duomo dome, Battistero, & Museo Storico dell'Opera del Duomo: $$$

operaduomo.firenze.it
ilgrandemuseodel
duomo.it
duomofirenze.it

Note: If you want to see the city's key sights—the Uffizi and "David"—it's essential to pre-purchase timed tickets to avoid very long lines (see sidebar p. 111).

Piazza del Duomo

Piazza del Duomo is the city's religious heart, home to the Duomo (Santa Maria del Fiore), which is flanked by its Campanile, or bell tower. In the Duomo's shadow stands the Battistero di San Giovanni, Florence's oldest building. Some of the art produced for these buildings has been removed for safekeeping to the Museo Storico dell'Opera del Duomo behind the cathedral.

INSIDER TIP:

In Florence, business addresses are suffixed with "r," which stands for *rosso* (red). These numbers are displayed in red on the street.

—MARINA CONTI
National Geographic Italy editor

Santa Maria del Fiore: The Duomo, Europe's fourth largest cathedral, was begun in 1296 by Arnolfo di Cambio (1245–1302). Its vast scope was designed to reflect Florence's burgeoning importance and to outshine the cathedrals of rivals Siena and Pisa. Consecrated in 1436, it was crowned with the largest dome since antiquity, a masterpiece of medieval engineering designed

by Filippo Brunelleschi (see pp. 98–99). The multicolored facade dates from 1887, Arnolfo di Cambio's quarter-finished frontage having been pulled down in 1587.

Highlights in the far more restrained interior start with three paintings on the left (north) wall: "Dante Explaining the Divine Comedy" (1465) is by Domenico di Michelino; the other two are equestrian portraits of the mercenary soldiers Sir John Hawkwood (1436) and Niccolò da Tolentino (1456) by Paolo Uccello and Andrea del Castagno, respectively.

Colorful frescoes (1572–1579) by Giorgio Vasari of the "Last Judgment" adorn the interior of the dome, below which on the left as you face the high altar is the **Sagrestia Nuova,** or New Sacristy, decorated with exquisite 15th-century inlaid wood and protected by bronze doors (1446–1467) designed by Michelozzo and Luca della Robbia. In the central apse is a magnificent **bronze reliquary** (1432–1442) by Lorenzo Ghiberti that holds the remains of St. Zenobius, Florence's first bishop.

In the crypt you can see the remains of **Santa Reparata,** an earlier church on the site. For insight into Brunelleschi's engineering genius and a glorious panorama of Florence and its surrounding countryside, climb the **dome.**

Battistero di San Giovanni:

Constructed on the site of a first-century Roman building, the Baptistery probably dates from the sixth or seventh century, although much of its classically inspired decoration is from 1059 to 1128. By far its most eminent features are its **doors.** Andrea Pisano, a Pisan sculptor, designed those on the south face (1328–1336), which are decorated with 28 panels depicting scenes from the life of Florence's patron saint, St. John the Baptist, to whom the building is dedicated. The north doors

sophistication. The panels are copies—the originals are in the Museo Storico dell'Opera del Duomo (see p. 100).

Inside, the highlight is a majestic mosaic-covered **ceiling,** a largely 13th-century work begun by Venetian craftsmen. Its complex narrative embraces episodes from the lives of Christ, Joseph, the Virgin, and John the Baptist. To the right of the apse lies Donatello and Michelozzo's

High Heel Art

The high heel, or stiletto from the Italian for "little dagger"—is said to have been invented in Florence by Catherine de' Medici, who attempted to compensate for her diminutive stature by wearing 2-inch (5 cm) heels at her wedding in 1533 (aged 14) to the future King Henry II of France. How appropriate, then, that Florence should also be home to a temple to the shoemaker's art, the **Museo Salvatore Ferragamo** (*Via dei Tornabuoni 2, tel 055 336 0846, closed Tues., $$*), devoted to Salvatore Ferragamo (1898-1960).

Ferragamo was born in Naples. He emigrated to the United States at age 15, later making his name—and fortune—in Hollywood by creating shoes for Greta Garbo, Vivien Leigh, Rudolph Valentino, and Gloria Swanson, among others. On his eventual return to Italy he opened a store in Florence, still home to the headquarters of the company that bears his name. The company's museum is a shoe-lover's dream, featuring more than 16,000 pairs of shoes, exhibited in rotation.

(1403–1424) were commissioned from Ghiberti after a competition in 1401; while following Pisano's earlier 28-panel scheme, they display far greater artistic ambition—their subjects are episodes from the life of Christ, the Evangelists, and Doctors of the Church.

Still greater refinements appear in Ghiberti's east doors (1425–1452), the **Gates of Paradise,** whose ten panels depict Old Testament scenes with a previously unseen measure of narrative and technical

tomb of Antipope John XXIII, an adviser to the Medici who died in the city in 1419. Note the interior's granite columns, probably removed from the old Roman Capitol, and the marble pavement, where the outline of the original font can still be seen.

Campanile: The Campanile is the cathedral's bell tower. It was begun in 1334 under the guidance of the painter Giotto, then the city's master of works, who completed the first of (continued on p. 100)

Brunelleschi's Dome

Planning a dome for Florence's cathedral was one thing; building it was another. Earlier medieval domes had been constructed on wooden frames, raised to hold the structures' stone in place until the mortar set. A frame the size of the cathedral's dome, however, would have required most of the wood in Tuscany. Worse still, medieval masons had no experience with a dome this size and no notion of how to contain its estimated 25,000 tons of lateral thrust.

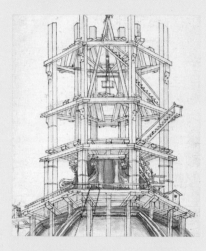

Construction of the lantern atop the dome began in 1446. A contemporary drawing shows the elaborate scaffolding.

All manner of ideas were put forth, including supporting the dome on a mound of earth laced with coins that would be dug away on completion by greedy Florentines. In a despairing mood, the city's elders mounted a competition in 1418 to devise a solution. Filippo Brunelleschi (1377–1446) narrowly beat out Lorenzo Ghiberti, the victor over Brunelleschi in the competition to design the Battistero doors in 1401.

Ghiberti was a poor loser, joining the chorus of doom-mongers who ridiculed Brunelleschi's plans as unworkable. An exasperated but canny Brunelleschi eventually feigned illness as an excuse to abandon the project, upon which Ghiberti took over, only to find himself out of his depth. By

1423, Brunelleschi had been reinstated as the dome's sole "inventor and chief director."

Engineering Genius

Brunelleschi's engineering solutions were ingenious. Some are still not understood today, but in essence they boiled down to the construction of two shells: a light outer covering about 3 feet (1 m) thick and a robust inner shell around 13 feet (4 m) thick. More important, the inner shell used a herringbone pattern of bricks, whose cantilevered rings were very strong and allowed the dome to support itself as it rose.

No detail was too small for Brunelleschi, who created a honeycomb of corridors to speed up movement around the dome and provided scaffolding hooks to make cleaning and repairs easier for future generations. Other innovations included lightweight materials, fast-drying mortar, and special tools, some of which can be seen in the Museo Storico dell'Opera del Duomo (see p. 100).

Completion of the dome in 1436 allowed for the cathedral's consecration on March 25 of the same year. The present lantern, however—the very top of the cupola—was still not built, mainly because many critics believed the dome would collapse if subjected to any further weight. Brunelleschi, after winning yet another competition, began work on the lantern a few months before his death in 1446. Only the exposed brickwork of a proposed gallery now remains unfinished, abandoned after criticism of the plan by one of the dome's most fervent admirers—Michelangelo.

Brunelleschi's solution to the problem of constructing the cathedral's huge dome was to design two shells, an inner one and an outer one. A system of cantilevered rings and bricks enabled the structure to support itself as it rose.

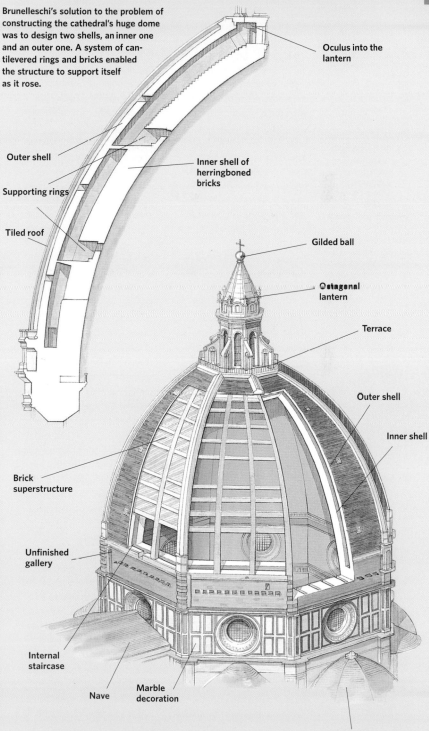

Oculus into the lantern

Outer shell

Supporting rings

Inner shell of herringboned bricks

Tiled roof

Gilded ball

Octagonal lantern

Terrace

Outer shell

Inner shell

Brick superstructure

Unfinished gallery

Internal staircase

Nave

Marble decoration

Apse

Museo Storico dell'Opera del Duomo

- ◭ Map p. 95
- ✉ Piazza del Duomo 9
- ☎ 055 230 2885
- 🕓 Closed Sun. p.m.
- 💲 $$; combined ticket with Santa Reparata, Campanile, Duomo dome, & Battistero: $$$

operaduomo.firenze.it

NOTE: The Museo Storico dell'Opera del Duomo is closed for renovation and expansion; it is scheduled to reopen in late 2015.

the tower's five stories before his death in 1337. Most of the first-story reliefs—the tower's decorative highlights—were executed by Andrea Pisano, Luca della Robbia, and assistants. The present reliefs are copies (the originals reside in the Museo Storico dell'Opera del Duomo). The 414-step climb (there is no elevator) up the 269-foot (82 m) tower rewards with sensational views.

Museo Storico dell'Opera del Duomo: The Opera del Duomo was a body created in 1296 to care for the fabric of the cathedral. Today its former home is a fine museum whose principal space is the

The Museo Storico holds masterpieces from the Duomo.

Orsanmichele

- ◭ Map p. 95
- ✉ Via dell'Arte della Lana
- ☎ 055 210 305

courtyard where Michelangelo carved much of his "David." This is now the setting for the panels from Ghiberti's Gates of Paradise doors on the Battistero. Elsewhere are a host of statues, most rescued from Arnolfo di Cambio's demolished cathedral

facade, including a figure of "St. John" by Donatello and two works by di Cambio: the "Madonna of the Glass Eyes" and an almost comical statue of "Pope Boniface VIII."

Be sure to seek out Michelangelo's **"Pietà Bandini"** (ca 1550), a late work probably intended for the sculptor's own tomb. Michelangelo became disillusioned by the piece and smashed Jesus Christ's left arm and leg. A pupil repaired the damage, but it's impossible to miss the discrepancy in styles.

The upper floor contains two sublime **choir lofts,** one by Donatello (1433–1439), the other by Luca della Robbia (1431–1438). Close by are Donatello's famous wooden statue of "Mary Magdalene" (1455) and the Old Testament prophet "Abacuc," or Habbakuk (1423–1425), one of 16 figures removed from the Campanile. Other sections include paintings, reliquaries, and a fascinating area devoted to Brunelleschi and the equipment used during the cathedral dome's construction.

Orsanmichele

Walk south from Piazza del Duomo along Via dei Calzaiuoli to the church of Orsanmichele, known for the sculptures that adorn its exterior. As early as 1339, the city's guilds had been entrusted with the building's decoration, each of the exterior niches to be filled with a statue of a particular guild's patron saint. Some of the great names of early Renaissance sculpture worked on the niches, among them Donatello, Ghiberti, Verrocchio, and Luca della Robbia (some of the present works are copies). Patches of frescoes in the peaceful interior also portray the guilds' patron saints. To the rear of the church stands a magnificent **tabernacle** (1348–1359) by Andrea Orcagna, built partly to house a painting of the "Madonna and Child" (1347) by Bernardo Daddi, a work said to have miraculous powers.

Piazza della Signoria

Florence's second great square, Piazza della Signoria, is home to the Palazzo Vecchio, the seat of city government for seven centuries, and to several notable pieces of public sculpture.

Palazzo Vecchio: The fortress-like Palazzo Vecchio was begun in 1299, probably to a plan by Arnolfo di Cambio. Initially it housed the Priori, or Signoria, the city's ruling council, but in 1540 it became home to Grand Duke Cosimo I. Cosimo later moved to the Palazzo Pitti (see p. 110), at which point his old (vecchio) palace acquired its present name. Today the palace again houses the city's council, but much of its interior and the tower are open to the public.

Enter via the inner **courtyard** (1555–1574), beautifully decorated by Giorgio Vasari, and then climb to the vast **Salone dei Cinquecento,** designed for the republic's ruling assembly. Its ceiling painting,

the "Apotheosis of Cosimo I," and wall paintings of Florentine military triumphs are the work of Vasari. Of greater interest are Michelangelo's statue, "Victory" (1525), almost opposite the room's entrance, and the **Studiolo di Francesco I** (1569–1573), a study decorated by more than 30 artists.

Turn left on the stairs from the Salone and a suite of rooms, the Quartiere degli Elementi, leads to the **Terrazzo dei Saturno,** which offers city views. Turn right and you enter the **Quartiere di Eleonora,** the apartments of

Cosimo I's wife. The highlight here is the tiny **Cappella di Eleonora** (1540–1545), sumptuously decorated by Bronzino. The **Sala dell'Udienza** offers views over the piazza and a glorious ceiling (1472–1476) by Giuliano da Maiano. The neighboring **Sala dei Gigli** is graced by another fine Maiano ceiling, a fresco sequence (1481–1485) by Domenico Ghirlandaio, and by Donatello's sublime statue of "Judith and Holofernes" (1455–1460).

Piazza della Signoria

A Map p. 95

Palazzo Vecchio

A Map p. 95

✉ Piazza della Signoria

☎ 055 276 8325

🕐 Closed Thurs. p.m.

💲 Palazzo: $$$; tower: $$$; palazzo & tower: $$$$

museicivicifiorentini .comune.fi.it

Piazza della Signoria Statues

From left to right as you face the Palazzo Vecchio, the statues on Piazza della Signoria's eastern flank are "Cosimo I" (1587–1594), an equestrian monument by Giambologna; "Neptune" (1565–1575) by Ammannati, a work ridiculed by Michelangelo; copies of Donatello's "Il Marzocco" (1418–1420), Donatello's "Judith and Holofernes," and Michelangelo's "David"; and "Hercules and Cacus" (1534), Bandinelli's companion piece for the "David."

Florence's Mighty Medici

The Medici banking fortune was established by Giovanni de' Medici (1360–1429) and consolidated by Cosimo de' Medici, also known as Cosimo the Elder (1389–1464). Its fruits were enjoyed by Cosimo's heir, Lorenzo de' Medici, better known as Lorenzo the Magnificent (1449–1492). The enlightened patronage of the Medici and others, together with an upsurge in classical and humanist scholarship, provided the spur for the Renaissance, a long-flowering artistic reawakening that found a fertile breeding ground in Florence, then Europe's most dynamic, cosmopolitan, and sophisticated city.

Galleria degli Uffizi

🅰 Map p. 95

✉ Piazzale degli Uffizi 6

☎ 055 238 8651; reservations: 055 294 883 or online at firenzemusei.it

🕐 Closed Mon. & some holidays

💲 $$; $$$ during exhibitions

uffizi.org

NOTE: The Galleria degli Uffizi is currently undergoing renovation. During this time, only some rooms are open to the public, and some artwork may have been relocated and/or rooms renumbered.

Loggia della Signoria: The large loggia on the piazza's southern side was begun in 1376 to shelter officials from the weather during public ceremonies. Today, it houses Benvenuto Cellini's prodigious bronze "Perseus" (1545–1553) and, to the right, Giambologna's "Rape of the Sabine Women" (1583). Despite its title, this latter sculpture was originally intended as a study of old age, male strength, and female beauty.

Galleria degli Uffizi

Located on Piazzale degli Uffizi, which extends south from Piazza della Signoria, the Uffizi holds the world's finest collection of Renaissance paintings. All the famous names of Italian art are here as well as works by artists from farther afield.

The building that houses the collection was designed in 1560 as a suite of offices (*uffizi*) for Cosimo I, the Medici's first grand duke, while the collection itself, accumulated by the family over the centuries, was bequeathed to the city in the 18th century by Anna Maria Luisa, sister of the last grand duke, Gian Gastone Medici.

The gallery begins with three depictions of the **Maestà,** or Madonna Enthroned, by Italy's three finest 13th-century artists—Giotto, Cimabue, and Duccio—each of whom pioneered a move away from the rigid conventions of Byzantine art that had dominated Italian and other art for centuries.

Paintings from Italy's Gothic masters fill **Rooms 3–6,** beginning with works from the city of Siena, where painters continued to borrow heavily from Byzantine art. Finest of all are Simone Martini's "Annunciation" (1333) and works by the brothers Pietro and Ambrogio Lorenzetti. Then come exponents of the International Gothic, a highly detailed and courtly style exemplified by Gentile da Fabriano's exquisite "Adoration of the Magi" (1423).

The first flowering of the Renaissance is seen in **Room 7,** which presents works by early iconoclasts such as Masaccio, Masolino, and Fra Angelico. Nearby hang well-known portraits (1460) by Piero della Francesca of Federico da Montefeltro, Duke of Urbino, and his wife, Battista Sforza.

Rooms 10–14 are given over to the gallery's most famous paintings; Botticelli's "Primavera" (1478) and "The Birth of Venus" (1485). The latter, the famous woman in a half shell, was the first pagan nude of the Renaissance and, like the "Primavera" ("Spring"), drew heavily on classical myth and contemporary humanist scholarship.

INSIDER TIP:

Avoid the street vendors selling fake "designer" goods around places like the Uffizi. It is illegal to buy such goods, and police can fine you.

—TIM JEPSON
National Geographic author

Room 15 contains two of only a handful of paintings in Florence attributed to Leonardo da Vinci: an "Annunciation" (1475) and the "Adoration of the Magi" (1481). The octagonal **Tribune** beyond was built by the Medici to house their most precious art, among which the "Medici Venus," a first-century B.C. Roman statue, figured large.

Well over halfway around the gallery you come to Michelangelo's "Doni Tondo" or "Holy Family" (1504), whose obscure meaning, contorted composition, and virulent coloring influenced a style of painting known as mannerism, a genre whose leading lights are represented

in **Rooms 16–19.** Look for Parmigianino's "Madonna and Child with Angels" (1534–1540), famous for the Virgin's peculiarly long neck.

Room 66 is dedicated to another late Renaissance painter who influenced the mannerists: Raphael. Notable works here are the "Madonna of the Goldfinch" (1506) and unflinching portraits (1506) of the Medici pope Leo X and cardinal Giulio de' Medici. Raphael also influenced Titian, whose infamous "Venus of Urbino" (1538), one of the most explicit nudes in Western painting, led Mark Twain to describe it as the "foulest, the vilest, the obscenest picture the world possesses." Titian's works can be seen in **Room 83.**

Other rooms hold masterpieces by Van Dyck, Rubens, Caravaggio, and Rembrandt.

Museo Nazionale del Bargello

If medieval sculpture and the decorative arts appeal, then the Bargello, a few minutes' walk northeast of the Galleria degli Uffizi, is for you. The museum takes its name from its building, the Bargello (1255), once the seat of the *podestà*, the city's magistrate, and later home to the *bargello*, or chief of police.

The ground floor contains three works by Michelangelo: the drunken "Bacchus" (1497), carved when the sculptor was 22; a delicate tondo of the "Madonna and Child" (1503–1504); and a proud-faced bust of

Museo Nazionale del Bargello

 Map p. 95

✉ Via del Proconsolo 4

☎ 055 238 8606

🕐 Closed 2nd & 4th Mon. of the month & some holidays

💲 $; $$ during exhibitions

museodelbargello.it

Santa Croce

 Map p. 95

✉ Piazza Santa Croce

☎ 055 246 6105

🕓 Closed Sun. a.m., some national holidays, & some religious holidays

💲 $$ (includes entry to Museo dell'Opera di Santa Croce & Cappella dei Pazzi)

santacroceopera.it

"Brutus" (1539–1540). Benvenuto Cellini was responsible for a "Bust of Cosimo I" and several preparatory bronzes for his great statue of "Perseus" in the Loggia della Signoria (see p. 102). Giambologna is represented by his famous winged "Mercury," an image that has become the standard representation of the god.

Sculptural Masterpieces:

Across the Bargello's courtyard, once a place of execution, stairs lead to the first floor and a wonderful menagerie of bronze animals by Giambologna. A right turn then opens into the **Salone del Consiglio Generale,** whose sculptures represent the pinnacle of Renaissance achievement, including the famous bronze **"David"** (1430–1440) and other works by Donatello, plus a pair of **reliefs depicting the "Sacrifice of Isaac"** by Ghiberti

and Brunelleschi. These were the joint winning entries of a 1401 competition to choose a sculptor for the Battistero's doors (see pp. 96–97). Also here are works from most of the great names of Renaissance sculpture—Michelozzo, Vecchietta, Agostino di Duccio, Desiderio da Settignano, and more.

Decorative Arts:

Most of the rest of the first floor and the entire second and third floors display a ravishing collection of carpets, tapestries, silverware, arms and armor, miniature bronzes, enamels, ivories, glassware, and other objets d'art spanning many centuries. Highlights include the frescoed **Cappella di Santa Maria Maddalena** (1340), with a pulpit, lectern, and stalls (all 1483–1488) carved for the church of San Miniato al Monte (see pp. 110–111).

Cappella dei Pazzi

Santa Croce's Cappella dei Pazzi is one of Florence's architectural highlights, commissioned as a chapter house and mausoleum in 1429 from Filippo Brunelleschi by Andrea de' Pazzi, a scion of one of the city's then leading banking families.

The chapel's austere interior is notable for how its decoration complements its simple geometric forms. Note the glazed terra-cotta tondi (decorated roundels) in the cupola, for example, which depict the Evangelists and are the work of Luca della Robbia (ca 1400–1482), possibly to designs by Donatello and Brunelleschi. Della Robbia also created the 12 tondi of the Apostles around the walls, as well as the garland of fruit clasping the Pazzi coat of arms.

Santa Croce

Florence's most important church stands just a few minutes' walk southeast of the Bargello. Santa Croce is not only an artistic shrine—with frescoes by Giotto and others—but also the burial place of 270 of the city's most eminent inhabitants.

The church was commissioned by the Franciscans and probably designed by Arnolfo di Cambio. Vast sums were spent on its creation after 1294, as rich Florentines saw it as an act of humility to be involved with, and better still buried among, the humble Franciscans.

This patronage accounts for the ostentation of the many chapels and tombs, which begin as soon as you enter with Giorgio Vasari's 1570 **monument to Michelangelo** (on the south wall). Alongside stands a cenotaph to Dante—the poet is buried in Ravenna—and beyond it the **tomb of Niccolò Machiavelli** (1787). Past a Donatello relief of the "Annunciation" (1435) are the tombs of the opera composer Gioacchino Rossini (1792–1868) and the 15th-century humanist scholar Leonardo Bruni. Moving back down the church on the north side, look for the **tomb of Galileo** (1737), near the entrance opposite the monument to Michelangelo.

Galileo's tomb in Santa Croce was erected in 1737, nearly a century after the man of science had died.

Frescoes & Other Art: The church's pictorial highlights are the **Cappella Bardi** and **Cappella Peruzzi,** both right of the high altar and frescoed by Giotto. The murals (1315–1330) in the latter chapel portray scenes from the lives of St. John the Baptist and St. John the Evangelist; those in the former depict episodes from the life of St. Francis.

The area around the high altar to the left of the Cappella Bardi is frescoed with the "Legend of the True Cross" (1380) by Agnolo Gaddi (ca 1350–1396). The same artist was responsible for the Cappella Castellani (in the south transept), while the Cappella Baroncelli to its left contains a cycle (1332–1338) by Agnolo's father, Taddeo, devoted mostly to scenes from the life of the Virgin.

Be sure to see the **Cappella dei Pazzi** (see sidebar opposite) in the church's cloister, a masterful work of early Renaissance architectural design aesthetics.

San Lorenzo & Around

To see Florence's oldest church—founded in 393—return to Santa Maria del Fiore and walk a little bit north. San Lorenzo served for many years as the city's cathedral. It was also the Medici's parish church, and vast grants from the family in the 15th century helped transform it into the present-day structure, a restrained Renaissance masterpiece designed by Brunelleschi.

The church's first highlight is Rosso Fiorentino's painting of the **"Marriage of the Virgin"**

San Lorenzo
- Map p. 95
- ✉ Piazza San Lorenzo
- ☎ 055 214 042
- 🕐 Closed Sun. Nov.–Feb. & Sun. a.m. March–Oct.
- 💲 $$ (includes entry to Biblioteca Medicea Laurenziana)

operamedicea laurenziana.it

Artists commonly show off their talent on the streets around the church of San Lorenzo.

Cappelle Medicee

- 🅰 Map p. 95
- ✉ Piazza Madonna degli Aldobrandini 6
- ☎ 055 238 8602
- 🕐 Closed 2nd & 4th Sun. & 1st, 3rd, & 5th Mon. of the month, & some holidays
- 💲 $$; $$$ during exhibitions

(1523) in the second chapel on the south wall. In the middle of the nave stand **two pulpits** (1460), their superb bronze reliefs among the last works of Donatello, who is buried in the church. Beneath the dome an inscription marks the tomb of Cosimo de' Medici, the church's main benefactor. More Medici tombs lie to the left of the altar, in the **Sagrestia Vecchia,** or Old Sacristy (1421–1426), where Cosimo's father, Giovanni, and his wife are buried beneath the central marble slab. The pair's grandsons, Giovanni and Piero, lie in a tomb (1472) to the left of the entrance.

Exit the church at the top of the north aisle, pausing to admire Filippino Lippi's altarpiece of the "Annunciation" (1440). Before the cloister, a door on your right leads to the **Biblioteca Medicea Laurenziana,** created to house the 15,000 manuscripts accumulated by Lorenzo and

Cosimo de' Medici. Michelangelo designed the vestibule (1559–1571), with its black steps, as well as the reading room at the top of the stairs.

Cappelle Medicee: The Medici Chapels form the Medici mausoleum, a three-part complex annexed to San Lorenzo. Beyond the ticket hall lie the bodies of 49 of the Medici's lesser lights, most of them placed here in 1791 by Grand Duke Ferdinand III. Steps lead from here to the **Cappella dei Principi,** or Chapel of the Princes, the most expensive project ever undertaken by the Medici. Begun in 1604, it was still being paid for when the family line died out in 1743. Its interior features the gaudy tombs of the six Medici grand dukes—Cosimo I first adopted the ducal title in 1570. Note the stone **coats of arms** around the walls of the 16 major Tuscan towns under Medici control.

More beautiful examples of Medici patronage are found in the **Sagrestia Nuova,** designed by Michelangelo, who was also responsible for the sacristy's **three tombs** (1520–1534): The one on the right belongs to Lorenzo, grandson of Lorenzo the Magnificent, depicted here as a man of thought. Opposite stands the tomb of Giuliano, Lorenzo the Magnificent's youngest son, portrayed as a man of action. The third sculpture, an unfinished "Madonna and Child," was intended to grace the tombs of Lorenzo the Magnificent and his brother, Giuliano.

Palazzo Medici-Riccardi: This palace (1462) around the corner from San Lorenzo was built for Cosimo de' Medici and remained the Medici's family home and business headquarters until 1540, when Cosimo I moved to the Palazzo Vecchio. Today's visitors come for the **Cappella dei Magi,** a tiny chapel decorated with a charming three-panel fresco cycle (1460) by Benozzo Gozzoli.

Ostensibly, its subject is the "Journey of the Magi." Its actual subject is probably the annual procession of the Compagnia dei Magi, the most prestigious Florentine medieval confraternity. Several Medici were members of the order, and many of the family feature in the paintings. The figure on a white horse is believed to be Piero; the red-hatted figure astride a mule may be Cosimo de' Medici; the gold-cloaked king riding the gray horse is probably Lorenzo the Magnificent. Gozzoli himself stands on the left a couple of rows from the rear with the words "Opus Benotti"—the work of Benozzo—picked out in gold on his red cap.

Galleria dell'Accademia

Crowds flock to the Accademia gallery, a block northeast of the Palazzo Medici-Riccardi, for one thing: Michelangelo's **"David,"** commissioned in 1501 by the Opera del Duomo, the body responsible for the upkeep of the cathedral. Michelangelo's achievement becomes more

remarkable when you learn the statue was carved in just three years from a single piece of marble—a thin and fault-riddled block—that was considered too damaged to be workable and had lain unused for some 40 years.

The 17-foot (5 m) statue remained in Piazza della Signoria until 1873; its long exposure to the elements resulted in the loss of the gilding that once adorned its hair and chest. What remain

INSIDER TIP:

Plan a lunch trip to the stalls of the covered Mercato Centrale, a block from San Lorenzo, where you can find everything from tripe to cheeses to breads.

—CAROLINE HICKEY
National Geographic Travel Books project editor

are the figure's strange proportions—notably the disproportionately long arms and overly large head and hands—created to emphasize the statue's monumentality in its original outdoors setting.

Away from the "David," the gallery contains a variety of pleasing paintings and other works by Michelangelo, notably a statue of "St. Matthew" (1504-1508) and four **"Slaves,"** all originally intended for the tomb of Pope Julius II.

Palazzo Medici-Riccardi

- Map p. 95
- Via Cavour 3
- 055 276 0340
- Closed Wed.
- $$
palazzo-medici.it

Galleria dell'Accademia
- Map p. 95
- Via Ricasoli 58-60
- 055 238 8609; reservations: 055 294 883 or online at firenzemusei.it
- Closed Mon. & some holidays
- $$; $$$ during exhibitions
firenzemusei.it

Santa Maria Novella

🅰 Map p. 95

✉ Piazza Santa Maria Novella, Piazza della Stazione 4

☎ 055 219 257

🕐 Closed a.m. Sun. & Fri.

💲 $$

chiesasanta marianovella.it
museicivicifiorentini .comune.fi.it

Santa Maria Novella

Located near the railway station, Santa Maria Novella is Florence's most important church after Santa Croce; its interior was completed in 1360, its Romanesque facade in 1456. Inside on the left, Masaccio's fresco of the "Trinity" was one of the first Renaissance works in which the new ideas of perspective were successfully employed. The first of three major fresco cycles lies in the **Cappella di Filippo Strozzi.**

with numerous portraits and a wealth of insights into the daily life of 15th-century Florence.

The third cycle is in the **Cappella Strozzi.** Its paintings (1350–1357) are the work of Nardo di Cione (died 1366). The principal frescoes depict "Paradiso" and a pictorial version of Dante's "Inferno." A separate church museum features frescoes (1425–1430) by Paolo Uccello and provides access to the **Cappellone degli Spagnoli,**

Performers in Florence's annual June Calcio Storico (historic football) games take a break.

The paintings (1489–1502) are the work of Filippino Lippi and deal with episodes from the life of Strozzi's namesake, St. Filippo the Apostle (Filippo is Philip).

The **chancel** holds the second, and most important cycle, a work by Domenico Ghirlandaio. Here the themes are the "Life of John the Baptist" and the "Life of the Virgin" (1485–1490), although the cycle is crammed

or Spanish Chapel, adorned with magnificent paintings (1367–1369) by Andrea da Firenze.

Ponte Vecchio & the Oltrarno

The Ponte Vecchio spans the Arno River and links Florence's downtown to the quieter Oltrarno district. With its overhanging buildings, it is one of Florence's most familiar images,

Cappella Brancacci

 Map p. 95

✉ Santa Maria del Carmine, Piazza del Carmine (entrance to right of church)

☎ 055 238 2195 or 055 276 8558; obligatory timed 15-minute reservations: 055 276 8224

🕐 Closed Sun. a.m., Tues., & some holidays

💲 $$

museicivicifiorentini .comune.fi.it

INSIDER TIP:

Enjoy a delicious ice cream from La Carraia (Piazza Nazario Sauro 25r) while admiring a view of the Ponte Vecchio at night from the Ponte alla Carraia, just a couple blocks west of Santa Trìnita.

—BEATRICE LAGHI
Hotel Brunelleschi front desk

and over the centuries it has survived countless floods and the havoc of war and civil strife.

There has probably been a bridge here since Etruscan times. Under the Romans it carried the Via Cassia, an important highway to the north, and for centuries thereafter it remained the city's only trans-Arno link, although its wooden structure was replaced often in the wake of floods. The present bridge was built in 1345, taking the name Ponte Vecchio (Old Bridge) to distinguish it from the Ponte alla Carraia (1218), then known as the Ponte Nuovo (New Bridge).

Shops first appeared during the 13th century. Most were fishmongers and butchers attracted by the river, a convenient dump for their waste. Next came tanners, who used the river to soak their hides. In time, a space was opened at the center of the bridge—still there today—to allow the tipping of garbage straight into the water. In 1593 Grand Duke Ferdinando I

banished what he called the practitioners of these "vile arts" and installed jewelers and goldsmiths instead, many of whose descendants still trade from the bridge's pretty wooden-shuttered shops.

Cappella Brancacci: Art lovers flock to the Santa Maria del Carmine church, in the heart of the Oltrarno district, for the sublime frescoes in its Cappella Brancacci. Executed on the cusp of the Renaissance, the frescoes were painted with a realism, dramatic narrative, and mastery of perspective that would influence painters for generations to come. If you wish to see them, you must book timed tickets.

Commissioned by Filippo Brancacci, a silk merchant, the paintings were begun in 1424 by Masolino (1383–1447) and his assistant, Masaccio (1401–1428). In 1426 Masolino was called to paint in Budapest, and in his absence Masaccio's genius blossomed: When Masolino returned in 1427 he became the junior partner. Masaccio was responsible for the cycle's most famous image, "The Expulsion of Adam and Eve from Paradise" (left of the entrance arch as you look at the frescoes). Compare this with Masolino's more anodyne rendering of "Adam and Eve" on the opposite wall.

Masaccio would die aged just 26, and in 1428 Masolino was called to Rome, never to return. It would be some 50 years before Filippino Lippi completed the frescoes.

A cluster of houses and workshops—many more than 400 years old—overhangs the Ponte Vecchio.

Palazzo Pitti (Galleria Palatina & Appartamenti Reali)

 Map p. 95

✉ Piazza de' Pitti 1

☎ 055 238 8614

🕐 Closed Mon.

💲 $$$; $$$$ during exhibitions

www.palazzopitti.it

Museo degli Argenti

☎ 055 238 8709 or 055 238 8761

🕐 Closed 1st & last Mon. of month

💲 $$

Giardino di Boboli

 Map p. 95

☎ 055 294 883

🕐 Closed 1st & last Mon. of month & some holidays

💲 $$

NOTE: The admission ticket bought at the Museo degli Argenti or Giardino di Boboli is a combination ticket good for entrance to the other site as well as a couple other museums.

Palazzo Pitti: Few palaces are as colossal as the Palazzo Pitti, just up Via de Guicciardini from the Ponte Vecchio. Begun by the Pitti family, a banking dynasty, in 1460 and later bought by the Medici, today it contains a cluster of museums—on a short trip, concentrate on the **Galleria Palatina,** where six ornate state rooms contain most of the Medici collection not in the Uffizi. The gallery has no fewer than 11 works by Raphael, the finest being the "Madonna della Seggiola" (1515) and the "Donna Velata" (or "Veiled Woman"; 1516). The most celebrated of 14 paintings by Titian is the "Portrait of an Englishman" (1540). Don't miss Cristofano Allori's erotic and curiously bloodless "Judith and Holofernes" (1610–1612), which hangs in one of seven smaller rooms parallel to the state rooms. Other painters represented include Caravaggio, Filippo Lippi, Andrea del Sarto, Rubens, and Tintoretto.

The ticket for the gallery also admits you to the **Appartamenti Reali,** the palace's lavishly decorated state apartments. A separate ticket is required for the **Museo degli Argenti,** a collection of silverware and other decorative arts.

Behind the Palazzo Pitti lies Florence's principal park, the **Giardino di Boboli,** or Boboli Garden, begun by Cosimo I in 1549. Open to the public since 1766, the park's trees, formal gardens, walkways, and fountains provide a green and peaceful retreat.

San Miniato al Monte: San Miniato is the most beautiful church in Florence, but because of its outlying position atop a hill on the Oltrarno's leafy fringes it is difficult to see on a short visit unless you take a taxi. Moments away is Piazzale Michelangelo, rightly noted for its views over the city.

On the church's lovely **facade** note the mosaic depicting "Christ Between the Virgin and St. Minias" (1260) and the eagle (1401) with its bale of cloth, a symbol of the Arte di Calimala, the cloth merchants' guild entrusted with the church's upkeep.

The interior's beautiful pavement dates from 1207, while many of the pillars and capitals were salvaged from Roman and Byzantine buildings. Michelozzo's Cappella del Crocefisso (1448) fills the center of the nave, with painted panels (1394–1396) by Agnolo Gaddi. The raised choir is dominated by a superlative Romanesque pulpit, screen (1207), and glittering apse mosaic (1297). Off the north aisle see the **Cappella del Cardinale del Portogallo** (1473), one of Italy's great Renaissance ensembles of sculpture and paintings. ■

San Miniato al Monte

Map p. 95

Via del Monte alle Croci–Viale Galileo Galilei

055 234 2731

Bus 13 to Piazzale Michelangelo

sanminiatoalmonte.it

NEED TO KNOW

Port Logistics: Livorno

Cruise ships dock at the **Port of Livorno** (portolivorno2000.it) for trips to Florence (Firenze), Pisa, Siena, Lucca, San Gimignano, Volterra, and the Tuscan countryside. The vast port has good facilities, but the town has few attractions. If you're not organizing your own excursions, tours with operators based outside Livorno are often better value. Avoid tours offered by Livorno taxis and port touts.

Livorno to Florence

Livorno's railroad station is 2 miles (3 km) from the port. You could take a taxi (€10–€15) directly to the station. Alternatively, take the port shuttle (allow 30 min.) or walk the half mile (1 km) or longer (it depends on where in the port your ship docks) to Piazza del Municipio. From here, walk two blocks on Via Cogorano to Piazza Grande and pick up bus 1 (10 min.) to the station.

Trains depart for **Firenze Santa Maria Novella** station hourly (journey time 82 min.). Taxis cost around €150–€200 one way or €40–€50 per person sharing an eight-seat minibus. Check whether drivers charge an hourly wait-fee in Florence when booking return trips and confirm all prices before departure. Most cruise lines offer transfer-only trips to Florence for around €70–€100.

Prepurchase Tickets

Be sure to secure advance timed-entry tickets (at least 24 hours in advance) for the Uffizi. Use the official ticketing site: **Firenze Musei** (tel 055 294 883, firenze musei.it). There is a booking fee on top of the entrance fee. Collect your ticket from the Uffizi office across the piazza from the gallery entrance. Miss your time slot and you forfeit the right to skip the lines.

Tickets can also be booked for the Galleria dell'Accademia, Museo Nazionale del Bargello, Cappelle Medicee, and Galleria Palatina in the Palazzo Pitti. The Firenze Musei website offers additional information.

Florence Highlights

You can spend your entire port of call time at any one of these destinations, but here are some suggested times to help with your planning. Note, these do not allow for travel time to and from and/or waiting in line:

- Duomo, Campanile, Battistero di San Giovanni, & ascent of the cathedral dome or Campanile: 1.5 hours
- Orsanmichele, Piazza della Signoria, Palazzo Vecchio, & Ponte Vecchio: 1 hour
- Galleria degli Uffizi, with booked timed ticket: 1 hour
- Michelangelo's "David," with booked timed ticket: 30 minutes
- Santa Croce: 30 minutes

Pisa

Most people know Pisa's famous Leaning Tower. Few know that it's just one component in a lovely ensemble of medieval buildings; fewer still know that the rest of the city, while modern in places—the result of bombing during World War II—has a historic core that is also worth exploring. Allow an hour to see the tower and its surroundings, and about the same again to explore Pisa's other medieval sights.

The tower once leaned 17.5 feet (5.5 m) from the vertical. Engineers in the 1990s reversed the lean by 10 percent.

Pisa has Etruscan and Roman roots, but its heyday came in the 11th and 12th centuries, when far-flung trading links turned it into one of the Mediterranean's maritime powers. The wealth from this era yielded the Leaning Tower and other monuments, although the city declined following defeat by Genoa in 1284 and the silting up of its harbor. Florence assumed control in 1406, accelerating Pisa's transformation into a quiet center of science and learning—the Pisan-born Galileo Galilei was the most famous alumnus of the city's university, founded in 1343.

Campo dei Miracoli

The **Torre Pendente** (Leaning Tower) is one element of the Campo dei Miracoli, or Field of Miracles, a large, grassy piazza that also contains Pisa's Duomo (cathedral), Baptistery, and Camposanto (cemetery). The tower was begun in 1173 as the cathedral's bell tower, and it started to lean almost immediately, the result of the weak, sandy subsoil under its foundations. The lean intensified during the 20th century. At its worst, the tilt was 17.5 feet (5.5 m) from vertical. In 1999 engineers began the task of

INSIDER TIP:

For your best luck, book your tour for the Leaning Tower at least two weeks out. Tours are strictly timed and require climbing 300 steps.

—TIM JEPSON
National Geographic author

successfully reversing the process using weights, steel cables, and sophisticated underpinning techniques. The lean stabilized, the tower reopened to visitors *(opapisa.it, $$$$)*.

The **Duomo** was begun in 1064, and with its array of pillars, columns, and colored marbles became the model for similar "Pisan-Romanesque" churches across central Italy. The exterior's highlight is the **Portale di San Ranieri** (1180), 24 bronze panels by Bonanno Pisano portraying stories from the New Testament.

Inside, the star turn is Giovanni Pisano's exceptional **pulpit,** the last and finest of the series of pulpits created by Nicola and Giovanni Pisano, father and son, across Tuscany. An equally staggering pulpit by Nicola stands in the **Battistero** (begun in 1152); Nicola, with Giovanni, was also responsible for much of the exquisite carving on the Baptistery's exterior.

The Campo's last component, the **Camposanto** cloister, is a medieval cemetery (begun in 1278) that according to

legend was filled with earth brought back from the Holy Land during the Crusades. It is filled with tombs.

Artistic treasures from the Campo can be seen in the **Museo dell'Opera del Duomo** in the piazza's southeast corner. Highlights include Giovanni Pisano's "Madonna del Colloquio," a carved group of the Madonna and Child with saints, and the noted "Croce dei Pisani," a cross carried by Pisan troops in the First Crusade.

The Rest of the Town

Visit **Piazza dei Cavalieri,** a square ringed by medieval buildings, then take Via Dini to Borgo Stretto, home to many of Pisa's stores, and the river beyond. Turn left on Lungarno Mediceo and you come to the **Museo Nazionale di San Matteo,** which has a wide-ranging collection of works of art, most removed from Pisa's churches. ∎

Pisa
88 D2
Visitor Information
Piazza Vittorio Emanuele II 16
050 42 291
pisaunicaterra.it

Museo Nazionale di San Matteo
Piazza San Matteo in Soarta (Lungarno Mediceo)
050 541 865
Closed Sun. p.m., Mon., & some holidays
$$$, combined ticket with Museo Nazionale di Palazzo Reale: $$$

NEED TO KNOW
Livorno to Pisa
Trains from Livorno to Pisa *(2-3 times hourly)* take 15-20 minutes *(trenitalia.com)*. They arrive at **Pisa Centrale,** a mile (1.6 km) from the Campo dei Miracoli. Take a taxi from the rank outside the station or the "LAM Rossa" bus *(4-6 times hourly)* from the stop in front of the NH Cavalieri hotel to Torre/Piazza Manin; buy tickets on board (correct change required, €1.50) or from the kiosk in the station. To return, there is a taxi stand in the Campo by the Bar Duomo; or take the bus (direction "Stazione Centrale") from the stop by the BNL bank.

Lucca

Henry James once described sleepy Lucca as "overflowing with everything that makes for ease, for plenty, for beauty, for interest and good example" (*Italy Revisited,* 1877). Little has changed since. Peaceful, urbane, and embraced by tree-topped walls, the city today is still an attractive mix of atmospheric piazzas, tiny churches, museums, galleries, and cobbled lanes. Among Tuscan towns and cities, only Florence and Siena are more compelling.

Diners enjoy an alfresco meal at one of Lucca's many charming streetside restaurants.

Lucca

🅰 88 D3

Visitor Information

✉ Vecchia Porta di San Donato, Piazzale Verdi

☎ 0583 583 150 or 0583 442 944

www.luccatourist.it www.comune.lucca.it luccaterre.it luccaitinera.it

San Michele in Foro

✉ Piazza San Michele

🕐 Closed 12 p.m.– 3 p.m.

Lucca owes the gridiron plan of its center to the Romans. It rose to medieval prominence as a result of a trade in silk. After the 14th century, the city declined in status, but it retained its independence until the arrival of Napoleon. Today, everything you want to see lies within the old walls. Start either in the central square, Piazza San Michele, and work north, or at the Duomo and work east.

San Michele in Foro

Few churches are quite as breathtaking at first glance as San Michele in Foro, built on the site of the old Roman *foro,*

or forum. Its **facade** combines the marble-striped veneer that distinguishes most Pisan-Romanesque buildings with an astounding confection of miniature loggias, blind arcades, and twisted columns. Lucca's own Giacomo Puccini (1858–1924) was born a stone's throw from the church. The famous composer's birthplace, **Casa di Puccini,** contains a museum.

Duomo di San Martino

Another wonderful facade (1060–1241) fronts the Duomo di San Martino, in Piazza San Martino. The cathedral's most important feature is a series of 13th-century carvings around the atrium and the entrance doors. The left-hand door reliefs are by the Pisan sculptor Nicola Pisano, while the panels between the doors on the "Life of St. Martin" are the work of the facade's principal architect, Guidetto da Como.

Inside, the **Tempietto,** a chapel created by local sculptor Matteo Civitali (1435–1511), houses the much venerated Volto Santo (Holy Face), a cedar crucifix said to be a true likeness of Christ carved by Nicodemus, an eyewitness to the Crucifixion. In truth, it is probably a 13th-century copy of an 8th-century work.

Of greater artistic merit is the "Tomb of Ilaria del Carretto" (1410), dedicated to the wife of Paolo Guinigi, one of Lucca's leading medieval rulers, and housed in the **sacristy** (*$*). The masterpiece of Sienese sculptor Jacopo della Quercia, it is one of Italy's loveliest sculptures.

The Rest of the Town

Just south of the Duomo is a good place to climb to Lucca's magnificent, broad, traffic-free **walls** (1544–1645). You can rent a bike at the visitor center and cycle the entire 4-mile (6.4 km) circuit, a magical and easy 25-minute ride.

Walk north from the Duomo and you come to Lucca's strangest sight, the **Casa Guinigi,** a town house built by the Guinigi, Lucca's preeminent medieval family. It is best known for its tower and the pair of holm oaks sprouting from the roof. Another former Guinigi dwelling houses the **Museo Nazionale di Villa Guinigi,** an extensive collection of archaeological remains, medieval paintings, sculptures, textiles, and other applied arts.

From here, or Piazza San Michele, pick up Via Fillungo, Lucca's main street, which leads close to **Piazza dell'Anfiteatro,** a square whose medieval houses were built into the oval of the old Roman amphitheater. Just north of Via Fillungo is **San Frediano** (1112–1147), a church distinguished by its 13th-century facade mosaic and interior treasures that include a sublimely carved 12th-century font and Amico Aspertini's 16th-century frescoes of the "Arrival of the Volto Santo in Lucca." ∎

Casa di Puccini
- ✉ Corte San Lorenzo 9 (Via di Poggio)
- ☎ 0583 584 028
- ⏰ Closed Tues.
- 💲 $$

puccinimuseum.org

Duomo di San Martino
- ✉ Piazza San Martino
- ☎ 0583 957 068
- ⏰ Closed Sun. 10:45 a.m.–12 p.m.

Museo Nazionale di Villa Guinigi
- ✉ Via della Quarquonia
- ☎ 0583 496 033
- ⏰ Closed Sun. (open a.m. July–Aug.)–Mon.
- 💲 $$

luccamuseinazionali.it

San Frediano
- ✉ Piazza San Frediano
- ⏰ Closed 12 p.m.–3 p.m.

NEED TO KNOW

Livorno to Lucca

It is possible to see Lucca and Pisa in a day from Livorno using public transit. Make for Lucca first and allow two hours to explore the town: Trains run roughly hourly and take between an hour and 90 minutes, with a change of train at **Pisa Centrale** (*trenitalia.com*). Lucca's station is just south of the walled center: On exiting, head for the walls and entry to the old town at Porta San Pietro. Return to Pisa by train; or take bus R008 or P731 (direction "Pisa Aeroporto") from Piazzale Verdi (*every 40 min. to 1 hour, 30-min. ride, vaibus.com*), just inside the walls by the visitor center.

Siena

Siena is Italy's most perfect medieval town. At its heart lies the Campo, Italy's finest square and the stage for the city's renowned annual horse race—the Palio—as well as the art-filled chambers of the majestic Palazzo Pubblico. Nearby are the Duomo, one of Italy's finest Gothic buildings, and the treasures of the cathedral museum, while all around a magical labyrinth of palace-lined streets and peaceful corners provides for hours of exploration.

Siena's magnificent Duomo sits on a site originally occupied by a Roman temple to Minerva.

Siena

🅰 89 E1

Visitor Information

✉ Piazza del Campo 56

☎ 0577 280 551

terresiena.it
www.comune.siena.it

NOTE: The multisight Opa Si Pass (*$$$$*) provides entry to the Duomo, Battistero di San Giovanni, and Museo dell'Opera del Duomo; buy it at the Museo dell'Opera ticket office.

Siena began as an Etruscan and then Roman colony before banking and textiles in the Middle Ages made it one of Europe's most important cities. In 1554, after centuries of conflict, the city fell to Florence, which resulted in the town declining into a backwater—one reason for its remarkably unsullied appearance today.

Il Campo

Your first stop in Siena should be the Campo—literally the "field"— a scallop-shaped piazza that has long served as the city's civic and

social heart. At its lowest point is the Palazzo Pubblico (1297–1342), now the town hall. Inside is the **Museo Civico,** full of frescoes and paintings. Its two most significant rooms lie side by side: the Sala del Mappamondo and Sala della Pace. The end walls of the former are decorated with a beautiful "Maestà" (1315) by Simone Martini and an equestrian portrait (1328?) of Sienese general Guidoriccio da Fogliano. In the Sala della Pace is the city's most renowned fresco cycle, Ambrogio Lorenzetti's faded "Allegories of Good and Bad

Government" (1337–1339). Turn left in the palazzo's courtyard and climb the 503 steps of the 330-foot (102 m) **Torre del Mangia** (1338–1348) for some magnificent city views.

Piazza del Duomo

The façade (1284–1296) of Siena's **Duomo** is one of the most beautiful things in Tuscany, a fitting prelude to an equally glorious interior, where highlights are the ceiling (the sculptured heads depict countless popes), the marble pavement (56 narrative panels created by leading medieval artists), and the Piccolomini Altarpiece (1503), whose lower four niche statues are the work of Michelangelo. Alongside the last lies the entrance to the Libreria Piccolomini, with a fresco cycle (1502–1509) by Pinturicchio that portrays episodes from the life of local-born Aeneas Piccolomini (Pope Pius II). Also don't miss Nicola Pisano's celebrated pulpit and its reliefs of episodes from the "Life of Christ" (1266–1268).

Opposite the cathedral stands the fascinating **Santa Maria della Scala** (*tel 0577 534 571, santamariadellascala.com, $$*), which for almost 800 years served as Siena's main hospital. Today, it is a leading cultural center. In situ works of art include an extraordinary fresco cycle (1440) by Vecchietta and his fellow Sienese artist Domenico di Bartolo (1400–1445) detailing the hospital's history.

Before you leave the piazza, visit the **Museo dell'Opera del Duomo** (*Piazza del Duomo 8,*

tel 0577 283 048, operaduomo .siena.it, $$) for its outstanding artworks, notably Duccio's monumental "Maestà," painted for the high altar in 1313. Steps to the museum's left lead down to the subterranean **Battistero di San Giovanni** (*tel 0577 283 048, $*), with a baptismal font (1417–1430) executed by Lorenzo Ghiberti and Jacopo della Quercia, the most exalted Florentine and Sienese sculptors of their day.

The Rest of the Town

Simply wandering Siena's streets is a pleasure, but you could aim for the **Pinacoteca Nazionale,** Siena's main art gallery, which offers an in-depth look at the city's Gothic school of painting, and the church of **Santa Maria dei Servi,** known for its views and frescoes (the latter is about a 20-minute walk from the Campo). At the opposite, northern end of the city is **San Domenico** (begun in 1226), a church closely associated with St. Catherine of Siena, patron saint of Siena. A chapel inside contains frescoes (1526) by Sodoma of scenes from her life. ∎

Museo Civico & Torre del Mangia
 Palazzo Pubblico, Piazza del Campo
 0577 292 223 or 0577 292 342
Museum: $$$; tower: $$; museum & tower: $$$$
museisenesi.org

Duomo
Piazza del Duomo
0577 283 048
Closed Sun a.m.
$; Sept.–Oct. (when pavement is on view): $$
operaduomo.siena.it

Pinacoteca Nazionale
Via di San Pietro 29
0577 286 143 or 0577 281 161
Closed p.m. both Sun. & Mon., & all day some holidays
 $$
www.spsae-si.beni culturali.it pinacotecanazionale .siena.it

NEED TO KNOW
Livorno to Siena
Viatour (*viatour.com*), among other operators, offers private 9-hour guided tours to Siena (with San Gimignano) from Livorno, with a guaranteed return to your ship for departure. Using public transit is difficult, as the minimum journey time by train is a prohibitive 2 hours one way.

San Gimignano

Tuscany's most famous village is often called a "medieval Manhattan" after a skyline that bristles with ancient stone towers. Although popular—perhaps too much so in summer—it is a place that retains its charm. Visit not only for its towers but also for a fascinating art gallery, some beautiful views of the Tuscan landscape, and a pair of superb fresco-filled churches.

The famous towers of San Gimignano: Most Italian towns would once have had a similar skyline.

San Gimignano
🗺 89 E2
Visitor Information
✉ Piazza del Duomo 1
☎ 0577 940 008
🕐 Closed 1 p.m.– 3 p.m. March– Oct. & 1-2 p.m. Nov.–Feb.

sangimignano.com

NOTE: A combined ticket (*$$$*) is available to principal sights such as the Museo Civico and Torre Grossa (but not the Collegiata).

San Gimignano existed in Etruscan and Roman times, and then developed during the Middle Ages thanks to its location on the Via Francigena, a trade and pilgrimage route between Rome and the north. The famous towers began to appear around 1150 as status symbols and defensive retreats, as they did in many villages across Tuscany. Plague and internal squabbles eventually weakened the village, which in 1348 placed itself under the protection of Florence. This undermined the power of local nobles, one reason so many towers survived (as they posed no

threat, there was no need to tear them down).

Exploring the village is easy—you can walk from one end to the other in a few minutes. Start at the southern gateway, the Porta San Giovanni, and then walk north on Via San Giovanni. At the top of this street, a medieval arch ushers you into the first of two linked squares, **Piazza della Cisterna** and **Piazza del Duomo.** The latter is home to the village's two principal sights: the Collegiata and Museo Civico.

Collegiata di Santa Maria Assunta

The Collegiata (or Duomo di San Gimignano) was founded in the tenth century. Beyond the blandest of facades (1239) lies an extraordinary interior almost completely covered in frescoes. Three principal cycles adorn the walls, beginning on the rear (entrance wall) with the **"Last Judgment"** (1410) by leading Sienese painter Taddeo di Bartolo (1363–1422); "Inferno" is portrayed on the left, "Paradiso" on the right. Between these two scenes, which are painted on protruding walls, is a fresco by Benozzo Gozzoli of "St. Sebastian" (1465), a saint invoked against infectious diseases and often painted during or after plague epidemics.

The church's second cycle (1356-1367), on the left (north) wall, was executed by Bartolo di Fredi and depicts scenes from the Old Testament, with biblical scenes from the Creation in the lunettes above. The cycle of New Testament scenes on the opposite wall is earlier (from around 1333) and is attributed to one of two Sienese artists, either Lippo Memmi or Barna da Siena.

INSIDER TIP:

Don't leave San Gimignano without buying a bottle of the famous Vernaccia di San Gimignano, an ancient and noble white wine.

—FEDERICA ROMAGNOLI
National Geographic contributor

Elsewhere in the church, the **Cappella di San Gimignano** (left of the high altar) contains an altarpiece by Benedetto da Maiano. The **Cappella di Santa Fina,** off the south aisle, is dedicated to one of San Gimignano's patron saints, the subject of lunette frescoes (1475) by the Florentine painter Domenico Ghirlandaio (1449-1494).

Museo Civico

San Gimignano's civic museum is divided between the museum proper and the **Torre Grossa,** the only one of San Gimignano's

towers currently open to the public. The former opens with the Sala del Consiglio, dominated by Memmi's majestic "Maestà" (1317). Upstairs is the picture gallery, crammed with masterpieces by Sienese and Florentine painters, most notably Gozzoli and Filippino Lippi. The most beguiling pictures, the work of local painter Memmo di Filippuccio, hang in a separate room (turn left at the top of the stairs): The early 14th-century panels portray three wedding scenes, including two vignettes in which the couple share a bath and then a bed.

The Rest of the Town

Spare a few moments to explore the remains of the **Rocca,** or castle (1353), and its peaceful public gardens to the west of Piazza del Duomo. Next, take a circuitous route north from there—enjoying some of the pretty backstreets en route—to San Gimignano's third major set piece, the church of **Sant'Agostino.** Frescoes adorn much of its walls, but Gozzoli's stunning "Life of St. Augustine" cycle (1463-1467) around the high altar outshines all. ∎

Collegiata di Santa Maria Assunta
- ✉ Piazza Luigi Pecori 1-2
- ☎ 0577 940 316
- 🕐 Closed Sun. a.m., 2nd half of Nov., & some holidays
- 🅢 Church & Cappella di Santa Fina: $

Museo Civico
- ✉ Palazzo del Popolo, Piazza del Duomo 2
- ☎ 0577 990 312
- 🅢 $$ (Includes entry to Torre Grossa)

Sant'Agostino
- ✉ Piazza Sant'Agostino
- ☎ 0577 907 012
- 🕐 Closed 12 p.m.-3 p.m.

NEED TO KNOW

Livorno to San Gimignano

It is difficult to reach San Gimignano by public transit, but many companies offer bus tours of up to 9 hours, with pickups from Livorno, often with a stopover en route in Siena or the medieval hilltop town of Volterra.

Two cities with some of Europe's greatest art and ancient monuments, and the sightseeing highlights of Pompeii, Capri, and the Amalfi Coast

Rome & Naples

Introduction & Map   122-123

Rome   124-143

A Walk Around Central Rome   136-137

Need to Know: Civitavecchia   143

Bay of Naples   144-151

Need to Know: Naples   151

Capri   152-155

Need to Know: Capri   155

Amalfi Coast   156-157

Need to Know: Visiting the Amalfi Coast   157

Restaurants   286-291

The wide staircase commonly known as the Spanish Steps leads up to the Renaissance church Trinità dei Monti, thus the stairs' official name: Scalinata della Trinità dei Monti.

Rome & Naples

Rome (Roma) and Naples (Napoli) are two of the Mediterranean's greatest cities, one the seat of an empire that shaped much of the Western world, the other an almost equally fascinating city that provides a springboard for visits to Pompeii and Herculaneum, two of the world's most celebrated archaeological sites, and to Capri, an island of fabled beauty.

Fontana dei Quattro Fiumi, centerpiece of Piazza Navona, Rome

No other city can match Rome for its artistic, historical, or architectural riches, and no city presents quite such an intimidating sightseeing prospect—visiting the absolute highlights alone will take you several days. And you'll have to grapple with modern problems, too: noise, traffic, pollution, and, especially in summer, crowds that may seem too bustling for comfort. This note serves only as gentle warning—it is easy to forget that both Rome and Naples are cities with a problematic present as well as a glorious past.

Rome

Bear this in mind when planning a short visit. Central Rome is quite compact, but do not try to see it all. Long lines mean that if you insist on touring the Musei Vaticani (Vatican Museums) and the interior of the Colosseo (Colosseum), you will have very little time left over. That said, if you set off early and are prepared to walk, then you can cover a lot of ground.

Start in Piazza Venezia and walk to Piazza del Campidoglio and then down to the Foro Romano. Spend an hour here and walk around the Colosseo, which is adjacent, perhaps with half an hour in the remarkable church of San Clemente nearby. Then take a taxi to the easily seen Spanish Steps and walk to the Fontana di Trevi (Trevi Fountain). From here it is a few minutes' stroll to the Pantheon, Piazza Navona, and Campo de' Fiori at the heart of the medieval, Renaissance, and baroque city. If you want just a small taste of Rome's museums and galleries, the nearby Palazzo Altemps or Palazzo Doria Pamphilj are good candidates.

Finally, walk through the fine old streets west of Piazza Navona to the Basilica di San Pietro (St. Peter's), where you'll need an hour or so to deal with the lines and to see the vast interior (longer if you wish to ascend the dome).

Naples & Points South

Central Naples is compact enough for much of it to be seen on a brisk day's walking tour, as its highlights are fewer. The one world-class sight is the Museo Archeologico Nazionale, which contains many of the treasures excavated at Pompeii and Herculaneum, the Roman towns a few miles south of Naples that were buried by the eruption of Mount Vesuvius in A.D. 79. Both these archaeological sites will mean much more if combined with the museum. Note that the immensely popular Pompeii covers a vast area, and that Herculaneum, while less famous, offers a more manageable,

Area of map detail

Rome

Mediterranean Sea

0   60 kilometers
0   30 miles

5 ▷ Montalto di Castro
     Tarquinia Marta Viterbo
     Vetralla L. di Vico
Civitavecchia Civita Castellana
Santa Marinella Bracciano 691m Monte Soratte
                 Bracciano Monte Soratte
            Cerveteri Campagnano di Roma
     Ladispoli SS4
4 ▷   A12 Veio A1
          VATICAN Monterotodo
          CITY
Fiumicino (Tiber) ROMA LATIUM A24
Lido di Ostia (ROME) Arsoli Carsoli
          Tivoli
     Marino Frascati
          Laziale Palestrina 2156m
                              Monte Viglio
△   Aprilia Velletri Monti Simbruini
A   Cisterna di Latina Cori Anagni
     Anzio Nettuno Alatri
3 ▷ Torre Astura Latina SS156 Frosinone Sora
                              SS214 P.N. ABRUZZI
     Pontinia Ceccano
     P.N. CIRCEO Ceprano 2247m
     Sabaudia Pico La Merta
          Terracina Ceprano
          541m Fondi Pontecorvo Isernia
     Monte Circeo Sperlonga Monti Aurunci Venafro Monti del Matese
          Formia 1533m A1 Campobasso
     I. Palmarola Gaeta Monte Petrella Roccamonfina
       I. Zannone Sessa Aurunca MOLISE
     I. di Ponza Golfo Teano Piedimonte Matese
        Ponziane di Mondragone Sparanise Calore
              Gaeta Capua
2 ▷   I. Ventotone Santa Maria Caserta
              Aversa Maddaloni Benevento
          NAPOLI A1 SS7
          (NAPLES) 1281m Nola
     I. d'Ischia Monte Altavilla
△   Ischia P.N. Vesuvio A16
B   Golfo di Napoli VESUVIO Sarno Avellino
          Herculaneum Pompeii Atripalda
          Torre Annunziata
          Castellammare Nocera
     I. di Capri Sorrento Ravello Inferiore 1809m
          Capri Positano Amalfi Salerno Monte Cervialto
                         Golfo CAMPANIA
                         A3
                    Battipaglia Eboli
1 ▷   di Salerno Sele
                    Paestum Capaccio
△   Agropoli
C   Castellabate △
                              D

but equally fas-
cinating insight
into the past.

The sheer weight
of visitors is one factor to
consider in Capri, the other
obvious alternative for a day's
excursion from Naples. A good plan
of attack is to take the earliest, quickest
ferry from Naples to Capri town and immediately take a boat tour to the Blue Grotto
(at its best in the morning light). Then
take a bus or taxi from above the grotto to
Anacapri, one of Capri's two towns, and ride
the funicular up Monte Solaro and see Villa
San Michele before taking a bus or taxi back
to Capri town.

Capri can also be seen under your
own steam from Sorrento, a town on the
north side of the peninsula that forms the
southern arm of the Golfo di Napoli (Bay of
Naples). Sorrento is also the springboard
for the towns, landscapes, and dramatic

roads of the Amalfi Coast, found along
the peninsula's southern shore. A drive
and boat tour, plus the towns of Positano
and Ravello (less so Amalfi itself), are the
things to see and do, but the practicalities of
making an independent trip in a short time
are difficult: It is far better here to take an
organized excursion. ∎

Rome

Rome is many things—the mother of Western civilization, a religious center, a modern capital; the city of Caesars and popes, of romance and *la dolce vita*—the soft, easy life. It is also the city of long, languorous sunny days and countless churches, museums and art galleries, of grand squares and medieval lanes, of piazzas, palaces, and majestic monuments to a golden age of empire.

Views east from the Basilica di San Pietro stretch across Bernini's magnificent Piazza San Pietro.

NEED TO KNOW p. 143

Rome

🅰 123 B4

Visitor Information

✉ Tourist Information Point (PIT) booths are all over Rome, including on Via dei Fori Imperiali & Piazza delle Cinque Lune (Piazza Navona)

turismoroma.it
museiincomuneroma.it

Layers of history are literally visible at every turn: Renaissance apartments sit atop Roman amphitheaters, baroque statues support ancient Egyptian obelisks. The modern, the medieval, and the ancient are juxtaposed, not always to happy effect—a Rome whose streets were built for carts and chariots can be ill suited to the demands of a modern city, not least those made by its cars and commuters.

But for the most part, the vivid sense of walking through history and the wonderful contrasts between the city's majestic sights—Basilica di San Pietro, the Colosseo, and the Pantheon—and its more intimate beauties are enough to counter any reservations one may have.

Rome also shares the more simple pleasures of most Italian towns and cities. It is intrinsically beautiful for a start—just stand on one of the Tiber bridges at dusk, or walk the backstreets at night, to see how. Then there's the coffee and ice cream—good as any in the country—and while the food and wines might be earthier than elsewhere, the simple joy of indulging in them in this great city, preferably under a starry sky on a balmy evening, is beyond compare.

Ancient Rome

Ancient Rome stretches for almost half a mile in the east of the present city from the Capitolino (Capitoline Hill), the most important of the city's original Seven Hills. It encompasses the Foro Romano (known simply as the Foro), the later Fori Imperiali, the Palatino (see sidebar this page), and, at the end of the Foro, the Colosseo.

Start your visit atop the Capitolino, then make your way down to the Fori Imperiali, then the Foro Romano—geographically, it makes sense to visit the Fori Imperiali first—and finally the Colosseo.

Capitolino: The climb to the top of the Capitolino begins in **Piazza Venezia,** the square at the heart of Rome. The square is dominated by the **Monumento a Vittorio Emanuele II,** a vast white shrine to Italian unification whose construction destroyed countless medieval buildings and altered forever the contours of the Capitolino. On the right (west) side of the monument, a shallow-stepped

---

Palatino

The hilly area above the Foro Romano is the Palatino (Palatine), one of Rome's original Seven Hills. It was also the site of the city's earliest settlement—predating the forum—and the spot on which the legendary she wolf is said to have suckled the twins Romulus and Remus.

One of Rome's earliest residential districts, the hill later became a favored location for the city's grandest imperial palaces (the word "palace" shares the same root as the Latin *palatium*). Its ruins, views, lovely gardens, shady orange groves, and peaceful corners make this a wonderful area in which to take a break from sightseeing (*tel 06 0608, Via di San Gregorio 30 or from within the Foro Romano, $$$ includes entry to Foro Romano & Colosseo).*

---

ramp, designed by Michelangelo, heads straight up the hill.

Inhabited since the Bronze Age, the Capitolino's southern summit once contained the city's most venerated temple, a shrine to Jupiter, while its northern promontory housed the Arx, Rome's earliest defensive citadel. Today, its main focus is **Piazza del Campidoglio,** completed to an original design by Michelangelo in the 17th century. Palaces on either side contain the linked **Musei Capitolini** (Capitoline Museums), home to some remarkable pieces of Roman and Greek statuary. The most impressive of all is the second-century A.D. equestrian statue of Emperor Marcus Aurelius, installed in the portico of the Palazzo del Museo Capitolino on your right (the one in the square is a copy).

Capitolino
- Map p. 126

Musei Capitolini
- Map p. 126
- Piazza del Campidoglio 1
- Reservations 06 0608 or online at omniticket.it
- Closed Mon. & some holidays
- $$$

museicapitolini.org

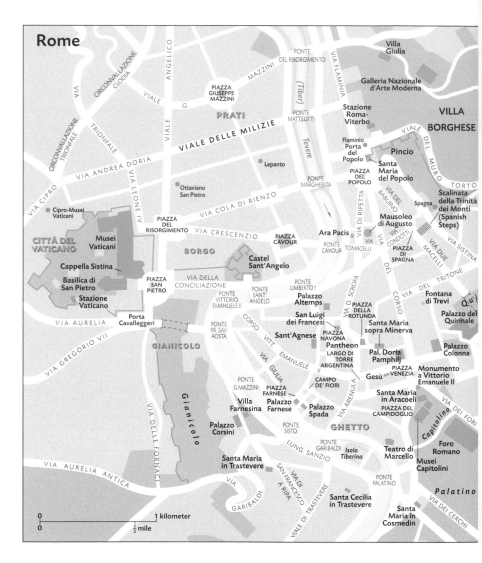

Rome

PONTE DEL RISORGIMENTO

Villa Giulia

Galleria Nazionale d'Arte Moderna

VILLA BORGHESE

VIA ANGELICO

VIA MAZZINI

VIA FLAMINIA

PIAZZA GIUSEPPE MAZZINI

PRATI

(Tiber)

PONTE MATTEOTTI

Stazione Roma-Viterbo

VIALE G.

VIALE

CIRCONVALLAZIONE CLODIA

VIALE DELLE MILIZIE

Tevere

Flaminio Porta del Popolo

Pincio

VIALE DEL MURO

TORTO

VIA TRIONFALE

CIRCONVALLAZIONE TRIONFALE

VIA ANDREA DORIA

Lepanto

PONTE MARGHERITA

Santa Maria del Popolo

PIAZZA DEL POPOLO

Scalinata della Trinità dei Monti (Spanish Steps)

Spagna

VIA DEL BABUINO

VIA CIPRO

VIA LEONE IV

Ottaviano San Pietro

VIA COLA DI RIENZO

Mausoleo di Augusto

VIA DI RIPETTA

VIA CONDOTTI

PIAZZA DI SPAGNA

VIA SISTINA

VIA DUE MACELLI

Cipro-Musei Vaticani

PIAZZA DEL RISORGIMENTO

VIA CRESCENZIO

PIAZZA CAVOUR

Ara Pacis

PONTE CAVOUR

VIA TOMACELLI

VIA DEL CORSO

VIA DEL TRITONE

CITTÀ DEL VATICANO

Musei Vaticani

BORGO

Castel Sant'Angelo

VIA DELLA CONCILIAZIONE

PONTE UMBERTO I

VIA D. SCROFA

Fontana di Trevi

Qui

Cappella Sistina

PIAZZA SAN PIETRO

PONTE VITTORIO EMANUELE II

PONTE SANT' ANGELO

Palazzo Altemps

PIAZZA DELLA ROTUNDA

Palazzo del Quirinale

Basilica di San Pietro

San Luigi dei Francesi

Santa Maria sopra Minerva

Stazione Vaticano

Porta Cavalleggeri

PONTE PR. SAV. AOSTA

CORSO VITT. EMANUELE

Sant'Agnese

PIAZZA NAVONA

Pantheon

Palazzo Colonna

VIA AURELIA

GIANICOLO

VIA GIULIA

LARGO DI TORRE ARGENTINA

Pal. Doria Pamphilj

PIAZZA VENEZIA

Monumento a Vittorio Emanuele II

VIA GREGORIO VII

CAMPO DE' FIORI

Gesù

VIA DEI FORI

Gianicolo

PONTE G.MAZZINI

PIAZZA FARNESE

Villa Farnesina

Palazzo Farnese

Palazzo Spada

VIA ARENULA

Santa Maria in Aracoeli

PIAZZA DEL CAMPIDOGLIO

Capitolino

Palazzo Corsini

PONTE SISTO

GHETTO

Foro Romano

VIA DELLE FORNACI

PONTE GARIBALDI

Isola Tiberina

Teatro di Marcello

Musei Capitolini

VIA AURELIA ANTICA

Santa Maria in Trastevere

LUNG. SANZIO

VIA SAN FRANCESCO A RIPA

VIA DI TRASTEVERE

PONTE PALATINO

Palatino

VIA DEI CERCHI

VIA GARIBALDI

Santa Cecilia in Trastevere

Santa Maria in Cosmedin

0 _____ 1 kilometer
0 _____ ½ mile

In the piazza's northeast corner, a flight of stairs lead up to a side entrance of the church of **Santa Maria in Aracoeli.** Inside, the church has a musty, magical charm and works of art that include Pinturicchio's frescoes on the "Life of San Bernardino" (1486), in the first chapel in the south aisle. If you exit the church's west facade, a long, steep set of stairs links the church with Piazza Venezia.

Returning to Piazza del Campidoglio, walk down the lane to the rear left of the piazza for some memorable views over the Foro Romano and then bear left and down to the wide road below, Via dei Fori Imperiali.

scythed through the area by Mussolini in 1932.

The **Colonna Traiana** dominates Trajan's forum, the first forum on the left if you walk down this road from Piazza Venezia. The top of the 97-foot (30 m) pillar was once the same height as the surrounding land, emphasizing the scale of the quarrying required to excavate the forum. The monument was raised in A.D. 113 to commemorate Trajan's victories over the Dacians, a tribe from present-day Romania. An intricate spiral frieze 656 feet (200 m) in length winds around the column's 18 marble drums. Woven into its majestic marble narrative are 2,500 figures and scenes from Trajan's campaigns.

Foro Romano: Walking south from the Fori Imperiali along Via dei Fori Imperiali, turn right onto Largo della Salara Vecchia to enter the Foro Romano—for almost a thousand years, the heart of ancient Rome. Today, all that remains is a jumble of romantic ruins, although its wistful beauty and myriad historical echoes still make it Europe's most important archaeological site. Altered and rebuilt over many centuries, its monuments—one superimposed on another—are often confusing but still hint at past glories.

The forum began life as a marshy valley between the Palatino and Capitolino hills. During the Iron Age it served as the cemetery on the fringes of a

Foro Romano

Map p. 126

Entrance at Largo della Salara Vecchia (junction of Via dei Fori Imperiali & Via Cavour)

06 0608; non-compulsory reservations: 06 3996 7700 or online at coopculture.it

$$$ (includes entry to Colosseo & Palatino)

Fori Imperiali: The Fori Imperiali (Imperial Forums), all off Via dei Fori Imperiali, are five areas created by Julius Caesar and his successors after the original Foro Romano (see below) became too full for further building. Many of their monuments now lie entombed beneath the Via dei Fori Imperiali, a road

village, a location that perhaps gave rise to the name (in Latin, *forum* means "open space"). Later, it became a communal marketplace. Its first distinct monuments probably appeared in the seventh century B.C.

As the empire flourished, so the forum began to accumulate all the structures of civic, religious, and political life. Patrician houses, shops, temples, and markets jostled for space, and politicians and emperors competed to fill the area with magnificent monuments.

INSIDER TIP:

While waiting in line, you can use Mobile Ticketing on your smartphone to purchase a combination ticket good for the Foro Romano, Colosseo, and Palatino.

—FEDERICA ROMAGNOLI
National Geographic contributor

By the second century A.D., most available room had been taken up, and new building shifted to the Fori Imperiali.

After Rome's fall, time began to take its toll. Fire had ravaged the site in the third century, followed by earthquakes and the assaults of barbarian invaders in the fifth century. During the Middle Ages, stone was pillaged for churches and palaces and precious marbles reduced to dust in the lime kilns of builders.

Silt and debris from numerous floods buried the monuments. Coherent excavations only began toward the end of the 18th century and continue to this day.

From the main entrance on Via dei Fori Imperiali, bear right on the Via Sacra, the ancient forum's most important street, and follow a roughly counterclockwise route. The first temple on your left on the Via Sacra, the **Tempio di Antonino e Faustina** (A.D. 141), is one of the forum's best preserved, largely because it was converted in the 11th century into the church of San Lorenzo in Miranda. The emperor Antoninus Pius raised the original temple in honor of his wife, Faustina. Beyond, on the right, lies the **Basilica Aemilia** (179 B.C.), once a business and banking complex.

At the end of the Via Sacra stand the austere, brick-built **Curia** and the **Arco di Settimio Severo.** The Curia was home to the Roman senate and its 300 senators (it became a church in the seventh century). The *arco* (A.D. 203), or arch, was raised to celebrate the military triumphs of the emperor Septimius Severus, its four principal reliefs decorated with battle scenes, the goddess of victory, and panels lauding Septimius' sons, Geta and Caracalla.

Below the arch stretches a brick wall, all that remains of the **Imperial Rostra,** orators' platforms that took their name from the bronze ships' rostra, or prows, used to ram other

Dusk falls on the scattered ruins of the Foro Romano, the heart of ancient Rome.

boats in battle. Such prows were taken as spoils of war and once adorned the platforms. It was here that Mark Antony reputedly delivered his "Friends, Romans, and countrymen" speech after the murder of Julius Caesar. Behind the arch to the left stand the eight red-gray columns of the **Tempio di Saturno** (479 B.C.), the oldest and most venerated of the forum's early temples. It was dedicated to Saturn, god of agriculture.

With your back to the temple, the area in front of you to the right is the **Basilica Giulia** (54 B.C.), once a central courthouse. Beyond it are the three lonely columns of the **Tempio di Castore e Polluce.** Farther beyond lie two of the forum's most evocative sights, the **Tempio di Vesta** and **Atrium Vestae,** respectively the Temple of Vesta, goddess of the hearth,

and the House of the Vestal Virgins (see sidebar p. 132). The former held Rome's eternal sacred flame, a symbol of the city's well-being.

On the left beyond the Atrium rises the **Basilica di Massenzio** (A.D. 306), whose vast vaults are one of the forum's most physically impressive sights. The **Arco di Tito** near the site's eastern limit is an arch built in A.D. 81 to commemorate the capture of Jerusalem by the emperor Titus. Its reliefs show Titus's triumphal return to Rome and the removal of treasures from the holy city.

Colosseo: The Colosseo (Colosseum), at the southern end of Via dei Fori Imperiali, is the Roman world's largest surviving structure, its majestic impact undimmed by the passage of time. Once its walls echoed to

Colosseo

- Map p. 127
- Piazza del Colosseo
- 06 0608; reservations: 06 3996 7700 or online at coopculture.it
- $$$ (includes entry to Palatino & Foro Romano)

the sounds of gladiatorial combat and the roar of the Roman mob, and later to the chink of hammers as its stones were pillaged to build Rome's medieval churches and palaces.

The structure was the brainchild of the emperor Vespasian in A.D. 70, who wanted a monument to celebrate his military triumphs in the Middle East. Vespasian's son, Titus, continued the project and the

The Colosseo's exterior was originally covered in travertine.

inauguration took place in A.D. 80. Its present name may derive simply from its size, or, more probably, from the presence of the nearby Colossus of Nero (now lost), once the world's largest bronze statue.

More than a million cubic feet (100,000 cubic meters)

of travertine marble gilded its surfaces, a decorative veneer held in place by 300 tons of iron brackets (these brackets were wrenched out in A.D. 664, hence the puzzling holes that pockmark the building's exterior).

The completed amphitheater was a model of simplicity and function, providing a template not only for other Roman amphitheaters but also for numerous stadiums of the modern age. Some 50,000 spectators could enter and leave by any one of the 80 numbered *vomitoria*, or exits, while 240 wooden masts on the upper story supported a broad *velarium,* or sailcloth awning, swung into place to protect crowds from the sun. Sand covered the amphitheater's floor, its purpose to prevent combatants slipping and to soak up the blood of gladiatorial combat (the Latin *arena* [sand] would be used from this time on to describe places of spectacle). All manner of under-stage tunnels, pulleys, and lifts enabled animals and contestants to be brought to the arena, while conduits and aqueducts were used to flood the arena to allow the staging of mock sea battles.

A fire in A.D. 240 destroyed much of the stage and upper seating. Further conflagrations and earthquakes compounded the damage over the next two centuries. After Rome's fall, a small church was built nearby and the stage area used as a cemetery. Some parts of the monument then became a fortress, others homes or shops. Stone was ruthlessly plundered from the site, finding its way into palaces, churches, and bridges. Two-thirds of the monument vanished over the years—more would have gone had it not been for Pope Benedict XIV, who consecrated the site in 1749 in honor of the Christians supposedly martyred here (evidence suggests few, if any, Christians died here).

Those who did die here were gladiators, who had originally fought in ritual combat to prepare for battle. Individuals initially sponsored the events, but by Domitian's time, the games were so important that they were the gift of emperors alone. Gladiatorial contests survived until A.D. 438, while the last animal extravaganza was recorded in A.D. 523.

Arco di Costantino:

Immediately alongside the Colosseo stands the Arco di Costantino, a triumphal arch built in A.D. 315 to celebrate the emperor Constantine's victory three years earlier over his rival, Maxentius. One of Imperial Rome's last great monuments, it features many decorative reliefs pilfered from earlier classical buildings.

San Clemente: The fascinating church of San Clemente is just a five-minute walk beyond the Colosseo and is well worth the detour. Here, three phases of Rome's long religious history lie layered one above another.

The first is encapsulated by a peerless medieval church (1108–1130), beneath which lies an older church, founded in A.D. 392, perhaps earlier. Below this again are the ruins of a temple dedicated to one of Rome's most important pre-Christian cults.

INSIDER TIP:

In order to avoid waiting in line for tickets to the Colosseo, first visit the much less crowded Foro Romano, where you can purchase a combination ticket for both sites.

—BRIDGET A. ENGLISH
National Geographic Books editor

The most eye-catching highlights of the medieval church are the nave's **choir screen, pulpits,** and parts of the *baldacchino,* or altar canopy. A 12th-century **mosaic** behind the altar depicts "The Triumph of the Cross," below which stands a 14th-century marble tabernacle by Arnolfo di Cambio. Important paintings on the "Life of St. Catherine" (1428), the work of Florentine artist Masolino, swathe a chapel next to the church's side entrance.

Steps lead down to the older church, built in honor of San Clemente, Rome's fourth bishop and pope and destroyed by the

Arco di Costantino

🔺 Map p. 127

San Clemente

🔺 Map p. 127

✉ Corner of Via di San Giovanni in Laterano & Via Labicana

☎ 06 774 0021

🕐 Closed 12:30 p.m.–3 p.m., Sun. a.m., & holidays a.m.

💲 Second & third levels: $$

basilicasan clemente.com

Piazza Navona
Map p. 126

Normans in 1084. The church was discovered in 1857.

More steps go down to the oldest area of the complex (first century A.D.), a series of chambers and tunnels that include the remains of a **Mithraic temple** and the partially excavated remains of a Roman street, warehouse, and patrician palace. The sound of running water comes from an underground stream that runs to the Cloaca Maxima, ancient Rome's principal sewer.

Campo Marzio & Around

In Roman times the Campo Marzio, or Campus Martius (Field of Mars), stretched from the Quirinal Hill to the Tiber River. Now the name is identified primarily with the area tucked into the curve of the Tiber that faces St. Peter's Basilica. This is one of the oldest parts of "modern" Rome, home to the wonderful Piazza Navona, the sculptured-filled Palazzo Altemps, and the bustling Campo de' Fiori.

Piazza Navona: Piazza Navona is Rome's loveliest square, ideal for people-watching, day or night. Broadly elliptical in shape, it has an outline which matches that of the Circus Agonalis—from which the square's name derives—a vast 30,000-seat stadium inaugurated by the emperor Domitian in A.D. 86.

In 1644 Pope Innocent X embarked on a radical program of baroque rebuilding. Chief among the resulting monuments were two outstanding fountains by Gian Lorenzo Bernini, the **Fontana del Moro** (at the square's southern end) and the central **Fontana dei Quattro Fiumi,** or Fountain of the Four Rivers. Statues on the latter symbolize the four Rivers of Paradise—the Danube, Nile, Plate, and Ganges—and Asia, Africa, Europe, and the Americas.

Vestal Virgins

Vestal Virgins tended Rome's sacred flame, a perpetually burning symbol of Rome's eternal character kept in the Tempio di Vesta. All were aged between six and ten at induction and were chosen only from the grandest families. The virgins served 30 years before being awarded a state pension and allowed to marry. Ten years were spent in learning, ten in performing ritual tasks, and ten in teaching.

Incumbents who lost their virginity—a vestal's blood could not be spilled—were buried alive, and the offending male flogged to death. Those allowing the flame to die were whipped by the Pontifex Maximus, Rome's high priest, and forced to rekindle the fire using sacred pieces of wood.

In return for their services the virgins enjoyed high social esteem and had special rights, among them the power of mercy over condemned criminals, the right of way on all streets, and permission to drive in carriages within the city limits (a right usually granted only to empresses). Any injury inflicted on a virgin was punishable by death.

Palazzo Altemps: A few minutes' walk north of Piazza Navona is the Palazzo Altemps, the seat of the Museo Nazionale Romano. It holds some of the greatest of all Roman sculpture, while the sublime Renaissance palace itself is worthy of a visit in its own right. On the **ground floor,** around the courtyard and flanking salons, the highlights are the Room of the Hermes, closely followed by the "Ludovisi Athena," showing the goddess taming a serpent.

On the **upper floor,** the palace's pretty chapel (Sant'Aniceto) and northern loggia are outstanding. In the adjoining rooms, you'll find the first-century B.C. "Ludovisi Orestes and Electra" by Menelaus, along with the "Ludovisi Ares," a seated figure. Also here is the "Ludovisi Throne," one of the city's most celebrated sculptures; though some claim it is a fake, it is generally considered a fifth-century B.C. Greek work brought to Rome.

now the French Embassy; Michelangelo contributed to the facade. Be sure to explore **Via Giulia,** one of Rome's most elegant streets, to the rear of the palace.

The Pantheon & Around

The area around the Pantheon is an unusual mélange of ancient, medieval, and Renaissance history, notable for the Pantheon itself, a pagan

Palazzo Altemps

A slice of Roman life on the edge of the Foro Romano

Campo de' Fiori: Campo de' Fiori ("field of flowers"), several minute's walk south of Piazza Navona, has a wonderful street market (every morning except Sunday) and in the evening is the focus for often boisterous nightlife. **Piazza Farnese,** a bright, open square to the south, provides a counterpoint to the Campo's more cramped charms. Here all is decorum and refinement, thanks mainly to the **Palazzo Farnese** (1515),

temple turned national monument; the church of Santa Maria sopra Minerva; and the magnificent Palazzo Doria Pamphilj.

Pantheon: The pristine grandeur of the Pantheon, on Piazza della Rotonda, provides Rome's most powerful illustration of how ancient Rome might have looked. Emperor Hadrian completed the Pantheon in A.D. 128—probably to his own

Palazzo Altemps

- Map p. 126
- ✉ Via di Sant'Apollinare 8
- ☎ 06 687 2719 (ticket office); reservations: 06 3996 7700 or online at coopculture.it
- 🕐 Closed Mon.
- 💲 $$; $$$ during exhibitions

Campo de' Fiori

- 🅰 Map p. 126

Pantheon

- 🅰 Map p. 126
- ✉ Piazza della Rotonda
- ☎ 06 6830 0230
- 🕐 Closed p.m. on public holidays & all Jan. 1, May 1, & Dec. 25

pantheonroma.com

The Pantheon's large oculus lets in rain as well as light. There are drainage holes in the floor.

Santa Maria sopra Minerva

- Map p. 126
- Piazza della Minerva 42
- 06 679 3926
- Closed during services

design—replacing much of an earlier temple on the site raised in 27 B.C. by Marcus Agrippa, son-in-law of the emperor Augustus. Hadrian retained the pediment's inscription, which attributed the building to Agrippa: The Latin text reads, "Marcus Agrippa, son of Lucius, consul for the third time, built this." The building's miraculous state of preservation stems from its conversion to a Christian church in 609.

Today the Pantheon is still a church, and its look remains virtually unchanged from the second century. Not all the interior marbles are original, but their patterning and arrangement are believed to conform to Hadrian's original scheme. Around the walls lie the **tombs** of Raphael and two Italian kings, Umberto I and Vittorio Emanuele II.

The **dome** is one of the masterpieces of Roman engineering. Bigger than St. Peter's, it was the largest concrete construction undertaken until the 20th

century and the world's largest freestanding dome until as recently as 1960. The dome's oculus, the circular hole that opens to the sky, was a key feature of Hadrian's original plan, its purpose being both practical—it helped illuminate the interior—and spiritual, allowing those in the temple direct contemplation of the heavens.

Santa Maria sopra Minerva: This church directly behind the Pantheon has a plain Gothic facade that is unique in Rome, a city where most churches were reworked along baroque lines during the 16th and 17th centuries. Note Bernini's **elephant statue** (1667) in front of the church, an idiosyncratic work in which the elephant is supposed to represent piety and wisdom, Christianity's founding virtues; the Egyptian obelisk on the elephant's back dates from the sixth century B.C. The present church (1280) was built over (*sopra*) an earlier Roman temple to Minerva—hence its name.

Pride of place among the interior's many paintings goes to a series of frescoes (1488–1492) by the Florentine artist Filippino Lippi (first chapel of the south transept), and the church's sculptural masterpiece is Michelangelo's "Redeemer" (1519–1521), criticized on its unveiling for appearing like a pagan god.

INSIDER TIP:

Every May the azaleas bordering the Spanish Steps bloom in a blaze of pink glory, creating an absolutely unforgettable sight.

—FEDERICA ROMAGNOLI
National Geographic contributor

Palazzo Doria Pamphilj:
This thousand-room palace four blocks east of Santa Maria sopra Minerva still belongs to the Pamphilj, one of Rome's preeminent medieval families. Part of the palace is given over to the family's art collection, one of the finest in the city. The paintings are ranged around part of the palace, their beautifully appointed setting almost as splendid as the works of art themselves. Guided tours around other areas of the palace are sometimes available.

The pictorial highlights are many. Make a point of seeking out Velázquez's celebrated portrait of "Innocent X" (1650), a member of the Pamphilj dynasty, a picture that captures all too

clearly the man's suspicious and feebleminded nature. Pope Innocent himself is said to have complained that the portrait was "too true, too true." Also here are works by Titian, Tintoretto, Filippo Lippi, and Caravaggio, as well as Raphael's magnificent "Portrait of Two Venetians."

Fontana di Trevi & the Spanish Steps

East of Piazza Navona, Rome's central Tridente neighborhood includes the instantly recognizable Fontana di Trevi (Trevi Fountain), tucked away on Piazza di Trevi; Piazza di Spagna, home to the famous Spanish Steps; and the more peripheral art-filled church of Santa Maria del Popolo and the Villa Borghese, a large park. It is also a prime shopping district.

Fontana di Trevi: The first fountain on this site was built in 1453 for Pope Nicholas V, taking its waters from the Roman-era Acqua Vergine, an aqueduct. The present fountain, modeled on the Arco di Costantino (see p. 131), was built between 1732 and 1762 for Pope Clement XII. Few sights in Rome are as lovely at first glimpse, narrow lanes suddenly opening up to reveal the *fontana* ranged across an entire wall of the Palazzo Poli. The fountain's name derives from these lanes—the *tre vie* (three streets) that meet here.
(continued on p. 138)

Palazzo Doria Pamphilj

 Map p. 126

✉ Via del Corso 305

☎ Reservations: 06 679 7323, or online at ticketeria.it for exhibition tickets

💲 $$$

dopart.it

Fontana di Trevi

 Map p. 126

✉ Piazza di Trevi

A Walk Around Central Rome

Central Rome covers a relatively small area that can easily be explored on foot, even on a brief visit. This walk includes some of the city's key highlights and leaves you well placed to then explore the Foro Romano, Colosseo, and Arco di Costantino.

An equestrian statue of Emperor Marcus Aurelius sits at the center of Piazza del Campidoglio.

Start by enjoying the view at the top of the Scalinata della Trinità dei Monti, better known as the **Spanish Steps ❶** (see p. 138). Walk down the steps to **Piazza di Spagna ❷** and admire its quaint fountain, **Fontana della Barcaccia** (1627).

To the west is Via dei Condotti, Rome's premier shopping street. But bear left out of the south side of the piazza, taking the right fork (with Via Borgonona on your right) onto Via di Propaganda and then along Via di Sant'Andrea delle Fratte before turning right on Via del Nazareno to Via del Tritone. Across the road, bear right on Via della Stamperia to the **Fontana di Trevi ❸** (see pp. 135 & 138).

From the fountain, take Via dei Crociferi and Via dei Sabini to Via del Corso and Piazza Colonna, where you can admire the **Colonna di Marco Aurelio ❹** (A.D. 180–196), a column that contains a frieze celebrating the military triumphs of the Emperor Marcus Aurelius.

NOT TO BE MISSED:

Spanish Steps • Fontana di Trevi • Pantheon • Piazza Navona • Santa Maria sopra Minerva • Il Gesù

Walk a few moments south on Via del Corso and turn right on Via di Pietra to Piazza di Pietra to see the extraordinary sight of the **Temple to the Deified Hadrian ❺** (A.D. 145), now part of a later building.

Take the alley at the left side of the temple as you face it and within seconds you'll be in Piazza Sant'Ignazio, a charming square named after the church on its southern flank, **Sant'Ignazio ❻,** a tour de force of baroque decoration.

From here, follow gloomy Via del Seminario to visit the **Pantheon ❼** (see pp. 133–134). Then take Via Giustiniani, pausing to see the three paintings by Caravaggio (1599–1602) in the church of **San Luigi dei Francesi** 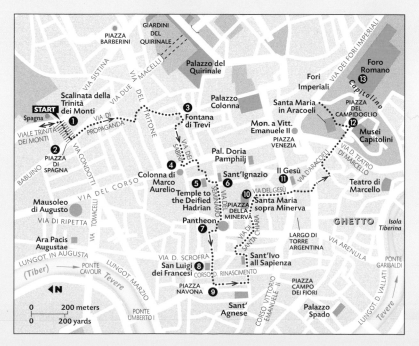. Continue west on Via del Salvatore and explore **Piazza Navona** (see p. 132).

Turn left (east) on tiny Via Canestrari out of the south end of the piazza, following it across Corso del Rinascimento and into Via dei Sediari and round left into **Piazza Sant'Eustachio.** Turn around to admire the eccentric church spire of **Sant'Ivo all Sapienza** (1642–1660).

Take Via di Santa Chiara to Piazza della Minerva to see the church of **Santa Maria sopra Minerva** (see pp. 134–135). Walk down the right of the church and turn right on Via del Gesù to see **Il Gesù** (1568–1580), ahead on the left. The Jesuits' main church in Rome, this is one of the most sumptuously decorated buildings in the city.

Now take the small Via Celsa right from Piazza del Gesù to Via San Marco. Cross this road, walk left a few paces and then take the first right off it onto Via dei Polacchi. This will bring you to a pretty corner on the fringes of Rome's old **Jewish ghetto**.

From here, turn left a few steps to Via d'Aracoeli, turn right and take care crossing the busy road to walk up the ramp to **Piazza del Campidoglio** (see p. 125). Pop into the church of **Santa Maria in Aracoeli** for frescoes (1484–1486) by Pinturicchio in the Cappella Bufalini and then take the lane at the rear left of the piazza for a stupendous view over the **Foro Romano** (see pp. 127–129). Then follow the lane left and down and turn right on the broad Via dei Fori Imperiali for the entrance to the Foro itself.

- Also see area map pp. 126–127
- Spanish Steps
- 2 miles (3.2 km)
- 2.5 hours
- Foro Romano

Piazza di Spagna & the Spanish Steps
 Map p. 126

At the fountain's center stands a statue of the Greek Titan god Oceanus, god of all waters, flanked by horse-riding Tritons that symbolize a stormy sea (left) and the sea in repose (right). The statues in the niches behind Oceanus represent Health and Abundance, and the pediment statues represent the four seasons with their gifts.

Baroque in style, the Fontana di Trevi is the most beautiful of the city's many fountains.

Keats-Shelley Memorial House
✉ Piazza di Spagna 26
☎ 06 678 4235
🕒 Closed 1 p.m.–2 p.m. Mon.–Sat., all Sun., & some of Dec.
💲 $$

keats-shelley-house.org

Piazza di Spagna & the Spanish Steps:
Several blocks north of the Fontana di Trevi, both Piazza di Spagna and its famous flight of steps—Scalinata della Trinità dei Monti—take their name from the Palazzo Spagna, built in 1622 as the residence of the Spanish ambassador to the Holy See.

The English Romantic poet John Keats, who came to Rome in 1821 seeking a cure from tuberculosis, died in a house alongside the steps. Today the building is known as the **Keats-Shelley Memorial House,** a museum given over to Keats, Percy B. Shelley (who also died in Italy), and other 19th-century literary figures.

The square's little **Fontana della Barcaccia,** at the foot of the steps, was designed—possibly by Bernini—to resemble a half-submerged boat. Upscale designer stores abound on surrounding streets.

Santa Maria del Popolo:
Santa Maria fronts Piazza del Popolo, reached taking Via del Babuino north from Piazza di Spagna. Church and square both take their name from the *populus,* or hamlet, that stood here during the Middle Ages. Santa Maria was founded in 1099 over the tomb of Emperor Nero, its purpose to reclaim for Christianity ground sullied by contact with the pagan demagogue.

The interior's most prized sight is the **Cappella Chigi** (1513), commissioned from Raphael by the Sienese banker Agostino Chigi, who instructed the artist that his chapel should "convert earthly things into heavenly." All its decoration is by Raphael, except for a few Bernini medallions on the Chigi tombs and an altarpiece painting. Other treasures include two works by Caravaggio (north transept), a set of **frescoes** (1485–1489) by Pinturicchio behind the high altar, and a pair of tombs (1505–1507) in the choir by Andrea da Sansovino.

Villa Borghese: It is unlikely you'll have time on a short trip to see Rome's main park, nor the Galleria Borghese located at its heart, but both are essential on longer visits. Located just east of Piazza del Popolo, the park, the first of its kind in Rome, was laid out between 1613 and 1616 for the Borghese family to provide them with a shady country retreat during Rome's hot summers.

The **Galleria Borghese** (prebooked timed entry tickets compulsory) at its heart was once the Villa Borghese's *casino* (little house), the name given to the principal building of an Italian country estate. Although smaller than many galleries in Rome, the Borghese's art collection is widely considered the city's most ravishing.

Many of the works were commissioned by Cardinal Scipione Borghese and bought by the state in 1902. Scipione was a great patron of Bernini, one of the baroque's leading lights, whose works dominate the gallery's sculpture sections. The most notorious sculpture, however, is by Antonio Canova: an erotic statue (1805–1808) of Paolina Borghese, sister of Napoleon and wife of Camillo Borghese. Among the many valuable paintings are exquisite works by Raphael, Titian, Botticelli, and Caravaggio.

Il Vaticano

The Basilica di San Pietro is the center of Roman Catholicism and the external face of Vatican City, the world's smallest independent city-state. Despite its tiny size, Il Vaticano (the Vatican) wields immense power and influence and is home to many incomparable works of art, including the Cappella Sistina, most of which are on view in the immense Musei Vaticani.

Basilica di San Pietro:

St. Peter's Basilica can hardly fail to impress: It can accommodate an estimated 60,000 people, serves as a seminal point of pilgrimage, and is crowned by a stupendous Michelangelo-designed dome that offers sweeping views across much of the Eternal City. The church owes its site and spiritual legitimacy to Peter the Apostle, the first pope, who is believed to have been buried here after his crucifixion in either A.D. 64 or 67.

Roman Coffee & Gelato

A debate rages about which café serves Rome's best cup of coffee. Some say the **Tazza d'Oro** (*Via degli Orfani 84, tel 06 678 9792 or 06 679 2768, tazzadorocoffee shop.com*), moments from the Pantheon, just off Piazza della Rotonda. Others say the nearby **Caffè Sant'Eustachio** (*Piazza Sant'Eustachio 82, tel 06 6880 2048, santeustachioilcaffe.it*). More people agree on the city's best ice cream, which comes courtesy of **Il Gelato di San Crispino**, either at its original home (*Via della Panetteria 42, tel 06 679 3924, ilgelatodisancrispino .it*), near the Fontana di Trevi, or the second outlet (*Piazza della Maddalena 3, tel 06 9760 1190, closed Tues. mid Sept.–mid-March*), just north of the Pantheon.

Santa Maria del Popolo

 Map p. 126

✉ Piazza del Popolo 12

☎ 06 361 0836

🕐 Closed 12 p.m.–4 p.m. Mon.–Sat. & 1:30 p.m.–4:30 p.m. Sun.

santamariadel popolo.it

Galleria Borghese

 Map p. 127

✉ Piazzale del Museo Borghese 5

☎ 06 841 3979; reservations: 06 32810 or online at tosc.it

🕐 Closed Mon. & some holidays

💲 $$$; $$$$ during exhibitions

galleriaborghese.it

Basilica di San Pietro

🗺 Map p. 126

✉ Piazza San Pietro

☎ Basilica: 06 6988 3731 or 06 6988 3462; Ufficio Pellegrini e Turisti, Piazza San Pietro: 06 6988 1662

🕐 Closed during religious services

vatican.va

NOTE: A dress code applies—no shorts, short skirts, or bare shoulders. Lines for security screening can be long at peak times.

The first church here for which records survive was begun around 326 by Pope Sylvester I during the reign of Constantine, the first Christian emperor. This church survived until 1452, when its perilous state prompted Pope Nicholas V to commission a new basilica. Almost 200 years elapsed before this church was completed; it was finally consecrated in 1626, exactly 1,300 years after the original basilica, in the majestic setting of Piazza San Pietro (see sidebar this page), designed by Bernini.

Inside the basilica, your first breathtaking impression is of its staggering size, all cascades of marble, somber tombs, and mountains of baroque decor. However, the interior is surprisingly bereft of major works of art. One notable exception is Michelangelo's masterpiece, the statue of the **"Pietà"** (1499), located in the first chapel off the south aisle.

The crossing is dominated by the bulk of the *baldacchino* (1678), or **altar canopy,** a work created by Bernini using bronze melted down from the Pantheon's ancient atrium. Behind it, at the rear of the church, lies the **Cathedra Petri** (1656), also by Bernini, an ornate throne crafted to enclose a wood and ivory chair reputedly used by St. Peter to address his first sermon to the Romans (scholars believe the chair actually dates from the fourth century).

Don't miss the bronze **statue of St. Peter,** attributed to Arnolfo di Cambio and located by the front right of the crossing's four pillars. It is an unmistakable work, thanks to its worn right foot, caressed by millions since Pius IX granted a 50-day indulgence to anyone kissing it following confession.

Finally, consider climbing the **dome** (*$$*) for unforgettable views of Piazza San Pietro and the city beyond. Its entrance lies off the south aisle; access is by stairs or elevator.

Piazza San Pietro

In contrast to the eponymous basilica, there is no doubt about who created Piazza San Pietro (St. Peter's Square). With its elliptical shape and its two semicircular colonnades, Gian Lorenzo Bernini's design, commissioned by Pope Alexander VII Chigi (1655–1667), has been universally acclaimed as an architectural masterpiece.

The square features 284 gigantic Doric columns in the colonnade, 88 other pilasters, and 140 statues. Statues of Jesus, John the Baptist, and 11 Apostles decorate the church facade. Three sets of steps, flanked by statues of St. Peter and St. Paul, lead to the entrance. In the middle of the piazza are two fountains, one by Carlo Maderno and a copy created in 1677 by Bernini, and an Egyptian obelisk, placed there before the creation of the colonnade. Halfway between the obelisk and each fountain is a plain stone disk reading "Centro del Colonnato." Stand on one and see the four rows of columns in the corresponding hemicycle miraculously line into one.

Musei Vaticani: Other galleries may match the broad span and myriad origins of the artifacts in the Musei Vaticani (Vatican Museums), but none also offers entire rooms painted by Raphael and the ceiling frescoes of the Cappella Sistina. Exhibits are scattered around many museums and several hundred rooms; to see them all involves a walk of some 5 miles (8 km).

See the obvious highlights—Museo Pio-Clementino, Stanze di Raffaello, and Cappella Sistina—and then make for museums that reflect your own interests. The Pio-Clementino is at one end of the Vatican palace, while the Stanze di Raffaello and the Cappella Sistina are both at the opposite end. It is easy to get lost: Pick up a museum guide and map to help you get around. Whatever your choice, prebook tickets online (*museivaticani.va*), allow plenty of time, and arrive early—the high-season crowds can be overwhelming. It is a 15-minute walk from Piazza San Pietro to the entrance of the Musei Vaticani on Viale Vaticano (follow the Vatican wall north).

Museo Pio-Clementino:

The Museo Pio-Clementino, whose finest pieces are arranged in the Cortile Ottagono, or **Octagonal Courtyard**, is famed for its classical sculpture. Here you'll find the famous **"Laocoön,"** carved on the island of Rhodes in 50 B.C. but only rediscovered close

Bernini's bronze altar canopy at the heart of San Pietro stands above the supposed tomb of St. Peter the Apostle.

to the Colosseo in 1506. The sculpture exerted much influence on the art of the High Renaissance, as did another of the courtyard's works, the celebrated **"Apollo Belvedere,"** a Roman work of A.D. 130 copied from a Greek original (330 B.C.). In the adjoining room is the first-century B.C. **"Belvedere Torso,"** a work that greatly impressed Michelangelo.

Stanze di Raffaello: In 1503
Pope Julius II commissioned

Musei Vaticani
- 🅰 Map p. 126
- ✉ Viale Vaticano
- ☎ 06 6988 3332, 06 6988 4676, or 06 6988 3145
- 🕐 Closed Sun. (except 9 a.m.– 2 p.m. last Sun. of month) & religious & public holidays
- 💲 $$$$; free last Sun. of month

museivaticani.va

The Hellenistic "Belvedere Torso," in the Musei Vaticani, greatly influenced late Renaissance and baroque artists.

Cappella Sistina: Soon after leaving the Stanze di Raffaello you'll encounter the Cappella Sistina (Sistine Chapel), Western art's most famous masterpiece, which started life as a chapel built for Pope Sixtus IV in 1475. Its earliest decoration dates to 1481, when the lower walls were painted by a group of leading artists who included Botticelli, Perugino, Pinturicchio, and Luca Signorelli. The ceiling remained relatively unadorned until 1508, the year Pope Julius II approached Michelangelo to begin one of the world's most celebrated paintings.

The **ceiling** art took four years. More than 300 figures populate the scenes, which divide into nine basic central sections. Each is read chronologically in the order you walk through the chapel. First come the five seminal events from the Book of Genesis: the "Separation of Light and Darkness," the "Creation of the Heavenly Bodies," the "Separation of Land and Sea," the "Creation of Adam," and the "Creation of Eve." These are followed by the "Fall and Expulsion from Paradise," the "Sacrifice of Noah," the "Flood," and the "Drunkenness of Noah."

Rome was a different city and Michelangelo a different man when he painted the chapel's other masterpiece, the vast fresco of the **"Last Judgment"** (1534–1541), which covers the rear wall. As a result, the painter's vision of the Day of Judgment is dark and uncompromising, its content a departure

Raphael, then just 26, to decorate a suite of four modestly sized rooms. The result was the Stanze di Raffaello (Raphael Rooms), a quartet forming one of the supreme masterpieces of Western European art.

Raphael first painted the **Stanza della Segnatura** (1508–1511), Julius's library and the room where papal bulls, or documents, received his signature (*segnatura*). The principal paintings here explore the themes of Theology, Poetry, Philosophy, and Justice. Raphael then moved to the **Stanza d'Eliodoro** (1512–1514), a private antechamber, where the theme of Divine Providence intervening to defend Faith is depicted. Raphael's manner of painting markedly changed in the next room, the **Stanza dell' Incendio del Borgo.** Raphael's death in 1520 cut short his work in the final room: Only one painting in the **Sala di Costantino** (1517–1524) is based on his drawings.

from earlier interpretations. The doomed are shown sinking to their fate on the painting's right, faces and bodies contorted with terror, while the saved—merely relieved rather than overjoyed at their salvation—rise powerfully on the painting's left.

Other Vatican Attractions: Other areas worth seeing in the Musei Vaticani, if you have the time, include the **Pinacoteca,** or art gallery, whose 20 or more rooms contain the cream of the Vatican's collection of medieval and Renaissance paintings, and the **Galleria delle Carte Geografiche,** whose walls are decorated with a 40-panel sequence of pictorial maps (1580). The **Cappella di Niccolò V,** close to the Raphael Rooms, contains frescoes by Fra Angelico on the "Life of St. Stephen and St. Lawrence" (1447-1451), while the nearby **Appartamento Borgia** features equally celebrated frescoes by Pinturicchio. The **Museo Gregoriano Etrusco** boasts the world's finest collection of Etruscan art after Rome's Villa Giulia, and the **Museo Gregoriano Egizio** is a treasure chest of Egyptian artifacts. ∎

NEED TO KNOW

Port Logistics: Civitavecchia

If you are visiting Rome from a cruise ship, you will dock at the **Port of Civitavecchia** (*civitavecchiaport.org*), 45 miles (72 km) north of Rome. Shuttle buses take ship passengers to and from the port gate on Largo Plebiscito every 15 minutes. The Cruises Services Center at the gate offers information. Taxis are not recommended for trips to Rome or for the short ride to the town's railroad station. Trains are cheaper and more reliable, in terms of ensuring you are back in port for your ship's departure. To reach the railway station (*Viale della Repubblica 2*), walk from the port gate up Viale Giuseppe Garibaldi, with the sea on your right, and turn left uphill at Hotel de La Ville (*10-min. walk; some cruise lines offer shuttles*).

Civitavecchia to Rome

Some trains from the Civitavecchia station run to **Roma San Pietro** (for easy access to the Basilica di San Pietro), and all go to Rome's main **Stazione Termini.** Trains run three times an hour. Journey time on Frecciabianca or InterCity trains is 41 minutes; Regionale trains take 1–1.5 hours. Book tickets online (*trenitalia.com*) or buy Regionale tickets at the station or port Cruises Services Center. The BIRG Day Pass includes travel on Regionale trains and unlimited travel on Rome's buses, trams, and metro. **Can't Be Missed Tours** (*cantbemissedtours.com*) offers guided tours to Rome using the train.

Rome Highlights

You can spend your entire port of call time at any one of these destinations, but here are some suggested times to help with your planning. Note, these do not allow for travel time to and from and/or waiting in line:

- Campidoglio, Foro Romano, & exterior of Colosseo: 1.5 hours
- San Clemente: 30 minutes
- Spanish Steps, Fontana di Trevi, & Pantheon: 1 hour
- Piazza Navona, Campo de' Fiori, & stroll: 1 hour
- Basilica di San Pietro: 1 hour

Bay of Naples

The area around the Bay of Naples (Golfo di Napoli) has much to offer. Naples (Napoli), southern Italy's largest city, sprawls along the Tyrrhenian coast, full of cultural and other attractions. Nearby, and easily accessible as excursions, are Pompeii and Herculaneum, which both preserve a slice of Roman life, buried under tons of ash in A.D. 79 during an eruption of the still active Mount Vesuvius.

Naples

Poets and painters have celebrated Naples since classical times as one of the most beautiful and blessed places on Earth. Latterly, crime, poverty, pollution, and traffic chaos have taken their toll, but progress has been made on several fronts, and today the city is becoming more amenable.

This edge and character, of course, are among the city's most distinctive features. Naples is so Italian as to be almost clichéd—a city of pizza, opera, busy markets, soccer, religion, Sophia Loren (born nearby), family, organized crime, petty crime, and the sort of washing-hung streets used as visual shorthand for Italy in countless movies.

The vibrancy of Naples's streets and citizens is matched by a huge artistic and archaeological patrimony, the result of the city's long history (Naples is at least 3,000 years old) and a succession of rulers and settlers that included the Greeks, Romans, Normans, French, Aragonese, Spanish, and Bourbons.

A good plan of attack is to take a cab to the Museo Archeologico Nazionale, one of Europe's preeminent archaeological museums and the city's single must-see sight. Then walk south through the most atmospheric part of the old city, the Spaccanapoli (meaning

Naples's Duomo, built in the shape of a Latin cross, has a lavish baroque interior.

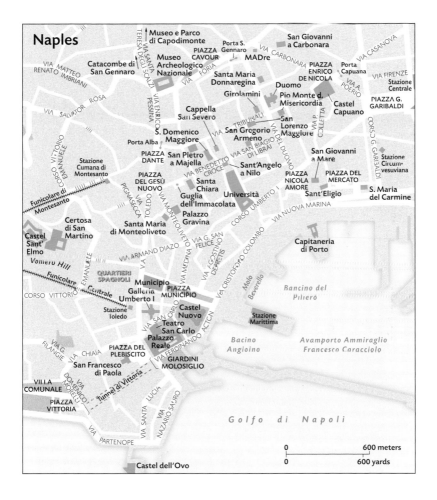

Naples

- Museo e Parco di Capodimonte
- PIAZZA S. Gennaro
- Porta S. Gennaro
- Catacombe di San Gennaro
- Museo Archeologico Nazionale
- MADre
- San Giovanni a Carbonara
- PIAZZA ENRICO DE NICOLA
- Porta Capuana
- Stazione Centrale
- Santa Maria Donnaregina
- Duomo
- Girolamini
- Pio Monte d. Misericordia
- Castel Capuano
- PIAZZA G. GARIBALDI
- Cappella San Severo
- San Lorenzo Maggiore
- S. Domenico Maggiore
- San Gregorio Armeno
- San Giovanni a Mare
- Porta Alba
- PIAZZA DANTE
- San Pietro a Majella
- Sant'Angelo a Nilo
- PIAZZA NICOLA AMORE
- PIAZZA DEL MERCATO
- Stazione Cumana di Montesanto
- PIAZZA DEL GESÙ NUOVO
- Santa Chiara
- Università
- Sant'Eligio
- S. Maria del Carmine
- Funicolare di Montesanto
- Guglia dell'Immacolata
- Palazzo Gravina
- Certosa di San Martino
- Santa Maria di Monteoliveto
- Castel Sant' Elmo
- Vomero Hill
- Capitaneria di Porto
- Funicolare
- QUARTIERI SPAGNOLI
- Municipio
- Galleria Umberto I
- PIAZZA MUNICIPIO
- Bancino del Piliero
- Stazione Centrale
- Stazione Toledo
- Castel Nuovo
- Teatro San Carlo
- Palazzo Reale
- Stazione Marittima
- San Francesco di Paola
- PIAZZA DEL PLEBISCITO
- GIARDINI MOLOSIGLIO
- Bacino Angioino
- Avamporto Ammiraglio Francesco Caracciolo
- VILLA COMUNALE
- PIAZZA VITTORIA
- Tunnel di Vittoria
- Golfo di Napoli
- Castel dell'Ovo

0 — 600 meters
0 — 600 yards

"split Naples"), the area around Via Tribunali and Via Benedetto Croce. Then continue south to arrive at the sights close to the port and waterfront.

Museo Archeologico Nazionale:
This archaeology museum and its collection of Greek and Roman antiquities, many of them recovered from Pompeii and Herculaneum, is superb. The ground floor is devoted primarily to sculpture, with most of the highlights in the first 15 of the floor's 40 or more rooms. Of particular note are statues of Athena, Harmodius and Aristogeiton, Aphrodite, and the much praised Doryphorus, or javelin thrower. More striking still are the "Farnese Hercules," the museum's finest statue, and the "Farnese Bull," the largest surviving sculpture from the ancient world. Much of the mezzanine

NEED TO KNOW p. 151

Naples
🅰 123 C2
Visitor Information
✉ Piazza del Gesù Nuovo 78, Naples
☎ 081 551 2701
🕐 Closed Sun. p.m.

inaples.it
www.campaniarte card.it

Museo Archeologico Nazionale

- 🗺 Map p. 145
- ✉ Piazza Museo Nazionale 19, Naples
- ☎ 081 442 2149
- 🕐 Closed Tues. & some holidays
- 💲 $$$

cir.campania.beni
culturali.it

Duomo

- 🗺 Map p. 145
- ✉ Via del Duomo 147, Naples
- ☎ 081 449 097 or 081 449 065
- 🕐 Closed 12:30 p.m.–4:30 p.m. Mon.–Sat. & 1:30 p.m.–5 p.m. Sun.
- 💲 Archaeological zone & baptistery: $$

is devoted to fabulous mosaics from Pompeii.

Further treasures grace the first floor, among them the west wing's collection of vases and the **Sale della Villa dei Papiri,** given over to papyrus, statues, and other exhibits removed from the Villa dei Papiri at Herculaneum. Equally absorbing are the Sala degli Affreschi, with wall paintings removed from Pompeii, Herculaneum, and elsewhere.

The Duomo & Other Churches: Wend east through the streets below the museum to the **Duomo,** best known for the relics of San Gennaro, a fourth-century martyr and the city's patron and protector. The saint's chapel (closed Sun. p.m.–Mon.) contains a vial of blood that is paraded three times yearly— failure of the blood to liquefy during the ceremony bodes ill for the city.

The church of **Santa Maria Donnaregina Vecchia** (Via Luigi Settembrini 80–Vico Donnaregina 26, Naples, tel 081 1931 3016 or 081 562 4561, closed Tues.), just to the north, has Tino di Camaino's "Tomb of Mary of Hungary" (1326) and early 14th-century frescoes by Roman painter Pietro Cavallini.

West of the Duomo stands Gothic **San Lorenzo Maggiore** (Via dei Tribunali 316, Naples, tel 081 454 948 or 081 290 580, www.sanlorenzomaggiorenapoli.it, closed Sun. p.m.), distinguished by Tino di Camaino's "Tomb of

> ## What Lies Beneath
>
> One of southern Italy's most memorable experiences involves exploring the ancient tunnels, cellars, and sewers that riddle subterranean Naples. Some tunnels date back to Greek times but have been extended throughout history for storage, drainage, and similar purposes. **Napoli Sotterranea** (*Piazza San Gaetano 68, Naples, tel 081 296 944, $$$*) runs English-language tours.

Catherine of Austria" (1323) to the right of the high altar. To the south rises **San Gregorio Armeno** (Via San Gregorio Armeno 1, Naples, tel 081 552 0186, closed p.m.), one of the most opulent of Naples's many baroque churches.

Farther west is **San Domenico Maggiore** (Piazza San Domenico Maggiore 8a, Naples, tel 081 459 298 or 081 459 188), worth visiting for its funerary sculpture. Across the square, **Sant'Angelo a Nilo** (Piazzetta Nilo 23, Naples, tel 081 211 0860 or 081 290 034, closed 1 p.m.–4:30 p.m. & Sun. p.m.) contains Michelozzo's "Tomb of Cardinal Bracciano" (1428). Just off the piazza stands the **Cappella San Severo** (Via Francesco de Sanctis 19–21, Naples, tel 081 551 8470, museosansevero.it, closed Tues. & p.m. Sun., $$), also celebrated for its sculpture, in particular Giuseppe Sammartino's virtuoso "Dead Christ" (1753) above the altar. **Santa Chiara** (*Via Santa Chiara 49, Naples, tel 081 797 1231 or 081 797 1224, closed 1 p.m.–4:30 p.m., $$*) has three 14th-century royal tombs by Tino di Camaino and other Florentine sculptors, as well as a pretty cloister.

South & North of Naples's Center:
Explore south by taking Calata Trinità Maggiore from near Santa Chiara, being sure to see the church of **Santa Maria di Monteoliveto** (*Piazza Monteoliveto 44, Naples, tel 081 551 333, closed 12:30 p.m.–4:30 p.m. & Sun. p.m.*). Begun in 1411, it houses more exemplary Florentine tombs and sculptures. Then visit the teeming Quartieri Spagnoli west of Via Toledo, full of archetypal Neapolitan street scenes, or continue

to the waterfront and Piazza del Plebiscito. The latter is dominated by **San Francesco di Paola** (*tel 081 764, closed Sun. p.m.*), a neoclassical church modeled on Rome's Pantheon, and by the **Palazzo Reale** (*Piazza del Plebiscito 1, Naples, tel 081 580 8111 or 081 400 547, closed Wed. & some holidays, $$*), a 17th-century Spanish palace with lavish royal apartments.

Via San Carlo leads to the **Castel Nuovo,** built in 1282. Its stolid ramparts, offset by the delicacy of a lovely entrance arch (1454–1467), conceal several grand salons and a modest civic museum.

North of the center are the **Museo e Parco di Capodimonte,** Naples's key attractions after the archaeological museum, but you will need to take a cab here. Begun by the Bourbons as a hunting lodge

Castel Nuovo

- Map p. 145
- Piazza Municipio, Naples
- 081 420 1241
- Closed Sun.
- $$

Museo e Parco di Capodimonte
- Map p. 145
- Via Miano 2, Naples
- 081 749 9111
- Closed Wed.
- Museum: $$$

A sea of lights at night, Naples sits under the profile of Mount Vesuvius, a still active volcano.

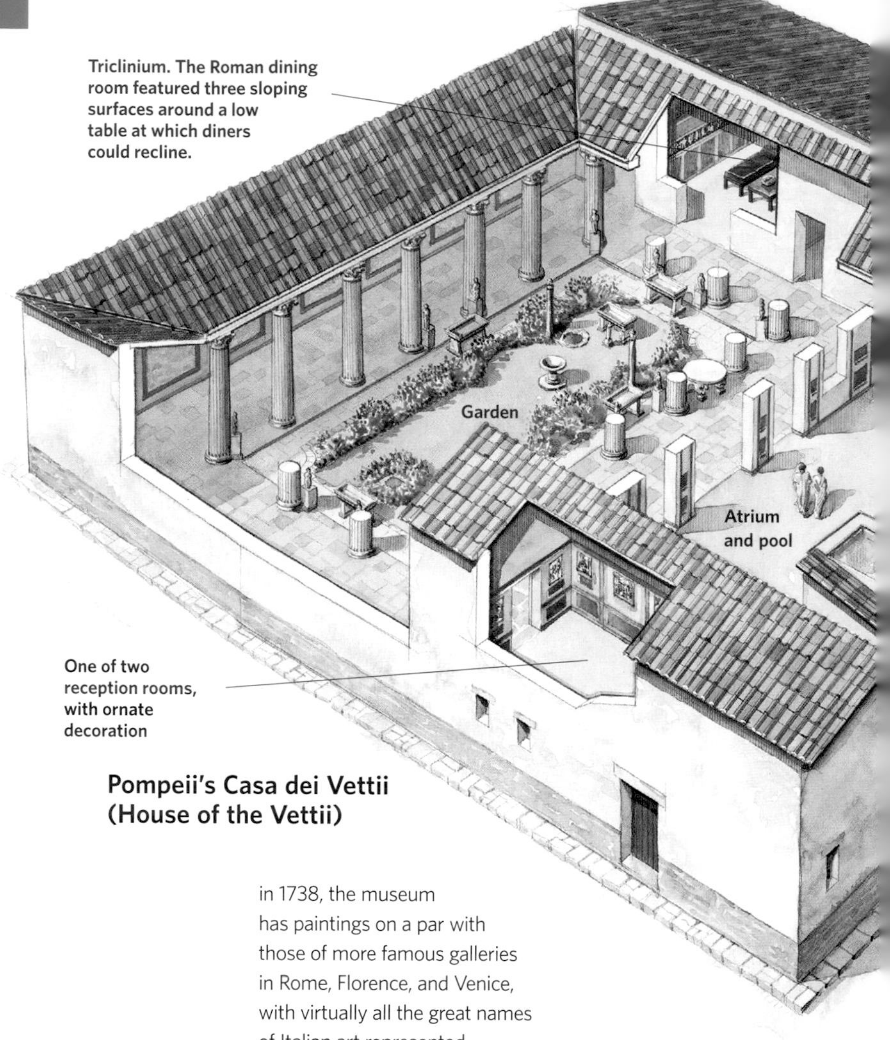

Triclinium. The Roman dining room featured three sloping surfaces around a low table at which diners could recline.

Garden

Atrium and pool

One of two reception rooms, with ornate decoration

Pompeii's Casa dei Vettii (House of the Vettii)

in 1738, the museum has paintings on a par with those of more famous galleries in Rome, Florence, and Venice, with virtually all the great names of Italian art represented.

Herculaneum

In A.D. 79, Herculaneum (Ercolano)—an exclusive residential district, built to exploit the site's cooling breezes and far-reaching views—was engulfed by the same volcanic eruption that devastated nearby Pompeii (see p. 149). Like Pompeii, Herculaneum remained entombed until the 18th century, and remains only half-excavated today. Where

it differs from Pompeii is in its more modest and manageable size. You should allow about two hours for the site. Located roughly 10 miles (16 km) south of Naples, it is about a 15-minute ride from Naples on the Circumvesuviana train line (see sidebar p. 151).

Beyond the entrance an avenue passes through the ruins of the **Palestra,** or gymnasium. Nearby are the **Casa dell'Atrio,**

Shrine

Entrance. Visitors were greeted by a fresco of Priapus, god of fertility, signifying the wealth and good fortune of the occupants.

which still boasts its mosaic pavements, and just beyond it, on the left, the **Casa a Graticcio** (House of the Wooden Trellis) and **Casa del Tramezzo Carbonizzato** (House of the Burned Partition). Beyond the latter, at the town's major intersection, stands a former dyer's shop (No. 10), known for its superbly preserved wooden clothespress.

Across the street stretch the ruins of the **Terme,** or baths. The plan of the **Casa Sannitica** opposite is typical of simpler dwellings built by the Sannites, a local Italic tribe absorbed by

the Romans. Next door is an old weaver's shop, and a couple of doors down is the wonderful **Casa del Mosaico di Nettuno e Anfitrite,** noted both for its shop and the blue-green mosaic adorning its rear living quarters. Other outstanding structures include the lovely **Casa del Bel Cortile** (House of the Beautiful Courtyard); the **Pistrinum,** a bakery with oven and flour mills; and the **Casa dei Cervi** (House of the Deer), the most sumptuous house in Herculaneum.

Pompeii

But for one of history's most famous cataclysms, Pompeii (Pompei in Italian) would have been one more minor Roman colony lost to the ravages of time. Instead, it was preserved for posterity by the eruption of Vesuvius in A.D. 79, when it and many of its inhabitants were buried beneath volcanic debris. There they remained until the 18th century, when the study of old texts suggested Pompeii's existence. Nowhere in Italy so vividly evokes the reality of the Roman world. "Nothing is wanting but the inhabitants," wrote diarist Henry Matthews in 1820.

Pompeii, about 18 miles (30 km) south of Naples, is a half-hour train ride from Naples on the Circumvesuviana line (see sidebar p. 151). The main entrance for visitors is the old **Porta Marina,** on the site's seaward (western) flank. Exploring the huge site—Pompeii had a

Herculaneum
- 123 C2

Visitor Information
- Via IV Novembre 82, Herculaneum
- ☎ 081 857 5347
- Closed Sat. Nov.–March & p.m.

Herculaneum ruins
- Corso Resina 6, Herculaneum
- ☎ 081 732 4311
- $$$; combined ticket with Pompeii: $$$$

pompeiisites.org

NOTE: The range of different buildings, and their generally superior state of preservation, make Herculaneum the better site to visit if you are forced to choose between Pompeii and Herculaneum.

Pompeii
- 123 C2

Visitor Information
- Via Sacra 1, Pompeii
- ☎ 081 850 7255
- Closed Sat. p.m.–Sun.

pompeiturismo.it

Pompeii ruins
- Entrances at Piazza Porta Marina, Piazza Esedra, & Piazza Anfiteatro
- ☎ 081 857 5347
- $$$; combined ticket with Herculaneum: $$$$

pompeiisites.org
coopculture.it

The casts of bodies captured where they fell in A.D. 79 are some of Pompeii's most compelling sights.

population of around 25,000—requires some forethought. Only about half of the area has been excavated, yet even this requires a day's sightseeing. Set off early and be prepared for crowds, for this is one of southern Italy's most popular excursions. Make for the highlights first, and don't become bogged down with the lesser streets, where the small houses soon look all alike.

Pompeii Highlights: Just beyond the entrance, you come to the town's old forum, ringed by many of the site's most imposing civic structures: the **Tempio di Apollo, Tempio di Giove,** and the **Basilica,** Pompeii's largest building. To the north lie the site's most famous houses: **Casa del Fauno** and **Casa dei Vettii.** The latter

is particularly interesting. It was once the property of rich merchant brothers, and its painted friezes are some of the finest of their kind. Among the scenes is a mural of a famously rampant Priapus, one of many phallic representations around the site (most probably representing superstitious attempts to ward off the evil eye).

The equally well-preserved Casa degli Amorini Dorati lies just to the east, while to the west you should hunt out the **Casa del Poeta Tragico,** known for its famous mosaic and graffiti—*"Cave canem"* ("Beware of the dog"). Some distance out to the west, through the Porta Ercolano, a tomb- and cypress-lined lane (Via delle Tombe) leads to a pair of villas, **Villa di Diomede** and **Villa dei Misteri.**

Return to the forum and then head east on Via dell'Abbondanza, formerly a busy commercial street, to reach the rest of the site. Off to the right after a short distance (on Via dei Teatri) are the **Teatro Grande,** a 5,000-seat open-air theater, and the smaller 800-seat **Teatro Piccolo,** or Odeon, the name given to a smaller covered theater. Two blocks north, on the corner with Vico del Lupanare, stretch the ruins of the **Terme Stabiane,** the town's main bath complex. At the end of Vico del Lupanare, once a thriving red-light district, is another visitors' favorite—a small **brothel** complete with bed stalls and frescoes illustrating the various services available.

Continue down Via dell'Abbondanza a block, then make a right turn to reach the **Casa del Menandro,** another outstanding patrician house adorned with mosaics and wall paintings. Back on Via dell'Abbondanza, two more fine houses, both with beautiful gardens, lie on the right toward the end of the street: **Casa di Loreius Tiburtinus** and **Villa di Giulia Felice.** Closing the eastern end of the site is the **Anfiteatro,** one of the oldest (80 B.C.) and best preserved Roman amphitheaters in existence. ■

NEED TO KNOW

Port Logistics: Naples

Naples's main cruise terminal, **Stazione Marittima** (porto.napoli.it), is on the waterfront close to the historic district. Taxis outside the terminal offer competitive, set-rate (tariffa predeterminata) trips to sights within the city and to Pompeii and Herculaneum as well as city tours. These can be economical with four in a taxi, but confirm prices beforehand.

Getting to Herculaneum & Pompeii

Herculaneum and Pompeii are both easily reached from Naples and Sorrento, where some cruise ships dock, too (see below). From Naples, take a tram or taxi to the **Porta Nolana–Corso Garibaldi** railroad terminus to catch a Circumvesuviana train (vesuviana.it). Tickets are sold at tabaccai and newsstands, including those in the cruise terminal. Remember to validate tickets in the yellow boxes. Look for trains to Sorrento or Pozzuoli (2–3 hourly). Both services stop at Ercolano (Herculaneum; 18–20 min., $) and Pompei Scavi (25–40 min., $).

From Sorrento, take trains headed toward Naples. It takes 25–30 minutes to reach Pompei Scavi, a little more to Ercolano. Cruise ships in Sorrento tender passengers to the **Marina Piccola;** from here it's a steep 15-minute walk to the central Piazza Tasso; or take the small blue shuttle (every 15 min.; buy ticket from driver, $) or red-and-white B or C EAV bus (every 20 min.; tickets from tabaccai, $). From Piazza Tasso, walk east for 5 minutes on Corso Italia to the railway station.

In Pompei, turn right from Pompei Scavi station for the one-block walk to the Pompeii entrance. In Ercolano, walk from the station down Via IV Novembre, then make a right on Corso Resina to reach the site entrance. Both stations and trains are favorites with thieves, so beware.

Capri

Capri is one of the most enchanting places in the Mediterranean, a beautiful little island of walks, views, and villages where the sea shimmers and the sky is a glorious blue; frangipani and lemon groves scent the air; bougainvillea provides floral cascades of color; whitewashed villas dazzle against tree-swathed slopes; and cliffs plunge on a thrilling coastline.

Capri has long been a sybaritic retreat for emperors, artists, writers, and the international jet set.

NEED TO KNOW p. 155

Capri
🅰 123 C1
Visitor Information
capritourism.com

Capri Town
Visitor Information
✉ Piazza
Umberto I, Capri town
☎ 081 837 0686
🕓 Closed 1:15 p.m.–3 p.m. Nov.–Easter & Sun.

No one should forgo the pleasures of Capri, but be aware that in high season— July, August, and weekends in May, June, and September— you will join up to 6,000 day-trippers, 3,000 hotel guests, and 12,000 residents, all squeezed onto an island that measures just 4 square miles (10 sq km). Catch the earliest possible boat to the island.

The main town, Capri, is in the east and its other town, Anacapri, is in the west. Between the two towns is 1,932-foot (589 m) Monte Solaro, the island's highest

point. The best attractions are a ride in the chairlift up Monte Solaro, the Villa San Michele in Anacapri, and the Grotta Azzurra (Blue Grotto) just below Anacapri. Note the pronunciation of the island's name—CA-pree, not ca-PREE.

Capri Town

At the heart of Capri town is Piazza Umberto I, the island's diminutive social hub, known as the **Piazzetta**—"Little Square." Invest in an expensive drink and settle back to enjoy people-watching. Streets around the square are

Blue Grotto

The Blue Grotto, or Grotta Azzurra, is one of the best known sights in Italy, never mind Capri. The cavern's otherworldly blue light has mesmerized generations of travelers, but given the crowds and the rigmarole involved in a visit, it's debatable whether you should make the effort, at least in high summer. If in doubt, take a circular boat tour of the island instead.

First you must reach the grotto, which you can do by boat from Marina Grande or by bus or cab from Anacapri to the parking lot above the grotto. Once you are at sea level and outside the cave, you have to wait to climb aboard a rowboat, the only way to enter the grotto owing to the low height of the cave entrance (under 3 feet/1 m). Tours are cancelled in seas with any significant swell. You must pay a fee to enter the grotto and a similar amount again for the rowboat; both of these fees are on top of the cost of the boat from Marina Grande, if that is the way you have come. At busy times, the lines of boats can be long, and because of the number of people wishing to experience the cave, you will have only a few minutes inside.

filled with souvenir stores, but you'll also find a greater concentration of designer boutiques than in any equivalent area in the world. Lose yourself in the lanes off these main thoroughfares, however, and you will begin to appreciate some of Capri's charm.

Start with Via Madre Serafina—a lane at the top of the steps by **Santo Stefano,** the church on the Piazzetta's south side—which offers magnificent views. Bear right and follow steep Via Castello and you come to the **Belvedere Cannone,** with a panorama of the Faraglioni, a trio of sea stacks. Just around the Piazzetta from Santo Stefano is the tiny **Museo Ignazio Cerio** (Piazzetta Cerio 5, Capri town, tel 081 837 6681, closed Sun.-Mon.), with exhibits on the island's archaeological and natural history, housed in a building dating to 1372.

To the left of Santo Stefano, take Via Vittorio Emanuele and Via Federico Serena, then turn right on Viale Matteotti. The last street provides another lovely viewpoint, embracing olive groves, the sea, and the **abbey of San Giacomo.**

Back on Viale Matteotti, continue west to reach the **Giardini di Augusto,** the Gardens of Augustus, so named because they were laid out over the ruins of an ancient Roman settlement. Capri has Greek or possibly Phoenician roots, its name deriving from the Greek kapros (boar) or the Romano-Italic word capreae, meaning "island of goats" (scholars dispute the precise origins).

The panoramic municipal gardens here were created as part of an estate belonging to Friedrich Alfred Krupp (1854-1902), a German arms manufacturer who also paid for the celebrated Via Krupp, a twisting path that winds down the cliff to the **Marina Piccola,** a lovely little bay that has seafront

The floor of San Michele Arcangelo in Anacapri is made up of more than 2,500 hand-painted tiles.

Anacapri

Visitor Information

- ✉ Via Giuseppe Orlandi 59, Anacapri
- ☎ 081 837 1524
- 🕐 Closed Sun. Nov.–Easter

cafés and several private beach concessions (the free, central area of the beach is a popular place from which to swim).

Head back to Capri town (or walk from the Piazzetta) to pick up Via Camerelle, a street that heads east into Via Tragara, the route of the townspeople's *passeggiata,* or evening stroll, and which ends in a lovely viewpoint at the **Belvedere di Tragara.** From here, most people return the way they have come (a 20-minute round-trip), but a paved path descends from the belvedere, then curves up and loops around the coast, a pleasing circular walk of about an hour.

Another excursion is the stroll on the road and easy trail to the ruins of the **Villa Jovis** (*closed 1st & 2nd Tues. of month & 3rd & 4th Sun. of month, $*) on the island's northeast tip, about 1.5 miles (2.4 km) from Capri town. The villa was Emperor Tiberius's Capri hideaway.

Anacapri

Anacapri has a different feel than Capri town, thanks to its more rugged position at the foot of Monte Solaro and the more Arabic feel of its square, whitewashed houses, but the number of visitors and designer outlets is similar.

From Piazza della Vittoria, the main square, it is a short walk, via a signed pedestrian path at the top of the stairs, to the must-see **Villa San Michele** (*Viale Axel Munthe 34, Anacapri, tel 081 837 1401, closed at 3 p.m. Nov.–Feb., at 4:30 p.m. in March, & at 5 p.m. in April, $$*). Built on the site of a Roman villa, the current villa was the creation of Axel Munthe (1857–1949), a Swedish doctor who brought the villa, and with it the charms of Capri, to a wider audience with the publication of *The Story of San Michele* (1929). It is hard to resist the allure of the gardens or the impact of the views. Note that you can follow the Scala Fenicia steps from the chapel of Sant'Antonio just below the villa all the way down to Marina Grande in Capri town.

Before you leave Anacapri, however, stop by the **Casa Rossa** *(Via Giuseppe Orlandi 78, Anacapri, tel 081 838 2193, closed Mon., & 1:30–5:30 p.m. June–Sept., $)*, a folly built in 1876 by a former Confederate soldier,

J. C. MacKowen, and the **San Michele Arcangelo** *(Piazza San Nicola, Anacapri)*, the town's parish church (1719). The latter has a pretty majolica floor (1761).

Monte Solaro: From the summit of Monte Solaro, sublime panoramic views embrace Vesuvius and the gulfs of Naples and Salerno. To reach the top, you can hike (it takes about an hour to walk up) or take the chairlift *(tel 06 081 9430 0001, capriseggiovia.it, $$)* from the south side of Piazza della Vittoria. A good idea is to ride up and walk down (or back to Capri town). ∎

NEED TO KNOW

Getting to Capri
Ferries and hydrofoils for Capri leave from Naples's **Molo Beverello**. Exit the Naples cruise terminal and turn left on Via Cristoforo Colombo; you will come immediately to it. Several companies offer services, but prices and departures are similar *(2 boats hourly, 45 min., $$$$$)*. Check the display by the ticket building for all imminent departures as individual lines only advertise their own sailings. Buy a return ticket and book a seat if possible, and double-check services to ensure a timely arrival back in Naples. Visit *snav.it, alilauro.it,* or *gescab.it* (for the fastest services) for information and online ticketing.

Prices and service frequency are similar if you are visiting Capri from Sorrento, but the journey time is around 10 minutes shorter. Boats leave from Sorrento's **Marina Piccola** *(portoturis ticosorrento.com)*, the same dock used

by tenders from cruise ships docking in Sorrento. Timetables can be found at *sorrentotourism.com.*

Port Logistics: Capri
All ferries and boats to Capri dock at **Marina Grande**, the port below Capri town. Arriving here in high season is no fun. It's a drab place, and you will have to run the gauntlet of your fellow visitors, hotel barkers, and trashy souvenir stalls.

From the Marina Grande you have several options: Take a boat trip to the Blue Grotto—the earlier you can make this trip, the better (see sidebar p. 153)—or around the island (a trip highly recommended); ride a bus to Capri or Anacapri towns (expect lines); take a cab to your destination (again, expect lines); ride the funicular to Capri town; or make the steep 10-minute walk up the path or Via San Francesco to Capri town.

Amalfi Coast

The Amalfi Coast, or Costiera Amalfitana, contains Italy's most beautiful maritime landscapes, a mild-weathered enclave of towering cliffs, idyllic villages tumbling colorfully to the sea, precipitous corniche roads, luxuriant gardens, and magnificent vistas over turquoise waters and green-swathed mountains.

The sheltered waters of the Marina Piccola, Sorrento

The coast lies along the southern flanks of the Sorrento Peninsula, the promontory that closes the southern reaches of the Bay of Naples. Sorrento, on the north side of this promontory, is the obvious base for excursions. Of the key coast towns, Positano is the prettiest and Ravello has the best views, but it is the drive along the littoral—especially the section west of Positano—or a boat tour, that will give you the best idea of why this coast is so celebrated.

Positano & Beyond

Positano, some 11 miles (18 km) east of Sorrento via the Amalfi Coast road, is supremely pretty from afar, its jumble of white houses tumbling down a cliff. But be warned: Its maze of tiny alleys becomes very crowded. There is a small beach here of gray (volcanic) sand.

Continuing east, the spectacular corniche road passes the **Vallone di Furore,** one of the coast's most impressive gorges, then the **Grotta dello Smeraldo,** a marine cave of emerald waters that you can visit by boat, elevator, or rock-cut steps. Soon afterward, the road leads into Amalfi, once the seat of a powerful maritime republic.

Amalfi

Amalfi's old center has charm. Pride of place goes to the **Duomo di Sant'Andrea** *(tel 089 871 059),* founded in the 9th century and fronted by an intricately patterned 12th-century facade that includes superb 11th-century Byzantine bronze doors. Access is via the adjacent 1268 **Chiostro del Paradiso,** or Cloister of Paradise *(tel 089 871 324, closed Jan.–Feb., $ incl. visit to Duomo),* whose somber Romanesque tone is enlivened by the Arab elements in its sinuous columns.

You can escape some of Amalfi's hustle by walking away from the main square toward the **Valle dei Mulini,** a steep-sided ravine dotted with ruined water mills—*mulini*—once used to make paper, an industry for which Amalfi was, and still is, famous. The small **Museo della Carta** *(Palazzo Pagliara, Via della Cartiere 22, Amalfi, tel 089 830 4561, museodellacarta.it, closed Mon. Nov.–Feb., $$)* offers displays related to the industry.

Ravello

The views from Ravello make it one of the most romantic small towns imaginable. Perched on steep, terraced slopes above Amalfi, it is a place blessed with luxuriant gardens, quiet lanes, sleepy, sun-drenched corners, and a lofty position at 1,148 feet (350 m) that provides an unforgettable panorama over the azure coast below. If you don't have a car, from Amalfi you can take a bus or, if your legs are willing, walk up—it takes 30 to 45 minutes to walk up, depending on path taken and your fitness level *(hiking map at the tourist office).*

At Ravello's heart lie an 11th-century cathedral and the **Villa Rufolo** *(Piazza del Vescovado, Ravello, tel 089 857 621, $$).* Built in the 13th century, the villa has received guests that included popes and emperors. Views from its idyllic gardens are magnificent, as are those from the nearby **Villa Cimbrone** *(Via Santa Chiara 26, Ravello, tel 089 857 459 or 089 858 072, $$).* ∎

NEED TO KNOW p. 157

Positano
 123 C1
Visitor Information
✉ Via del Saracino 4, Positano
☎ 089 875 067
🕐 Closed Sun. & p.m. Nov.–March
aziendaturismo positano.it

Amalfi
123 C1
Visitor Information
✉ Corso delle Repubbliche Marinare 27, Amalfi
☎ 089 871 107
🕐 Closed 1 p.m.– 3 p.m. year-round, & Sun. & p.m. in winter
amalfitouristoffice.it

Ravello
123 C1
Visitor Information
✉ Via Roma 18 bis, Ravello
☎ 089 857 096
🕐 Closed Sun. & 1 p.m.–2 p.m.
ravellotime.it

NEED TO KNOW
Visiting the Amalfi Coast

Because of the time involved, and the probability of traffic congestion en route, it is not easy to see the Amalfi Coast in a day from Naples. If you want to make the trip, use a specialist such as **See Amalfi Coast** (seeamalficoast.com), which is used to dealing with cruise passengers.

Trips from Sorrento are more realistic, and while it is possible to use buses (or irregular ferries) to see the key towns and the scenic drives between them, it is still tempting fate. Take a cruise excursion—preferably one that includes Ravello—to be sure of a timely return to your ship or hire a car with driver: Visit sorrentosilverstar.com or benvenutolimos.com for further information. For a boat tour along the coast, visit gruppobattellieriamalfi.com. Allow a day for a tour that includes Positano, Amalfi, and Ravello.

From the rich historic pasts of Sicily and Malta to the ancient caves of Matera and the mysterious *trulli* of Puglia in southern Italy

Sicily, Malta, & Puglia

Introduction & Map   160-161

Sicily   162-169

Need to Know: Taormina & Palermo   169

Malta   170-173

Need to Know: Valletta   173

Puglia   174-177

Need to Know: Bari   177

Restaurants   291-293

The clear blue waters surrounding Malta are a haven for scuba divers.

Sicily, Malta, & Puglia

In Sicily, Malta, and southern Italy's Puglia the Mediterranean begins a transition, moving from the past and present cultures of Western Europe toward the lands and historical and other legacies of North Africa and the Middle East. The pivotal positions of Sicily and Malta, at the crossroads of civilizations across centuries, make them especially rich places to visit; and in Puglia, southern Italy shows that it has sights to match those of northern Italy's better known towns and cities.

Sicily

Sicily is a world apart, an island separated from the rest of Italy not only by the sea but also by centuries of different history, politics, and cultural experience—all the result of geography. The largest island in the Mediterranean Sea, it has provided a tempting prize for traders and invaders. It has played host to ancient Greek and Roman settlements, was under Arab control between the ninth and tenth centuries, and has been in thrall, at one time or another, to Normans, Vandals, Byzantines, Bourbons, French, Spanish—and even the British.

The result is an extraordinarily rich heritage, from art and architecture to language and cuisine, a heritage you'll sample in abundance even on visits to just two of the island's main centers. Balmy, bucolic Taormina on the east coast is

galleries, museums, and some of Italy's most fantastically ornate baroque churches. On the outskirts of the city lies the not-to-be-missed cathedral at Monreale, a mosaic-filled masterpiece to rival almost any religious building in Italy or beyond.

Malta

Even more ancient remains can be found on tiny Malta, a legacy, like Sicily (which is just 75 miles/120 km north), of a position that made the isle a natural prize or port of call for settlers, traders, and invaders over several millennia. Temple and burial complexes on this island nation date back 5,600 years, and they complement some fine medieval monuments—not least some redoubtable walls—in the capital, Valletta. This small city is also known for its connections with the once powerful Knights of St. John, or Knights Hospitallers, who made Malta their headquarters in the 16th century, and who added a fascinating strand to the island's history.

Puglia

From Malta, skirting past the toe of the Italian "boot," you come to Puglia, the region that makes up the heel of the boot. Even by Italian standards it is a rich and varied patchwork, dotted with pretty countryside, quiet bays and beaches, Romanesque churches, mysterious fortresses, Crusader ports, baroque cities, and the strange conical dwellings—unique to this area—known as *trulli*.

Many of these attractions are easily seen from Bari, a town with a fine old historic quarter that is worth an hour or so in its own right, though on a short visit you might be tempted to devote most of your time to Matera, in the neighboring region of Basilicata, a beautiful town increasingly visited for its ancient cave dwellings and quiet, honey-stoned medieval streets. ∎

known primarily as a resort town, a favorite with writers, artists, and celebrities for more than a century, but it also boasts a superlative Greek theater, part of a cultural heritage that dates back well over 2,000 years. The town also serves as a springboard for visits to Mount Etna, a still active volcano and one of the single greatest landforms in the Mediterranean.

Palermo, Sicily's vibrant and slightly battered capital, is a very different place: more edgy and more varied but even more fascinating from a historical and cultural point of view. Monuments to its period of Arab and Norman splendor more than a thousand years ago still survive, along with

Sicily

Sicily's chicest resort town is the charming east coast town of Taormina, which also serves as a gateway to Etna, Europe's greatest active volcano, a smoldering peak of brooding majesty. The capital Palermo, on the northern coast, offers a vibrant mix of history and faded grandeur.

A café beckons at the foot of Taormina's stately church of San Giuseppe.

NEED TO KNOW p. 169

Taormina

 160 C2

Visitor Information

✉ Palazzo Corvaia, Piazza Santa Caterina–Piazza Vittorio Emanuele II, Taormina

☎ 0942 23 243

🕐 Closed Sun. & 1:30 p.m.–4 p.m.

www.regione.sicilia.it/turismo

Taormina

This beguiling hill town has been a favored winter and summer retreat for more than a century, offering flower-scented piazzas, charming streets, chic boutiques, subtropical gardens, fine sea views, and broad vistas of nearby volcanic Etna.

Taormina's extraordinary site curves around a natural terrace 669 feet (204 m) above the sea and has been inhabited for at least three millennia. Its first documented settlement was the Greek colony of Tauromenion, founded in 403 B.C. It then prospered under the Romans and fell to the Arabs in 902 and the Normans in 1078. Thereafter

it slumbered for centuries until 1866, when it was linked to Messina by rail.

The village became a favored winter resort to rival similar retreats on the French Riviera, drawing the likes of Orson Welles, John Steinbeck, Greta Garbo, Rita Hayworth, Cary Grant, and Salvador Dalí. Tennessee Williams penned *A Streetcar Named Desire* and *Cat on a Hot Tin Roof* here.

Today, Taormina is extremely popular: Between about June and September, visitors cram the beaches and tiny streets. April, May, and October are better, but winter and spring reveal the town at its picturesque best.

The Heart of Town: Most visitors arrive on Via Luigi Pirandello and the **Porta Messina gateway,** which marks the beginning of Taormina's single main street, the gently climbing **Corso Umberto I,** lined with boutiques, souvenir shops, elegant cafés, flower-filled balconies, antiques stores, several churches, and lots of pretty historic buildings.

Once through the gateway, the Corso opens onto **Piazza Vittorio Emanuele II,** built on the site of the old Roman forum. The **Shaker Bar** here was a favorite of Tennessee Williams. The square's principal building is the 14th-century **Palazzo Corvaia** (or Corvaja) on the right, with a central Moorish tower from the tenth century, decorated in the black lava and white pumice characteristic of many local buildings.

The palace houses the town's visitor center and the **Museo Siciliano di Arte e Tradizioni Popolari,** an entertaining and occasionally eccentric collection of folk art and artifacts. The palace's main salon, the Norman-era Sala del Parlamento, is so called because it was the seat of the Sicilian parliament in 1410.

To the left of the palace is the 17th-century church of **Santa Caterina,** partly built over the remains of the **Odeon,** a first-century Roman theater, part of which can be seen behind the church and built into its nave.

On the opposite side of the square, Via del Teatro Greco leads to the **Teatro Greco** (or Teatro Antico), Taormina's main sight (see p. 164).

For now, continue along the Corso, then turn onto a tiny side street on the left (Via Naumachia) that leads quickly to the **Naumachie,** the remains of what was probably a Roman cistern or gymnasium.

In Corleone's Footsteps

Are you a fan of Francis Ford Coppola's film *The Godfather*? Do you remember the part where Michael Corleone (Al Pacino) is sent to Sicily, where he marries the ill-fated Apollonia? Much of this sequence was shot in and around Savoca (a village in the Monti Peloritani that's a 20-minute drive northwest of Taormina), not least in the village bar, the Vitelli, where you can still stop for coffee or a lemon granita (a local crushed-ice treat).

A visit here—and to other of the region's sleepy villages, such as Forza d'Agrò and Casalvecchio Siculo—reveals a fascinating slice of the old Sicily, with landscapes and ways of daily life that have changed little over the centuries.

Rejoining the main street, you come to **Piazza IX Aprile,** the place to see and be seen. Its name refers to the date in 1860 on which Taormina's citizens revolted against Bourbon rule during the battle for Italian unification. The halfway point down the Corso is a good place to stop, day or night, for a drink, albeit at a price. The money is well spent, however, both for the superb views to Etna and the sea and for the chance to take in the square's human spectacle. The most prestigious

Museo Siciliano di Arte e Tradizioni Popolari

✉ Palazzo Corvaia, Piazza Santa Caterina-Piazza Vittorio Emanuele II, Taormina

☎ 0942 610 274 or 0942 610 206

🕐 Closed Mon. & 1 p.m.–4 p.m.

 $

Teatro Greco

✉ Via del Teatro Greco 40, Taormina

☎ 0942 23 220 or 0942 24 291

$ $$$

spots are Caffè Wunderbar and the Mocambo.

Borgo Medioevale: Beyond the square and its clock tower, the Corso enters the Borgo Medioevale, the oldest part of town, full of medieval palaces and the odd architectural remnant of the town's Arab past.

Castelmola

This rock-top hamlet about 3 miles (5 km) north of Taormina is a popular excursion (lovely off-season, horribly crowded at other times) thanks to its views and celebrated almond wine. It is easily reached from Taormina by bus *(bus station on Via Luigi Pirandello),* or you could walk. Winston Churchill used to come here to drink and paint, settling down at the **Caffè San Giorgio** *(Piazza Sant'Antonio 1, tel 0942 28 228, closed Tues. in winter),* founded in 1907 and still in business. Signatures in the visitors' book include those of John D. Rockefeller and Mr. Rolls and Mr. Royce of luxury automobile fame.

Piazza del Duomo is the site of a lackluster cathedral, though the piazza is noteworthy for its **fountain** (1635), topped by a strange female centaur—the town's symbol. The Corso ends a few steps away at the **Porta Catania gateway** (1440). On the left is Via del Ghetto, part of the town's Jewish quarter until the Jews were expelled from Sicily and other Spanish possessions in 1492. A lane leads to the **Palazzo dei Duchi di Santo Stefano,** a fine 15th-century palace that hosts art and other exhibitions.

Bearing left past the palace, you come to **Piazza San Domenico,** home to the San Domenico Palace hotel, opened in 1894 and still one of Taormina's top hotels. The hotel was targeted by Allied bombing in July 1943 after it was designated the German headquarters of Field Marshal Kesselring.

Teatro Greco: Taormina's fourth-century B.C. Greek theater is carved from the surrounding rock and has a panorama that embraces Etna, the highlands of the Sicilian interior, the Ionian Sea, and the shadowy mountains of the Italian mainland. "Never did any audience, in any theater," said German writer J. W. von Goethe in 1787, "have before it such a spectacle."

Despite its Greek origins, most of the present structure dates from the Roman period, and from alterations between the first and third centuries A.D. This is when, among other things, the still well-preserved brick stage buildings were added and the shape of the auditorium was altered to stage gladiatorial games. Today, the theater hosts performances during the **Taormina Arte** *(taormina-arte.com)* arts festival, held July through August.

Below the theater are delightful gardens of **Parco Duca di Cesarò** *(Via Bagnoli Croce, off Corso Umberto I, Taormina),* also called Giardini della Villa Comunale, an oasis created in 1899.

Visible from far and wide, the still active volcano Etna looms over the Plain of Catania.

Etna

Etna is Europe's highest volcano—and it's still very active. Ancient mariners believed its summit was the world's highest point. To the Arabs, it was simply the "Mountain of Mountains," while the Greeks called it Aitho (meaning "I burn"). A visit close to its summit, which rises to circa 10,922 feet (3,330 m), and its striking, lunar landscapes, is highly memorable.

Etna is a youngster, geologically speaking. Formed about 60,000 years ago, it sprang from undersea eruptions on what is now the Plain of Catania. Unlike many volcanoes, it tends to rupture rather than explode, creating huge lateral fissures instead of a single crater—some 350 fissures have appeared to date. About 90 major and 135 minor eruptions have been documented.

Volcanic activity alters the means of access and the areas you can safely approach. Guided tours are possible from Taormina and elsewhere using minibuses and off-road vehicles.

Independent access to the area is difficult unless you rent a car to drive to the Rifugio Sapienza, a mountain refuge, where you can take a cable car (funiviaetna .com) to the upper slopes, and then walk (allow a full day). Be sure to wear strong boots and bring warm- and wet-weather clothing. Many tour operators provide clothing.

Palermo

Battered and bustling Palermo is not to all tastes, its traffic and decaying baroque grandeur not for the fainthearted. At the same time, it is one of Italy's most atmospheric cities, founded by the Phoenicians in the eighth century B.C. and still bearing the stamp of its later Arab, Norman, and Spanish rulers.

Monuments to past glories rise amid the modern tenements and cramped backstreets, fighting for space in a city whose Arab bazaars, flourishing port, seedy dives, and teeming thoroughfares offer a dramatic and vibrant contrast between past and present.

Etna
🔼 160 C2
Visitor Information
www.parcoetna.ct.it
etnaguide.com
guidetnanord.com

Palermo
🔼 160 B3
Visitor Information
✉ Piazza Castelnuovo 34, Palermo
☎ 091 605 8351
🕒 Closed Sat.–Sun.
palermotourism.com

Palazzo dei Normanni & Cappella Palatina

- ✉ Piazza Indipendenza, Palermo
- ☎ 091 626 2833
- 🕐 Palace: closed p.m. Sun. & holidays, & Dec. 25–Jan. 1; chapel: closed a.m. Sun. & holidays; royal apartments: closed Tues.–Thurs.
- $ Palace: $$$ (Tues.–Thurs. $$); chapel: $$; palace & chapel: $$$

www.ars.sicilia.it
fondazionefederico
secondo.it

San Giovanni degli Eremiti

- ✉ Via dei Benedettini, Palermo
- ☎ 091 651 5019
- 🕐 Closed Sun. p.m.
- $ $$

Many sights cluster in the city center, but they will still require plenty of walking—the Palazzo dei Normanni, La Martorana, and Vucciria markets are highlights if time is short. Others, such as the Duomo di Monreale and the eerie Catacombe dei Cappuccini, will require a taxi or bus journey (aziendasicilianatrasporti.it).

INSIDER TIP:

You won't be allowed to enter the Norman-era Cappella Palatina if you have bare shoulders or are wearing a short skirt, shorts, or low-cut top.

—TIM JEPSON
National Geographic author

Palazzo dei Normanni:
The Palazzo dei Normanni, or Palazzo Reale, occupies the site of the city's ninth-century Saracen fortress, a building enlarged by the Normans and transformed into a palace complex that became one of Europe's leading royal courts. Its 12th-century **Sala di Re Ruggero,** or Hall of Roger II, is a chamber adorned with mosaics of hunting scenes. Roger, a Norman king, was also responsible for the magnificent **Cappella Palatina** (1132–1140), one of Palermo's highlights, a glittering private chapel that encapsulates the composite

Roman-Arab-Byzantine architectural style that flourished in Sicily under the Normans. The chapel's mosaics are considered to be among Europe's finest. Also see the palace's gardens, the Villa Bonanno, if they are open.

Palermo had more than 200 mosques during its period of Arab rule (831–1072). Many were subsequently replaced by Christian buildings, including the lovely **San Giovanni degli Eremiti,** a deconsecrated church, built between 1132 and 1148 to the south of the Palazzo dei Normanni. The cloister and unkempt garden of palms, lemon trees, and subtropical plants here are equally beautiful.

A Riot of Churches: Moving east along Via Vittorio Emanuele II, you come to Palermo's great **cathedral** (begun in 1184; closed Sun. a.m.), another Norman monument. Its interior was much altered in the 18th century, but the exterior has retained its exotic blend of early architectural styles. Note, in particular, the Gothic main portal, a 15th-century work, and, inside, the royal tombs of Henry IV, Roger II, and Holy Roman Emperor Frederick II and his wife, Constance of Aragon (located in two chapels in the south aisle).

Palermo's heart is marked by Via Vittorio Emanuele's intersection with Via Maqueda, known as the **Quattro Canti,** or Four Corners. Just south

Via Vittorio Emanuele II and the streets around the Quattro Canti, the hub of historic Palermo

is **Piazza Pretoria,** a ring of medieval and Renaissance buildings centered on a 16th-century fountain known as the "Fountain of Shame" after its lascivious nude figures. To the south in Piazza Bellini stands the church of **La Martorana** (Santa Maria dell'Ammiraglio), whose baroque alterations spared the church's sensational Greek-crafted 12th-century dome mosaics.

Alongside La Martorana lies the 12th-century Norman church of **San Cataldo,** whose external architecture bears marked Moorish leanings. The interior, like most of Palermo's smaller churches, is a riot of baroque overelaboration. Another example of baroque exuberance is the 1612 **San Giuseppe dei Teatini** *(closed p.m.)* on the Quattro Canti, whose plain-faced exterior

conceals an interior of decorative splendor.

East of Quattro Canti: From the Quattro Canti head east to a cluster of sights to the south. Chief among these is the **Galleria Regionale di Sicilia** *(Via Alloro 4, Palermo, tel 091 623 0011, closed Mon. & p.m. Sat.–Sun., $$$),* an important art collection whose highlights are Antonello da Messina's 1473 "Annunciation" painting and an exquisite 1471 bust of Eleonora of Aragon by Francesco Laurana.

Immediately north in Piazza Marina stands the **Palazzo Chiaramonte** (1307), a Gothic palace best known for its garden's mighty magnolia fig trees, and the **Palazzo Mirto** *(tel 091 616 4751, closed Sun. p.m.–Mon.),* filled with gloriously decorated period rooms.

La Martorana

✉ Piazza Bellini 3, Palermo

☎ 091 616 1692 or 345 828 8231

🕐 Closed Sun., 1 p.m.–3:30 p.m., & religious holidays

💲 $$

museodiocesanopa.it

San Cataldo

✉ Piazza Bellini, Palermo

☎ 091 637 5622 or 091 611 8168 (Amici dei Musei Siciliani)

🕐 Closed 12:30 p.m.–3 p.m.

💲 $

museodiocesanopa.it
amicimuseisiciliani.it

Catacombe dei Cappuccini

✉ Convento dei Cappuccini, Piazza Cappuccini (off Via Pindemonte), Palermo

☎ 091 652 4156, 091 212 117, or 329 415 0462

⊖ Closed Sun. p.m. Nov.–Feb. & daily 12:30 p.m.– 3 p.m.

$ $

For something more unusual, head to the Corso's eastern end and the **Museo Internazionale delle Marionette Antonio Pasqualino** (*Piazzetta Antonio Pasqualino 5, Palermo, tel 091 328 060, museomarionettepalermo.it, hours vary, $$*). The museum has a fine collection of puppets from across Sicily—where they were long a source of traditional satire and entertainment—and other parts of the world.

The Monreale cathedral represents the pinnacle of Arab-Norman-Byzantine art and architecture.

North of the Corso: You could now make your way back toward the port, pausing to explore Palermo's vibrant market area in the streets around Piazza San Domenico. This highly colorful district is known as the **Vucciria,** from a dialect phrase meaning a place of noise and confusion.

While in the area, stop by **San Domenico** (*Piazza San Domenico, Palermo, tel 091 589 172 or 329 425 9159, closed Mon.*

except May & Oct., & p.m.), the nearby **Oratorio del Rosario** (*Via Bambinai 2, Palermo, tel 091 609 0308, closed p.m. & Sat.-Sun., $$*), and the **Oratorio di Santa Cita** (*Via Squarcialupo, Palermo, closed Sun., $$*). All three churches offer object lessons in the finer points of Sicilian baroque decoration.

Farther north, just off Via Roma, Sicily's leading archaeological museum, the extensive **Museo Archeologico Regionale "Antonino Salinas"** (*Via Bara all'Olivella 24, Palermo, tel 091 611 6806, closed p.m. except Tues. & Fri., $$*), is a repository for art and artifacts removed from the island's myriad ancient sites.

Catacombe dei Cappuccini:

Long after other memories of your Italian visit have faded, chances are you will recall the unusual and macabre sights of the **Convento dei Cappuccini,** west of the city center—any cab driver knows how to get there.

Preserving the dead using lime, arsenic, and the drying effects of the sun was a Capuchin tradition and one seen in the convent's subterranean corridors. Rows of bodies are hung in gruesome poses. Each cluster of corpses is divided according to rank and profession: priests, monks, commoners, aristocrats—even children. All wear the clothes they died in, the effect morbid and comical by turns—bones and yellowing flesh poke through moldering gloves; tufts of hair sprout from crumbling top hats.

Duomo di Monreale:

Monreale, a town 6 miles (10 km) from Palermo's city center and now almost subsumed by Palermo's suburbs, has one of Europe's supreme cathedrals, a monument to the greatest traditions of Arab, Norman, and Byzantine art and architecture. The Duomo di Monreale, and its mosaics in particular, constitutes Sicily's single greatest treasure.

Founded in 1172 by the Norman king William II, the Duomo drew on French, Islamic, and Byzantine models for its design and decoration. A finely carved portal frames its main bronze doors (1186), which are adorned with 42 biblical scenes.

Inside, the building shimmers with gold leaf, paintings in rich tones, and colored marbles, its nave and wooden ceiling supported by columns salvaged from earlier classical buildings. A glorious mosaic pavement mirrors the greater mosaics in the main body of the church, a cycle completed around 1182. The royal tombs of kings William I and II lie in a chapel to the right of the apse.

The Duomo's interior alone would be worth the trip, but the adjacent monastery's Norman cloister is an added bonus. Some 228 twin columns, most sinuously carved or inlaid with colored marbles, support the quadrangle's Arab-style arches. To the rear, a pleasing terrace and garden offer views of the basin cradling the city of Palermo below. ∎

Duomo di Monreale

- ✉ Piazza del Duomo (Piazza Guglielmo II 1), Monreale (outskirts of Palermo)
- ☎ Duomo: 091 640 4413 or 091 640 2424; cloister: 091 640 4403
- 🕐 Duomo: closed 12:30 p.m.–2:30/3:30 p.m. Mon.–Sat. & 10 a.m.–3 p.m. Sun.; cloister: closed Sun. p.m.–Mon., & holidays
- 💲 Duomo: $; cloister: $$

duomomonreale.it

NEED TO KNOW

Port Logistics: Taormina & Etna

Some cruise ships visiting Taormina dock at **Giardini-Naxos**, the port immediately below Taormina. From here, buses, taxis, or a small cable car run to Taormina on the hill above (*taorminaservizipubblici.it*).

Most cruise ships, however, put in at **Messina**, a largely modern port well to the north. Trains run from **Messina Marittima** station at the port to Messina Centrale (*5 min.*), where you can change for trains to **Taormina-Giardini** (*1–2 hourly, journey time 37–80 min., trenitalia .com*); or take a 5-minute taxi transfer directly to Messina Centrale for additional connections.

Allow at least 5 hours to see Taormina, with transfers, and a full day if an excursion to Etna is included. Sicily

TravelNet (*sicilytourguides.net*) offers tours from Messina and Taormina.

Port Logistics: Palermo

Palermo's **port and cruise terminal** (*portpalermo.it*) is just north of the historic center, which can be reached on foot, but beware scam artists and pickpockets in the immediate port area. Free shuttles operate inside the terminal, but not beyond. Taxis are available at the gates, but overcharging is rife. Ask taxis to drop you at the Palazzo dei Normanni and work your way back toward the waterfront, seeing the sights on and just off the main Via Vittorio Emanuele II.

You can get a taste of the city in a half-day, along with the great cathedral at Monreale, 6 miles (10 km) southwest of the city center.

Malta

The island of Malta is the Mediterranean's gateway, poised in the narrow straits between Sicily and Tunisia, and between the countries of Western Europe on one side and those of the near and Middle East on the other. Its capital, Valletta, has a wonderful walled old quarter, while the island beyond is rich in ancient sites that testify to thousands of years of human history.

Grand Harbor, Valletta, Malta

Malta's position has made it prey to virtually every invader that ever sailed or lived between Gibraltar and the Middle East. Phoenicians, Romans, Arabs, Normans, the Aragonese, the French, the British, and many others all left their mark.

These successive waves of invaders account in large part for the majestic walls and fortifications of Valletta, but it was a very different type of occupier that left the most lasting impression on the city and the island beyond.

The Knights of the Order of St. John, or the Knights Hospitallers, were founded in Jerusalem around 1023 with the aim of providing care for Christian pilgrims. When a Christian army took Jerusalem in the First Crusade in 1099, the Knights were given the task of protecting the Holy Land under a papal charter, and their role acquired a military dimension. When Muslim forces invaded the Holy Land the Knights moved their headquarters to Rhodes and eventually, in 1530, to Malta, awarded to them by Charles V of Spain. It was on the island that they would fight and win their last great battle, holding off an immense Ottoman force during the "Great Siege of Malta" in 1565.

Valletta

The main entrance to old Valletta is on the south side of the fortifications, at the City Gate, by Triton's Fountain (the end point of bus services). Walk through the gate and you are on Triq Repubblika, or **Republic Street,** the main south-north street of the old quarter's grid-plan layout. Much of what you want to see is on or just off this street, but for good shopping—such as the island's distinctive glass, silver, and lace—delve into the city's quieter backstreets.

Walk three short city blocks, to the **National Museum of Archaeology** (Republic St., Valletta, tel 021 221 623, heritage malta.org, $$) on your left, housed in a former hostel of the Knights of St. John. Here you'll find artifacts from across the island in extraordinarily ancient tombs, catacombs, and other monuments, such as Tarxien, Hagar Qim, and Mnajdra (these sites are all managed by Heritage Malta; check heritagemalta .org for details on visiting them).

A block farther up Republic Street, at Great Siege Square, turn right to see the 1578 **St. John's Co-Cathedral** (Pjazza San Gwann, St. John St., Valletta, tel 021 239 628, closed Sat. p.m.– Sun., stjohnscocathedral.com, $$), Malta's main highlight. Once the church of the Knights of St. John, its gloriously ornate interior is home to many past Knights, buried under fine marble tombstones, as well chapels commissioned and adorned by

individual "hostels" of the order in different countries. Many of the paintings and interior decoration are the work of the 17th-century Maltese master Mattia Preti, but the standout work of art is Caravaggio's "The Beheading of St. John" in the Oratory. The cathedral also contains one of the world's finest collections of Flemish tapestries as well as rich vestments and illuminated manuscripts.

A short walk farther north on Republic Street brings you to Palace Square, where you'll find the 1571 **Grand Master's Palace** (tel 021 249 349, cityofvalletta .org, closed during parliamentary sessions, $$$$). Currently home to the office of the Maltese president, it contains more outstanding tapestries, an armory full of arms and armor, and a main salon decorated with frescoes depicting scenes from the history of the Knights and the Great Siege of 1565.

Malta's George Cross

The George Cross is a British medal awarded for only the greatest acts of heroism and courage in the face of extreme danger. It is a civilian medal— the equivalent of the military Victoria Cross. It has only twice been awarded collectively, the first time to the people and "Island Fortress of Malta" in 1942 for withstanding a siege, blockade, and repeated naval and air attacks from the Nazis and Italian forces desperate to capture one of the Mediterranean's most important strategic strongholds. The medal is incorporated into the Maltese flag to this day.

NEED TO KNOW p. 173

Valletta
- 160 B1

Visitor Information
- ✉ Pinto Wharf, Valletta waterfront
- ☎ 021 220 633
- 🕑 Closed outside cruise ship visits

- ✉ 229 Merchants St., Valletta
- ☎ 022 915 440
- 🕑 Closed Sun. p.m.

- ✉ Inquisitor's Palace, Main Gate St., Birgu
- ☎ 021 800 145
- 🕑 Closed Sun. p.m.

visitmalta.com
cityofvalletta.org

Colorful, traditional fishing boats bob in Marsaxlokk's harbor, awaiting their next outing.

A lane to the east, Old Theatre Street, leads to Valletta's market and, just around the corner, to the church of **St. Paul's Shipweck** (*St. Paul's St., Valletta, tel 021 245 350, maltadiocese.org*), named after the story that St. Paul was shipwrecked on Malta in A.D. 60 and brought Christianity to the island. Behind the church's dull 19th-century facade is an earlier interior (1639–1680) full of treasures, including a reliquary said to contain bones from the saint's wrist, an ornate wooden statue (1657) of the saint (carried around the city's streets on February 10), and a fragment of the column on which St. Paul is said to have been beheaded in Rome.

Walk north from the church on St. Paul's Street and you come to the **Sacra Infermeria** (*St. Elmo's Bastions, Mediterranean St., Valletta*), now a conference center, but built by a Grand Master of the Knights of St. John in 1574 as a hospital. It's a remarkable building, nowhere more so than in the Great Ward, an immense stone-vaulted hall more than 500 feet (155 m) long. A theater in the complex offers **"The Malta Experience,"** an hourly audiovisual presentation on the history of Malta (*tel 021 243 776, themaltaexperience.com, shows*

INSIDER TIP:

The Maltese town of Marsaxlokk is as pretty as can be. Don't miss the painted "evil eyes" warding off trouble on the colorful boats in the harbor.

—LARRY PORGES
National Geographic Travel Books editor

*11 a.m.–4 p.m. Mon.–Fri. & 11 a.m.–
1 p.m. Sat.–Sun. & holidays, $$$).*

Walk west back to Republic Street, then turn left to reach the **Casa Rocca Piccola** *(74 Republic St., Valletta, tel 021 221 499, closed Sun., $$$)*, near the junction with St. Dominic Street. One of the capital's few historic town houses still privately owned and occupied, it is open to visitors on hourly guided tours; it contains a wealth of period material, from paintings and antiques to the bomb shelter used during Nazi air raids in World War II.

The Rest of the Island

Some 5 miles (8 km) east of Valletta across the water, on the opposite side of the island's great natural harbor, are the so-called **Three Cities—** Vittoriosa (or Birgu), Senglea, and Cospicua—settlements ringed by walls from the 1570s on fingers of land that push into the bay.

Boat tours and ferries *(vallettaferryservices.com)* from Valletta's waterfront access the "Cities," which were the first areas settled by the Knights of St. John when they came to the island. It was also here that much of the fighting took place during the Great Siege of 1565. **Vittoriosa** takes its name from the Knights' victory of that year and is home, among other things, to the church of San Lawrenz in the main square and the 16th-century Inquisitor's Palace (1530s), originally the Knights' law courts and now an ethnographic museum. Each of

the "Cities" offers lovely views back to Valletta, but some of the best are from the Gardjola Gardens *(Triq Portu Salvu)* on the edge of Senglea.

If time is short, however, consider traveling inland from Valletta, to the World Heritage site of **Hal Saflieni Hypogeum,** 3 miles (4.8 km) south of the capital in Paolo; it's easily reached by public transportation from Valletta. A labyrinth of subterranean chambers on three levels, it is a rare example of a Neolithic underground temple and burial area some 5,600 years old. It's a fascinating place, but also a popular one: *Book the very expensive tours several weeks in advance.*

If archaeology does not appeal, visit **Marsaxlokk,** a quaint fishing village 5 miles (8 km) southeast of the capital, where fishermen still work their boats and mend their nets, and where waterfront cafés and restaurants, often housed in pretty old stone cottages, serve their catch. To get there, take bus 81 or 85 from Valletta. ∎

Hal Saflieni Hypogeum

✉ Burial St., Paola
☎ 021 805 018
🕓 Tours (daily) must be booked
💲 $$$$$
🚌 Bus: 81, 82, 83, or 85 from Valletta

heritagemalta.org

NEED TO KNOW
Port Logistics: Valletta
Cruise ships dock on Valletta's eastern side, at the sleek Valletta Waterfront Facility *(vallettawaterfront.com).* Avoid the steep walk to the city in favor of the elevator (Barrakka Lift; $) or bus 130 *(publictransport.com.mt, $),* one of several services that operate from the promenade in front of the terminal: Buy tickets from booths on this strip.

Puglia

Puglia is the heel of the Italian "boot," a long narrow region of endless plains and rolling hills. Bari, the principal port of call, has an atmospheric old town and provides easy access to the extraordinary town of Matera and the strange *trulli* dwellings around Alberobello. Farther-flung attractions include the 13th-century Castel del Monte and the scenic Gargano, the boot's spur.

Traditional *trulli* houses mix with more recent buildings in the Puglian town of Alberobello.

Bari

Almost everything to see in Bari is in the labyrinth of streets and alleys that make up the **Città Vecchia** (Old Town). Most of the houses have been restored, and many small bars, restaurants, and stores have opened.

Bari's roots go back to the Bronze Age or earlier, with periods of Roman, Saracen, Lombard, and Byzantine domination; however, it was the arrival of the Normans in 1071 that fully established the city. Its status was further enhanced in 1087 when a group of Baresi merchants in Antioch, learning that the Venetians intended to steal the sacred relics of St. Nicholas (then interred in modern-day Turkey), stole the relics themselves.

Holy relics had great value in the Middle Ages, and after St. Nicholas's arrival in Bari it was only natural that a suitably splendid home should be created in which to house them. The result was the **Basilica di San Nicola** *(Piazza San Nicola–Largo Abate Elia 13, Bari, tel 080 573 7111, basilicasannicola.it),* consecrated in 1197 and one of the earliest and finest monuments of Puglian-Romanesque architecture.

The exterior highlight is the glorious carved main portal, a medley of Arab, Byzantine, and classical styles. Inside, note the painted wooden and gilt ceiling (1661–1674) and the beautiful canopied ciborium (1150). Almost equally magnificent is the Bishop's Throne from 1089. The remains of St. Nicholas are found in the crypt.

Just south of the basilica stands **San Sabino** (*Piazza dell'Odegitria 1, Bari, tel 080 521 0605, closed 12:30 p.m.–4 p.m. Mon.–Sat. & 12:30 p.m.–5 p.m. Sun.*), a virtual copy of San Nicola. Begun in 1170, this cathedral was designed to replace one destroyed when the Norman king William II razed the city in 1156, sparing only San Nicola. Like its near neighbor, this is a superb Romanesque building, still with its original wooden ceiling and another fine ciborium and episcopal throne. Close by is the vast 13th-century **Castello Svevo** (*Piazza Federico II de Svevia, Bari, tel 080 528 6261, closed Wed.*), which hosts exhibitions.

North of both churches is the **Pinacoteca Provinciale** (*Palazzo della Provincia, Via Spalato 19– Lungomare Nazario Sauro 27, Bari, tel 080 541 2420, pinacotecabari .it, closed Sun. p.m.–Mon. & holidays, $*), which is in the new town but worth the journey. Its collection includes several major works by Renaissance masters such as Tintoretto and Veronese as well as a good selection of southern Italian artists.

Trulli Country

Southwest of Bari stretches one of southern Italy's most distinctive landscapes: vineyards, oak woods, olive groves, and cherry orchards dotted with *trulli*, strange conical dwellings of mysterious origin that are unique to this small corner of Italy. Ferrovie Sud Est trains service the region from Bari (see sidebar p. 177); the ride

to Alberobello, the region's "capital," takes about 1.5 hours.

There's no escaping the fact that **Alberobello,** a UNESCO World Heritage site, is a touristy spot. At the same time, the 1,500 trulli in and around the walkable town make it somewhere that has to be seen. Just aim to come early or late, and try to wander around the quieter rural hinterland, where the trulli form a lovely and organic part of the age-old landscape.

INSIDER TIP:

For an uncrowded experience, summer is the time to visit Matera, as most tourists prefer to go to southern Italy's beaches then.

—TINO SORIANO
National Geographic photographer

From Alberobello it is 5 miles (8.7 km) to the area's second major town, **Locorotondo,** whose streets are arranged on a circular plan around a conical hilltop—hence its name ("round place"). Even without the nearby trulli, this would be a pleasing town, well worth a few minutes' exploration for the views over the fields and hills.

A short way south is **Martina Franca,** a place with modern outskirts but an appealing historic core. Northwest of here is **Cisternino,** a prettier and more

NEED TO KNOW p. 177

Bari
- 161 E4

Visitor Information
- ✉ Piazza Aldo Moro 33/A, Bari
- ☎ 080 524 2361 or 080 524 2244

infopointbari.com
agenziapuglia
promozione.it

Alberobello
- 161 E4

Visitor Information
- ✉ Pro Loco, Via Monte Nero 3, Alberobello
- ☎ 080 432 2822 or 080 432 2060
- 🕑 Closed p.m. & Sat.–Sun.

prolocoalberobello.it

Locorotondo
- 161 E4

Visitor Information
- ✉ Pro Loco, Piazza Vittorio Emanuele 27, Locorotondo
- ☎ 080 431 3099

prolocolocorotondo.it

Martina Franca
- 161 E4

Visitor Information
- ✉ Piazza XX Settembre 3, Martina Franca
- ☎ 080 480 5702 or 366 126 6045

prolocomartinafranca.it

Outstanding baroque architecture has made Lecce famous.

Ostuni
🅰 161 F4
Visitor Information
✉ Corso Mazzini 8, Ostuni
☎ 0831 301 268

✉ Corso Vittorio Emanuele 39, Ostuni
☎ 0831 307 219

Matera
🅰 161 E4
Visitor Information
✉ Via Domenico Ridola 60/67, Matera
☎ 0835 311 655
🕐 Closed 2:30 p.m.–4 p.m.
aptbasilicata.it

authentic sightseeing experience than Alberobello—and at the heart of some of the region's loveliest scenery.

Above all, though, try to see **Ostuni,** one of Puglia's most appealing hilltop towns. Known as the "white city" after its mantle of Greek-style white-washed, flat-roofed houses, it has a heart of twisting alleys in which you are guaranteed to become pleasantly lost.

Elsewhere in the region, **Castellana Grotte** is notable for its grottoes (tel 080 499 8221, grottedicastellana.it, hours vary, open Nov.–Feb. by reservation only, $$$–$$$$), the finest caverns in Italy open to the public. Tours take place roughly every

half hour and are divided into 50-minute visits of just over half a mile (1 km) and two-hour tours of around 2 miles (3 km).

Matera

Matera is one of Italy's most alluring towns, thanks to its extraordinary sassi, or cave dwellings—more than 3,000 houses and 150 cave churches that form the largest and most complex troglodyte city in the Mediterranean. A byword for extreme squalor and poverty until the 1950s, when their inhabitants were rehoused, they were awarded UNESCO World Heritage status in 1993 and today have been restored as homes, cafés, and galleries that have become some of southern Italy's foremost visitor attractions.

Matera occupies a lofty site on one of the typical gravine (ravines) that characterize the low hills of eastern Basilicata, the region west of Puglia, and is easily incorporated into a tour of trulli country. (If traveling independently, take a train from Bari; you'll need to walk or taxi from the Matera station to reach the sassi district.) Its origins date back at least 7,000 years, when humans took advantage of the area's easily excavated stone and inhabited the ravine's natural caves and early niche-cut dwellings.

You could easily spend a morning wandering the sassi in the lower district of the town—Sasso Barisano—being sure to venture into the still unrestored areas for a glimpse of how life might have been just a generation ago. But the Sasso Caveoso district on the ridge above is also a delight, a largely traffic-free labyrinth of unspoiled lanes full of picturesque medieval nooks and crannies. Be prepared to negotiate plenty of steps.

The **Sasso Caveoso** district boasts many of Matera's more than 45 **cave churches** (*chiese rupestri*), most of which were carved into the rock by monks between the 8th and 12th centuries. The 10th-century **Santa Lucia alle Malve** (*Via del Corso–Via la Vista, Matera, $ or $$ combined ticket with Santa Maria de Idris*) is distinguished by Byzantine frescoes from 1250. The 10th-century **Santa Maria de Idris** (*Via Madonna dell'Idris, Matera*) has medieval frescoes and is connected via a tunnel (also frescoed) to an earlier chapel, **San Giovanni** in Monterrone.

Farther Afield

Other options that are often included in tours from Bari are the towns of **Molfetta, Barletta,** and **Trani.** Each has a pretty historic core with churches in the distinctive Romanesque style typical of Puglia.

Inland from these towns is the **Castel del Monte,** a vast 13th-century fortress that sits in splendid isolation in open countryside. Distinguished by a mysterious obsession with the number eight, it was the only octagonal fortress among some 200 quadrilateral castles commissioned by Emperor Frederick II on his return from the Crusades. It is a World Heritage site.

Two other options require several hours' driving, leaving little time on a short trip for exploration or visits elsewhere. **Lecce,** 94 miles (150 km) southeast of Bari, is a large town rightly celebrated for its baroque architecture and Roman remains. About the same distance in the other direction is the **Gargano promontory,** the spur of the Italian "boot." Its hilly, wooded interior is a national park, and the fine coastline is dotted with charming small resorts; many visitors also come for the busy religious shrines in and around Monte Sant'Angelo. ∎

Castel del Monte
- ▲ 161 E4
- ✉ Andria
- ☎ 0833 569 997
- 🅂 $$
- casteldelmonte.beniculturali.it

Lecce
- ▲ 161 F3

Visitor Information
- ✉ Piazza Duomo 2, Lecce
- ☎ 0832 521 877
- 🕐 Closed 1:30 p.m.–3:30 p.m.

NEED TO KNOW

Port Logistics: Bari

Bari's **cruise terminal** (*aplevante.org*) is directly north and a short walk from the town's old historic hilltop center. Allow 2 hours to explore this old town. **Bari Centrale** railroad station (*trenitalia.com*) is 12 long city blocks south of the old center for connections to Trani (*1–3 hourly, journey time 32–46 min.*). Trains to Alberobello (*1–2 hourly, 90 min.*) run on the private **FSE line** (*fseonline.it*).

Bari is well placed for a wide-ranging tour of several sights. **Viator** (*tourguides.viator.com*) offers almost 40 local tours. Gianluca Guadagnino on Viator's site is a qualified and recommended guide. Matera and Alberobello can both be seen in the course of a day.

Venetian splendor, the magnificent ports of Split and Dubrovnik, and the glories of the Croatian and Balkan coasts

Venice &
the Adriatic

Introduction & Map   180–181

Venice   182–205

Feature: Building Venice   190–191

A San Marco & Dorsoduro Stroll   196–197

Feature: Gondolas   200

Need to Know: Venice   205

Split   206–207

Need to Know: Split   207

Dubrovnik   208–215

Dubrovnik Walking Tour   210–211

Need to Know: Dubrovnik   215

More Ports to Visit on the Adriatic   216–217

Restaurants   293–297

The canals of Venice teemed with more than 10,000 gondolas in the 16th century. Today, there remain but a few hundred.

Venice & the Adriatic

The Adriatic Sea has long been a crossroads in the Mediterranean, a meeting point of eastern, western, and middle European countries and cultures. History has bequeathed it a mixed hand, and the legacy of Greek, Roman, Byzantine, Venetian, Ottoman, Austro-Hungarian, Communist, Italian, Balkan, and other invaders and occupants has created a fascinating but also fractured heritage.

In the west, the Adriatic's dominant culture is Italian and its key player, past and present, is Venice, a city founded on maritime prowess and pioneering trade routes to the Orient. It is one of the world's most beautiful and singular cities, and an obvious target for visitors, but other historic cities on the Adriatic's eastern coast are also worthy of attention, not least Split and Dubrovnik in Croatia, both of which were longtime medieval vassals of Venice.

As Venice declined, the result of new trade routes to the Americas and the rise of the Ottoman Empire, so Split and Dubrovnik fell to new powers such as the Austro-Hungarian Empire. More recently, they became embroiled in the bitter upheavals that accompanied the breakup of the former

Yugoslavia in the 1990s. Both cities have bounced back, and both are superb ports of call, with small, self-contained historic quarters perfect for short visits. Both, however, are very popular: Expect crowds in high summer.

Much the same goes for Venice. Most visitors on a short trip to the city will be tempted to make for the obvious targets of Piazza San Marco (St. Mark's Square) and the Palazzo Ducale (Doge's Palace), but outside the winter months this is a very busy city indeed, and one whose crowded main attractions may leave you disenchanted.

More than 400 bridges span the countless waterways that weave through Venice.

But Venice is not just for tourists: There are squares where kids play soccer, where mothers sit to chat, where Venetians come to shop. There is also a tangle of quieter streets and alleys—beware of getting lost—along with superlative churches, galleries, and other sights many visitors ignore.

And there are strategies to cope. To get a sense of the city, take a water-bus ride on the Canal Grande, then walk as much as you can. Even on a short visit, make first for the city's periphery—to the quieter Castello and Cannaregio districts of the north, or the sleepy streets of Dorsoduro in the south—where you'll get a sense of Venice's more magical qualities before a head-on confrontation with the Basilica di San Marco (St. Mark's Basilica).

Adriatic Idylls

Leaving aside Venice and Dubrovnik, the Adriatic also offers some beautiful scenery, not least along much of the Croatian coast, which is a labyrinth of islands, bays, and inlets interspersed with forests, beaches, and mountains, as well as a succession of pretty and still virtually unknown smaller towns and villages. ∎

Venice

Venice, Italy, rarely disappoints. The city casts its magic spell year-round—whether you visit in the depths of winter, an icy mist spreading chill over the encircling lagoon, or in the shimmering, enervating heat of summer, when the canals, ancient churches, and endless palaces are dappled with the shifting light of the sun.

Venice's main corridor of transportation, the Canal Grande makes a large S-formation as it winds through the city.

NEED TO KNOW p. 205

Venice
 180 A4

Visitor Information

✉ Stazione Ferroviaria Santa Lucia (railroad station)

✉ Piazzale Roma

✉ Calle dell'Ascensione 71/f

☎ All visitor centers: 041 529 8711 or 041 529 8700

turismovenezia.it
visitmuve.it

Canal Grande

There is no more beautiful urban thoroughfare than the Canal Grande (Grand Canal), the broad waterway that makes a serpentine loop through the heart of Venice. Your first thought on arriving in the city should be to board one of the lumbering vaporetti, or water-buses, that ply its palace-lined length, providing an eye-opening first glimpse of the waterborne eccentricities of Venetian daily life.

To the Rialto: Board a boat at Piazzale Roma, signed for "San Marco" and/or "Lido SME" (see sidebar p. 205). The first church on your left beyond the

bridge by the railroad station is Santa Maria di Nazareth, better known as the **Scalzi,** designed in 1656 by Baldassare Longhena (1598–1682), the architect of the canal's Santa Maria della Salute church and several of its most prestigious palaces. Farther down on the left stands **San Geremia,** home to the prized relics of St. Lucy, a fourth-century martyr. On the opposite (south) bank, the arched **Fondaco dei Turchi,** now a natural history museum, was the headquarters between 1621 and 1838 of Turchi (Ottoman) merchants, while the plain 15th-century Deposito del Megio to its left served as an emergency grain store for use during famine or siege.

The **Palazzo Vendramin-Calergi,** one of the canal's most famous palaces, is now home to the Casinò. Another great palace lies a short way beyond, the **Ca' d'Oro** (see pp. 202–203), now a museum of medieval art. Almost opposite the Ca' d'Oro stands the neo-Gothic **Pescheria** (fish market), heralding the arrival of the Rialto, the city's ancient heart, and the unmistakable outlines of the 16th-century **Ponte di Rialto** (Rialto Bridge).

Beyond the Rialto, the 13th-century **Palazzo Loredan** and

Palazzo **Farsetti** on the left form Venice's town hall. The poet Lord Byron lodged close by, in one of four palaces owned by the Mocenigo family on the Volta del Canal, the canal's great bend. On the opposite bank, right on the bend, stands the **Ca' Rezzonico** (see p. 193), now devoted to a museum of Venice in the 18th century.

On the left, beyond the Ponte dell'Accademia, last of the canal's four bridges, stands the 15th-century **Palazzo Barbaro,** bought in 1885 by the Curtis family, a Boston dynasty whose guests included Claude Monet, John Singer Sargent, Cole Porter, and Henry James. The modern mosaics on the palace almost opposite mark the **Palazzo Barbarigo,** now owned by a glass company. A short way down on the same bank stands the truncated Palazzo Venier dei Leoni, where the **Collezione Peggy Guggenheim** (see pp. 195 & 198) is housed. Immediately beyond is the leaning **Palazzo Dario,** a charming-looking palace but one Venetians have long considered cursed. A glass company also owns the mosaic-fronted **Palazzo Salviati** two palaces down. Just beyond

Canal Grande

Map p. 183

1, 2

Single journey: $$

actv.it

NOTE: Vaporetto 1 stops at every landing stage on the Canal Grande; the faster 2 makes fewer stops.

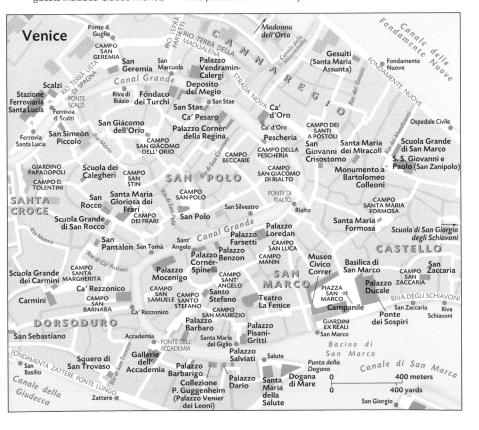

Crowds and pigeons flock to Piazza San Marco, Venice's cultural heart.

Piazza San Marco

 Map p. 183

1, 2, 4.1, 5.1, & other services to San Marco or San Zaccaria

the Santa Maria del Giglio landing stage on the right rises the immense church of **Santa Maria della Salute** (see p. 198). Soon afterward comes the first glimpse of the Palazzo Ducale and Piazza San Marco.

Piazza San Marco

"The most beautiful drawing room in Europe," said Napoleon of Piazza San Marco (St. Mark's Square), Venice's famous central square. In the heart of the San Marco district, it provides the setting not only for two of the city's foremost buildings—the Basilica di San Marco and Palazzo Ducale—but also for historic cafés, the Campanile, and the Museo Civico Correr.

The square's most distinctive smaller monuments are the two

columns near the waterfront, brought from the eastern Mediterranean in 1170. One is topped with the lion of St. Mark, the other with St. Theodore (one of Venice's patron saints), flanked by a creature of unknown significance. The area between the pillars was once a place of execution; Venetians still consider it an unlucky spot to walk.

To the west lies the **Zecca** (1545), the city's mint until 1870 and one of the few buildings in the city built entirely of stone as a precaution against fire. Alongside stands the **Libreria Sansoviniana** (1588), the state library.

To the left (north) of the basilica, look up at the **Torre dell'Orologio** (tel 848 082 000 or visit torreorologio.visitmuve.it for reservations & guided tours, $$$$), a clock tower built in 1499 whose Latin legend translates "I number only the happy hours." The two distinctive bronze figures are known as I Mori, or the Moors, after their dark patina.

Flanking the piazza on three sides are the **Procuratie,** the arcaded buildings that once served as offices for the upper tier of Venice's bureaucracy. Within part of these buildings is the **Museo Civico Correr,** whose exhibits offer a wonderful and often eccentric survey of Venice's long history.

INSIDER TIP:

Follow in the footsteps of the locals and grab a well-priced sandwich and beer at tiny Mio (Frezzeria 1176). It's only a one-minute walk from Piazza San Marco's southwest corner.

—SHEILA F. BUCKMASTER
National Geographic Traveler
magazine editor at large

Campanile: Venice's tallest building, at 323 feet (98.5 m), provides one of Europe's most entrancing viewpoints, but when it was built around 912, it had three different purposes: to act as bell tower for the basilica, to provide a lookout for the harbor below, and to serve as a

lighthouse for ships at sea. Over the centuries it received all manner of minor alterations, none of them, unfortunately, directed at the foundations—which were barely 65 feet (20 m) deep.

Lashed by wind and rain, corroded by salt water, and struck repeatedly by lightning, the tower became ever weaker. When it finally collapsed on July 14, 1902, the only wonder was that it had not crumbled earlier. Within hours the city council vowed to rebuild the tower *dov'era e com'era* (where it was and how it was). The pledge was realized in 1912, when a new tower, identical but for the fact it was 600 tons lighter and better supported, was inaugurated.

Basilica di San Marco: It is hard to imagine another building in western Europe more richly embellished with the architectural and artistic legacy of the centuries than the Basilica di San Marco (St. Mark's Basilica), on the piazza's east side. A magnificent hybrid, it served for almost a thousand years as the tomb of St. Mark (the Venetians stole the saint's relics from Egypt in 828), the private chapel of the doges (Venice's rulers), and the spiritual fulcrum and ultimate symbol of the power, authority, and continuity of the Venetian state.

The first resting place for St. Mark was a modest chapel within the Palazzo Ducale, a sanctuary replaced in 832, and again in 978. In 1063 Doge Domenico Contarini instigated

Museo Civico Correr
- **Map p. 183
- Procuratie Nuove-Ala Napoleonica, Piazza San Marco, San Marco
- ☎ 848 082 000
- $ Combined ticket with Palazzo Ducale: $$$$$

correr.visitmuve.it

Campanile
- **Map p. 183
- Piazza San Marco, San Marco
- ☎ 041 522 4064
- $ $$$

NOTE: Arrive early to avoid lines. Ascent is by elevator.

Basilica di San Marco
- **Map p. 183
- Piazza San Marco, San Marco
- ☎ 041 522 5697 or 041 270 8311; reservations: online at venetoinside.com
- Closed Sun. until 2 p.m.
- $ Sanctuary: $; treasury: $; museum: $$
- 1, 2, & services to San Zaccaria

basilicasanmarco.it

NOTE: Large bags are not permitted in the basilica.

a fourth building, demanding a church that would be "the most beautiful ever seen." Work on this nonpareil culminated in 1094, when the new basilica was consecrated. This is more or less the building you see today, although in 1094 it had yet to acquire its array of artistic and architectural embellishment. Work on the mosaics began around 1100, but the bulk of the ornamentation appeared in 1204, much of it looted by the Venetians from Constantinople during the Fourth Crusade.

The basilica has three facades: Start your visit beneath the right (south) facade, the side facing the water, where the outline of what was once the basilica's main entrance can still be seen.

The two columns against this facade, fifth-century Syrian works, came either from Constantinople or from Acre (in present-day Israel), where the Venetians defeated a Genoese force in 1256. The smaller column stump nearby, the **Pietra del Bando,** probably hails from Acre and was

Baldacchino

Pala d'Oro

Porta dei Fiori

Basilica di San Marco

Rood screen

used to proclaim state decrees; it was also used to display the heads of executed criminals. High on the facade is a small mosaic Madonna flanked by ever burning oil lamps, probably originally lit to mark executions, when the condemned would turn to the Madonna with the cry of "Salve Regina."

Many of the apparent treasures on the main facade are copies, most notably the famous **bronze horses** (the originals are inside) and the vast majority of the mosaics, only one of which is original: the "Translation of the Body of St. Mark to the Basilica" (1260–1270), above the door on the extreme left. The facade's greatest works are the 13th-century **Romanesque carvings** above the central (third) portal.

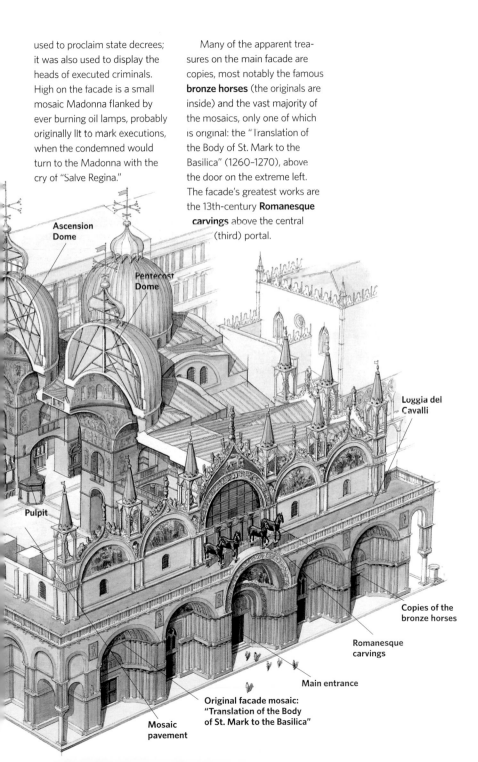

Ascension Dome

Pentecost Dome

Loggia del Cavalli

Pulpit

Copies of the bronze horses

Romanesque carvings

Main entrance

Original facade mosaic: "Translation of the Body of St. Mark to the Basilica"

Mosaic pavement

Mosaics—some more than 900 years old—cover almost every surface of the basilica's interior.

or late in the afternoon. And note that while admission is free to the main interior space, you will need separate tickets to view most of the basilica's real treasures.

Almost every available surface of the basilica— some 43,000 square feet (4,000 sq m) in all—is blanketed with golden-hued **mosaics,** an artistic medium, like the church's Greek cross plan, that was adopted from the Byzantine tradition. The earliest date from around 1100, but additions were still being made 700 years later. Down the centuries, the leading artists of their day, notably Titian, Tintoretto, and Veronese, often contributed designs for new panels. Mosaics in the basilica's interior largely portray episodes from the New Testament, while those in the narthex, or vestibule, the first area you come to inside the basilica's main door, depict scenes from the Old Testament.

Stairs from the narthex lead to the **Loggia dei Cavalli,** an external balcony that is home to the basilica's famous **bronze horses,** brought from Constantinople in 1204—or rather copies of these horses, as the originals are now kept in the adjoining *museo,* or Galleria Marciano. Part of a quadriga, or four-horsed chariot team, the gilded creatures are the only such artifact to have survived from classical antiquity, although whether they are of Greek (fourth century B.C.) or Roman (third century A.D.) provenance is uncertain.

Sights on the oft-ignored north facade include the **Porta dei Fiori,** or Door of Flowers, whose arches enclose a charming nativity scene. Alongside is the tomb of Daniele Manin (1804-1857), leader of a heroic but unsuccessful 19th-century uprising against the Austrians.

Crowds and services within the basilica are such that you can rarely wander at will or choose which of the many treasures you wish to see. Aim to arrive early in the morning

The basilica's next most compelling sight is the area behind the high altar—the sanctuary—and its monumental **Pala d'Oro** (Screen of Gold). This altarpiece lies to the rear of the altar, reputed final resting place of St. Mark, although many claim the saint's relics were destroyed in a fire in 976. The Pala, begun in 976, is Europe's greatest piece of medieval gold and silverware, its dazzling frontage adorned with 15 rubies, 100 amethysts, 300 sapphires, 300 emeralds, 400 garnets, 1,300 pearls, and some 200 other stones.

Booty from the Fourth Crusade makes up much of the collection in the basilica's *tesoro,* or treasury, located off the transept midway down the church's right (south) side. Comprising mostly religious and other early Byzantine silverware, the collection is the finest of its kind in Europe, and would have been finer still—some 55 gold and silver ingots were all that remained once Napoleon had melted down the cream of the collection. Note the large throne by the turnstile, the so-called **Throne of St. Mark,** carved in Alexandria and given to one of the lagoon's earliest religious rulers in 690.

Palazzo Ducale: The Palazzo Ducale (Doge's Palace), next door to the Basilica di San Marco, was home for almost a thousand years not only to Venice's doges, secret police, and principal law courts but also to its prisons, torture chambers, and many administrative institutions.

It is one of the world's finest Gothic buildings, with an exterior that beautifully mingles columns, quatrefoils, and intricately patterned marbles. The interior is a labyrinth of gilt- and painting-smothered rooms, as well as a series of dark and intimidating dungeons.

The first palace, a fortress-like structure, was built in 814, but it succumbed to fires in 976 and 1106. The present building was begun in 1314, when work started on a great hall for the Maggior Consiglio, the Republic's parliamentary lower house. Three years after this was completed, in 1422, remaining parts of the older palazzo were razed to make way for the palace's present main facade. Thereafter, the interior was constantly modified as the machinery of government grew, the palace attaining more or less its present shape in 1550.

(continued on p. 192)

Caffè Florian

Florian is expensive, certainly, and often busy, but it's worth treating yourself at least once to enjoy Venice's oldest and most opulent café—its beautiful old interior has barely altered since it opened for business in 1720. In that time it has served coffee, hot chocolate, and more to the likes of Casanova, Charles Dickens, and Marcel Proust. Visit in the evening or in winter, if possible, when it is less busy *(Piazza San Marco 56–59, tel 041 520 5641, caffeflorian.com, closed Wed. in winter).*

Palazzo Ducale

🅰 Map p. 183

✉ Porta del Frumento-Piazzetta San Marco, San Marco

☎ 848 820000

$ Combined ticket with Museo Civico Correr: $$$$$. Guided tours (Itinerari Segreti): $$

🚤 1, 2, & other services to San Zaccaria

palazzoducale .visitmuve.it

Building Venice

Venice may appear to float on the water, but that's exactly what its inhabitants didn't want. The ingenuity with which the city has been constructed is almost more impressive than its charm. Venice is built on about a hundred small muddy islets, threaded with myriad canals, and the greatest challenge to the early settlers was to create a firm foundation that would reliably support the weight of the structures.

Venice's canals require constant maintenance in order to keep the city above water.

There were two methods for preparing the ground, both involving wooden piles. From the 15th century onward, construction methods utilized piles that were about 13 feet (4 m) long and rounded, measuring about 8 inches (20 cm) in diameter, and were made of oak, bay oak, or larch. In the rare cases where there was a hard clay substratum under a building site, the piles would be driven down until they rested firmly on it. More commonly, a bulkhead or caisson would first be constructed around the area, then the land would be drained, and finally the piles would be "planted," as they say, working from the outside toward the center, with about nine piles per square yard. The piles were pounded by hand (even up until the early years of the 20th century), with several

men at a time holding on to a chunk of wood with which they pounded the pile slowly downward, often chanting as they went to set the rhythm. When the piles would go no deeper, and they were all level across the top, heavy beams were laid across them, which were in turn covered by two layers of larchwood strips filled in with a reinforced cement aggregate that contained pieces of stone or brick. This is still a common form of Venetian flooring and can be seen in many palaces.

Prior to the 15th century, the early Venetians had used basically the same approach, but their results were somewhat less reliable because the piles were of alder, and were only about a yard (meter) long. The floor was constructed only from a layer of larch or elm.

Venetian Know-How

With all this in mind, it becomes clear that Venetian architects, especially those of the Byzantine and Gothic eras, had many stratagems for minimizing the weight of a building. The use of wood, large windows, slender columns, and brick covered by only slim slabs (rather than blocks) of stone all helped. It also goes some way to explaining why some bell towers have developed a list, or have even collapsed, the most recent being the Campanile of San Marco itself, which fell in 1902 (see p. 185).

Ancient piles pulled out during a restoration have been found in perfect condition. Unlike the piles that mark canals, which are exposed to damaging cycles of wet and dry, the submerged piles have been completely protected for centuries by the mud.

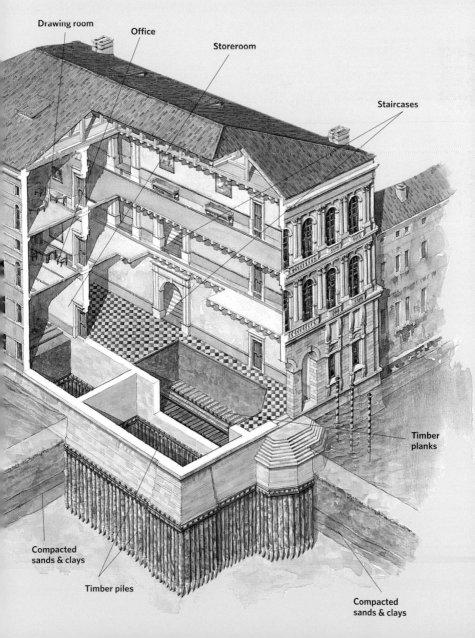

Drawing room

Office

Storeroom

Staircases

Timber planks

Compacted sands & clays

Timber piles

Compacted sands & clays

Start your visit by walking to the **Ponte della Paglia,** at the far end of the palace's waterfront facade. From this little bridge, you can admire the **Ponte dei Sospiri** (1600), or Bridge of Sighs, reputedly named after the sighs of condemned men being led from the palace to the city's prisons. Then look up to the left to admire "The Drunkenness of Noah," one

INSIDER TIP:

While on a tour of the Palazzo Ducale, don't miss the vivid, artistic graffiti left behind by unfortunates on the walls of the prisons.

—PATRICIA DANIELS
National Geographic contributor

of three statues adorning three corners of the palace—the other two represent "Adam and Eve" and "The Judgment of Solomon." Walking back along the facade, note the statue of "Justice" (1579) above the central window. The capitals of the pillars below are carved with allegories of the vices and virtues.

Around the corner, on the palace's other principal facade, look up to the loggia and its two anomalous red columns, reputedly stained by the blood of the tortured criminals who were hung here before execution.

Left of the palace's ornate doorway, the **Porta della Carta** (1443), stand the famous **Tetrarchs,** a group

of maroon-colored porphyry knights, probably fourth-century statues representing the emperor Diocletian and three co-rulers of the Roman Empire.

Now enter the palace. In the courtyard is the **Scala dei Giganti** (1501), or Giants' Staircase, named after sculptor Jacopo Sansovino's statues of Mars and Neptune (1567), emblems of Venice's command of land and sea respectively. Climb Sansovino's **Scala d'Oro** (1550), or Golden Staircase, to the start of an itinerary through the palace's succession of magnificently decorated rooms.

The first of these, the **Sala dell'Anticollegio,** acted as an anteroom for visiting dignitaries, who, while awaiting an audience, could admire paintings by Tintoretto and Veronese. The same painters decorated the **Sala del Collegio,** home to the Collegio, Venice's ruling council, and the Signoria, the Collegio's more powerful inner sanctum.

Highlights among the rooms that follow include the gilt-laden **Sala del Senato** and the **Sala del Consiglio dei Dieci,** the latter a meeting place for the Council of Ten, magistrates and overseers of Venice's feared secret police.

The **Sala della Bussola** next door contains a Bocca di Leone (Lion's Mouth), a form of mailbox into which citizens could drop accusations against fellow Venetians. The room's rear door led to a small inner courtroom, and from thence to the torture chamber and prisons.

The palace's star turn is

the immense **Sala del Maggior Consiglio,** dominated by Tintoretto's immense "Paradiso" (1592). The old prisons follow, reached via the Bridge of Sighs, strikingly dark and somber after the preceding splendor.

To see more than just the public rooms, take one of the Itinerari Segreti, the palace's guided tours. Tickets must be booked 48 hours in advance, though you can ask at the box office if any places remain on that day's tours.

Dorsoduro

Wedged between the Canal Grande and Canale della Giudecca, Dorsoduro—one of Venice's six *sestieri* (districts) —holds many attractions, notably a slew of art in the Ca' Rezzonico, Gallerie dell'Accademia, and Santa Maria della Salute.

Ca' Rezzonico: Venice
has enjoyed many a colorful period, but few have been as striking as the decadent years of its 18th-century dotage, a period when, according to one popular adage, the "Venetians did not taste their pleasures but swallowed them whole." The Ca' Rezzonico, or Museo del Settecento Veneziano, on the Canal Grande, is devoted to the period, its displays and interior fashioned to reflect the artistic and social tastes of the city during its often frivolous decline.

Highlights include the magnificent ballroom; the

Sala dell'Allegoria Nuziale, with 18th-century ceiling frescoes by Giovanni Battista Tiepolo (1696–1770); rooms adorned with portraits by Rosalba Carriera, Flemish tapestries, and beautiful lacquerwork furniture; and, In the art gallery, Francesco Guardi and Pietro Longhi's fascinating snapshots of Venetian daily life and Giandomenico Tiepolo's satirical frescoes (1793–1797), a sequence moved here from the artist's country villa.

Ca' Rezzonico

- 🅰 Map p. 183
- ✉ Fondamenta Rezzonico, Dorsoduro 3316
- ☎ 041 241 0100
- 🕐 Closed Tues.
- 💲 $$$
- 🚋 1 to Ca' Rezzonico

carezzonico.visit muve.it

Glittering chandeliers and beautifully decorated ceilings are a feast for the eyes in the Ca' Rezzonico.

Gallerie dell'Accademia:
Walking east along the Canal Grande, you'll soon come to where some of Venice's greatest works of art are gathered in a single gallery, the Gallerie dell'Accademia. Many of the famous paintings are in Rooms 1–5, in Rooms 10 and 11, and amid the two *storie,* or narrative fresco cycles, that provide the Accademia's grand finale.

The star turn in the splendid opening room is the **"Coronation**

Gallerie dell'Accademia
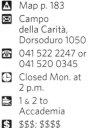
- 🅰 Map p. 183
- ✉ Campo della Carità, Dorsoduro 1050
- ☎ 041 522 2247 or 041 520 0345
- 🕐 Closed Mon. at 2 p.m.
- 🚋 1 & 2 to Accademia
- 💲 $$$; $$$$ during exhibitions

gallerieaccademia.org

of the Virgin" (1365), by Paolo Veneziano. One of the city's first great painters, Veneziano played a prominent role in transforming Venice's previous artistic preoccupation with mosaic into a preference for painting.

Moving to Room 2, you skip a century to find yourself among early Renaissance masterpieces: Giovanni Bellini (1435–1516), perhaps the most sublime of all Venetian painters, is represented by the

INSIDER TIP:

To find warmth on a cold sunny day after visiting the Accademia, weave through the narrow streets for about three minutes to the Zattere, the wide promenade on the Canal della Giudecca.

—SHEILA F. BUCKMASTER
National Geographic Traveler
magazine editor at large

"Madonna and Saints" (1485), while another big name, Vittore Carpaccio (ca 1460–1526), makes an early appearance with the **"Presentation of Jesus in the Temple"** and the graphic **"Ten Thousand Martyrs of Mount Ararat."** The latter alludes to the legend of 10,000 defeated Roman soldiers martyred by Armenian rebels.

Rooms 4 and 5 contain some of the Accademia's most notable paintings. Among them is Giorgione's **"The Tempest"** (1500), a work so enigmatic that no one has been able to explain its meaning (if one exists). Nearby is Giorgione's **"Col Tempo,"** a more easily understood allegory of old age and passing time. Piero della Francesca (1416–1492), an equally enigmatic painter, is represented by a curious **"St. Jerome,"** arranged alongside an almost indecent number of paintings by Giovanni Bellini— a painter heavily influenced by Piero—the most beguiling of which is the **"Madonna and Child with Saints."**

It is hard to miss Paolo Veronese's colossal **"Supper in the House of Levi"** (1573) in Room 10. It was originally intended as a depiction of the Last Supper, but Veronese (1528–1588) was forced to change the painting's title—but not its content—when the Inquisition objected to its inappropriate portrayal of what it termed "buffoons, drunkards, Germans, dwarfs, and similar indecencies." Nearby is Titian's **"Pietà"** (1576), a masterpiece painted by the artist when he was more than 90 years old: The red-cloaked figure to the right of Christ is probably a self-portrait.

The **"Miracles of the True Cross"** (1494–1510) in Room 20 is an eight-painting sequence created by a variety of artists for the city's Scuola Grande di San Giovanni Evangelista. Each work

Venetian Vocabulary

Understanding some of the words you'll encounter time and again on the streets of Venice will add to your understanding and enjoyment of the city. *Campo,* for example, is the name given to a square, from the Italian for "field"—note that Venice has only one "piazza," Piazza San Marco. A small square is a *campiello* or *campazzo,* and a courtyard or dead-end alley is a *corte. Rio* means "canal," *rio terà* a canal that has been filled in. A *calle* is a street, *ruga* an important street or one lined with stores, and a *fondamenta* or *riva* (bank) is a wide street running along a canal where a boat can dock. *Salizada* refers to a paved street (which were once rare), and a *ramo*—from the word for "branch"—is a short alley or the extension of another street. A *sotoportego* is an arcade or arched passage under a building.

ostensibly portrays a miracle associated with a fragment of the cross from the Crucifixion owned by the *scuola* (a type of confraternity), although much of the paintings' charm derives from the cycle's wonderful narrative detail. Gentile Bellini's **"Procession of the Holy Relic,"** for example, offers a marvelous portrait of Piazza San Marco as it appeared in 1496.

Another painting cycle, with similar narrative appeal, fills Room 21, but this time the nine-work sequence is by a single artist, Carpaccio, and the theme is the life and grisly **death of St. Ursula.** Daughter of a Breton king, Ursula promised to marry an English prince on condition he accompany her and a train of 11,000 virgins on a pilgrimage to Rome. Carpaccio portrays a variety of scenes, often compressing several events into a single frame. Each is crammed with the sort of detail for which Carpaccio is famous (his little dog was a favored motif). Few scenes are as action-packed as the penultimate panel, which combines the martyrdom of the saint and her followers in Cologne—massacred by the Huns then besieging the city— and her subsequent funeral.

Collezione Peggy Guggen-heim: A few minute's walk east of the Gallerie dell'Accademia is more art, in the Collezione Peggy Guggenheim. Peggy Guggenheim adored Venice and Venice adored her in turn, making the American-born heiress an honorary citizen of the city she adopted as her own in 1949. Born in 1898, she moved to Europe in 1921, where she became a collector of the finest avant-garde art of her day. Much of her collection is now on show in the Palazzo Venier dei Leoni.

The **palace gardens,** on the banks of the Canal Grande, are a delight, thanks to their scattered works of sculpture, including pieces by Paolozzi, Giacometti, and Henry Moore. The 18th-century palace was never completed—hence its nickname, the "Non finito," the Unfinished.

Most broad movements within 20th-century art are *(continued on p. 198)*

Collezione Peggy Guggenheim

- Map p. 183
- Fondamenta Venier dei Leoni, Dorsoduro 701
- 041 240 5411
- Closed Tues.
- $$$
- 1 & 2 to Accademia or Salute

guggenheim-venice.it

A San Marco & Dorsoduro Stroll

This walk runs west from Piazza San Marco through the heart of Venice, crossing the Accademia Bridge to explore the Dorsoduro district before reaching the Scuola Grande dei Carmini, headquarters of the Carmelite confraternity.

Leaving **Piazza San Marco ❶** (see pp. 184–193), walk past the **Palazzo Ducale** (see pp. 189 & 192–193) to the waterfront and bear right. Go past the Giardini ex Reali and turn right up Calle del Ridotto to the church of **San Moisè,** noted for its baroque facade created by Alessandro Tremignon in 1668. Cross the bridge over the Rio di San Moisè to reach shop-lined Calle Larga XXII Marzo. Head west, making a short detour north on Calle delle Veste to **Teatro La Fenice,**

NOT TO BE MISSED:

Santo Stefano • Collezione Peggy Guggenheim • Santa Maria della Salute

Venice's opera house, to Campo Santa Maria Zobenigo, where **Santa Maria del Giglio** stands, crammed with a bizarre medley of saintly relics. Continue west through Campo San Maurizio to Campo Santo Stefano.

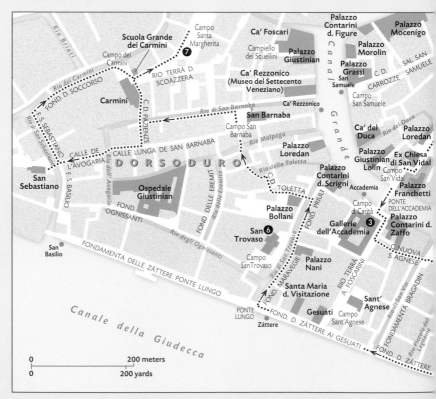

Leave this square after seeing the church of **Santo Stefano ❷** *(closed Sun., $),* with its fine ceiling and calm interior. Campo San Vidal leads from the square's southern flank to the **Ponte dell'Accademia,** a bridge over the Canal Grande offering mesmerizing views.

Follow the street Rio Terà A. Foscarini to the left of the **Gallerie dell'Accademia ❸** (see pp. 193–195), then bear left on Calle Nuova Sant'Agnese. Continue due east, past the **Collezione Peggy Guggenheim ❹** (see pp. 195 & 198), to emerge at **Santa Maria della Salute ❺** (see p. 198). Follow the waterfront promenade around the Punta della Dogana and the Zattere. Turn north on Fondamenta Maravegie along the Rio di San Trovaso canal. Note the *squero* (gondola boatyard) across the canal in front of the church of **San Trovaso ❻** *(closed Sun. & a.m.).*

Cross the second bridge and follow Calle della Toletta to emerge in Campo San Barnaba. Follow the canal left from the top of the square. Cross the bridge before the canal bends left and take Calle de le Pazienze north to the church of the **Carmini** *(closed Sun. & a.m.),* which has paintings by Lorenzo Lotto and Cima da Conegliano. Opposite stands the **Scuola Grande dei Carmini** *(tel 041 528 9420, scuolagrandecarmini.it, $$),* noted for Tiepolo's 18th-century ceiling frescoes.

A loop west on Calle de le Pazienza, Calle Lunga de San Barnaba, and Calle de l'Avogaria takes you to **San Sebastiano** *(closed Sun., $),* with paintings by Veronese. Continue north on Fondamenta San Sebastiano and east on Fondamenta del Soccorso, past the Carmini, to reach **Campo Santa Margherita ❼**, one of Venice's prettiest piazzas.

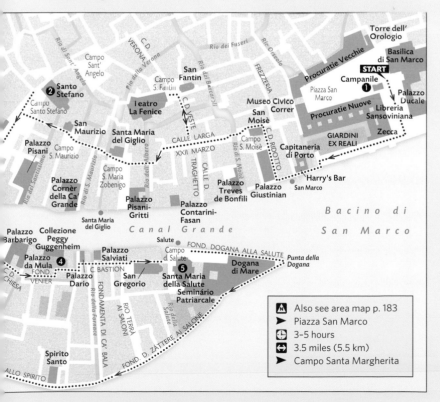

The Collezione Peggy Guggenheim boasts an impressive collection of 20th-century art.

Santa Maria della Salute

Map p. 183

✉ Campo della Salute, Dorsoduro 1

☎ 041 274 3928

🕐 Closed 12 p.m.–3 p.m.

🚤 1 to Salute

seminariovenezia.it

represented. Thus Picasso and Braque fly the flag for cubism, Francis Bacon for English modernism, and Mondrian, Malevich, and Pevsner for constructivism. Among the surrealists, one of Guggenheim's chief passions, the works of Dalí, Max Ernst, and Magritte stand out, as do those of Americans such as Pollock, Willem de Kooning, and Rothko.

Santa Maria della Salute:

Remove the church of Santa Maria della Salute from Venice and you would lose one of the city's most distinctive landmarks. Perched at the mouth of the Canal Grande, just minutes from the Collezione Peggy Guggenheim, the great white-domed edifice has occupied a pivotal point on the Venetian skyline for more than 350 years.

Santa Maria was built in 1631 to fulfill a pledge to create a church in honor of the Virgin should she deliver Venice from a plague that had claimed more than 45,000 of the city's population. It was christened the Salute, meaning both "health" and "salvation" in Italian.

The impact of the interior is as great as that of the exterior, with a beautiful marble pavement at your feet and a soaring dome above. The high altar features the "Virgin Casting Out the Plague" (1670): The figure on the Virgin's left symbolizes Venice, the figure to the right the banished plague. Other highlights include major works by Titian and Tintoretto.

San Polo

San Polo, Venice's smallest district, is well known for its churches—chief among them Santa Maria Gloriosa dei Frari, second only to the Basilica di San Marco in terms of importance—and its ornately decorated small palaces and other buildings.

Santa Maria Gloriosa dei Frari: Begun around 1250, this colossal Gothic church was created for the Franciscans, from whom it takes its colloquial name, the Frari, a corruption of *frati*, meaning "friars." It boasts much sculpture and three of Italy's greatest Renaissance paintings.

The first of these, Titian's gargantuan **"Assumption"** (1518), dominates the church from its position above the high altar. Everything in the Frari contrives to focus attention on the work, most notably the 124-stall wooden choir (1468)—itself a masterpiece—whose arched entrance frames the painting from the church's rear.

The Frari's second great painting could hardly be more different. **Giovanni Bellini's triptych** (1488) in the sacristy is the essence of meditative calm. It portrays the Madonna and Child between Sts. Peter, Nicholas, Mark, and Benedict, the namesakes of those who commissioned it—Pietro Pesaro and his sons Niccolò, Marco, and Benedetto.

The Frari's third major painting is Titian's **"Madonna di Ca' Pesaro"** (1526). Commissioned by Iacopo Pesaro, who lies in a tomb to the right, the work contains several portraits of the Pesaro family. The most obvious is Iacopo's nephew and heir, Lunardo, the small boy who stares out at the onlooker. Pesaro was a bishop and admiral, and, in 1502, led a campaign against the Turks on the prompting of the Borgia pope, Alexander VI. This accounts for the Borgia and Pesaro coats of arms on the red banner and the turbaned Turk and slave on the left being led toward St. Peter, symbolizing their conversion and the Christian impulse behind Iacopo's campaign.

There is no mistaking the huge white **marble pyramid** created in honor of Antonio Canova (1827). All that remains of the noted neoclassical sculptor within it, however, is his heart, the rest of his remains having been removed to his birthplace in Veneto. To the right of Canova's pyramid stands the extraordinary **monument to Doge Giovanni Pesaro** (died 1659), a kitschy but oddly beguiling tomb.

Santa Maria Gloriosa dei Frari

 Map p. 183

✉ Campo dei Frari, San Polo 3072

☎ 041 275 0462 or 041 272 8611

🕐 Closed Sun. until 1 p.m.

💲 $

⛴ 1 & 2 to San Tomà

basilicadeifrari.it
chorusvenezia.org

Dogana di Mare

The Dogana di Mare, Venice's beautiful former customhouse, sits on the Punta della Dogana, the finger of land at the point where the Canal Grande and Canale della Giudecca meet. After a couple decades of sitting vacant, it reopened in 2009, having been beautifully restored by world-renowned Japanese architect Tadao Ando as an exhibition space—Palazzo Grassi–François Pinault Foundation *(Punta della Dogana, Dorsoduro 2, tel 199 139 139, palazzograssi.it, vaporetto 1 to Salute, $$$$$)*—for the collection of contemporary art belonging to François Pinault, the building's co-owner and benefactor. The works exhibited change from time to time, but around a hundred pieces are generally on view, including most of the big names of modern art, among them Cy Twombly, Jeff Koons, Cindy Sherman, Maurizio Cattelan, and Luc Tuymans.

Gondolas

Dark, silent, and oddly sinister, the gondola, for all its romantic allure, is an equivocal vessel. Nothing summons Venice so swiftly to mind as the gondola's sleek shape and its easy gliding motion along mirror-smooth canals. Yet few objects so emblematic of a city are so mysterious in their origins, so rigid in their present-day appearance, or so convoluted in their evolution over the centuries.

A couple rides in the world's most romantic vessel through the world's most romantic city.

Gondolas today are remarkably uniform. All weigh around 1,500 pounds (700 kg), have 280 components, and employ eight different types of wood—lime, larch, oak, fir, cherry, walnut, elm, and mahogany. All have an oar—made from beech—and a *forcola,* or carved oarlock, each of which is custom-made to suit individual gondoliers and allows the oar to be manhandled in eight distinct maneuvers. All are 35.5 feet (exactly 10.87 m) long and 4.5 feet wide (exactly 1.42 m), and all have one side 10 inches (24 cm) longer than the other. This final feature, oddly enough, was one of the last in the boat's evolutionary process. Added by a boatyard during the 19th century to compensate for the weight of the gondolier, the imbalance lends the gondola its distinctive lean and lopsided appearance.

Other refinements are much older. Some scholars say the vessel dates back to 697. Most agree on a first documentary reference

in 1094, when the word appears in part of a decree regulating boats in the lagoon. The name is a matter of debate—some claim Maltese or Turkish origins, others that it derives from the Greek for "cup" or "mussel." The most macabre theory links the name to classical mythology and the ferry used by Charon to carry the dead to the underworld.

An Icon Takes Shape

In reality the gondola's evolution was gradual. The lagoon's shallows and mud-flats required a shallow-drafted vessel. In the 13th century the requisite boat had 12 oars; by the 15th century the "gondola" had shrunk in size but acquired a *felza,* or cabin. By 1562 it had accumulated such a wealth of decoration that a law banning ostentation of almost any kind was introduced. Henceforth, gondolas became a uniform black, while their exteriors were restricted to just three decorative flourishes—a curly tail, a pair of sea horses, and a multipronged *ferro,* or prow.

The origin and symbolism of the prow are even more contentious than the gondola's origins. Some *ferri* have five prongs, some six—emblematic perhaps of Venice's six districts. The single prong facing aft is described alternatively as a symbol for the Palazzo Ducale, the Giudecca, Cyprus (part of Venice's former empire), or Piazza San Marco. The broad-edged "blade" above may represent the sea, a lily, a doge's hat, a Venetian halberd, or the Rialto Bridge. And the ferro was inspired by Roman galleys, the funerary barges of ancient Egypt, or a judicial axe.

Gondola Rides

Venice's cheapest gondola rides involve the *traghetti* (ferries) that ply the Grand Canal at regular intervals. (A Venetian stands up, but a *foresto*, or outsider, usually finds it safer to sit.) Tariffs are set for the "genuine" gondola excursions. You pay more between 8 p.m. and 8 a.m., and additional rates apply for every 25 minutes over the standard 50-minute ride.

Musical entertainment also costs more. In practice, gondoliers are open to negotiation—you may want to follow a particular route, for example—but always confirm the price and trip length before setting out. Prices are per boat (not per person), up to a five-passenger limit. To avoid rip-offs, consult visitor centers for rates and locations of official stands.

Three tombs occupy the end wall of the south transept: Paolo Savelli was a Roman *condottiere*, or mercenary, who died of the plague in 1405 while leading Venice's army against Padua. Benedetto Pesaro was a Venetian admiral who died in 1503 in Corfu, hence the reliefs of ships and naval fortresses adorning his tomb. The pretty tomb (1437) of Beato Pacifico, a religious figure, is a rare Florentine work.

Scuola Grande di San Rocco:

The Scuola Grande di San Rocco, behind Santa Maria Gloriosa dei Friari, was founded in 1478 in honor of San Rocco (St. Roch), a French-born saint widely invoked against infectious diseases. These credentials made him a prime candidate for veneration in plague-battered Venice and the obvious inspiration for an institution devoted to healing the sick, hence the large sum paid by the scuola to bring his relics from Germany to Venice in 1485.

In 1564 Tintoretto won a commission to decorate the **Sala dell'Albergo,** beginning an association with San Rocco that would last 25 years and produce 54 extraordinary paintings. To follow Tintoretto's progress through the scuola, make first for this room, a small annex on the first floor. Decorated between 1564 and 1567, it features the ceiling painting of "St. Roch in Glory"—for which he won the commission—and his vast "Crucifixion" (1565), which is widely considered one of the finest paintings in Italy.

The rest of the upper floor, the **Sala Superiore,** features the main body of Tintoretto's work (1575-1581). The artist began his labors on the ceiling, where a multitude of paintings depict episodes from the Old Testament. All were selected to draw some parallel with the scuola's humanitarian aims—thus the relevance of such scenes as "The Feeding of the Five Thousand" or "Christ's Healing of the Paralytic."

The ten wall paintings deal with episodes from the New Testament, their volatile composition, unworldly coloring, and generally iconoclastic approach making them some of the city's

Scuola Grande di San Rocco

- Map p. 183
- Campo San Rocco, San Polo 3052
- 041 523 4864 or 041 524 2820
- $$$
- 1 & 2 to San Tomà

scuolagrandesan rocco.it

Ca' d'Oro

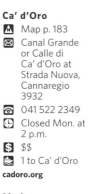

Map p. 183

Canal Grande
or Calle di
Ca' d'Oro at
Strada Nuova,
Cannaregio
3932

041 522 2349

Closed Mon. at
2 p.m.

$$

1 to Ca' d'Oro

cadoro.org

Madonna dell'Orto

Map p. 183

Campo
Madonna
dell'Orto,
Cannaregio
2372-2626

041 719 933

Closed Sun. a.m.

$

4.1, 4.2, 5.1, &
5.2 to Madonna
dell'Orto

chorusvenezia.org

most striking works of art. Don't miss the wonderful collection of 17th-century wooden carvings around the walls. The two most famous are the "Painter," a caricature of Tintoretto, complete with brushes (near the altar), and "Curiosity," a macabre, spy-like figure in cocked hat, with one sinister eye peering over his cloak (left and below Tintoretto's "Resurrection").

Eight huge canvases (1583–1587) in the **Sala Terrena** (lower hall) pick up from the New Testament scenes upstairs. The painter's invention here is equally breathtaking, notably in the "Annunciation," where the Virgin's home is a chaos of splintered wood and shattered brick, her expression one of startled disbelief as the angel Gabriel descends from the heavens with a cohort of dive-bombing cherubs.

Cannaregio

Cannaregio is mostly a quiet, peaceful residential neighborhood, worth a wander for a sense of everyday Venetian life. Notable sights are the Ca' d'Oro, a sumptuous palace now housing an art museum; and the churches of Santa Maria dei Miracoli and Madonna dell'Orto.

Ca' d'Oro: The Ca' d'Oro (House of Gold), on the Canal Grande, takes it name from the veneer of gilt and other precious materials that once adorned its facade. Begun in its present guise in 1420, the

palace endured a succession of lackadaisical owners and clumsy restorations before being bequeathed to the state in 1927. The interior now houses the Galleria Franchetti.

The gallery's works of art are not numerous, although they are often exquisite, none more so than the first floor's pictorial masterpiece, Mantegna's **"St. Sebastian"** (1506). As a saint invoked against disease, Sebastian was a popular pictorial subject in plague-ridden Venice.

INSIDER TIP:

Don't miss the Ghetto area in the Cannaregio district, near the Santa Lucia train station, with its unique atmosphere, its unusual tall buildings, and historic synagogues.

—FEDERICA ROMAGNOLI
National Geographic contributor

Other highlights include the 15th-century "Bust Of Young Couple" by Tullio Lombardo, six 15th-century bronze reliefs by Andrea Briosco (also known as Andrea Riccio), paintings by Carpaccio, Titian, Giovanni Bellini, and Antonio Vivarini, and works of art by Florentine masters such as Luca Signorelli and Antonio da Firenze.

Madonna dell'Orto: Tranquil in its setting and blessed with a beautiful redbrick Gothic facade,

Madonna dell'Orto, north of the Ca' d'Oro and near the Canale delle Fondamente Nuovo, was the parish church of Tintoretto. The first church here was founded in 1350 and dedicated to St. Christopher, whose statue still stands above the main portal. It was rededicated to the Madonna in 1377 following the discovery of a statue of the Virgin with miraculous powers in a nearby *orto* (vegetable garden).

The church's highlight is Cima da Conegliano's painting of **"St. John the Baptist"** (1493) on the first altar of the south wall. Almost every other work of note belongs to Tintoretto, who is buried in the chapel to the right of the choir. The choir itself contains two of the painter's masterpieces, the towering **"Last Judgment"** and **"The Making of the Golden Calf."** The artist completed all the church's paintings free, asking only for the cost of his materials.

Santa Maria dei Miracoli:

On the southeastern end of Cannaregio is Santa Maria dei Miracoli. This half-hidden jewel of a church, swathed inside and out in precious colored marbles, has one of Venice's loveliest exteriors. Pietro Lombardo (1438–1515), one of the leading architects of his day, began Santa Maria in 1480, its purpose to house a miraculous image of the Virgin painted in 1409. Lombardo ignored structural complexity in favor of a church that relied for its exterior effect almost entirely on color.

Inside the barrel-vaulted church, he was responsible, along with sons Tullio and Antonio, for the fine carving on the pillars of the **nuns' choir** (near the entrance) and the pillars and balustrade of the raised **choir** by the altar. On the altar is the miracle-working image of the Virgin that gave the church its name (*miracoli* means "miracles").

Castello

The largest of Venice's districts, Castello boasts the churches of Santi Giovanni e Paolo and San Zaccaria, as well as the Scuola di San Giorgio degli Schiavoni (see sidebar p. 204), a tiny scuola founded in 1451 to serve the city's large Slav population. All three contain spectacular works of art.

Santi Giovanni e Paolo:

Just a few minutes' walk east from Santa Maria dei Miracoli is Santi Giovanni e Paolo. This church—also called San Zanipolo—was

Santa Maria dei Miracoli

 Map p. 183

 Campiello dei Miracoli, Cannaregio 6075

☎ 041 275 0462

🕐 Closed Sun.

💲 $

🚏 1 to Ca' d'Oro or 1 & 2 to Rialto

chorusvenezia.org

The Ca' d'Oro facade was once gilded in gold leaf, meant to make it the most magnificent building on the Canal Grande.

Santi Giovanni e Paolo

 Map p. 183

✉ Campo Santi Giovanni e Paolo, Castello 6363

☎ 041 523 5913

🕐 Closed Sun. a.m.

💲 $

🚏 1 & 2 to Rialto

www.basilicasanti giovanniepaolo.it

Scuola di San Giorgio degli Schiavoni

Few works of art in Venice are as charming as the painting cycle of the tiny Scuola di San Giorgio degli Schiavoni in eastern Castello (*Calle dei Furlani, Castello 3259/a, tel 041 522 8828, closed Sun. at 1 p.m., Mon. a.m., & daily 1 p.m.–2:45 p.m., $$*), founded in 1451 to serve the city's large Schiavoni (Slav) population. The work of Carpaccio, the cycle deals mainly with events from the lives of Dalmatia's three patron saints: George, Tryphon, and Jerome. The nine-painting cycle (1502) starts on the left wall with "St. George Slaying the Dragon." Panels to the right portray "The Triumph of St. George," "St. George Baptizing the Gentiles," and the "Miracle of St. Tryphon," which captures the boy-saint exorcizing a demon. The central saintly theme, abandoned in the next paintings, "The Agony in the Garden" and "The Calling of St. Matthew," is picked up again in the last three pictures, each of which recalls an episode from the life of St. Jerome.

the mother church of the city's Dominicans, who began the present building in 1333. Its fame rests on a wealth of superb funerary monuments—25 doges are buried here.

On the way in, you pass the **tomb of Doge Giacomo Tiepolo** (died 1249), buried in the most ornate of the four tombs on the exterior facade. Three more tombs range across the facade's interior wall, all devoted to members of the Mocenigo family and all sculpted by Pietro, Tullio, and Antonio Lombardo, three of the most accomplished sculptors of their day. The finest belongs to Doge Pietro Mocenigo, remarkable for the fact that it contains barely a hint of the religious iconography often found in church tombs.

The second altar on the south wall features the church's greatest painting, Giovanni Bellini's **"St. Vincent Ferrer With Sts. Christopher and Sebastian"** (1465). Across the nave, on the north wall, stands Pietro Lombardo's **"Monumento al Doge Nicolò Marcello"** (died 1474): a mature Renaissance work that contrasts with the same sculptor's canopied Gothic tomb—three altars to the right—of Doge Pasquale Malipiero (died 1462), carved some 15 years earlier.

The south transept features three eye-catching paintings: Alvise Vivarini's **"Christ Carrying the Cross"; "The Coronation of the Virgin,"** attributed to Cima da Conegliano; and Lorenzo Lotto's marvelous **"St. Antoninus Peruzzi Giving Alms to the Poor"** (1542). Moving to the high altar, note the **tomb of Doge Michele Morosini** (died 1382) on the right-hand wall, a beautiful Byzantine-Gothic hybrid. High up on the opposite wall is an almost equally lovely Gothic tomb, the five-figured **"Monumento al Doge Marco Corner"** (died 1368); to its right lies the **"Monumento al Doge Andrea Vendramin"** (died 1478), a vast white marble edifice by Antonio and Tullio Lombardo.

The north transept walls belong to the Venier, once among Venice's leading patrician families. The most eminent family member interred here is Doge Sebastiano Venier (died 1578), victorious commander of the fleet that confronted the Turks at the Battle of Lepanto (1571). A door leads to the **Cappella del Rosario,** where the best artworks are the ceiling panels by Veronese.

San Zaccaria: This Castello church, which is actually east and very close to the Basilica di San Marco, is dedicated to Zacharias, the father of St. John the Baptist. The church's facade bears both Gothic and Renaissance elements. Inside, the second altar on the left contains Bellini's "Madonna and Saints" (1505), one of the city's finest altarpieces. Across the nave, the second altar on the north wall contains the reputed relics of St. Zacharias.

The vaults in the **Cappella di San Tarasio** feature important early Renaissance frescoes (1442) by the Florentine artist Andrea del Castagno, while around the walls are three glorious altarpieces (1443) by the Venetian painters Antonio Vivarini and Giovanni d'Alemagna. ■

San Zaccaria

🄰 Map p. 183
✉ Campo San Zaccaria, Castello 4693
☎ 041 522 1257
🕐 Closed Sun. a.m. & daily 12 p.m.–4 p.m.
💲 Chapels & crypt: $
🚏 1, 2, & other services to San Marco & San Zaccaria

NEED TO KNOW
Port Logistics: Venice

Most ships dock at the **Stazione Marittima** (*www.vtp.it*) on the west side of Venice, which has six terminal buildings (*1–2, 103, 107, 108, 117, & 123*). Some ships dock at nearby terminal **San Basilio 22.**

There are three recommended ways to get to Piazza San Marco from Stazione Marittima. The most direct route is on the **Alilaguna ferry** (*Linea Blu service, tel 041 240 1701, alilaguna.it, 2 hourly 7:50 a.m–5:20 p.m., journey time 30 min.*) from in front of terminal 103. It fills quickly, and lines can be long (*tickets from kiosk, $$*). On your return, board a service going in the direction of Terminal Crociere. Avoid the small water taxis: They are fast but cost €80 or more for this short ride.

Alternatively, you could head to Piazzale Roma to pick up the 1 or the quicker 2 vaporetto, a water-bus (*actv.it, 11 hourly, journey time 30–40 min.*), along the Canal Grande to San Marco. This involves a 15-minute walk or a 3-minute ride on the "People Mover" monorail (*station near terminal 103, tickets from machines at monorail entrance, avmspa.it, $*) that links Tronchetto (Venice's parking lot), the Stazione Marittima, and Piazzale Roma.

You could also walk to Piazza San Marco: Allow an hour.

Venice Highlights

You can spend your entire port of call time at any one of these destinations, but here are some suggested times to help with your planning. Note, these do not allow for travel time to and from and/or waiting in line:

• Canal Grande vaporetto ride: 1 hour
• Campanile, Basilica di San Marco, San Zaccaria, & Scuola di San Giorgio degli Schiavoni: 2 hours
• Walk, Santi Giovanni e Paolo, & Santa Maria dei Miracoli: 1 hour
• Walk, Rialto Bridge & markets, & Gallerie dell'Accademia: 1.5 hours
• Walk & Santa Maria Gloriosa dei Frari: 1 hour

Split

Modern Split, in Croatia, is a sprawling, no-nonsense city with a gem at its heart. The Roman remains here, notably, the palace of Emperor Diocletian (A.D. 245–313), are some of the finest outside Italy, while the tiny streets that eventually grew up in and around the palace are a wonderfully atmospheric maze of cafés, restaurants, galleries, and medieval nooks and crannies.

The Cathedral of St. Dominus's bell tower looms over the Peristyle of Diocletian's Palace.

NEED TO KNOW p. 207

Split

 181 E2

Visitor Information

✉ Peristil bb

☎ 021 345 606, 021 339 899, or 021 348 600

visitsplit.com

Virtually all you want to see is in the small Old Town (Stari Grad): Diocletian's Palace and its streets, plus an equivalent medieval area to the west that evokes the city's period under Venetian rule from 1420 to 1797. Leave time to stroll the Riva waterfront in front of the Old Town and to visit a couple of outlying museums.

Diocletian's Palace

Emperor Diocletian was born in Salona, a Roman colony close to modern-day Split. He built a palace there, and moved there on his retirement in 305. Much of the palace has survived or shaped the streets that grew up within its

walls after the fall of Rome. The **harbor-facing walls** of the palace originally formed the rear of the palace, home to Diocletian and his family; the "front" of the palace, on the opposing side, housed the 700 guards, slaves, and servants that manned the household.

Walk through the "Brass Gate" (Mjedena Vrata) in the center of the walls. On your left is the entrance to the vaulted **Cellars** (Podrumi; *closed Sun. p.m. Nov.–April, $*), built partly as the palace's foundations and to level the sloping ground to the sea. Later filled with refuse and debris, they were

INSIDER TIP:

Go where the locals go for bargains. Spend some time cruising the open-air market next to Diocletian's Palace.

—GRACE FIELDER
National Geographic contributor

partially excavated after World War II, providing a graphic illustration of the palace's former scale.

Opposite the Cellars entrance is the **Ethnographic Museum** (Etnografski Muzei), whose setting—a beautifully restored medieval palace—is as alluring as its folk art, culture, costume, and other exhibits.

Carry straight on and you come to the **Vestibule**, the entrance to Diocletian's living quarters: It's a deliberately awe-inspiring space. Beyond this is the **Peristyle** (Peristil), a square that marks the palace's former heart. To the left a small lane runs to the remains of a temple to Jupiter, later converted into a Christian **baptistery**.

More impressive is the **Cathedral of St. Dominus** (Katedrala Sv. Duje) on the Peri-style's right, built as Diocletian's mausoleum but converted into a church after 652. Highlights include the main door's wooden reliefs (1214); the dome base reliefs (which may contain portraits of Diocletian and his wife, Prisca); the 13th-century stone pulpit; and the adjacent

bell tower, which you can climb (\$) for expansive views.

Return to the street and continue straight (north); turn down Majstora Jurja, the last street on the left before exiting the palace confines, for some pretty cafés and specialist stores.

The Rest of the Town

The heart of the Old Town west of the palace is Narodni Trg, or **People's Square.** Gradska Kavana here is Split's most famous old café: It's a great spot to sit out with a coffee. Bear west a block from the square and take in the **Fish Market** (Peskarija) before walking to the **Riva** waterfront, recently restored with a contemporary edge, and turn right for the Fishermen's Port.

Around a 15-minute walk (or taxi or bus 12 from the Riva) west is Split's main highlight after the palace, the **Meštrović Gallery,** a showcase for the work of the eponymous 20th-century Croatian sculptor. A 5-minute walk away is the **Kaštelet Chapel** (Kaštelet-Crikvine), which houses the artist's striking series of panels illustrating the life of Christ. It's in a 16th-century summer palace. ■

Ethnographic Museum

  Iza Vestibula 4/ Severova 1

☎ 021 344 164 or 021 344 161

🕐 Closed Sun. p.m. June–Sept. & Sat. p.m.–Sun. Oct.–May

💲 \$

etnografski-muzej -split.hr

Cathedral of St. Dominus

✉ Kraj Svetog Duje 5

☎ Cathedral: 021 342 589; treasury: 021 305 444 (treasury)

🕐 Closed Sun.

Meštrović Gallery & Kaštelet Chapel

✉ Šetalište Ivana Meštrovića 46

☎ Meštrović Gallery: 021 340 800; Kaštelet Chapel: 021 358 185

🕐 Closed Mon.

💲 Combined ticket: \$\$

mdc.hr/mestrovic/ galerija/index-en.htm

NEED TO KNOW

Port Logistics: Split

Ships dock on the east side of Split's harbor (*portsplit.com*): Leave the terminal, turn left toward the distinctive bell tower, and a few minutes' walk brings you to the Old Town. Tenders drop on a smaller pier off the Riva, the waterfront promenade in front of the Old Town itself.

Dubrovnik

Croatia's best known city is an unforgettable place, with a wealth of fascinating sights crammed within its outstanding medieval walls. Highlights include the old streets, a walk around the walls themselves, and the view from the hills above the town. But be aware that in high season the town becomes extremely crowded: An early start, or low season visit, is highly recommended.

The Old Town of Dubrovnik is protected by its world-famous walls.

NEED TO KNOW p. 215

Dubrovnik

 181 F1

Visitor Information

✉ Brsalje 5

☎ 020 323 887 or
020 312 011

tzdubrovnik.hr
croatia.hr

In its medieval heyday, Dubrovnik—known as Ragusa until 1918—was a major maritime and trading power. An earthquake in 1667 destroyed much of the town, later rebuilt on largely baroque lines, and was followed by 150 years of decline as European trade adopted new shipping routes. The town and its territories eventually passed to Austria until after World War I. The city suffered considerable damage during a ten-month siege in 1991–1992, when it was caught up in the "Homeland War" that accompanied the breakup of the former Yugoslavia.

Dubrovnik's now restored and pedestrian-only Old Town occupies a rocky headland, shadowed above by the prominent slopes of Mount Srđ and surrounded on all sides by majestic walls. Within, it is divided by the 1,000-foot-long (300 m) Stradun—an elegant main street—and its radiating smaller streets. Most of the many sights lie within the walls, making the city easy to navigate.

City Walls

Dubrovnik's walls (Gradske Zidine) bristle with towers and bastions and are among the best preserved in Europe, extending some 1.25 miles (2 km), rising to 82 feet (25 m), and reaching a thickness of 20 feet (6 m). A second, outer wall rises on the landward side, with additional bastions and fortresses. Begun during the 8th century, the ramparts encircled the town by the 12th century and were extended over the next 500 years, partly in response to threats from the Ottomans and Venice. The largest of the fortresses, St. John's (Tvrdava Sv. Ivana), was built between 1346 and 1557.

The main entrance onto the walls is inside the 15th-century **Pile Gate** (Vrata od Pile), but there are other entrances on Svetog Dominika (by the Dominican Monastery) and on Kneza Damjana Jude (by St. John's Fortress). The gate is reached by a wooden drawbridge and surmounted by a statue of St. Blaise (Sv. Vlaho), the city's patron saint and a figure with whom you will become familiar as you explore the town. Allow about 1.5 hours to make a complete circuit of the walls.

Stradun & Around

Pile Gate leads onto Stradun (known locally as Placa), a broad, straight thoroughfare that ends at Luža Square. It marks the ancient division—a marsh and then a canal before it was paved—between the area south of Stradun settled in the seventh century by the former inhabitants of Cavtat, a nearby Greco-Roman town, and the area settled later by Slavs (the steep streets to the north).

Just inside Pile Gate on the right is a small square with the 16-sided **Onofrio's Great Fountain,** created in 1444 as a cistern for the city's drinking water. It provided one of the only sources of water for the city during the 1991–1992 siege. It is named after the architect who designed it, Onofrio della Cava of Naples.

INSIDER TIP:

If looking for a small gift, try a locally made face cream from the old Franciscan Pharmacy on the Stradun (*Placa 2*) that's been in operation for more than 700 years.

—CAROLINE HICKEY
National Geographic Travel Books project editor

Behind the fountain is the former **Convent of St. Clare** (Sv. Klara), built in the 13th century and dissolved by Napoleon in 1806. Beyond this, along Garište, a street on the right, is the small 16th-century **Church of St. Roch** (Crkva Sv. Roka), built as a votive church against the frequent outbreaks of plague. On one of the exterior walls is carved the curious inscription,

(continued on p. 212)

Dubrovnik Walking Tour

With so much to see in Dubrovnik, any tour of the city is correspondingly long. This one falls easily into two parts that can be spread over two days or broken with a stop for lunch. In either case, walk around the city walls in the morning before it gets too hot, then head down Stradun for lunch before resuming the itinerary.

The vaulted loggia outside the Rector's Palace

Atop the Walls

Enter the Old Town through the **Pile Gate** ❶ (see p. 209), noting the first of many statues of the city's patron saint, St. Blaise. Then, after buying a ticket (*$$$*), follow the steps up to the left onto the city walls. After getting a good view of Stradun, turn left (south) and follow the walls toward **Bokar Fortress** (with views over the bay to St. Lawrence's Fortress) and on along the Old Town's seaward side. Notice the aqueduct here, part of Onofrio della Cava's system for supplying the city with water.

At the far (southeast) corner of the walls you reach the huge **St. John's Fortress** ❷,

NOT TO BE MISSED:

The medieval city walls • Luža Square • The Cathedral treasury • Gundulić Square • Dominican Church and Monastery

from which a massive protective chain once stretched across the old harbor. Toward the northeast corner of the walls, you have good views down on the **Dominican Monastery** (see p. 215). Climb up past **St. James (Sv. Jakov) Tower** ❸, which marked the eastern extremity of the walls until the 14th century. From here, along the northern section of the walls to the **Minčeta Fortress** ❹ (the highest point on the walls), you have unrivaled views over the Old Town. The best views of the **Franciscan Monastery** look down over the cloister from the following section of wall before the Pile Gate, where you will descend again.

Street Level

Stop to fill up your water bottles at **Onofrio's Great Fountain** (see p. 209) and continue onto **Stradun,** stopping first at the **Franciscan Monastery** ❺ (see p. 212) on the left, with its exceptionally fine cloister. Continue ahead to **Luža Square** ❻ (see pp. 212–213), the center of public life during the republic, where you will find the lovely **Sponza Palace** and the baroque **Church of St. Blaise.**

Turn right (south) onto Pod Dvorom, arriving first at the **Rector's Palace** ❼ (see p. 213), on the left, with a beautiful loggia,

followed by the **Cathedral** ❽ (see p. 213), whose **treasury** is filled with exquisite gold and silver filigree reliquaries of St. Blaise. Turn right to **Gundulić Square** ❾ (see p. 214), an open market square that makes the perfect spot for lunch. Backtrack to Luža Square and follow the narrow lane up to the right onto Old Sv. Domenika, where you will find the **Dominican Church and Monastery** ❿ (see p. 215).

From the church, turn west along Prijeko (or walk back along Stradun) as far as Antuninska, where you arrive at **War Photo Limited** ⓫ (see pp. 214–215), an excellent gallery showcasing the work of war photographers from conflict zones across the globe. Return to the Pile Gate along Stradun.

🅰	Also see area map p. 181
▶	Pile Gate
🕒	5 hours
↔	2.25 miles (3.5 km)
▶	Pile Gate

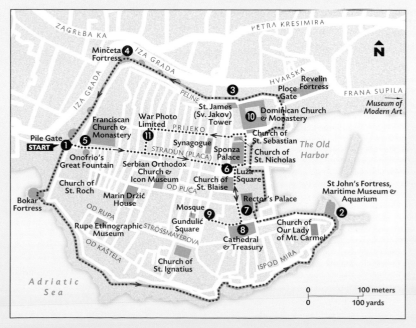

Franciscan Church & Monastery

⚑ Map p. 211

✉ Placa 2

☎ 020 321 410

$ $$

Sponza Palace

⚑ Map p. 211

✉ Svetog Dominika 1

☎ 020 321 032

$ $

in Latin: "Peace be unto you, but remember that you will die, you who are playing ball, 1597."

On the left inside the Pile Gate is the small 16th-century **Church of Our Savior** (Crkva Sv. Spasa), built in thanksgiving following an earthquake in 1520.

As you walk down Stradun, note the distinctive old shop fronts, with a door and window combined within a single arched frame, which allows the closed lower portion to function as a shop counter.

Beyond the Old Town

North of the Old Town is the steep, 1,352-foot (412 m) **Mount Srđ**, whose views make it one of the town's highlights after the walls, so either walk up, following a very steep path from Državna Cesta, or take the cable car from a block north of the Buža Gate (tel 020 325 393, dubrovnik cablecar.com, journey time 3 min., $$$).

Franciscan Church & Monastery: Just past the Church of Our Savior on the left, and entered through a late 15th-century carved portal, is Dubrovnik's wonderful Franciscan Church and Monastery (Franjevačka Crkva i Samostan), begun in 1343. The Croatian 17th-century poet Ivan Gundulić, whose statue you will find in Gundulić Square (see p. 214), is buried here.

The **cloister** of the monastery is outstanding and, unlike the church, survived the 1667 earthquake more or less intact. It features pairs of slender, octagonal columns with joint capitals,

each carved individually with different animals, birds, human heads, and fantastic beasts.

The arcades surround a small garden, a shady oasis of when Dubrovnik gets too busy. The **pharmacy,** established in 1317, is said to be the oldest surviving in Europe, and the small museum just off the cloister contains various old jars, manuscripts, pestles, and mortars from the 15th and 16th centuries. The **bell tower** dates mostly from the 15th century.

Luža Square: At the far end of Stradun is Luža Square, which has as its centerpiece **Orlando's Column** (1417), bearing a sculpture of a sword-wielding Roland (of the epic poem The Song of Roland), a symbol of the city's free status. Public proclamations were read from the top. Roland's forearm (and an equivalent length marked at the base of the column) was the standard unit of measurement in old Ragusa.

The **clock tower** (1444) on the square was rebuilt in 1929 when it began to lean, and its original mechanism—featuring two little green figures (called Zelenci) that strike the hour—was moved to the Sponza Palace (see below). Also on the square is **Onofrio's Small Fountain** (named after the same Italian engineer), with worn sculptures dating from the mid-15th century.

On the left (northern) side of Luža is the town's finest Renaissance-Gothic building, the **Sponza Palace** (Palača Sponza;

1522), which over the years has also served as the city's customhouse, mint, arsenal, and cistern. The building now houses a museum, including the clock tower mechanism, and the Memorial Room of the Dubrovnik Defenders, devoted to the siege of 1991–1992.

On the right (south) side of Luža is the baroque **Church of St. Blaise** (Crkva Sv. Vlaha), patron saint of Dubrovnik, built in 1706–1714. Inside there is a 15th-century silver gilt statue of the saint who holds a model of Dubrovnik as it looked in the late 1400s.

All visitors are entranced by Dubrovnik's Stradun main street.

Rector's Palace

South of St. Blaise's, across Pred Dvorom, is the Renaissance-Gothic Rector's Palace (Knežev Dvor), once home to the city's medieval, doge-like rulers, or rectors, and built on the site of an earlier, more heavily fortified construction by Onofrio della Cava, the man responsible for designing the city's public water supply.

The exterior consists of a beautiful loggia and the main entrance has another statue of St. Blaise. The arcaded inner courtyard has a statue of Miho Pracat (1528–1607), a 16th-century merchant from Lopud, who left a fortune to the city on his death. On the first floor is the Hall of the Great Council, at the entrance of which an inscription in Latin admonishes officials to forget their private affairs and concern themselves with business. The upper floor houses a dull museum of period furniture and paintings.

Among the other buildings on the east side of Pred Dvorom is the former town hall, now one of Dubrovnik's most famous cafés, **Gradska Kavana.**

Dubrovnik Cathedral

Dubrovnik's Cathedral (Katedrala) was built between 1672 and 1713 on the site of an earlier Romanesque cathedral destroyed during the great earthquake of 1667. Inside there is a large painting by the school of Titian above the unusual west-facing altar.

The well-guarded **treasury** (*$*)—there are three locks on the door—contains more than 130 relics dating from the 11th to the 19th century, including the head, arms, and leg of St. Blaise, brought from Byzantium in 1026 and contained in gold reliquaries made by local craftsmen during the 11th and 12th centuries.

Rector's Palace
- Map p. 211
- Pred Dvorom 3
- 020 426 469 or 020 321 497
- Closed Sun. & p.m. in winter
- $$

Dubrovnik Cathedral
- Map p. 211
- Držićeva Poljana
- 020 323 459
- Closed 12 p.m.– 3 p.m. in winter

Gundulić Square, named for poet Ivan Gundulić

St. John's Fortress
- Map p. 211
- Knesa Damjana Jude 12

Icon Museum
- Map p. 211
- Od Puča 8
- 020 323 283
- Closed Sun. & p.m. year-round & Sat. Nov.– April
- $

Pustjerna & Prijeko

Above the Cathedral, up in the streets that compose the area called Pustjerna, are the small 17th-century **Church of Our Lady of Mt. Carmel** (Crkva Gospe od Karmena) and the massive **St. John's Fortress,** which contains the city's **Aquarium** (Akvarij; tel 020 32 125 or 020 427 937, closed Mon., $$$) and **Maritime Museum** (Pomorski Muzej; tel 020 323 904, closed Mon., $$), which documents the city's extraordinary maritime history.

Behind the Cathedral, heading back toward Stradun, is the lovely old **Gundulić Square,** surrounded by restaurants and cafés and home most mornings to a small open-air market. At its center stands a statue (1892) of Ivan Gundulić, a Croatian poet born in Dubrovnik in 1589. The statue, created by Croatian sculptor Ivan Rendić (1849–1932), is decorated with scenes from Gundulić's best known work, the epic poem *Osman*.

South of Gundulić Square, a long flight of steps (modeled on the Spanish Steps in Rome) leads to the early 18th-century Jesuit **Church of St. Ignatius** (Crkva Sv. Ignacija).

West from the square on Od Puča, past Dubrovnik's small mosque *(džamija),* is the **Icon Museum,** with an outstanding collection of icons from the 15th to 19th centuries. The nearby **Serbian Orthodox Church** (Pravoslavna Crkva) dates from the late 19th century. South of here toward the city walls, the wonderful **Rupe Ethnographic Museum** (Etnografski Muzej Rupe) is housed in a cavernous 16th-century granary.

Prijeko: This restaurant-filled street running parallel to Stradun through the higher part of town to the north is best avoided around lunchtime, when waitstaff are busy.

On Antuninska, a narrow street leading up to Prijeko from Stradun, is the outstanding **War Photo Limited,** established in 2003 by New Zealand–born war photographer Wade Goddard, who came here during the "Homeland War." The collection includes images from conflict zones around the globe by some of the world's leading war photographers.

On Žudioska, a narrow street between the eastern ends of Stradun and Prijeko, is Dubrovnik's **synagogue** (and museum), the second oldest in Europe after Prague's. At the far end of Prijeko stands the small **Church of St. Nicholas** (Crkva Sv. Nikole), rebuilt in the 17th century but with some pre-Romanesque carvings in the interior.

Dominican Church & Monastery

Beyond the far end of Prijeko, on Svetog Dominika, are the **Dominican Church and Monastery** (Dominikanski Crkva i Samostan). The church, built in 1315, has been renovated several times. The monastery has suffered similarly through the ages, but has been beautifully restored. Note the cloisters, which still have the water troughs cut into

their walls by Napoleon's troops for their horses.

Inside the sizable church is a huge 14th-century Crucifixion by the Venetian painter Paolo Veneziano, together with other artworks and a 15th-century stone pulpit. The church's Romanesque south door, with its flight of steps cascading into the street below, is best appreciated from the city walls. Adjacent to the south door is the former **Church of St. Sebastian** (Sv. Sebastijana), built during the 15th century and used as a prison by Napoleon.

Dominican Monastery Museum: This interesting museum (Muzej Dominikanskog Samostana) has a 16th-century altarpiece by Titian showing St. Blaise and various works from the Dubrovnik school of the 15th and 16th centuries, including a restored triptych by Nikole Božidarevii (1460–1517), which shows St. Blaise holding a model of the old town and St. Dominic holding a model of the church and monastery. ∎

Rupe Ethnographic Museum

- 🅰 Map p. 211
- ✉ Od Rupa 3
- ☎ 020 412 545
- 🕐 Closed Sun. & p.m.
- 💲 $$$

mdc.hr/dubrovnik/eng/etnografski/index.html

War Photo Limited

- 🅰 Map p. 211
- ✉ Antuninska 6
- ☎ 020 322 166
- 🕐 Closed Nov.– April & Mon. May & Oct.

warphotoltd.com

Dominican Church & Monastery

- 🅰 Map p. 211
- ✉ Svetog Dominika 4
- ☎ 020 321 423
- 💲 Museum: $$

NEED TO KNOW
Port Logistics: Dubrovnik

Some smaller ships tender to the **Old Town** (Stari Grad), but most dock on a long strip at **Gruž** (*portdubrovnik.hr*), 2.5 miles (4 km) northwest of the Old Town, with exits at the Passenger Terminal or (more distant) Cruise Center buildings, 10 minutes' walk apart.

Some ships offer free shuttles to the Old Town. Otherwise, taxis wait outside

the terminal and buses 1, 1a, 1b, or 1c run to the Pile Gate (Vrata od Pila), the end of the line and the western entrance to the Old Town. Tickets are cheaper if you buy from the kiosk rather than on board; at the time of publication, only Croatian kuna are accepted. Only a few services and sights in town accept euros, so change a small amount of currency.

More Ports to Visit on the Adriatic

Korčula's fortified and beautifully situated Old Town resembles a small version of Dubrovnik.

Hvar, Croatia

Hvar is a 42-mile-long (68 km) island—the fourth largest on the Croatian Adriatic—often visited by cruise ships en route to nearby Split. Tenders land directly at **Hvar town** on its western tip, a well-heeled enclave increasingly visited by international celebrities. Cruise stopovers are usually brief, so most passengers will have time only to explore the pretty town, which centers on **St. Stephen's Square** (Trg Sv. Stjepana), Dalmatia's largest square, and its mostly 17th-century **St. Stephen's Cathedral** (Katedrala Sv. Stjepana).

North beyond the square, admire the Venetian Gothic facade of the unfinished **Hektorović Palace,** then climb through the pines to the 16th-century **Španjola Fortress** (*$*). The site has been fortified since at least Roman times and offers superb views. If you have more time, take a boat tour (20 minutes) to the 20 or so **Pakleni islands** or visit the town of **Starigrad**, a few miles east of

Hvar town, best known for **Tvrdalj,** a magical, fortified Renaissance villa; the gardens are open to the public (*closed Nov.–April, $*).
🅰 181 E2 **Visitor Information** *tzhvar.hr*

Koper, Slovenia

The town of Koper on Slovenia's sliver of Adriatic coastline—it's just 29 miles (47 km) long—is drawing an increasing number of smaller cruise ships. Boats dock below Koper's **Old Town,** whose appealing historic core dates mainly from its 15th- and 16th-century heyday under Venetian rule. Follow the cobbled streets from the seafront to **Titov Square** (Titov trg), the main square that is home to a cluster of period buildings, notably the cathedral, fronted by a Venetian Gothic facade.

If excursions are offered, the best bet is **Piran**, a medieval port whose Venetian-era center is almost perfectly preserved, or, if time allows, the longer trip to Ljubljana, the Slovenian capital. Closer to Koper is easygoing **Izola:** It's less built-up than Koper, but offers some excellent fish restaurants. Also popular is the **Lipica Stud Farm** (Kobilarna Lipica; *Lipica 5, Sežana, lipica.org*), founded in 1580 and the original source of Vienna's famous Lipizzaner horses. The horses are still bred here, and the stables and grounds are open to the public.

▲ 180 B4 **Visitor Information** *slovenia .info, koper.si*

Korčula, Croatia

Korčula is the most visited island in southern Croatian. Like many ports on the Adriatic, centuries under Venetian rule left the lovely old quarter of **Korčula town** with a wealth of fine art and architecture, not least **St. Mark's Cathedral** (Katedrala Sv. Marka; *Trg Sv. Marka, closed Šun., $*) on the main square; the adjacent 17th-century **Abbot's Treasury** (Opatska Riznica; *closed Sun., $*), which houses a collection of sacred Renaissance art; and the old **Land Gate** (Kopnena Vrata). The town also claims to be the purported birthplace of the Venetian explorer Marco Polo; you can visit the alleged **Marco Polo House** (Kuća Marca Pola; *Ul. Marka Pola, $*). Because Korčula is at the heart of Croatia's main wine-producing region, there's plenty of opportunities to taste and buy local vintages in stores and cafés.

Korčula—often described as Dubrovnik in miniature—is directly accessible to small cruise ships; larger boats tender ashore.

▲ 181 F2 **Visitor Information** *visitkorcula .eu, korculainfo.com*

Kotor, Montenegro

Kotor is a beautifully preserved walled old town on the bay of the same name and a UNESCO World Heritage site. Its historic core is a delight and is becoming an increasingly chic celebrity hangout.

A walking tour of the old quarter takes in the **main town gate** for its fine reliefs

and carvings; the Romanesque **St. Luke's Church,** built in 1195; the 19th-century neo-Byzantine style **St. Nicholas,** Kotor's main Orthodox church; and the glorious Romanesque **Cathedral of St. Tryphon** (*$*), begun in 1166 over an earlier chapel. Take a break in **Arms Square** (Trg od Oruzja), Kotor's vibrant main square, and then if time—and lungs—permit, climb the 1,300-odd steps to the hilltop **St. John's Fortress** (*$*) for sweeping views. Less energetic is the boat-taxi tour to **Perast,** 8 miles (13 km) to the northwest, and its two picturesque

A Dance With a Point

Korčula, in Croatia, is noted for a sword dance, the *moreška* (from "Moorish"), one of few surviving examples of a type of dance that for more than a thousand years was once widespread across the Mediterranean. The dance portrays the combat between Black and White kings and their followers, in dispute over a woman, Bula. Elsewhere, the combatants often symbolized the conflict between Muslim and Christian forces, but here they probably represent the rivalry between Arabs and the Ottoman Turks. Performances take place regularly in summer, with tickets available from local agencies.

islets, one of which is widely celebrated for its votive-filled church, **Our Lady of the Rock** (Gospa od Skrpjela; *gospa-od-skrpjela .me*), completed in 1630.

Ships dock immediately in front of the walls, or the town can be seen as a day trip from Dubrovnik, Croatia (see pp. 208–215), which is 28 miles (45 km) west: Use local tour operators or taxis; the latter can be expensive. Citizens of the United States, Canada, and any European Union countries do not need a visa to enter Montenegro.

▲ 181 G1 **Visitor Information** *tokotor.me*

The heart of ancient Greece, home to the Parthenon, and the watery outposts of Corfu, Santorini, Rhodes, and Crete

Athens & the Islands

Introduction & Map   220–221

Athens   222–235

Need to Know: Peiraiás   235

The Peloponnesus   236–239

Need to Know: Nafplio & Katakolon   239

The Islands   240–243

Need to Know: Corfu, Santorini, & Rhodes   243

Crete   244–247

Need to Know: Iraklio   247

Restaurants   297–300

Crescent-shaped Santorini—the remnant of an ancient volcano—is the southernmost isle of the Cyclades.

Athens & the Islands

Greece is one of the cradles of European civilization. In Athens, the capital, and at the sites at Olympia, Mycenae, and Epidavros you'll find superb ancient ruins and art-filled museums that showcase the Hellenistic legacy. Greece is also a land of immense natural beauty, from the mountains of Crete to the warm-water beaches of the islands that scatter the Aegean and Ionian Seas.

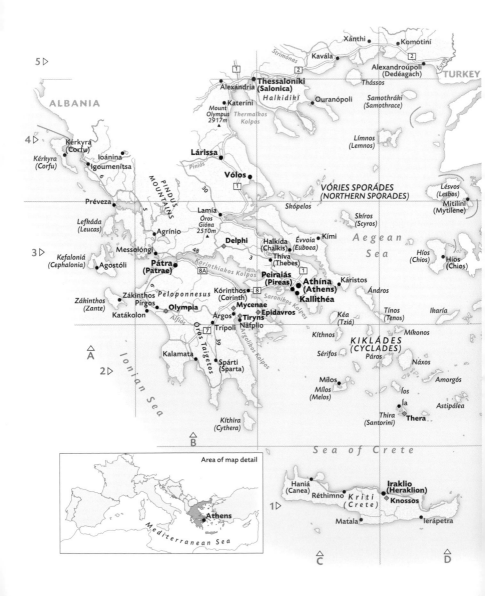

The second-century A.D. Herodes Atticus Theater (foreground), a Roman-style odeon, was built centuries after the Parthenon (right) and other major buildings on top of the Acropolis.

Athens provides a not altogether representative introduction to Greece, its often busy, noisy, and polluted streets at odds with the calm and beauty of the country's islands and mainland countryside. At the same time, the Greek capital is capable of unique and magical moments, for its streets are steeped in more than 2,500 years of history. You will want to visit the Parthenon, the great temple that dominates the Acropolis, the craggy outcrop at the heart of the city. But don't overlook other ancient sites and museums, notably the sleek new Acropolis Museum and the National Archaeological Museum, the latter one of the world's great collections of art and antiquities. Neither should you ignore the city's smaller city districts, especially those at the foot of the Acropolis, which still retain much of their Old World charm.

Beyond Athens

Away from Athens, most visitors, especially those traveling by sea, head first to the Peloponnesus—a peninsula west of Athens—and then to one or more of the country's many islands. Among many other things, the Peloponnesus contains several sites of ancient Greek culture and settlement, notably the great theater at Epidavros and the citadel of Mycenae—both accessible as excursions from the charming port town of Nafplio—as well as Olympia, birthplace of the Olympic Games, on the peninsula's opposite, western side.

Greece's islands run the gamut, from large and more verdant islands such as Corfu, the mainstay of the Ionian Sea on the country's western shore, to the dozens of drier and rockier islands and islets sprinkled across the Aegean, the sea that separates Greece from Turkey to the east. Yet another sea, the Sea of Crete, washes the shores of Greece's largest island, Crete, renowned above all for the remains of the Palace of Knossos, one of the great monuments left by the island's ancient Minoan civilization. ∎

Athens

Athens is two cities: one, the city of the ancient Greeks, imagined and glorious, the other, the rambunctious and often daunting modern city of the 21st century. Thus the greatest monuments of the past—the Acropolis and its jewel, the Parthenon—loom over anarchic rows of tightly packed apartment blocks and traffic-clogged streets. Although this is a city that can be hard to love at first sight, it is also a place of matchless treasures and—once you have spent some time here—many subtle and more hidden charms.

Detail of the Erechtheion, on the Acropolis

NEED TO KNOW p. 235

Athens
 220 C3
Visitor Information
✉ Amalias 26a, Syntagma
☎ 210 331 0716 or 210 331 0392
thisisathens.org
cityofathens.gr
odysseus.culture.gr

Acropolis & Around

The Acropolis, the heart of the ancient and modern metropolis, should be the first thing you visit on arriving in Athens. *Akro poli* means "upper city," and many Greek towns have an acropolis. Athens has the most famous, thanks to the Parthenon. Evidence of a settlement on the southern slopes of the Acropolis dates the first habitation in Athens to about 3000 B.C. But the Acropolis buildings that remain date mainly from the fifth century B.C., when ancient Athens reached its pinnacle, under the great statesman Pericles (r. ca 461–429 B.C.).

Atop this great crag you should visit the Parthenon, and then approach the medley of museums and other ancient ruins that lie below the temple, mostly to the south and north. The site's entrance is at its western end. Numerous paths lead up to it, including ones branching off the pedestrianized Dionysiou Areopagitou, which parallels the Acropolis to the south.

Before you go, know that a combination ticket purchased at the Acropolis also covers entry to other major ancient sites, including the Theater of Dionysos (see p. 225), ancient Agora (see pp. 226–227), Roman Forum (see p. 227), Hadrian's Library (see pp. 227–228), and Kerameikos cemetery (see p. 228). Lines to enter are long, especially from 10 a.m. to 12:45 p.m., with waits of 45 minutes or more possible. Arrive early (from 8 a.m.) or late to avoid the crowds and the heat (there is little shade). Wear sensible shoes: Surfaces are uneven. Wheelchair-users can take an elevator, but otherwise there is no way to avoid the steep, 10- to 20-minute walk to the site.

The Parthenon & More:
After entering the Acropolis via the U-shaped, multi-columned **Propylaia**, a grand gateway meant to inspire awe in those that entered the sacred site, most visitors head straight for the Parthenon.

The main temple of the Acropolis, the **Parthenon** took nine years to construct (it was finished in 438 B.C.). Flecks of iron in the locally quarried stone give the building its wonderfully warm golden glow in evening light. Note, however, that

ancient Athenians wouldn't have seen that: Evidence shows the temple was originally painted in vivid colors.

The Parthenon has no straight lines, its apparent symmetry created by gently tapering columns and steps, and is designed using repeated ratios of 9:4 for such aspects as the gap between columns in relation to the width of a single column, or the width of the building in relation to its height. Originally the temple's focus was a 40-foot-high (12 m)

Acropolis

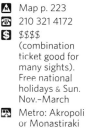

Map p. 223

☎ 210 321 4172

$ $$$$
(combination ticket good for many sights). Free national holidays & Sun. Nov.–March

🚇 Metro: Akropoli or Monastiraki

acropolisofathens.gr

Athens

[Map of Athens showing streets and landmarks including: AVEROF, MOUSEIO, LEOFOROS, ALEXANDRAS, National Archaeological Museum, LOFOS STREFI, VATHI, NEAPOLIS, METAXOURGEIO, National Theater, PLATEIA OMONOIAS, Opera, Theater Museum, LYKAVITTOS, Lykavittos Theater, Agios Georgios, Town Hall, National Library, University Academy, American School of Classical Studies, KOLONAKI, KERAMEIKOS, Central Market, Agii Theodoroi, Benaki Museum of Islamic Art, Athens Museum, Museum of Cycladic Art, War Museum, National Gallery of Greece, GAZI, Technopolis, PSIRRI, Historical Museum, Schliemann, Benaki Museum, Byzantine Museum, MONASTIRAKI, Temple of Hephaistos, Hadrian's Library, Great Mitropolis, PLATEIA SYNTAGMATOS, Vouli (Parliament), AGORA, Stoa of Attalos, Little Mitropolis of Greek Museum of Greek Folk Art, NATIONAL GARDENS, Presidential Palace, Agii Apostoli, Tower of the Winds, PLAKA, ANAFIOTIKA, Observatory, ACROPOLIS, Propylaia, Parthenon, Zappeion, Pnyka, Herodes Atticus Theater, LOFOS NYMFON, Theater of Dionysos, Acropolis Museum, Temple of Olympian Zeus, Stadium, LOFOS ARDITTOU, Agios Dimitrios, LOFOS FILOPAPPOU, Theater of Philopappos, Monument of Philopappos, PROTO NEKROTAFEION ATHINON]

0 ──── 600 meters
0 ──── 600 yards

gold-and-ivory statue of the goddess Athena Parthenos (Athena the Virgin), after whom the city is named.

Several other buildings atop the Acropolis are worth a closer look. To the right soon after you enter is the small **Temple of Athena Nike,** added in 427–424 B.C. to celebrate victories by the Athenians in their wars with the Persians. Athena Nike means Athena of Victory.

To your left as you approach the Parthenon is the **Erechtheion,** added between 421 and 395 B.C. It is said that the first olive tree in Athens sprouted here when the goddess Athena touched the ground with her spear. An olive tree has been kept growing here since 1917. The building includes the Porch of the Caryatids, where the six supporting columns have been sculpted in the form of maidens. Those on-site are copies: Five of

The Sanctuary of Pandion, dedicated to a mythical ruler of ancient Athens

The Parthenon, once home to a vast statue of Athena Parthenos

Acropolis

The Erechtheion, dedicated to several different gods. Behind it stands the site of the old temple of Athena.

The Propylaia is one of the ancient world's grandest secular structures.

Hephaistos was the god of many things, including fire, art, and metallurgy, and the temple was built in the metalworkers' quarter of the city.

On the far side of the Agora is the **Stoa of Attalos** (Stoa Attalou). A stoa is a roofed colonnade, and this two-story building is unique in Athens, as it is the only one that has been fully restored. The stoa was built in the second century B.C. by Attalos, King of Pergamon, but burned to the ground in A.D. 267. Inside it today is a small but fascinating museum, with a collection that brings to life the people and society of the Agora.

Just east of the ancient Agora is the less impressive **Roman Forum,** also known as the Roman Agora. It was originally an extension of the earlier Greek Agora, and was built by Julius Caesar (r. 59–44 B.C.) and Emperor Augustus (r. 44 B.C.– A.D. 4). While it looks scruffy in comparison with other sites nearby, it contains one of the most unusual and distinctive Athenian landmarks, the **Tower of the Winds** (Naos Aiolou).

This marble tower was built in the second half of the first century B.C. and its Greek name is Aerides, which means "the winds." Each of its eight sides faces one of the eight main compass points, and a decorative frieze at the top of each represents one of the eight winds of mythology. The North Wind, for example, is Boreas, warmly clad and with billowing cloak; his brother

Notos, the South Wind, brings rain, which he pours from a pitcher of water.

The other notable building in the Forum is the **Mosque of Fethiye Tzami** (see sidebar this page). A madrassa, where Muslim students were taught

Mosque of Fethiye Tzami

At a glance, the small stone building at the corner of Panos and Pelopida, at the northern end of the Roman Forum, seems like an unlikely cause for controversy. A closer look, however, reveals that this building—which is currently used as a storage shed—is an old Ottoman mosque. The Fethiye Mosque, as it is known, is the oldest mosque in Athens, built by Mehmed II in 1458. In a city with a Muslim population of 200,000 but no mosques, the building's current state makes many people angry.

Some Muslim community leaders hope that it can be restored, but they have so far struggled to get much political support. Their proposal received a boost in 2010, however, when it emerged that the Turkish government was pressing for the restoration of the mosque as part of a deal that would see several properties in Turkey returned to the Orthodox Church.

the Koran, once stood opposite what is now the entrance to the Roman Forum. It later became a prison, and a tree on the grounds was used for public hangings, but the building was almost completely destroyed after the prison closed.

At one time, **Hadrian's Library** (Vivliothiki Adrianou) stood on the edge of the Roman Forum, but it is now separated from the site by

Monastiraki
🅰 Map p. 223

Kerameikos cemetery
🅰 Map p. 223
✉ Ermou 148
☎ 210 346 3552
💲 $ or combined ticket with Acropolis
🚇 Metro: Kerameikos
odysseus.culture.gr

several streets. It was built around A.D. 132 by Emperor Hadrian to house his vast collection of books, the extent of which can be gauged by the fact that this was the largest building he erected in Athens. Little remains but the east wall, but the library once had a pool and a garden surrounded by a walled courtyard 400 feet by 270 feet (122 m by 82 m) with no fewer than 100 columns.

Monastiraki & Around

Centered on the square of the same name, rough and ready Monastiraki, bordering the pleasant Plaka district (see pp. 229–230), is a vibrant and exciting shopping area.

The Sunday flea market at Monastiraki Square offers bargain hunters a cornucopia of collectibles.

Monastiraki Square (Plateia Monastiraki) is not at all reminiscent of the peaceful monastery that once stood on this site and gave the place its name. Hundreds of shops line the streets, and the farther you go the more varied the shops become. If you want to find a genuine Greek coffeepot or a traditional bouzouki, this is the place to come. Shopkeepers will try to coax you in, but usually in a jovial manner. (Pickpockets can be more of a problem.) The biggest crowds and best spectacle are on Sunday morning, when the market expands, extending east from the square along Ermou Street to beyond the Kerameikos cemetery.

Try to visit the **Kerameikos cemetery,** whose name comes from the potters of the ancient city who once lay claim to this area. Keramos was the patron deity of potters: hence, "ceramics." The cemetery is a peaceful haven, with much greenery and wildlife. It first served as a burial ground in the 12th century B.C., and many old tombs still remain, most notably along the central Street of the Tombs.

Walk back along Ermou away from Kerameikos, past Monastiraki Square, and you reach another, much more peaceful and graceful square known as **Cathedral Square** (Plateia Mitropoleos). There are actually two cathedrals here: The **Little Mitropolis**

(Mikri Mitropoli) to the right is a charming, tiny church dating from the 12th century and dedicated to Agios (St.) Eleftherios. Next door is the **Great Mitropolis** (Megali Mitropoli), which is Athens's cathedral, constructed in the mid-19th century.

INSIDER TIP:

Visit the Monastiraki market on Sunday to absorb the local colors, sounds, and smells.

—EVA VALSAMI-JONES
National Geographic field scientist

Psirri & Gazi: Next door to Monastiraki, to the north of Ermou and west of Amerikis, is the gentrified district of Psirri, full of fashionable *ouzeries* and restaurants, bars, and clubs. Here, too, is now one of the city's best small museums, the **Benaki Museum of Islamic Art,** which houses all the Islamic items that used to be on display at the main Benaki Museum (see p. 231). It's a collection of exquisite items not to be missed.

West of Psirri is Gazi, the latest inner-city area to be transformed. A former gasworks has been turned into **Technopolis,** the kind of cultural center that would grace any capital city, housing changing art and photography exhibitions, with evening concerts, too.

The Plaka

A warren of mainly pedestrianized streets to the north and east at the foot of the Acropolis, the Plaka is the prime visitor area of Athens, a tourist-oriented enclave of small streets lined with stores and restaurants. Many of the buildings are old and beautiful. There are some good eating places, and the atmosphere is lively, day and night.

The area expanded in the 19th century and was home to many well-to-do Athenian families who built grand neoclassical mansions, several of which have been turned into museums or stores.

An essential stop on a stroll around the Plaka is the **Museum of Greek Musical Instruments** (Mouseio Ellinikon Mousikon Organon), housed in a mansion that was built in 1842. Its courtyard is used in summer for outdoor concerts. Inside on three floors are some of the 1,200 or so musical instruments amassed over the years by the Greek musicologist Fivos Anoyanakis (born 1915). It is a fascinating and fun museum, with audio that allows you to listen to many of the exhibits being played.

Another mansion, dating from 1884, houses the **Kanellopoulos Museum** (Mouseio Kanellopoulos), a collection of ceramics, statues, jewelry, icons, and more built up by Athenian collectors Paul and Alexandra Kanellopoulos. Exhibits cover the 3rd century B.C. through the

Benaki Museum of Islamic Art
 Map p. 223
Ag. Asomaton 22/Dipilou 12
210 325 1311
Closed Mon.-Wed.
$$ (free Thurs.)
Metro: Thissio
benaki.gr

Technopolis
 Map p. 223
Pireos 100, Gazi
210 346 1589 or 210 347 5518
Parts closed Mon.
Metro: Kerameikos
technopolis-athens.com

Museum of Greek Musical Instruments
Diogenous 1-3
210 325 0198
Closed Mon. & a.m. Wed.
Metro: Monastiraki
instruments-museum.gr

Kanellopoulos Museum
Theorias 12/Panos
210 324 4447 or 210 321 2313
Closed Mon.
Metro: Monastiraki, Acropoli, or Thissio
pakanellopoulos foundation.org
odysseus.culture.gr

Museum of Greek Folk Art

- 🅰 Map p. 223
- ✉ Kydathinaion 17
- ☎ 210 322 9031
- 🕐 Closed Mon. & from 2 p.m.
- 💲 $
- Ⓜ Metro: Syntagma

melt.gr

Syntagma Square

- 🅰 Map p. 223
- Ⓜ Metro: Syntagma

National Gardens

- 🅰 Map p. 223
- ✉ Amalias
- Ⓜ Metro: Syntagma

Benaki Museum

- 🅰 Map p. 223
- ✉ Vasilissis Sofias/ Koumbari 1
- ☎ 210 367 1000
- 🕐 Closed Mon.-Tues.
- 💲 $$ (free Thurs.)
- Ⓜ Metro: Syntagma

benaki.gr

19th century A.D., ranging across many Mediterranean civilizations (Minoan, Mycenaean, Roman, Persian, Egyptian, and Phoenician).

The Plaka's other principal museum is the **Museum of Greek Folk Art** (Mouseio Hellenikes Laikes Technes), a rather chaotic but fascinating spot, with intriguing nooks and crannies over five floors. Highlights include examples of the work of the primitive painter Theophilos, including an entire painted room transported from a house on the island of Lesvos, alongside a large collection of other folk costumes from most of Greece's islands and mainland regions. For anyone interested in embroidery or clothing generally, the museum is a must.

The Plaka wakes up slowly, but it is the perfect place for an outdoor lunch or an evening's entertainment, starting with a stroll, taking in a typical Greek meal, moving on to some music, and ending late with coffee and brandy in the warm night air. As a rule, avoid eating places with someone trying to persuade you inside. The better restaurants

have no need to pay someone to fill their seats.

Syntagma Square & Around

Syntagma Square (Plateia Syntagmatos) is the heart of Athens. *Syntagma* means "constitution" and the Greek parliament building, or **Vouli,** stands here, along with the **National Gardens** (see sidebar this page). Built as the royal palace, the Vouli was completed in 1842, and King Otto I proclaimed Greece's first constitution from its balcony.

In front of the Vouli, and marking the boundary of the square, is the **Tomb of the Unknown Soldier,** with a permanent guard of Greek soldiers known as Evzones. The best time to visit is on Sundays at 11 a.m., when the main Changing of the Guard ceremony takes place: The entire unit of guards, dressed in colorful traditional costumes, participates, as does a marching band. On other days, the guards, in their regular uniforms, change on the hour in a less pomp-filled but still elaborate routine.

National Gardens

The National Gardens (Ethnikos Kipos) are laid out alongside the Vouli, the Greek parliament building. Created in the 1840s, the gardens are a focal point for the city and were the creation of Amalia, wife of King Otto I. At 40 acres (16 ha), they are not quite big enough to get lost in but still a good size to explore.

On the south side, the grand 19th-century Zappeion is now a conference center, but it was originally built as an exhibition hall by Greek-Romanian cousins, Evangelos and Konstantinos Zappas. The café alongside, an Athenian institution, is the ideal place to stop for a frappé, ouzo, or *mezedes* (small plates of food).

Several cafés stand around the edge of the square, their shady awnings providing a retreat from the sun and a relaxing place to take a break.

Museums: Antoine Emmanuel Benaki (1873–1954) was a Greek cotton trader from Alexandria, Egypt. He spent much of his vast wealth amassing a varied collection of historical artifacts, now displayed on several floors of the **Benaki Museum,** housed in a neoclassical mansion that was once his family home.

The collection starts with statues from the fifth century B.C. On the second floor artifacts from the Greek islands and Asia Minor have pride of place. Greek culture and crafts feature on the third floor, including jewelry, wooden carvings, ceramics, and a sizable collection of Greek costumes. There are also Mycenaean jewelry and many religious items, such as early Gospels, church vestments, and some exquisite icons. Lord Byron's desk is a star exhibit, along with works by El Greco, the most famous Greek painter. Finally, don't miss the rooftop snack bar.

The **War Museum** (Polemiko Mouseio) catches your eye as you walk along Vasilissis Sofias because outside is a display of Greek military equipment, including tanks from World War I and several fighter planes, including a venerable Tiger Moth. Inside, over several large floors, the theme of war

The War Museum features a wide-ranging collection of arms and armor.

is given the broadest possible interpretation. The vast collections of rifles, swords, and other weapons might lack variety, but exhibits such as models of Greek castles and fortified towns should stir your imagination. Other models reenact significant battles from Greek history—and from more recent times there are displays covering the War of Independence, World War II, and Greece's bloody civil war.

Greece has never had money to invest in major works of art, so the **National Gallery of Greece** (Ethniki Pinakothiki), housed in a modern building a short walk east of the War Museum, relies largely on the work of local artists. There are some extraordinarily vivid works: Look for works by Nikos Hadjikyriakos-Ghika, who signs himself "Ghika," one of Greece's most prominent modern artists.

War Museum
- Map p. 223
- Vasilissis Sofias 22/Rizari 2
- 210 724 4464 or 210 725 2974
- Closed Mon.
- $
- Metro: Evangelismos

warmuseum.gr

National Gallery of Greece
- Map p. 223
- Vassileos Konstantinou 50
- 210 723 5937
- Currently closed for restoration until 2016
- Metro: Evangelismos

nationalgallery.gr

Byzantine Museum

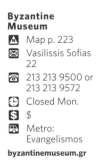

Map p. 223

Vasilissis Sofias 22

213 213 9500 or 213 213 9572

Closed Mon.

$

Metro: Evangelismos

byzantinemuseum.gr

You'll also find engravings and sketches by big-name European artists such as Cézanne, Brueghel, Caravaggio, Picasso, Braque, Rembrandt, and Dürer—and five pieces by El Greco.

The revamped **Byzantine Museum** (Vizantino Mouseio) is one of the city's brightest attractions. The underground wing is an astonishing architectural feat

moves on to display icons, jewelry, ceramics, illuminated manuscripts, Bibles, frescoes, embroideries, and sculptures. The galleries close on the fall of Constantinople in 1453.

Kolonaki & Lykavittos

As you approach the district of Kolonaki, nestled against the southern flank of the Lykavittos hill, from the Syntagma Square area, you become aware that you are entering a more upscale environs of Athens—with more galleries, antiques shops, and fashion stores. Tree-clad Lykavittos can be seen from everywhere in central Athens, and a visit there is a must if you have time.

If you walk toward Kolonaki along Neofytou Douka, you will come to the splendid **Museum of Cycladic Art** (Mouseio Kykladikis kai Archaias Ellinikis Technis), one of the city's most important but lesser known highlights. This modern museum houses a collection of art from the Cycladic islands that dates back 5,000 years. There are vases and glassware, as well as other sculptures in the museum, but it is the extensive range of Cycladic figurines that steals the show. The best works were produced at the height of the Cycladic civilization—about 3000–2000 B.C.

The Cycladic figurines—statues and face masks—are known for their graceful simplicity and are wonderfully

---

Metro Galleries

The underground construction of the Athens Metro in the 1990s spurred archaeological excavations and yielded more than 50,000 artifacts—many of which are now on display in six Metro stations: Among other things, the Syntagma station features artifacts from the Classical, sub-Mycenaean, and Byzantine eras, as well as portions of Roman baths and the Peisistratus Aqueduct. Kerameikos station has artifacts from two burial grounds dating to the beginning of the Peloponnesian War and the remains of ancient ceramic workshops. Monastiraki station displays a wealth of marble sculptures, mosaic floors, frescoes, pots, coins, and objects made from metal and bone. Akropoli station has finds dating to the third millennium B.C., and Evangelismos and Panepistimio stations have artifacts from ancient cemeteries.

Museum of Cycladic Art

Map p. 223

Neofytou Douka 4

210 722 8321

Closed Tues.

$$

Metro: Syntagma or Evangelismos

cycladic.gr

and an attractive home for the extended collection. Special exhibitions are displayed in one of the museum's former homes, a Florentine villa built in the 1840s.

The first gallery sets the collection in context by telling the story of the Byzantine Empire, beginning with the pre-Byzantine art of the Christian era, and

displayed, with subtle lighting bringing out every nuance of their shape and texture. You will immediately see how the figures inspired modern artists, including Spanish artist Pablo Picasso (1881–1973), British sculptor Henry Moore (1898–1986), and Italian painter and sculptor Amedeo Modigliani (1884–1920).

Lykavittos: The highest hill in Athens, 909-foot-high (277 m) Lykavittos—also spelled Lykabettos—dominates this part of central Athens and offers superb views toward the Acropolis and beyond to Peiraiás (Pireas) and the Aegean Sea. The summit can be reached on foot or by **funicular** *(top of Ploutarchou, tel 210 321 7116, $$, Metro: Syntagma)*. The walk to the top is pleasant but tiring, the path zigzagging through scented pinewoods. Think twice in the height of summer, or consider riding up and walking down.

At the top of the hill is the tiny whitewashed 19th-century chapel of **Agios Georgios,** or St. George, and, nearby, the excellent Orizontes Restaurant (there is also a café partway down Lykavittos).

Around Omonia Square

Omonia Square (Plateia Omonoias), northwest of the city center, is the second most important square in Athens after Syntagma; the two squares are linked by the 0.6-mile-long (1 km) Stadiou shopping street. If Syntagma is the city's European face, then Omonia is the Balkan/Middle Eastern counterpoint. It is loud and bustling, full of traders and cheap goods, and emphatically full of life. There are also busy cafés where you can soak up the real Athens atmosphere. And as a landmark for negotiating the city, Omonia can't be beat.

At night the square becomes Athens's equivalent of an older Times Square or London's Soho. Illegal immigrants cluster in Omonia and surrounding streets, selling

Lykavittos
🅜 Map p. 223

Omonia Square
🅜 Map p. 223
🅼 Metro: Omonia

Lykavittos rises high above central Athens.

National Archaeological Museum

- 🅰 Map p. 223
- ✉ Oktovriou 28 / Patission 44
- ☎ 213 214 4800 or 213 214 4890
- 🕐 Closed Mon. a.m. & Sun. after 3 p.m. year-round, Tues.–Sat. after 3 p.m. Nov.–March, & some holidays
- 💲 $$
- 🚇 Metro: Omonia or Victoria

namuseum.gr

imported goods or fake designer gear, but by and large the area is safe, with plenty of people about late into the night. At night Omonia also becomes the red-light district, with a few sleazy movie theaters showing erotic movies in the streets just off the square. However, this is so low-key that many visitors might not even notice it.

One of the liveliest places is a few blocks down Athinas, heading south from Omonia Square—the **Central Market** (Kentriki Agora), the city's main meat and fish market, but other goods are on display, too. It's busy from early in the morning through the afternoon.

INSIDER TIP:

Near Omonia Square, explore the Mediterranean Grocery at Sofokleous 1, a block off Stadiou, for a wide selection of local products.

—PENNY DACKIS
National Geographic publicist

In the evening it livens up again, as there are several ouzeries (where you can sample a variety of ouzos along with snacks) and music clubs in the area. Here you will find cheeses and olives, bread and fruit, fresh herbs and spices, along with flowers and vegetables and nuts and ouzos. In short, if you can eat it, then you'll find it here.

National Archaeological Museum: If you do only two things in Athens, see the Parthenon and visit the National Archaeological Museum (Ethniko Archaiologiko Mouseio), home to the finest treasures from Greek civilizations down the ages. It is a ten-minute walk north of Omonia Square. There is too much to take in on one long visit and it can be worth taking a guided tour.

Head first for the **Mycenaean Collection,** the treasures from the royal tombs at Mycenae, dating from 1500 B.C. They include gleaming gold masks, cups, dishes, and jewelry uncovered by archaeologist Heinrich Schliemann in 1874. Don't miss the exquisite golden burial mask believed by Schliemann to be that of King Agamemnon; in fact, it predates the Trojan War by 200 to 300 years.

You will also find a stunning collection of **Cycladic figurines** from 2000 B.C.

The museum's **sculptures** are equally impressive. Seek out the rudely exuberant statue depicting the gods Pan and Aphrodite, dating from the first century A.D. Also lovely are the remnants of a colossal cult statue of Zeus, found in 1916, and some delicate plaques of dancing girls from the Theater of Dionysos (see p. 225).

The **bronzes**—including some of the museum's largest works—are majestic, none more so than the huge figure of the sea god Poseidon, dating to around 460–450 B.C. The more delicate second-century B.C. "Jockey of Artemision" is one of the museum's most famous bronzes. Another brilliant piece is the "Youth of Antikythera," a bronze statue of a nude male that combines delicacy and power.

The collection of **Egyptian art** reminds the visitor of the ancient Greeks' close trading ties with the Egyptians. Among the works to admire are an alabaster statue of a pharaoh, dating from 2575–2155 B.C.; a granite statuette of Ramses II,

dating from 1290–1224 B.C.; and a stone stele from 664–525 B.C.

The museum also boasts the exquisite **Eleni and Antonios Stathatos Jewelry Collection.** This private collection includes beautiful work in turquoise, silver, bronze, and glass, ranging from the Bronze Age to the Byzantine era. Coin enthusiasts will want to see the **Numismatic Museum,** with its 600,000 coins from ancient Greece through Roman and Byzantine periods up to the present day. ∎

NEED TO KNOW
Port Logistics: Peiraiás

Most cruise ships dock in Peiraiás (Pireas), 7 miles (11 km) southwest of central Athens, at the far southern end of the port (olp.gr), at either **Cruise Terminal A or B.** There are also gates E11 and E12, respectively, of 12 numbered port gates; the other gates handle ferries.

Getting to Central Athens

Allow 90 minutes to get to and from Athens from Peiraiás; some means of transportation will be faster than others.

Cabs wait outside both cruise terminals: Note there is a cruise-terminal surcharge ($$) on top of the metered fare. The journey time to central Athens is 20–40 minutes or more, depending on traffic. Be sure the meter is on and note that drivers often pick up other passengers en route, who will also pay full fare.

The quickest way to central Athens is via the underground metro. Take Line 1 from the Peiraiás station, located between gates E6 and E7 (5- to 10-min. walk from Terminal A, 10- to 20-min. walk

from Terminal B). It's a 20-minute ride—beware pickpockets—to the Monastiraki stop (near the Plaka and many sights), in central Athens.

Alternatively, you can take bus 040 to Syntagma Square from the Apheteria bus stop on the main road between the two terminals. Several buses stop here, so check carefully before boarding. Bus and metro tickets ($) are valid for 90 minutes, including transfers (athens transport.com/english/tickets).

Athens Highlights

You can spend your entire port of call time at any one of these destinations, but here are some suggested times to help with your planning. Note, these do not allow for travel time to and from and/or waiting in line:
• Acropolis & Agora: 2–3 hours
• Acropolis Museum: 1 hour
• Walking (and taking lunch) in the Plaka district: 1–2 hours
• National Archaeological Museum: minimum 1 hour

The Peloponnesus

The Peloponnesus (Peloponnisos)—the large peninsula southwest of Athens—contains a wealth of ancient sites. On the east side of the peninsula are Tiryns, Argos, Epidavros, and Mycenae, all of them easily accessed from Nafplio, an elegant port town that is a charming place to explore in its own right. The important site of Olympia, on the peninsula's west coast, can be reached from the more modest port of Katakolon.

Bourtzi's island fort guards Nafplio.

NEED TO KNOW p. 239

Nafplio

Ⓜ 220 B3

Visitor Information

✉ Martiou 25, Nafplio

☎ 275 202 4444

nafplio.gr

Peloponnesian Folklore Museum

✉ Vasileos Alexandrou 1, Nafplio

☎ 275 202 8947

🕐 Closed Tues. & after 2:30 p.m.

💲 $

pli.gr

Nafplio & Around

Nafplio is beautifully sited next to the water with views across a gulf to the mountains of the eastern Peloponnesus. The narrow streets and pristine whitewashed houses of the Old Town are reminiscent of a Greek island.

On Nafplio's main square, Plateia Syntagma, is the **Archaeological Museum** (tel 275 202 7502, closed Mon., $), housed in an elegant 18th-century former Venetian warehouse. Its highlight is a circa 1500 B.C. suit of bronze armor that has survived virtually intact from Mycenaean times. Many items here were found at nearby Tiryns (see p. 237) and Mycenae (see p. 238).

The town's **Peloponnesian Folklore Museum** is excellent, with extensive displays of colorful traditional costumes and a wide collection of farming and domestic artifacts. The **War Museum** (Amalias 22, Nafplio, tel 275 202 5591, closed Mon.) is full of weaponry and documents and a large collection of photographs portraying the impact of World War II on Greece.

Three fortresses add to Nafplio's picturesque appeal. You can reach the hilltop **Palamidi Fortress** (tel 275 202 8036, $) either by climbing 999 steps or by an easier but longer route by road. The views from the top make the effort worthwhile. The main fortress is Venetian and dates from the 18th century, with three smaller fortresses inside the walls.

The **Akronafplia** (which is also known by its Turkish name, Its Kale) is slightly less dramatic. This was the site of Nafplio's original acropolis, and several castles have stood here over the centuries. There are few remains, but it is a pleasant place for a stroll. Another good walk leads around the headland on which the fortress stands.

The third fortress, the smaller **Bourtzi,** stands on an islet in the

Epidavros

The ancient **theater** at Epidavros *(map 220 C3, tel 275 302 2009, odysseus .culture.gr, $$)*, 18 miles (29 km) east of Nafplio, is one of the most wonderful sights in Greece. Built in the fourth century B.C. and considered a masterpiece of Greek architecture, it can hold 14,000 people. The acoustics are marvelous.

But there is more to Epidavros than the theater. The site was dedicated to the god of healing, Asklepios, the son of Apollo, and had a **temple** built in his honor, of which fragments remain. People brought their health problems to Epidavros and its medical practitioners; the site's museum contains, among other things, examples of the medical instruments used.

Another important building is the circular **tholos**, though its purpose is uncertain. It may have housed the sacred serpents used in some rites, or been a place where those rites were carried out. Near the tholos are the remains of the fifth-century B.C. **stadium;** some of the seating and the starting and finishing lines for races are visible.

---

hay. Built in the 15th century, at the time of the Venetian occupation, it owes its importance to the deceptive waters here. They look deep, but in fact there is only one navigable passage into Nafplio, which the Bourtzi guards could block by stringing chains from the islet to town.

Tiryns: Just a couple miles (4 km) northwest of Nafplio, ancient Tiryns is definitely worth a visit for its massive **walls.** It is easily reached via bus from Nafplio's center.

At the time of the Mycenaean civilization (ca 1600–1100 B.C.), Tiryns stood on the Aegean guarding Mycenae and neighboring Argos. Since then the sea has retreated, leaving Tiryns stranded inland. Homer described the town as having mighty walls, and these are still the first things you notice. Their remains—rebuilt in the 13th century B.C.—are 2,300 feet (701 m) in length, up to 26 feet (8 m) wide, and

33 feet (10 m) high, although they originally stood twice this high. The Mycenaeans used their characteristic cyclopean masonry technique to fashion the walls, piecing together the huge limestone blocks without the use of mortar.

Little remains of the **royal palace** *($)*, apart from foundations, although with the aid of a site plan it is possible to make out sections such as the royal apartments.

Argos: The former importance of Argos, a town that can be visited en route to Mycenae and Epidavros, can be seen at the site of **ancient Argos.** The principal attraction is the fourth-century B.C. theater, which seats a staggering 20,000 people. The site also has the remains of a Roman bath, theater, aqueduct, and large drainage channels.

Above the site a steep path leads to the fortress where the original Argos acropolis was

Tiryns
- 220 B3
- 2.5 miles (4 km) NW of Nafplio

Argos
- 220 B3
- 7 miles (11 km) NW of Nafplio

Mycenae

- 220 B3
- 14 miles (22.5 km) N of Nafplio
- 275 107 6585
- Closed after 3 p.m. Nov.–March
- $$$

odysseus.culture.gr

situated before being replaced by a medieval castle (although some of the walls date back to the sixth century A.D.). The views are superb.

In town, the **Archaeological Museum** (*Plateia Agiou Petrou/ Vasilissis Olgas 2, Argos, tel 275 106 8819, closed Mon., $*), close to the main square, has finds from Argos, Tiryns, and Mycenae.

The remains of Olympia's Palaestra, where athletes, in particular wrestlers, trained

Olympia

- 220 B3
- Odos 74 (0.25 mi/0.5 km outside modern Olympia), 18 miles (29 km) E of Katakolon
- 262 402 2517
- Closed after 3 p.m. Sat.–Sun. year-round & after 3 p.m. daily Nov.–March
- $$

odysseus.culture.gr

Mycenae: Once a major center of civilization, Mycenae (Mykinai) is the most important historical site on the Peloponnesus. Here, on a hilltop, stand the ruins of a great Bronze Age fortified palace known as the House of Atreus after the ruler of that name, the son of Pelops (who gave his name to the Peloponnesus). The whole is surrounded by immense walls and evidence of a large supporting community.

The first thing you see as you approach the site is the

14th-century B.C. **Treasury of Atreus,** one of several "beehive" tombs built on the slopes of the hill without mortar. Inside, the acoustics are startling, as is the lintel over the entrance, which weighs almost 120 tons.

To enter the Mycenaean citadel, you pass under the 13th-century B.C. **Lion Gate,** the massive carved lintel that straddles the entrance. Note the grooves in the floor, made by chariots, and the holes for bolts. Inside the gate and to your right are the circular remains of the **royal tombs.** In Grave Circle A, as it is known, six graves were detected, containing a total of 19 bodies. Archaeologist Heinrich Schliemann found here the glorious golden burial mask that he believed was buried with King Agamemnon. It and other masks, jewelry, crowns, and more discovered here now form one of the major attractions at Athens's National Archaeological Museum (see pp. 234–235).

You need a certain amount of imagination, and a map, to make the most of the rest of Mycenae. The palace was destroyed by fire in 1200 B.C.; the burn marks can still be seen on the foundation stones that remain. A century later, the site was abandoned and left to decay until its rediscovery by Schliemann in 1874.

Olympia

Birthplace of the Olympic Games and an important sanctuary of ancient Greece, Olympia is on the west side of the Peloponnesus. It is easily reached from the port town of **Katakolon** (see sidebar this page). The first games were held here in 776 B.C. and continued for more than a millennium. The Olympic flame of the modern games, resurrected in 1896, is still lit here, in front of the seventh-century B.C. **Temple of Hera,** close to the site's modern-day entrance.

You see much of ancient Olympia before reaching the Stadium where the games were held, revealing what a vast complex it was—the equivalent of modern Olympic villages. At its center was the fifth-century B.C. **Temple of Zeus,** marked by column bases and fallen pillars, which once contained a gold-and-ivory statue of Zeus made in the group of buildings whose foundations are in front of the temple. One of these buildings is marked as the **Studio of Pheidias,** the sculptor who crafted the statue. Nearby are the remains of the **Leonidaion,** the guesthouse used for distinguished visitors.

Behind the Leonidaion is the **Bouleuterion,** a meeting house where the equivalent of the modern International Olympic Committee would gather. It was also where the athletes swore to uphold the Olympic rules. From here the athletes made their way to the Stadium, passing rows of statues portraying past athletes who had broken the rules. Entrance to the **Stadium** was via a vaulted tunnel. Up to 50,000 spectators could watch the

athletes perform on a sporting area some 700 feet long by 94 feet wide (213 m by 28.5 m).

Museums: In present-day Olympia, opposite the site of Olympia, the **Archaeological Museum of Olympia** houses incomparable finds from the site. Pride of place goes to the sculptures and friezes that adorned the Temple of Zeus. Exhibits also include items used in the games, such as discuses, part of a starting block, and the stones used by the weight lifters. Also stop by the **Museum of the History of the Ancient Olympic Games** *(tel 262 102 9119, $)*, which focuses on the ancient Olympic Games and other athletics. ■

Archaeological Museum of Olympia

✉ Dytiki Ellada, Olympia
☎ 262 402 2529
💲 $$
olympia-greece.org/museum.html

NEED TO KNOW
Port Logistics: Nafplio
Cruise ships tender passengers directly to Nafplio's **Old Town waterfront.** From here, you could take a taxi to Tiryns, Argos, Mycenae, or Epidavros, or a bus *(bus station on Andrea Siggrou, a few blocks from waterfront, journey time 30–45 min., depending on destination),* but joining a cruise-based shore excursion to these sites may be easier if you wish to see more than one.

Port Logistics: Katakolon
Cruise ships dock at a **jetty** that is a 5-minute walk from the town of Katakolon (or Katakolo). Taxis *(taxikatakolon.gr)* charge high but negotiable rates for the 18-mile (29 km) trip to Olympia: Ship-organized tours can be cheaper. You could also take the **Katakolon Express bus** *(katakolon-express.com, book well in advance)* or the train *(1–4 daily, journey time 45 min., trainose.gr, $$$).*

The Islands

Greece has more than 6,000 islands, most graced with azure seas, fine beaches, pretty interiors, and—in the case of the 227 islands that are inhabited—a medley of often charming white-housed villages. Choosing which to visit on a short trip is a challenge, but verdant Corfu and Rhodes, two of the largest islands, feature on most cruise ship itineraries, and many ships put in to Santorini, the busy but beautiful archetype of Greece's smaller islands, as well as Crete (see pp. 244–247).

One of the many sheltered, sandy beaches on Corfu's north coast

NEED TO KNOW p. 243

Corfu

🗺 220 A4

Visitor Information

www.corfuvisit.net
zoomcorfu.gr

Corfu

Corfu, close to both Italy in the west and Albania in the east, has been touched over the years by several foreign cultures. The Greek name for the island is Kérkyra, while Corfu is an Italian version of the ancient Greek word *koryphai*, meaning "the hills," referring to two spots in Corfu town where the Old and New Fortresses were founded.

The island's fertility, size, strategic position, and natural beauty all contributed to its development. It was much coveted by the Romans and other powers over the centuries. The Venetians had the most impact as a result of their occupation from 1386 to 1797, not least in the Italianate architecture of Corfu town and elsewhere.

Corfu Town: Nowhere is the island's pan-European background more evident than in beguiling Corfu town. It may have Greek tavernas in the backstreets, but it also shows strong influences from Britain, France, and Italy. This cosmopolitan mix is most evident in the center of

The Venus de Milo

In 1820 farmer Giorgos Kentrotas was digging in the ruins of the ancient city of Milos (on the Cycladic island of the same name), searching for some building materials to repair his house, when he uncovered a well-preserved statue of the Greek goddess Aphrodite (known to the Romans as Venus). By a lucky coincidence, he was not the only one there. Olivier Voutier, a French naval officer and amateur historian, was also exploring the site. Together they uncovered the two halves of the broken statue and reassembled them for the first time in thousands of years, although they could find no trace of the statue's missing arms.

A few weeks later Voutier persuaded an eminent French classicist to examine the statue. He agreed to buy it from Kentrotas and ship it to the Louvre in Paris. Once on display the statue caused a sensation. It was hailed as a masterpiece and a rare surviving work of the great fourth-century B.C. sculptor Praxiteles. This latter assertion was proved wrong, however, when the inscription on the plinth (now lost) was translated and found to name the sculptor as Alexandros of Antioch, a traveling craftsman who lived in the first century B.C. The statue continues to attract thousands of visitors daily and is known the world over for its beauty.

town, around the **Esplanade** (Spianada), a combination park and town square centered on an English-looking cricket field, once a Venetian firing range. On its eastern side, on a promontory jutting into the Ionian Sea, stands the Venetian **Old Fortress** (Palaio Frourio; $), completed in 1559.

At the north end of the cricket field stands the **Palace of St. Michael and St. George** (Palaia Anaktora; closed Mon. a.m., $), built between 1819 and 1824 as the residence of the British High Commissioner. It was renovated in the 1950s and now contains administrative buildings, a library, and, in one wing, the **Museum of Asian Art.** This collection, unique in Greece, was built up from 10,000 items amassed by Grigorios Manos (1850–1929), a Greek diplomat from Corfu who traveled extensively in the Orient.

The **Liston,** a row of cafés and stores built by a Frenchman in 1807 at the request of Napoleon, who wanted its colonnades to echo the famous Rue de Rivoli in Paris, borders the western edge of the Esplanade. The cafés along the Liston are where everyone comes to socialize. Your coffee will cost more here than anywhere else in Corfu, but it's *the* place to be.

At the Esplanade's southern end is a park with a magnificent fountain and, nearby, the **Unification Monument** (Enosis Monument), which celebrates the occasion in 1864 when the Ionian islands were united with the rest of Greece after their final period of British rule.

The best excursions from Corfu town are to **Paleokastritsa,** a pretty but very touristy village 14 miles (22.5 km) to the northwest, with a good beach and the panoramic Theotokos

Museum of Asian Art

✉ Palaia Anaktora, Corfu town

☎ 266 103 0443

🕐 Closed Mon.

💲 $

matk.gr

Greek Orthodox clergy prepare for a holy day in Corfu town.

Santorini

■ 220 D2

Visitor Information

visit-santorini.com

Rhodes

■ 221 E2

Visitor Information

✉ Corner of
Alexander the
Great St. &
Street of the
Knights, Rhodes
town

☎ 224 107 4313

⏱ Closed Sun.

rhodes.gr

Monastery; and to **Achilleion**
(achillion-corfu.gr, $$), a sumptu-
ous hillside villa 6 miles (10 km)
south built for Empress Elisabeth
(1837–1898), wife of the
Habsburg emperor Franz Josef.

Santorini

Santorini (Thira) is dramatic
and unique, formed from the
remains of a volcanic crater.
The scenic village of **Oia** is the
island's highlight, dramatically
perched on the rim of the
caldera at the northern end
of the island. At the island's
southern extremity is **Akrotiri**
(tel 228 608 1939 or 210 331
0280, closed Mon. year-round
& Sun. Nov.–March, $$), the

remarkably well preserved
remains of a Minoan city devastated in the volcanic eruption
of 1625 B.C. that also destroyed
the old island, creating the
present one. On the east
coast, the remains of **Archaia
Thira,** or Ancient Thira (closed
Mon., $), overlook the sea. The
Archaeological Museum (tel
228 602 2217, closed Mon., $) in
Thira has finds from these and
other sites.

Santorini produces surprisingly
good wine—despite the climate,
the assyrtiko grape flourishes
here—and there are excursions
to local wineries (santowines.gr).
Fields of what at first look like
basket trees are actually vines
covered by cane baskets.

Tucked in and around
Santorini's caldera are several
red- and black-sand beaches
and tiny islands, accessible by
popular boat trips from Thira.
The largest islet, **Thirasia,** was
part of the main island until an
earthquake in 236 B.C. caused it
to split away. Like Santorini, it has
fertile volcanic soil. **Manolas** is
the island's harbor, with a choice
of places to eat.

Rhodes

Rhodes (Rodos) is the largest
of the Dodecanese group of
islands. Much of the northern
coast is developed for tourism,
but it also has great beaches,
perfect for sunbathing all day.
Most visitors, however, will want
to explore **Rhodes town,** whose
medieval walled Old Town is
a jewel of the Aegean and a
UNESCO World Heritage site.

Old Town: The historic quarter dates back to the arrival of the Knights of St. John in 1306—although a town has existed on the spot since 408 B.C.—who stamped their lasting identity by building the Old Town, which they ruled until 1519.

Some of the Old Town has turned into a tourist bazaar, but if you venture into the backstreets you see authentic life still going on. The imposing hilltop **Palace of the Grand Masters** and the cobbled **Street of the Knights** (Odos Ippoton) are the key sights. Heavily restored over the centuries, the latter is lined with Inns of the Order of the Knights of St. John. The inns were meeting places for different nationalities—hence the Inn of Italy, the Inn of France (the most elaborate), and so on.

Near the main entrance to the Old Town is the **Archaeological Museum,** within the former hospital of the Grand Knights. Rhodes is rich in archaeological sites, including Kamiros and Lindos, and the star exhibit is the Aphrodite of Rhodes, a sensuous first-century B.C. statue. (Many cruise ships and local operators offer tours to **Lindos** and its ruined acropolis, 35 miles/56 km south of Rhodes town, but it's a busy and only moderately interesting site.)

Other museums within the Old Town's thick walls include the **Decorative Arts Museum,** with a fine collection of works that are unique to the island, with decorative tiles from Lindos, and a reconstructed period house. ∎

Palace of the Grand Masters

 Odos Ippoton, Rhodes town

☎ 224 136 5270

🕐 Closed Mon. Nov.–March

💲 $$; combined ticket with Archaeological Museum & other sights: $$$$

Archaeological Museum

 Odos Ippoton, Rhodes town

☎ 224 136 5256

🕐 Closed Mon. Nov.–March

💲 $$; combined ticket with Palace of the Grand Masters & other sights: $$$$

Decorative Arts Museum

 Plateia Argyrokastrou, Rhodes town

☎ 224 136 5246

💲 $

NEED TO KNOW

Port Logistics: Corfu

Cruise ships berth at the **New Port** (*corfuport.gr*), a mile (1.6 km) from Corfu town's old quarter, a 20- to 25-minute walk along a single road (with the sea on your left); or take bus 2 from the terminal: To find the stop, exit the terminal and turn left past the long parking lot for taxis and rental cars.

Port Logistics: Santorini

Cruise ships tender to Santorini's old port, **Skala**. It's a very steep hike up the 587-step zigzag path to Thira, perched high above: Avoid the waiting donkeys for rent to help you and take the cable car (*scc.gr, $*), though lines can be long. Cruise passengers taking excursions are usually tendered to the ferry port at **Athinios** (*santorini-port.com*), 5 miles (8 km) south of Thira, for onward bus connections.

Port Logistics: Rhodes

Many cruise ships use the **harbor** at Rhodes town, docking at the port just outside the walls of the Old Town.

Crete

Crete (Kriti) is the largest island in Greece and the fifth largest in the Mediterranean after Sicily, Sardinia, Cyprus, and Corsica. Within its shores are high mountain ranges, the longest gorge in Europe, hundreds of excellent beaches, and one of Greece's most significant ancient sites: Knossos. Seeing this last site, along with the island's capital, Iraklio (Heraklion), will take up all the time of visitors who only have time for a short stay.

The redoubtable 16th-century Koules fort guards the entrance to Iraklio harbor.

NEED TO KNOW p. 247

Iraklio
🅰 220 D1
Visitor Information
✉ Xanthoudidou 1 (opposite the Archaeological Museum), Iraklio
☎ 281 022 8225 or 281 022 8203
🕐 Closed Sun.
heraklion.gr

Iraklio

Greece's fifth largest city has plenty to offer, but, as with Athens, you ideally need time to get acquainted. Iraklio suffered damage during World War II and now has many unappealing concrete buildings and a chaotic road system. But the city also has great character and a superb archaeological museum containing some of the world's most renowned antiquities.

Iraklio has been settled since Neolithic times, and it flourished as the harbor for the Minoan center at Knossos (see pp. 246–247), 3 miles (5 km) to the south. The Venetians conquered it in the 13th century and made it their Aegean capital, building a fort to protect the harbor. The **Koules fort** (*$*) that stands there today was built in the 16th century after the first was destroyed in an earthquake, and it played an important role in the city's history. It was the focal point when the Ottoman Turks beset the city in 1648, a siege that lasted until 1669, when the Venetians finally surrendered the island to the Turks.

On the southern side of the harbor is another Venetian structure, the **Arsenal,** constructed in the 16th century as the place where the fleet for the Aegean was built and repaired. Iraklio's magnificent **city walls** are from the same period.

Archaeological Museum & Around: The Archaeological Museum is Iraklio's sightseeing highlight. Rich finds have been made all over this large and historically important island, and most of them have ended up here. Among the most treasured artifacts are 1600–1400 B.C. frescoes from Knossos, such as the "Bull Leaping," "La Parisienne," the "Saffron Gatherers," and the "Blue Bird." Neolithic tools, pottery from prepalatial and early palatial times, jewelry, and vases, as well as the enigmatic 1600–1450 B.C. Phaistos Disk—a clay disk stamped with as yet undeciphered hieroglyphs—can also be seen.

The museum is close to **Plateia Eleftherias,** a large square that is the heart of Iraklio, a busy traffic hub with a pedestrianized and tree-shaded center. It comes alive in the evenings, when the bars and restaurants open and half the city seems to congregate here for the evening *volta* (communal stroll).

It is a short walk from Plateia Eleftherias to the city's other main square, **Plateia Venizelou,** known for its 17th-century Venetian fountain. There's a Turkish fountain on nearby Plateia Kallergon, where you will also find the 17th-century **Loggia,** once a meeting place for Cretan nobility, now City Hall.

Behind the Loggia is the church of **Agios Titos,** built in the tenth century and dedicated to the Island's patron saint, St. Titos, who brought Christianity to Crete, and whose relics it contains.

Other Museums: From Plateia Venizelou, Chandakos leads to the waterfront, where, just a few steps to the right, the **Historical Museum of Crete,** gives a good picture of Cretan life through the ages. There are examples of art from the Venetian period as well as an interesting collection of Byzantine art. The highlight is the only painting by El Greco (1541–1614) displayed on the island where he was born: the "Monastery of St. Catherine

Archaeological Museum

- ✉ Xanthoudidou 2, Iraklio
- ☎ 281 027 9000 or 218 027 9086
- 🕐 Closed Mon. a.m. year-round, after 3 p.m. Sun. April–Oct., & after 3 p.m. daily Nov.–March
- 💲 $$

Nikos Kazantzakis

If there is one fictional figure who typifies most people's idea of the exuberant, emotional Greek character it is Zorba, portrayed by Anthony Quinn in the 1964 movie *Zorba the Greek*. The character was created in the novel of the same name by Nikos Kazantzakis (1883–1957), the greatest modern Greek novelist. Born in Iraklio, he traveled widely in Europe, Africa, and Asia before starting to write. Best known for novels such as *Christ Recrucified* and *The Greek Passion* (both 1948), he also wrote essays, poetry, and plays. Martin Scorsese's 1988 movie of his novel *The Last Temptation of Christ* proved controversial in its attempt to depict the human nature of Jesus Christ. The tomb of Kazantzakis can be visited in Iraklio.

Historical Museum of Crete

- ✉ A. & M. Kalokairinos House, Sofokli Venizelou 27, Iraklio
- ☎ 281 028 3219 or 281 028 8708
- 🕐 Closed Sun. & after 3:30 p.m. Nov.–March
- 💲 $$

historical-museum.gr

Who actually used Knossos' so-called Throne Room and its "throne" (right) remains unclear.

Museum of Religious Art

 Agiou Mina / Plateia Agias Aikaterinis, Iraklio

☎ 281 028 8825

🕑 Closed Sat.-Sun.

💲 $

Natural History Museum of Crete

✉ Sofokli Venizelou, Iraklio

☎ 281 028 2740

💲 $$$

nhmc.uoc.gr

on Mount Sinai" (ca 1570). No museum on the history of Crete could ignore the events of World War II, and the museum tells the full story of the suffering on the island, which fell to the Germans in 1941.

Also worth seeing is the **Museum of Religious Art** (Museum of St. Aikaterini), next to the city's 19th-century cathedral of Agios Minas, with an extensive collection of Byzantine icons, frescoes, and manuscripts. The **Natural History Museum of Crete** has displays on the flora and fauna not only of Crete—which is incredibly well blessed in this respect—but of the whole Aegean.

Knossos

The remains of the vast Royal Minoan Palace at Knossos, 3 miles (5 km) south of Iraklio,

are Crete's major visitor attraction; they are easily reached by bus from Iraklio. Plan to spend at least two hours here if you hope to see much of the palace and surrounding town. Summer is a busy time, so arrive at the start of the day or in the early evening and consider being shown around by an official guide to make the most of what otherwise can be a bewildering site.

Today's remains are far from the earliest on the site, which was first settled about 6000 B.C. The first palace here has been dated to 2000 B.C. This was destroyed in an earthquake in about 1700 B.C. The most recent palace was built after that earthquake and survived until 1380 B.C., when it, too, was destroyed, this time by fire.

This palace was built on a vast scale, with some 1,300 rooms, and at the height of the Minoan civilization, it is estimated that there would have been 12,000 people living here, with four times as many in the immediate surroundings. The site is extensive, covering 185 acres (75 ha), but only a portion of it is open to the public.

One of the best known legends of ancient Greece originated here, that of the labyrinth and its guardian, the Minotaur. After the wife of King Minos of Knossos gave birth to a beast that had the head of a bull on the body of a man, the king imprisoned the Minotaur in a labyrinth beneath his palace and fed it with human sacrifices. Theseus, with the help of Minos's daughter, Ariadne, tracked down and slew the creature and, in so doing, liberated Athens from an oppressive bondage.

It was thought that King Minos was a legend, too, until British archaeologist Sir Arthur Evans (1851–1941) found the Minoan Palace at Knossos. In fact, the word "labyrinth" derives from *labrys,* which is a double-headed ax, a Minoan symbol seen throughout the palace.

Buildings scattered over the site today are reconstructions by Evans. His use of modern materials is still controversial, but it is fascinating to see some of the palace rooms brought to life. When you enter the site, you pass three large pits, probably used for storing grain. As you progress you will see on the right one of the famous symbols of Knossos, the **Horns of Consecration,** which represents the horns of the sacred bull that would originally have stood at the top of the palace. Left of the main path, almost opposite the Horns, are steps leading to the **piano nobile,** the upper floor, which has the remains of shrines and good views over much of the site.

There are many **frescoes** around the palace, but they are replicas of originals that have been removed for safekeeping to the Archaeological Museum in Iraklio (see p. 245). The "Lily Prince" fresco, just beyond the Horns of Consecration, is a highlight.

In the center of the site is a large, open **central courtyard,** where the sport of bull leaping took place. Sportsmen would face charging bulls head-on and leap over them by grasping their horns and performing a somersault. Beyond this area are the main parts of the palace, including the royal apartments. ∎

Knossos

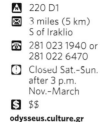

- 220 D1
- 3 miles (5 km) S of Iraklio
- 281 023 1940 or 281 022 6470
- Closed Sat.–Sun. after 3 p.m. Nov.–March
- $$

odysseus.culture.gr

NEED TO KNOW
Port Logistics: Iraklio

Ships dock at points around Iraklio's sprawling **port** *(portheraklion.gr),* with shuttle buses connecting to the terminal building a mile (1.6 km) east of the city center. Walk (partly uphill), take a taxi *($$),* or catch bus 1 *(4 hourly, journey time 15 min.)* to Plateia Eleftherias, a square close to the Archaeological Museum; bus 2 runs from the terminal to Knossos *(2 hourly, 30 min., bus-service-crete-ktel.com).*

From the Byzantine treasures and great Islamic monuments of Istanbul to the majestic Roman remains at Ephesus

Turkey

Introduction & Map   250–251

Istanbul   252–267

İstiklal Caddesi: Walking the Old Grande
   Rue de Péra   264–265

Need to Know: Istanbul   267

Ephesus   268–271

Need to Know: Kuşadası   271

Restaurants   300–303

Istanbul's Hagia Sophia—the name means
"divine wisdom"—was built in the sixth century.

Turkey

If you have been traveling through the Mediterranean, then Turkey, and Istanbul in particular, will look and feel very different to the places you have visited in Western Europe and the Balkans. And so it should, for most of this country belongs to a different continent: Asia. And it has been shaped by very different cultural, social, historical, and religious forces.

Young Istanbullus relax at a trendy café on the Galata Bridge, which spans the Golden Horn.

It is a commonplace to describe Istanbul as a symbol of Turkey as a whole, as a bridge between Europe and Asia, a meeting place of conflicting ideas and forces; a place where East meets West; and where traditional values clash with modernization and secularism is pitched against religious orthodoxy. But the crossroads metaphor is not just simplistic. It simply doesn't ring true. Turkey is not confused about its future, nor is Istanbul an ideological battleground. Rather, both the city and the country are on a direct path to prosperity, a new and confident regional power as well as one of the world's oldest and finest cultural centers.

Istanbul boasts some of the greatest pagan, Christian, and Islamic buildings in existence, the legacy of a history that saw it, among other things, a former capital of the

eastern part of the Roman Empire—when it would become known as Constantinople; the center of the Byzantine empire that emerged after Rome's fall; the object, in the 13th century—for all that it was a great Christian city—of a rapacious Crusader army; and then the focal point of the mighty Ottoman Empire that brought Islam to the city in the 15th century.

Ancient Roman and other ruins survive here, along with mosaic-swathed Byzantine churches that were later converted to mosques, as well as palaces of breathtaking splendor and new mosques—notably the Blue Mosque—raised by the Ottoman conquerors.

But beyond the sights, contemporary Istanbul is a fun and exciting city in its own right, a metropolis of 13 million that buzzes with life and individuality. Teeming

washed his hands after dispatching prisoners.

The twin-turreted **Gate of Salutation** (Bab-üs Selâm) leads to the **second courtyard,** once home to thousands of staff. Originally only persons on official palace business could pass through this vast portal. All visitors were also required to dismount, as only the sultan could proceed on horseback.

To the right of the courtyard are the **Palace Kitchens,** that fed up to 4,000 people a day, and twice as many if there was a banquet. Today the kitchens are filled with silver services, pots and pans, and a stunning display of Far Eastern porcelain, which was prized by the Ottomans, as the dye used in its production was supposed to neutralize poison.

Directly on the other side of the courtyard, inside the **old treasury,** is a vast display of vintage weaponry plundered from all over the Middle East, Europe, and Asia. In the north corner of the courtyard are the **Imperial Stables** (Istabl-ı Âmire), now a temporary exhibition space. The entrance to the harem (see p. 255) is beneath the Tower of Justice, the palace's tallest building.

Entrance to the **third courtyard,** or "inner palace," was strictly controlled. Even the grand vizier, the sultan's chief adviser, could only pass through the **Gate of Felicity** (Bab-üs Saadet) with special permission. The sultans would have spent their days in this courtyard's lush gardens and ornate buildings.

Topkapı Palace

🅰 Map p. 253

✉ Bab-ı I lümâyûn Caddesi, Sultanahmet

☎ 0212 512 0480; reservations: online at muze .gov.tr/buy_e_ ticket

🕐 Closed Tues.

💲 $$$$

🚇 Gülhane

topkapisarayi.gov.tr
muze.gov.tr/topkapi-en
muze.gov.tr/harem-en

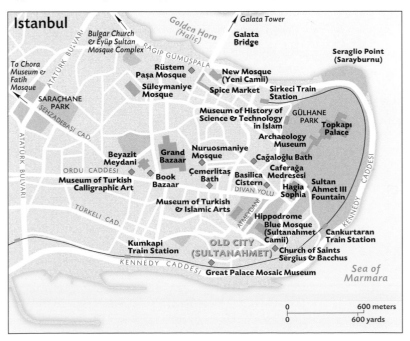

Behind the gate is the **Throne Room** (Arz Odası), where military leaders and imperial advisers would petition the sultan, who would receive news of his far-flung empire while reclining on a golden plinth in this lavishly decorated room.

Behind the throne room is the **Library of Ahmet III** (Enderûn Kütüphanesi). Its soaring dome is frescoed with an intricate weave of orange and blue flowers. Natural light filters through glass stained with Koranic inscriptions below İznik tiles thick with delicate tulips.

INSIDER TIP:

The harem at Topkapı Palace is very popular and books up quickly. Buy the separate timed entry ticket at the kiosk in front of it and view the palace's other sights while waiting for your time.

—SALLY McFALL
National Geographic contributor

To the left of the library is the **Chamber of the Sacred Relics** (Kutsal Emanetler Dairesi), one of the most arresting sights in the palace. The pavilion contains some of the most important relics in the Islamic world, most of which were brought back by Sultan Selim I (Selim the Grim, 1465–1520) from his campaign to subdue Arabia in 1517. These artifacts include a tooth and a footprint of the Prophet, the ancient keys to the Ka'aba—the most sacred site in Islam, found in Mecca—and one of Muhammad's finely inscribed swords. The star exhibit, protected behind glass, is the mantel once worn by Muhammad.

The **Imperial Treasury** (Hazine-ı Âmire) takes up the entire east wall of the inner courtyard. This shimmering collection of gems and gold has few rivals. Read each inscription carefully, as the story behind each emerald-encrusted sword or diamond headdress is fascinating. The most valuable exhibit is the Spoonmaker's Diamond, a brilliant 86-carat gem lit up by a surrounding double row of 49 additional diamonds.

The leafy **fourth courtyard** was a sanctuary for the sultan and his family, a welcome respite after the ostentatious overload of the third courtyard. The **Circumcision Room** (Sünnet Odası) is decorated with unusual Chinese-inspired tiles.

Next to the Circumcision Room is the golden **İftar Pavilion,** where the sultans would have broken their fast during the Muslim feast of Ramadan. The views are sublime. The nearby **Baghdad Kiosk** commemorates Murat IV's Baghdad campaign and capture of the Mesopotamian city in 1638. It's a classically Ottoman reclining room with fine carpets and cushions, where sultans would have chatted and smoked with friends and relatives.

Topkapı Palace was the primary residence of the Ottoman sultans for approximately 400 years.

Harem: The extra fee (*$$*) to visit the harem, where you get the chance to glimpse what was *haram*, or forbidden, for more than four centuries, is worth every cent. The harem served as the sultan's private chambers, as well as that of his close family, a fact made clear by the sheer level of opulence. The scores of small rooms, fine latticework, and stained-glass windows give the impression of a gilded cage, which is exactly what it was for several sultans-to-be, who were imprisoned in paradise lest they threaten the current sultan's throne.

The narrow **Golden Road** (Altınyol) connects the harem's key rooms, including the **Imperial Hall** (Hünkâr Sofası), a rococo playground for the sultan and his family, and the deliciously beautiful **Apartments of the Queen Mother** (Valide Sultan Dairesi), a central figure in Ottoman palace society.

Of key historical importance is the **Courtyard of the (Black) Eunuchs** (Harem Ağaları Taşlığı).

These castrated figures administered the harem. Although they couldn't physically take part in harem scandal, they were the instigators of many a conspiracy within what was literally a cut-throat world of several hundred women, all jockeying for supreme status and power.

Archaeology Museum: This world-class museum contains exquisite ancient artifacts, Roman splendors, and the finest treasures of the Ottoman world outside Topkapı Palace. It has two entrances, one in the first public courtyard of Topkapı Palace and the other in Gülhane Park.

Allow two hours for even a brief tour of the principal collection. As the Ottoman Empire spread over North Africa, the Levant, and present-day Syria, Iraq, and Saudi Arabia, the wonders piled up in Istanbul. Additional treasures from southern Turkey and present-day Lebanon were rounded up in the empire's dying days.

Archaeology Museum

🅰 Map p. 253
✉ Alemdar Caddesi, Osman Hamdi Bey Yokuşu Sok, Sultanahmet
☎ 0212 520 7740
🕐 Closed Mon.
💲 $$
🚈 Gülhane
muze.gov.tr/istanbul archaeological

Hagia Sophia

Map p. 253

Ayasofya Meydanı 1, Sultanahmet

0212 522 1750 or 0212 522 0989

Closed Mon.

$$$

Gülhane

ayasofyamuzesi.gov.tr
muze.gov.tr/hagia
sophia

The three-storied Archaeology Museum's most popular room contains a collection of grand Lycian, Egyptian, and Phoenician tombs. The most elegant is the **Alexander Sarcophagus.** Its splendor and decoration once confused curators, who wrongly ascribed it to Alexander the Great; it's now thought to be the resting place of a provincial governor. Carvings along the side depict Alexander routing the Persians and hunting lions.

Over rooms feature Hittite history, Roman jewelry, and 30 boats discovered and excavated from an archaeological dig that uncovered the remains of a Byzantine harbor.

Two ancillary museums on-site (admission included with Archaeology Museum) add other dimensions to the visit. The **Tiled Kiosk** (Çinili Köşk),

housing the **Museum of Islamic Art,** built as a pleasure palace by Mehmet the Conqueror in 1472, is filled with an unrivaled collection of Ottoman ceramics, stained glass, carpets, and porcelain. The **Museum of the Ancient Orient** is noted for its collection from pre-Islamic Arabia and its clay tablets inscribed with cuneiform script.

Hagia Sophia

Hagia Sophia, just steps from the Imperial Gate through which one enters Topkapı Palace, has dominated Sultanahmet's history, geography, and politics since its completion as the world's largest cathedral under Emperor Justinian in A.D. 537. Emperor Leo III (ca 685–741) banned the worship of graven images during the late 720s and the building's beautiful mosaics

The Alexander Sarcophagus, originally (and mistakenly) attributed to Alexander the Great

were removed. But they made a swift return, thanks to the icon-revering empress Irene (752–803). Christian crusaders in 1204 then desecrated the church as if it were a pagan temple. Gold leaf and silver artifacts were plundered, and relics were shipped off to churches across Europe.

The last Byzantine emperor, Constantine XI Dragases (1404–1453), uttered the cathedral's final Christian liturgy on May 28, 1453, as Ottoman forces pounded the city walls. The invasion's leader, Mehmet the Conqueror, rode directly to the Hagia Sophia after Constantinople's fall the next day. By the following Friday the cathedral had been converted into a mosque. The Ottomans kept it in perfect repair, adapting it without harming the original structure or its glorious decoration. In 1935 the mosque became a public museum.

Hagia Sophia's Interior:

Most visits begin in the long **gold-ceilinged narthex.** Look up for the **mosaic of Emperor Leo VI** bowing before Christ Pantocrator. To gauge the Hagia Sophia's grand scale it's worth heading straight up to the horseshoe-shaped **upper gallery.** A green disk marks where Byzantine empresses would place their thrones and gaze over proceedings.

Head right from here to the south gallery for a pantheon of glowing mosaics. First is the **Deësis mosaic,** depicting a humble Virgin Mary and

---

Gülhane Park

Gülhane, which means "rose house" in Turkish, is Istanbul's oldest public park. It lies just east of Topkapı Palace and shares the same entrance gate as the palace and the Archaeology Museum. A shady place for a stroll, its spacious landscape of trees and flower beds has long been a favorite with picnicking families and courting couples. The sultans used the park as a private domain and built boathouses, kiosks, and viewing platforms to watch the ships ferrying in trade from every part of their empire. A few teahouses occupy the place where sultans once pontificated.

---

fine-featured John the Baptist casting their eyes down at Christ. The **Empress Zoe mosaic** portrays Christ Pantocrator, supposedly flanked by Emperor Constantine IX Monomachus (1000–1055) and Zoe (978–1050), his beautiful empress. In fact, it's likely that Constantine's face was the third to grace the wall, with Zoe's first two husbands replacing each other in turn. The neighboring **Comnenus mosaic** depicts the Virgin and Child, flanked by Emperor John II Comnenus (1087–1143) and his wife, Empress Irene (1088–1134). From both sides of the upper gallery there is a wonderful view of the **Virgin and Child mosaic,** which dominates the apse.

The **ground floor** delights in equal measure. Even if you can't fathom every carved pillar, burial chamber, or mini-mosaic, revel in the space nonetheless. Look out for the **weeping column,** normally conspicuous by its line of hopefuls; it's said that if you

Basilica Cistern

🗺 Map p. 253

✉ Yerebatan Caddesi 13, Sultanahmet

☎ 0212 522 1259

💲 $$

🚇 Gülhane

yerebatan.com
kultursanat.org

twist your thumb around the hole in the moist rock, your wish may come true.

Remnants of Hagia Sophia's five centuries as a mosque are apparent throughout. Note the marble **minbar** (a large freestanding staircase from which the imam would preach; it's set at a diagonal near the apse), an ornate **ablutions fountain,** huge pendant **chandelier,** plus eight suspended **green disks** inscribed with the names of Allah, the Prophet Muhammad, the first four caliphs, and Muhammad's first two grandsons.

More than five million visitors share this sight each year, so it pays to arrive early, or just before closing.

Basilica Cistern

This vast subterranean space, one of the city's most visually arresting sights, occupies 105,000 square feet (9,500 sq m) almost directly underneath the Hagia Sophia. Like the Hagia Sophia, the Basilica Cistern (Yerebatan Sarnıcı) was constructed on the orders of Emperor Justinian (483–565). Around 7,000 slaves toiled on the project for years at a time. When it was completed, the cistern could hold 100,000 tons of water and was filled by an intricate series of aqueducts.

The cistern fell out of favor after the Ottoman Conquest of 1453, as the Turks preferred running water, not stagnant pools, in their palaces. The often used local idiom *"kadın sesi, para sesi, su sesi*—the sound of women, the sound of money, the sound of water" gives an inkling of the Turkish love of bathing

---

Secret Sites Around Hagia Sophia

Four free, little-visited sites ring the gated Hagia Sophia complex. Within the complex itself, but only accessible via a different entrance 100 yards (91 m) west of the main gate, is the Sinan-designed, 16th-century **mausoleum of Selim II,** plus the tombs of his son Murat III (1546–1595), grandson Mehmet III (1566–1603), and great-grandson Mustafa I (1591–1639). None of them was a model leader: Selim was a drunkard, Mehmet a bully (he murdered at least 39 family members), and poor Mustafa a neurotic weakling. But the exquisite tilework, so fine that the raised glaze can be caressed, plus the additional eerie graves of each sultan's family members (Selim's alone is circled by 44), makes for a fascinating tour.

The nearby **Hammam of Roxelana,** Sultan Süleyman the Magnificent's ever conspiring wife, is another Sinan-designed mini-masterpiece. The staff of Hagia Sophia would have used the hammam in times past, as the world's most powerful woman obviously had her own private bath in Topkapı Palace.

Farther around the complex is the **Çeşme of Sultan Ahmet III,** an ornate calligraphy-covered fountain that proudly proclaims itself "the most beautiful street fountain in Istanbul." Finally, turn left halfway down the cobbled street for a peek at the **Caferağa Medresesi** (tel 0212 513 3601), a former madrassa built in the 16th century that now serves as an exhibition center and workshop area for handicrafts.

The Ottomans transformed the Hagia Sophia, a centuries-old basilica, into a mosque in 1453.

and fountains, although the Ottomans still used the cistern's water for the palace gardens.

A moist, eerie silence greets visitors today. A wooden walkway now loops through the columns and the feeling is completely otherworldly. Families of carp swim around the complex. At the far end of the cistern, holding up two great pillars, lie two huge Medusa heads carved out of stone: They make for a great photo, with scores of hauntingly lit columns lined up behind them.

Blue Mosque

The Blue Mosque stands directly opposite the Hagia Sophia, across Sultanahmet Park with its large fountain. The Blue Mosque's official name, Sultanahmet Camii, comes from Sultan Ahmet I (1590–1617), the sultan under whom this grand temple was constructed. In part, the Blue Mosque served as an attempt to appease Allah for Ahmet I's losses against armies on the eastern and western flanks of the Ottoman Empire. Just as the mosque was completed, Ahmet I succumbed to typhus at the age of 27.

It's easy to imagine the mosque as two squares, one containing the interior, the other the courtyard. Inside, eyes are instantly drawn upward to the great dome and succession of semidomes, each one covered by spellbinding geometric frescoes (although these are not the mosque's original decoration). The **gallery,** just a short way above the carpeted floor, is ringed with more than 20,000 fine İznik tiles, the rich blue of which gave rise to the mosque's more familiar English name.

Of key importance are the **mihrab,** the carved niche that denotes the direction of Mecca, and the **minbar,** the pulpit used for Friday prayers. The upper gallery left of the mihrab contains the **royal loge,** where the sultans themselves would have prayed.

Be aware that the mosque is still a working one. A polite

Blue Mosque
- 🗺 Map p. 253
- ✉ Atmeydanı Sokak, Sultanahmet
- ☎ 0212 518 1319
- 🕐 Closed Fri. a.m. & during prayers
- 💲 $$ donation recommended
- 🚇 Sultanahmet

bluemosque.co

Museum of Turkish & Islamic Arts

- Map p. 253
- İbrahim Paşa Palace, At Meydanı Sokak 46, Sultanahmet
- 0212 518 1805
- Closed Mon.
- $$
- Sultanahmet

www.tiem.gov.tr
muze.gov.tr/turkish
islamic

notice asks visitors to stay hushed and be respectful, and not to take photographs of those at prayer. Shoes must be removed and female visitors must don a head scarf upon entering the inner sanctum (you can borrow one from the mosque's varied collection).

Hippodrome

Just east of the Blue Mosque is where the former Hippodrome stood. Present-day **Atmeydanı road** roughly follows its U-shaped track. When Emperor Constantine moved his capital from Rome to the shores of the Bosporus in A.D. 324, he embarked upon this vast racetrack, where a crowd of

The Blue Mosque, a legacy of Sultan Ahmet I (1590–1617)

100,000 could clamor for victory and charioteers careened around the *sphendonè* curve—above which the emperor sat.

Though the arena's seating has long disappeared, many of the various statues and spoils that were lined up in the Hippodrome's center, or *spina,* survive in situ in an area made into a park. The **Obelisk of Theodosius** was pilfered from Luxor in Egypt in A.D. 390 by Emperor Theodosius. The obelisk's hieroglyphics, still in near mint condition, celebrate Thutmose III's (died 1425 B.C.) victory in the distant Euphrates some 3,500 years ago. Scenes of Theodosius and his retinue toiling away are engraved on the obelisk's pedestal. The nearby **Walled Obelisk,** today little more than a very tall tower of bricks, was once covered in valuable bronze plaques. They were pillaged in the early 13th century during the Fourth Crusade.

Museum of Turkish & Islamic Arts

On the western side of the Hippodrome is the Museum of Turkish and Islamic Arts (Türk ve İslam Eserleri Müzesi), housed in a portion of the 16th-century **İbrahim Paşa Palace** (İbrahim Paşa Sarayı). It has a rich collection of more than 40,000 ancient ceramics, calligraphy artworks, miniatures, and carpets.

Upstairs, small rooms neatly chart Islamic art, beginning with carved ivory objects and mosaic fragments from Damascus'

Around the mosque, associated parks and buildings include a hospital, caravansary, madrassas (religious schools), a hammam, a library, a kitchen (now the excellent Dârüzziyafe restaurant; see Travelwise p. 302), plus rows of shops. At one time, more than 3,000 people worked in the complex.

Outside, ten balconies line the four minarets, representing Süleyman as the tenth sultan on the Ottoman throne. Inside, the main hall's four red columns were plucked from Alexandria in Egypt and Baalbek in present-day Lebanon. The central dome sits upon four elephant-leg pillars, supported by several half domes and columns. Look for the imperial balcony to the left of the mihrab, where sultans would have worshipped. The finely carved minbar, where Friday prayers are still delivered, stands to the right.

In the mosque's gardens, search out the **Tomb of Sultan** Süleyman. Many Turks visit here to utter a few solemn words by his resting place.

Southern Golden Horn

The southern Golden Horn, on the western fringes of Sultanahmet, is a beguiling neighborhood. Mass immigration from eastern Turkey has slowly turned it and areas west into the most conservative areas of Istanbul. Black burkas for women and flowing pajama robes for men are the norm.

Its winding streets of hidden churches and tumbling wooden houses are dominated by the vast **Fatih Mosque** (Fatih Camii), celebrated for the mausoleum of Mehmet the Conqueror (*fatih* in Turkish). The mosque's dome, frescoed with roses and fabulous patterns, is one of the most exquisite in the city.

Much the same can be said of the Kariye Mosque (Kariye

(continued on p. 266)

Süleymaniye Mosque

- **Map p. 253**
- Mimar Sinan Caddesi/Prof Sıddık Sami Onar Caddesi, Eminönü
- ☎ 0212 514 0139
- 🕐 Closed Fri. a.m. & prayers (tombs closed Mon.)
- 💲 $ donation recommended
- 🚇 Eminönü

Fatih Mosque

- **Map p. 253**
- Fevzi Paşa Caddesi, Fatih
- 🕐 Closed Fri. a.m
- 💲 $ donation recommended

Spice Market

The Spice Market (Mısır Çarşısı, or "Egyptian bazaar," in Turkish) was constructed in the 1660s to provide income for the nearby New Mosque complex. Both locals and visitors frequent the market, an enchanting domed structure with around 90 shops that originally sold only spices, herbs, and medicinal mixes. Today you can expect to find piles of *kırmızı pul biber* (spicy red pepper flakes), deep yellow turmeric, strings of tiny okra or preserved vine leaves, and dried eggplant shells for *dolmas*. Soft figs are stuffed with walnuts, and you can easily pick up a dozen different varieties of Turkish delight (see sidebar p. 266) or prized items such as Iranian saffron and caviar.

The streets twisting outward from the market merge into the alleys that pour downhill from the Grand Bazaar. The shops here often offer better value and are more interesting than those within the Spice Market itself. Continue west and you'll quickly enter a unique neighborhood selling food, scales, candy, and wooden handcrafted items. To the east is the fragrant **Flower Market** (Çiçek Pazarı).

İstiklal Caddesi: Walking the Old Grande Rue de Péra

The heart of 19th-century Istanbul, İstiklal Caddesi in the Beyoğlu (once called Péra) district is studded with former embassies, ornate art nouveau masterpieces, a few churches, and wiggling passageways. This now pedestrianized avenue has a distinct European flavor—note that the addresses refer to the red (new) numbers outside each building.

An ice-cream vendor on İstiklal Caddesi

NOT TO BE MISSED:

Galata Whirling Dervish Hall
• St. Anthony of Padua • Fish
Market • Hüseyin Ağa Mosque

Start at **Tünel Square ❶** (Tünel Meydanı), at the southern end of İstiklal Caddesi by the Tünel underground funicular entrance. Opposite, colored lights dangle from the trees marking the entryway to pretty Tünel Geçidi, a small passageway filled with bars and restaurants.

Around 50 yards (45 m) to the right (east), **Galata Whirling Dervish Hall ❷** (galatamevlevihanesimuzesi.gov.tr, closed Mon.) sits at the top of Galip Dede Caddesi. Visit the museum (Galata Mawlavi House), or poke around the shady, cat-filled courtyard.

Return to İstiklal Caddesi and head north; on the right at No. 235 is the seven-story **Botter House ❸**, an art nouveau masterpiece currently in a state of disrepair. Italian architect Raimondo D'Aronco designed the resplendent edifice in 1900 for Sultan Abdülhamid II's private tailor, Jean Botter.

Over the road at No. 172, the budget eatery Robert's Coffee sits on the site of the old **Markiz Patisserie,** once a hugely popular café that was established in 1940. As well as the sign above the passageway, French artist J. A. Arnoux's "Spring" and "Autumn" panels still adorn the café's interior.

Walking on, tall wrought-iron gates mark the entrance to the **Russian Consulate** at No. 219. The vast building, its massive columns best seen from the Bosporus shore below, was built under the Fossati brothers in 1845.

Santa Maria Draperis Church ❹ (tel 0212 244 0243, istancoreofm.org) at No. 215 is easy to miss: Look for the steep stairs that lead down to the entrance, underneath a golden mosaic of the Virgin Mary. Established during the late 16th century by Genoese resident Clara Bartola Draperis, the Catholic church was moved to this spot 100 years later.

Next door at No. 213, the **Borusan Culture and Arts Center Music Library ❺** (Borusan Sanat Kültür ve Merkezi's Müzik Kütüphane; tel 0212 336 3280, closed Sun.) houses the country's largest collection of Turkish music. Across the street, Borusan launched its contemporary exhibition space, **Müzik Evi,** in February 2010.

Map labels:
Haco Pulo Cafe
British Consulate
European Passage
TARLABAŞI BULVARI
St. Anthony of Padua Church ⑧
Fish Market ⑩
Holy Trinity Church
RAFIK SAYDAM CADDESI
İSTIKLAL CADDESI
Flower Passage ⑪
İSTIKLAL CADDESI
Borusan Culture Müzik and Arts Center Music Library
Evi ⑥
⑦
Galatasaray Square
Alkazar Sineması
Hüseyin Ağa Mosque
French Consulate
Markiz Patisserie ⑤
Netherlands Consulate
Mısır Apartmanı building
TÜNEL SQUARE
START ①
④
Santa Maria Draperis Church
YENİ ÇARŞI CAD
To Taksim Square & Military Museum
②
Galata Whirling Dervish Hall
Botter House ③
Russian Consulate
ÇUKURCUMA CAD
Firuzağa Mosque
ÇUKURCUMA

0   200 meters
0   200 yards

► Tünel Square
🕐 1.5 hours
↔ 0.6 mile (1 km)
► Hüseyin Ağa Mosque

Strolling north again, the **Netherlands Consulate** at No. 197, on the right, was also designed by the Fossati brothers and completed in 1855. Another 50 yards (45 m) along, the alley Perukar Çıkmazı leads left to the **Holy Trinity Church** ⑥ (Surp Yerrortutyun Kilisesi; *tel 0212 244 1382*). This Armenian Catholic church has been serving Beyoğlu since the 17th century, although the numbers attending Mass today are low, and the church often organizes mixed religious services.

About 80 yards (75 m) north, the redbrick **St. Anthony of Padua Church** ⑦ (*İstiklal Caddesi 182, tel 0212 244 0935*), the largest Catholic church in Istanbul, is visible on the right, dating from 1913. The next-door **Mısır Apartmanı building** (*İstiklal Caddesi 163*) was built for the Khedive of Egypt in 1910. Today, trendy bar **360** occupies its top floor.

Continue for another 80 yards (75 m) to **Haco Pulo Cafe** ⑧ on the left. A kiosk-cluttered entrance leads to a courtyard hemmed in by old buildings. In the early 20th century, the Young Turks, including future president Mustafa Kemal Atatürk, used to meet here. Pop through the opposite exit for a peek at the **British Consulate** (*Meşrutiyet Caddesi 34*), completed in 1855.

Galatasaray Square & Beyond

Galatasaray Square ⑨ is İstiklal Caddesi's approximate midway point. Artist Şadi Calık's abstract sculpture sits at its center, installed in 1973 on the 50th anniversary of the Turkish Republic. The bright white marble building over the road, a former post office, houses a museum dedicated to Galatasaray high school, established in the 15th century, and its offshoot soccer club.

Turn left onto Yeni Çarşı Caddesi, then a quick right into **European Passage** (Avrupa Pasajı) ⑩. Designed in 1874 by Austrian architect Pulgher, this long store-lined passageway is decorated with small, detailed statues above each doorway. Exit onto Sahne Sokak, home of Galatasaray's daily **Fish Market** (Balık Pazarı), which extends downhill to the left. Turn right and walk back to İstiklal Caddesi, passing **Flower Passage** (Çiçek Pasajı) ⑪ on the left-hand corner. Raucous *meyhanes* (tavernas) have replaced the fragrant stalls that once stood here 50 years ago.

To end your walk, follow İstiklal Caddesi on its kink eastward, keeping an eye out for the ornate 1920s facade of the **Alkazar Sineması** movie theater at No. 111. Another 130 yards (120 m) farther, the white walls of **Hüseyin Ağa Mosque** (Hüseyin Ağa Camii) ⑫, İstiklal's only mosque, appear.

Turkish Delight

This sweet—*lokum* in Turkish—is the country's most famous export. It's said that in the 18th century Sultan Abdülhamid I broke several teeth crunching through a favorite rock candy and, without his sugary fix, became inconsolable. Royal confectioner Ali Muhiddin Hacı Bekir quickly came to the rescue, and the delicacy we know today was born.

Traditionally flavored with rosewater and dusted with powdered sugar, lokum is created with a blend of sugar and starch. Try specialist varieties, including those made with fruit juice or sprinkled with pistachios. To buy, **Hacı Bekir** (*İstiklal Caddesi 83A, Beyoğlu, tel 0212 245 1375 or 0212 245 1376, hacibekir.com.tr*), just east of the New Mosque, is popular with locals. Alternatively, in the Spice Market, **Hayat** (*Mısır Çarşısı 8, tel 0212 528 4586, misircarsisi.org*) has a divine double honey and pistachio version.

Chora Museum

- Map p. 253
- Kariye Camii Sokak 18, Kariye Meydani, Edirnekapı
- 0212 631 9241
- Closed Wed.
- $$

choramuseum.com

Eyüp Sultan Mosque Complex

- Map p. 253
- Camii Kebir Sokak, Eyüp
- Closed Fri. a.m.
- $ donation recommended

Camii), several blocks west. Formerly the Church of St. Savior in Chora, it now houses the **Chora Museum** (Kariye Müzesi), the city's second largest collection of mosaics after the Hagia Sophia. Scenes of the nativity, the flight to Egypt, and Joseph's journey to Bethlehem look almost as if they were painted in gold.

Eyüp Sultan Mosque Complex:

Far north from the Chora Museum, in the Eyüp neighborhood, you'll find the Eyüp Sultan Mosque Complex, Istanbul's holiest site. It was founded near the Golden Horn on the burial site of Ebū Eyyūb el-Ensari, standard-bearer to the Prophet Muhammad.

During the first Arab siege on the city (A.D. 674–678), Ebū Eyyūb el-Ensari spearheaded the invasion and was killed during battle. His body was buried here, and a small shrine established. When Mehmet the Conqueror took control of Constantinople in 1453, he erected an elaborate new shrine, along with a mosque, school, and kitchens. The complex deteriorated over the centuries and was eventually reconstructed in 1800 under Sultan Selim III (1761–1808).

Passing through one of the complex's two large gates, visitors head to an internal courtyard: To the right is Eyüp Sultan Mosque, while **Ebū Eyyūb el-Ensari's *türbe*** (tomb) sits opposite. Inside, dazzling tiles create a brilliant backdrop to the crowds of devout pilgrims. In a corner to the left, the prophet Muhammad's sacred marble footprint is exhibited behind glass.

Remove your shoes before entering the türbe, as you would a mosque. Cover bare legs; women must also cover their heads. Scarves can be borrowed from a basket at the entrance.

European Istanbul

Located on the northern side of the Golden Horn, "European" Istanbul—also known as Beyoğlu—is mainly a residential area. From Sultanahmet, it is usually approached via the Galata Bridge. On a short visit most people will only have time to see the area's landmark Galata Tower.

Galata Bridge: Over the past 500 years, Galata Bridge (Galata Köprüsü) has taken various forms. The first real Galata Bridge came in 1845 and was replaced three times over the next century and a half. The bridge's fifth and present incarnation (built between 1992 and 1994) has two action-packed levels. On the lower one, restaurants, bars, and cafés face eastward across the Bosporus toward Asia, as well as up the Golden Horn, their west-facing terraces a rosy delight at sunset. Local fishermen drape lines from the bridge's upper level, as vendors pace back and forth with tea, snacks, and extra bait for sale.

Galata Tower: The Genoese built Galata Tower (Galata Kulesi) in 1348 at the center of what was then their walled city. Possession of the tower passed to Mehmet the Conqueror in 1453. Under the Ottomans, it functioned at various times as a jail, observatory, and fire lookout.

The tower is 200 feet (61 m) tall, its walls 12 feet (3.75 m) thick. Patrons can take an elevator to the upper floors and have refreshments in the tower's restaurant or café. (Beware: The stunning views from here make it very popular; therefore, it is difficult to get a table.) A nightclub on the top floor presents traditional Turkish entertainment. For a fee (*$$*), tourists may take the elevator as far as it goes then walk up another two flights of stairs to the ninth floor, where a slender balcony offers some of the city's most spectacular panoramas. ■

Galata Tower
- Map p. 253
- Büyük Hendek Sokak, Galata
- Karaköy

NEED TO KNOW

Port Logistics: Istanbul

Ships dock in Istanbul at a long waterfront bookended by two terminals, Karaköy and the more easterly Salipazarı. Most dock at the former, in the shadow of Galata Bridge; from here, walking across the bridge and continuing to Sultanahmet, Istanbul's main historic quarter, will take around 45 minutes. Taxis wait at the pier. Insist on the meter being turned on and only pay the metered rate, ignoring any alleged supplements. There are trams to Sultanahmet, but stops are difficult to locate from the terminals.

Istanbul Highlights

You can spend your entire port of call time at any one of these destinations, but here are some suggested times to help with your planning. Note, these do not allow for travel time to and from and/or waiting in line:
- Hagia Sophia, Blue Mosque, Topkapı Palace, Grand Bazaar, & Süleymaniye Mosque: each 45 min. to 1 hour
- Archaeology Museum: 2 hours (more if include Turkish & Islamic Arts Museum)
- Galata Tower & stroll down İstiklal Caddesi: 1.5–2.5 hours

Ephesus

Outside of Istanbul's sights, the ruins of ancient Ephesus attract the highest number of Turkey's visitors. Dating from around 1000 B.C., the initially small Greek settlement grew to boast the Temple of Artemis, one of the Seven Wonders of the Ancient World, and was at one point the Aegean's most important port (silting resulted in the town being moved to its present location in the third century B.C.). But it was the Romans who transformed the city into much of what is seen today, a place of perfectly preserved temples, merchants' houses, and theaters.

Architectural tricks were used to make the Library of Celsus seem more monumental than it is.

NEED TO KNOW p. 271

Ephesus

 251 B2

✉ Efes Örenyeri, Selçuk

☎ 0232 892 6010 or 0232 892 6011

☎ $$$

selcuk.bel.tr
muze.gov.tr/ephesus
-archaeological

During roughly four centuries of rule, beginning around 133 B.C., the Romans built more glorious buildings, including the magnificent Library of Celsus, and Ephesus was cultivated as a regional capital, growing in size to support thousands upon thousands of people. The settlement was also an early adopter of Christianity, and hosted St. Paul and St. John the Evangelist (and some say the Virgin Mary) during the first century A.D.

The Site

Entering from the **Upper Gate,** the path heads straight toward the upper **agora** (market), passing the **Baths of Varius** on the right before reaching the **Odeon,** or parliament. Clamber up the tiered rows, which seated 1,500 in the second century A.D., for views over the **Prytaneum** (Palace of Council) and two **temples** next door. Two statues of Artemis (now in Selçuk's Ephesus Museum; see p. 270), originally housed in the nearby **Temple of Arte-mis,** were discovered here.

The central colonnaded road dips downhill, before opening out onto the **Pollio Fountain** and **Domitian Temple** (both first century A.D.) on the left, and the first-century B.C. **Tomb of Mem-mius** and **Monumental Fountain** (first–fourth centuries A.D.) on the right. Keep an eye out for the **Gate of Hercules,** which flanks the start of **Curetes Street.** During Ephesus' heyday, this street was lined with shops, each vendor positioned between two columns.

Passing the first-century A.D. **Temple of Trajan** (its sculp-tures now in Selçuk's Ephesus Museum), the stunning **Temple of Hadrian,** built on the occasion of Emperor Hadrian's second-century A.D. visit to the city, was restored during the fourth century. Behind it are the public **latrines** and the **Baths of Sko-asticia.** The bathing complex—built in the second century A.D. and extensively remodeled by the eponymous Skolasticia in the fourth century—was originally three stories, but only the top floor is currently visible.

The **terraced houses** sit on the opposite side of Curetes Street. Although there is a supplemental charge, Terrace House 2—a warren of six first- and second-century A.D. luxury dwellings still undergo-ing restorations—is absolutely a must-see. The homes were abandoned after a series of severe earthquakes during the third century A.D., and their

Visiting Ephesus

Set out early to avoid the crowds and enter from the Upper Gate, in order to proceed slowly downhill as the heat of the day increases (bring hat and sunscreen, as there is very little shade). There's nowhere to buy drinks or snacks within the ruins, so pack a large bottle of water, no matter what the season. Although all major points of interest are labeled in Turkish and English, there are no detailed explanations save the lengthy descriptions posted within the ter-raced houses. History buffs may choose to rent an audio guide (*$$$*) or hire one of the many multilingual guides (*$$$$$ per group, 2 hours*) lingering near the site's entrance.

treasures have remained rela-tively undisturbed. Painstaking reassembly of the banquet hall's marble-lined walls (discovered shattered into 120,000 pieces) takes place in Unit 6, while Units 2 and 3 boast superb wall murals and mosaic floors.

Back in the brilliant sunshine, the impressive **Library of Celsus** is one of the site's highlights. Consul Gaius Julius Aquila (A.D. 110) commissioned the library in honor of his father, the proconsul of the province of Asia; it was completed in A.D. 135. Copies of the four sculptures representing intellectual virtues (the originals are in Vienna's Ephesus Museum) sit in niches on the library's facade. The building once held thousands of texts, but these were burned and destroyed by invading Goths during the third century A.D.

To the right of the library's entrance, the **Mazeus & Mithria-dates Gate** marks the entrance

Selçuk

🗺 251 B2

Visitor Information

✉ Atatürk Mah.
Agora Çarşısı
35

☎ 0232 892 6925

selcuk.bel.tr

Ephesus Museum

✉ Atatürk
Caddesi, Uğur
Mumcu Sevgi
Yolu 28, Selçuk

☎ 0232 892 6010
or 0232 892
6011

🕐 Closed Mon.

💲 $$

muze.gov.tr/ephesus

to the lower agora. Funded by former slaves Mazeus and Mithriadates, this 52-foot (16 m) triple archway was erected in imperial gratitude for freedom bestowed upon them.

Back up on **Marble Street** and heading northeast, visitors will pass the town's **brothel** on the right—note the etched footprint and female figure, an ancient advertisement for the world's oldest profession, on a left-hand paving stone. Ephesus' massive 25,000-seat **theater** (built in the first and second centuries A.D.) towers up to the right. From its upper tiers, there are excellent views over the town's **theater gymnasium** and **Harbor Street** (also referred to as the Arcadian Way), funneling visitors north and then east toward the **Lower Gate's** exit.

Around Ephesus

If you are docked in Kuşadası, the port of call for Ephesus, for a full day, it is possible to see the ruins and still have plenty of time for peripheral sites in and around the nearby town of Selçuk as well time for Kuşadası, which has plenty of **shopping** options (note that while these are often fun—some vendors can be aggressive—many are touristy, overpriced, and aimed predominantly at cruise passengers). Be especially aware when buying carpets: Very many stores, guides, and cruise companies operate a complex, mutually beneficial web of commissions, markups,

and middlemen that make for inflated prices.

Selçuk: For many non-cruise visitors, Selçuk is purely a dormitory for the nights before and after a day at Ephesus. However, there are reasons to linger. The town's dedicated museum, the **Ephesus Museum,** located just opposite the visitor information

INSIDER TIP:

Selçuk is famous for its çöp şiş—small lamb and vegetable kebabs. You don't need to visit a restaurant; the dish is best savored in portions of 10 or 12 skewers on sale at streetside snack bars.

—KEMAL NURYADIN
Executive editor, National
Geographic Turkey

office, displays ancient objects from nearby archaeological sites. Look for the diorama re-creating Roman daily life in a terraced house, the Pollio Fountain statues, and the tiny, perfect Eros-engraved oil lamps in the Eros Room. The real stars, however, are housed in the **Artemis Room:** three stunning sculptures of Artemis (first to second centuries A.D.), as well as a small model of the Temple of Artemis (Artemision). The remains of the actual temple are about a ten-minute walk west of

Visitors write notes on fabric or paper to add to the wishing wall at Meryemana.

the museum. One of the Seven Wonders of the Ancient World, today the site is almost empty dotted with just a few large stones and one column.

St. Jean Bazilikası: St. John the Evangelist was buried on Selçuk's Ayasuluk hilltop in the first century A.D. Three hundred years later, Emperor Constantine built a huge basilica over the tomb, with Emperor Justinian expanding it further during the sixth century. Today St. John's central tomb is well marked, as are the approximate church outlines. At sunset the ruins offer rosy vistas over Selçuk's mosque. **İsa Bey Camii** (14th century).

Meryemana: A site of both Christian and Muslim pilgrimage, this woodland chapel atop Mount Koressos, near Ephesus, is believed to be where

the Virgin Mary spent her last years. She is said to have traveled here with St. John the Evangelist. The house appeared in a vision to German nun Sister Anne Catherine Emmerich during the early 19th century, and was officially "discovered" by Christian clergy in 1891. ■

Meryemana
- 251 B2
- 5 miles (8 km) SW of Selçuk
- 0232 894 1012
- $$

NEED TO KNOW
Port Logistics: Kuşadası
Cruise ships dock at the port of Kuşadası, within walking distance of the town center and some 10 miles (16 km) from the ruins at Ephesus. If you are not taking a cruise excursion to Ephesus, taxis from the stand in front of the terminal are the most efficient way of getting there. However, prices are inflated, and you will need to pay for waiting time at the site, plus the return to Kuşadası. It is worth hiring a guide, who will meet you at the terminal, usually with a vehicle, but beware rip-offs: Reputable guides are booked early; visit *melitour.com* or *srmtravel.com* for contacts.

TRAVELWISE

Planning Your Trip 272–273 • Practical Advice 273 • Emergencies 273 • Restaurants
274–303 • Shopping 304–306 • Cruise Lines 307 • Language Guide 308–310

At sunset, tranquility descends upon a small coastal town in Montenegro.

PLANNING YOUR TRIP

Climate

Countries on the Mediterranean usually have mild winters and hot summers, but topography can produce a wide range of local conditions. Climate is generally warmer and drier the farther south you go. Winter across more northerly regions is shorter but otherwise broadly comparable to the colder climate of northern Europe. Spring tends to be short and fall more drawn out, but summer is hot—and more so in the south.

Winter daytime temperatures might range from around 15° to 59°F (-10° to 14°C), and summer temperatures from 65° to 90°F (18° to 33°C), although they may often exceed these extremes, especially in Greece, Turkey, and the south. Temperature is measured in degrees Celsius (°C). To determine degrees Fahrenheit, multiply °C by 9, divide by 5, and add 32.

What to Take

You should be able to buy anything you may need in most cities and main centers. Pharmacies offer a wide range of drugs, medical supplies, and toiletries, along with expert advice, but bring any prescription drugs you might need. A green cross outside the store generally indicates a pharmacy. It is also useful to bring a second pair of glasses or contact lenses if you wear them. Sunscreen and bug spray products are advisable in summer.

With regard to clothing, you only really need to dress up for the grandest city restaurants and casinos. Don't be too casual on nights out, however: Many locals dress more smartly than most U.S., Canadian, and northern European visitors. Always dress appropriately in places of worship—no bare shoulders or shorts for women. Note, too, that dress codes are more conservative the farther south you go and in most rural areas, and especially in Turkey. Bring a sweater, even in summer, for evenings can be chilly. Come prepared for some rain and cool temperatures outside midsummer.

Lastly, don't forget your passport, tickets, money, and insurance documents.

Passports & Visas

Passports with more than six months' validity before expiration are required for U.S., Canadian, U.K., and other visitors traveling to all the countries covered in this book.

U.S., Canadian, and many other nationals require a three-month "e-Visa" for Turkey: This must be obtained online before entry at *evisa.gov.tr*.

No visa is currently required for Croatia, but Croatian visa requirements are changeable: For the latest news visit *mvep.hr* and *travel.state.gov*.

PRACTICAL ADVICE

Conversions

1 kilo = 2.2 pounds
1 liter = 0.2642 U.S. gallon
1 kilometer = 0.62 mile
1 meter = 1.093 yards

Money Matters

The euro is the official currency of all the countries covered in this book with the exception of Croatia and Turkey. Euro notes come in denominations of 5, 10, 20, 50, 100, 200, and 500 euros. There are 100 cents to the euro. Coins come in denominations of 1 and 2 euros and 1, 2, 5, 10, 20, and 50 cents.

Croatia uses the kuna (abbreviated HRK, or KN locally), which is made up of 100 lipas. The kuna comes in note denominations of 5, 10, 20, 50, 100, 200, 500, and 1,000 and in coins of 1, 2, 5, 25. The lipa comes in coins of 1, 2, 5, 10, 20, and 50.

Turkey uses the lira (TL or TRY), which is made up of 100 kuruş. Coins come in denominations of 1, 5, 10, 25, and 50 kuruş and 1 lira. Note denominations are 1, 5, 10, 20, 50, and 100. The Yeni Türk Lira (new Turkish lira; YTL), used between 2005 and 2008, is no longer valid (but can

be redeemed at branches of the Central Bank of the Republic of Turkey until 2019); watch out for people passing off their YTL kuruş coins on you

Most major banks, airports, and railroad stations have automatic teller machines (ATM) for money cards and international credit cards (ask your credit card company for a PIN number to enable you to withdraw money). Currency and traveler's checks—best bought in euros—can be exchanged in most banks and Bureaux de Change *(cambio)*. In rural areas and small towns, ATMs and exchange facilities are rarer—and sometimes nonexistent.

Credit cards are accepted in restaurants in most major towns and cities. Look for Visa, MasterCard, or American Express stickers (Diners Club is less well known). Many businesses still prefer cash, and smaller stores, especially in rural areas, may not take credit cards. Always check before ordering a meal.

Restrooms

Few public buildings have restrooms, save maybe larger and more modern museums. You will find facilities in bars, railroad stations, shopping centers, and gas stations. Carry toilet tissue and tip attendants 25 to 50 cents. In Greece and Turkey (and elsewhere) toilets may be of the "squat" variety, and toilet tissue should be thrown in the garbage, not into the toilet itself, where it can block drains.

Tipping

Tip checkroom attendants up to 25 cents. Tip airport and railroad station porters up to 2 euros. Cab drivers expect around 10 percent. Tip church or other custodians 1 to 2 euros.

EMERGENCIES

Embassies

SPAIN
U.S.: madrid.usembassy.gov
Canada: spain.gc.ca
U.K.: gov.uk/government/world/organisations

FRANCE
U.S. france.usembassy.gov
Canada: france.gc.ca
U.K. gov.uk/government/world/organisations

ITALY
U.S.: italy.usembassy.gov
Canada: italy.gc.ca
U.K.: gov.uk/government/world/organisations

MALTA
U.S.: malta.usembassy.gov
Canada: travel.gc.ca/embassies/malta#H1
U.K.: gov.uk/government/world/organisations/

CROATIA
U.S.: zagreb.usembassy.gov
Canada: croatia.gc.ca
U.K.: gov.uk/government/world/organisations

GREECE
U.S.: athens.usembassy.gov
Canada: greece.gc.ca
U.K.: gov.uk/government/world/organisations

TURKEY
U.S.: turkey.usembassy.gov
Canada: turkey.gc.ca
U.K.: gov.uk/government/world/organisations

Emergency Phone Numbers

In all countries in this guide, dial 112 for emergencies. Additionally, in France dial 15 for an ambulance and 17 for police; in Croatia dial 94 for an ambulance, 93 for fire department, and 92 for police; and in Greece, dial 171 for the tourist police.

Restaurants

A wide variety of restaurants are available in the Mediterranean ports of call and beyond. They include small out-of-the-way places as well as the best known spots along the coast. The food reflects the individuality of the country and destination, and the wine selections are regional, providing an opportunity to taste varietals from the coast of Spain to the shores of Turkey.

Restaurants are organized by chapter and then alphabetically in descending order of price range. The following abbreviations are used:

L = lunch
D = dinner
AE = American Express
DC = Diners Club
MC = MasterCard
V = Visa

If a slash appears in the number of seats, the first number is the number of seats inside, the second the number of seats outside.

■ COASTAL SPAIN

Most restaurants provide a *menú del día:* starter, main course—usually meat or fish—dessert, and a drink. Often such meals are solid rather than gourmet experiences, but they tend to be good value; it is easy to eat for $12 to $20 (coffee is usually extra). At bars and cafés it is common to have tapas with beer and wine.

Always ask if the main course comes with vegetables, the *guarnició* in Catalan, or whether this has to be ordered separately. There are no hard-and-fast rules, and you are not obliged to eat more than one course if you do not wish to.

Lunch is from 2 p.m. to 4 p.m., although in many establishments you can start earlier (1 p.m.), though you probably won't be eating with many locals. Dinner is roughly from 9 p.m. to 11 p.m. or up to 1 a.m. Again, should you feel the need

to eat earlier, there is generally no problem.

Most restaurants shut for a day or two during the week, often Sunday night and Monday. Some also close at Easter, over Christmas, and for anything from two to four weeks in August. Times often change, however. Reservations are generally recommended, particularly Thursdays to Saturdays. You can often get away with just turning up on other days.

Service charges are occasionally, but by no means always, included in the check (sales tax, or IVA, is always included). Spaniards tend to be somewhat restrained about tipping. If service has not been included and you feel a tip is warranted, about 5 percent is sufficient.

BARCELONA

During the day, Barri Gòtic, the epicenter of Barcelona, overflows with people. At night parts of it become quiet, while others hum with the activity of restaurants and bars. As in other areas of the old city, you need to be aware that some streets are potentially risky by dark. Elsewhere, the area around Barcelona's most famous boulevard, La Rambla, hides some fine eating options, as does La Ribera to the east, but avoid La Rambla itself as restaurants tend to be tourist traps serving low-quality food. By contrast, the waterfront area, La Barceloneta, is full of

character-filled restaurants and tapas bars, and there are some good beachside options, too.

🍴 ALKIMIA
$$$$$
CARRER DE LA INDÚSTRIA 79
(NEAR LA SAGRADA FAMÍLIA)
TEL 93 207 6115
alkimia.cat
Jordi Vilà's creative seasonal Mediterranean cooking has been rewarded with a Michelin star. Dishes might include pickled oysters with glazed pork cheek and spinach sauté, or baked chicken cannelloni with almond béchamel and fresh salad. The lunch menu is well priced.
🪑 40 🕐 Closed Sat.–Sun., Easter, & 3 weeks in Aug.
🅿 🚫 DC, MC, V

🍴 CA L'ISIDRE
$$$$$
CARRER DE LES FLORS 12,
LA RAVAL
TEL 93 441 1139
calisidre.com
This charming restaurant on the edge of the Raval district serves traditional Catalan dishes that use local ingredients.
🪑 35 🕐 Closed Sun., holidays, & 3 weeks in Aug.
🚫 All major cards

🍴 CASA CALVET
$$$$
CARRER DE CASP 48,
L'EIXAMPLE
TEL 93 412 4012
casacalvet.es
This wonderful restaurant is ideal if you are on the Gaudí trail: It is on the first

floor of a Gaudí-designed, late 19th-century apartment block. Hide yourselves away in a booth for a menu that changes with the season. Jacket and tie are not a bad idea for men.
🍴 60 🕐 Closed Sun., holidays, 1 week in Aug., & Mon. June–Aug. 💳 All major cards

🍴 PASSADÍS DEL PEP
$$$$
PLA DEL PALAU 2, LA RIBERA
TEL 93 310 1021
passadis.com
One of the secret addresses that everyone should know, the Passadís is a paradise for fish lovers. Fresh fish is shipped in from up and down the coast to provide the raw materials for a marine feast, with no menu.
🍴 100 🕐 Closed Sun. & 2 weeks in Aug. 💳 All major cards

🍴 SET PORTES
$$$$
PASSEIG ISABEL II 14, LA BARCELONETA
TEL 93 319 3033
7portes.com
It seems remarkable that after so many years (since 1336) a restaurant can continue to maintain a good name. This is one of those cases, and, as a midrange option serving traditional Catalan dishes accompanied by a broad range of wines, it is a sure bet. It was long run by Paco Parellada, one of the leading lights in Catalan cuisine, and it remains in the family. Open 1 p.m. to 1 a.m.
🍴 300 💳 All major cards

SOMETHING SPECIAL
🍴 TORRE D'ALTA MAR
$$$$
TORRE DE SANT SEBASTIÀ, PASSEIG JOAN DE BORBÓ 88,

LA BARCELONETA
TEL 93 221 0007
torredealtamar.com
Of one thing you can be sure: Nowhere in Barcelona will you be able to match the views you'll get from this steel giant of a tower while treating yourself to a taste festival. Seafood dominates the menu, a fine wine list accompanies it, and the evening mood is perfect for romantics.
🍴 120 🕐 Closed L both Sun. & Mon. 💳 All major cards

🍴 CAN RAMONET
$$$–$$$$
CARRER DE LA MAQUINISTA 17, LA BARCELONETA
TEL 93 319 3064
grupramonet.com/canramonet
An oldie but a goodie. Can Ramonet has been serving food since 1763, according to its claim. It's a classic spot for seafood in the narrow lanes of La Barceloneta. Crowd inside around the upended barrels or grab a table outside across the lane in the hotter months. Paella and similar rice dishes are good here.
🍴 103 🕐 Closed Dec. 24–25 & D Dec. 31 💳 All major cards

SOMETHING SPECIAL
🍴 CASA LEOPOLDO
$$$–$$$$
CARRER DE SANT RAFAEL 24, LA RAMBLA
TEL 93 441 3014
casaleopoldo.com
Before they carved out the Rambla del Raval boulevard in 2000, this must have been hard to find, deep in the heart of the dingiest Raval. A timber-beamed ceiling frames the well-spaced tables. The fish hot pot (cazuela de

pescado) is tempting.
🍴 140 🕐 Closed D Sun., Mon., Easter, & mid-July–mid-Aug. 💳 All major cards

🍴 CAFÈ DE L'ACADÈMIA
$$$
CARRER DE LLEDÓ 1, BARRI GÒTIC
TEL 93 319 8253
A tiny restaurant squeezed into a magnificent 13th-century house that overlooks an equally quaint square, this spot has become a standing favorite with the local left. Hearty traditional meat and venison dishes dominate the menu. Try to reserve one of the few upstairs tables.
🍴 50 🕐 Closed Sat.–Sun. & 3 weeks in Aug. 💳 All major cards

🍴 CAL PEP
$$$
PLAÇA DE LES OLLES 8, LA RIBERA
TEL 93 310 7961
calpep.com
Known across the city, the bar in this establishment is almost always bursting with diners eager to feast on Pep's tapas, a cut way above the average. For most, a selection of these tasty little morsels accompanied by wine is enough, but you can also sit down to a full meal in a

---

🚭 Nonsmoking ❄ Air-conditioning 💳 Credit Cards

diminutive dining area.
🪑 44 🕐 Closed Sun., holidays, L Mon., D Sat., Easter, & 3 weeks in Aug. 💳 MC, V

SOMETHING SPECIAL

🍴 COMETACINC
$$$
CARRER DEL COMETA 5,
BARRI GÒTIC
TEL 93 310 1558
cometacinc.com
A duplex dining area in medieval obscurity. Just as the cuisine crosses all established boundaries, so the feel of the place is an almost disconcerting mix. A vibrant, urban staff whisks about the designer settings delivering anything from copious salads and Thai options to couscous and excellent carpaccio.
🪑 75 🕐 Closed L 💳 MC, V

SOMETHING SPECIAL

🍴 PLA
$$$
CARRER DE BELLAFILA 5,
BARRI GÒTIC
TEL 93 412 6552
restaurantpla.cat
An inviting decor with timber tables and muted lighting will lure you in here for a romantic dinner of fun fusion. You can expect options from adapted Asian dishes through to cheerful travesties of local favorites, such as the cod in green applesauce. The menu changes regularly.
🪑 60 🕐 Closed L 💳 MC, V

🍴 SUQUET DE L'ALMIRALL
$$$
PASSEIG JOAN DE BORBÓ 65,
LA BARCELONETA
TEL 93 221 6233
suquetdelalmirall.com
Although some will tell

you it's not as good as it was, this seafood establishment remains outstanding. The rice dishes and fish stews (cazuelas) are hard to resist.
🪑 80 🕐 Closed D Sun. & holidays, L Mon., & 2 weeks Aug. 💳 DC, MC, V

🍴 LOS CARACOLES
$$-$$$$
CARRER DE LOS ESCUDELLERES 14, BARRI GÒTIC
TEL 93 301 2041
loscaracoles.es
Perennially busy and serving guests since the 19th century, this is a remarkable locale, all timber and wine barrels and garlic hanging on the walls. You wait at the bar for a table out in back, where you will be served all sorts of things ranging from rice specialties to snails.
🪑 230 💳 All major cards

🍴 AGUT
$$-$$$
CARRER D'EN GIGNÀS 16,
BARRI GÒTIC
TEL 93 315 1709
restaurantagut.com
Presenting classic Catalan cooking in the labyrinth of alleys at the lower end of the Barri Gòtic, Agut combines a contemporary feel (inspect the art on the walls) with tradition in a homey setting. It offers a variety of meat and seafood, and is known for its bacallà (cod).
🪑 85 🕐 Closed D Sun., Dec. 24-25, & 2 weeks in Aug. 💳 All major cards

🍴 CAN CULLERETES
$$-$$$
CARRER D'EN QUINTANA 5,
BARRI GÒTIC
TEL 93 317 3022 OR 93 317 6485
culleretes.com
Founded in 1786, Can

Culleretes is Barcelona's oldest restaurant. Although a little stuffy, the steadfastly Catalan menu does not disappoint and the dark, timber decor and old-style, poker-faced service are a treat in themselves.
🪑 170 🕐 Closed D Sun., Mon., & 4 weeks in July-Aug. 💳 DC, MC, V

🍴 BAR PINOTXO
$-$$
MERCAT DE LA BOQUERIA
466-470, LA RAMBLA
TEL 93 317 1731
pinotxobar.com
The Mercat de la Boqueria is blessed with several busy food bars, where market workers, shoppers, and tourists crowd for tapas, drinks, and more substantial dishes. The food is fresh from the stalls around you, and the atmosphere always bustling. One of the locals' longtime favorites is Bar Pinotxo, near the main market entrance off La Rambla.
🪑 10 🕐 Closed D, Sun., & Aug. 💳 No credit cards

🍴 +ORGANIC
$-$$
CARRER DE LA JUNTA DE COMERÇ 11, LA RAVAL
TEL 93 301 0902
antoniaorganickitchen.com
A cavernous, bustling spot with a shop area where you can buy all sorts of organic products, this establishment is a vegetarian's taste of paradise. Order from a limited and frequently changing menu at the open kitchen and then pile on extras from the salad buffet. It also has an outlet in the Mercat de la Boqueria.
🪑 200 🛗 💳 DC, MC, V

🍴 GRANJA M. VIADER
$

CARRER D'EN XUCLÁ 4,
LA RAMBLA
TEL 93 318 3486
granjaviader.cat.mialias.net
Step back to more innocent
times in this century-old
granja (a kind of milk bar),
where the Viader family
sells delicatessen goodies.
Most people come to sit
at the little marble tables
and admire the beautiful
tile floor and old-fashioned
decor while sipping a thick
hot chocolate. The same
with whipped cream, called
a *suís*, is sinful.
🪑 75 🕐 Closed Sun. & holidays 💳 All major cards

VALENCIA

🍴 RICARD CAMARENA
$$$$$

CALLE DOCTOR SUMSI 4
TEL 963 355 418
ricardcamarena.com
In this pared-down,
contemporary dining room
Ricard Camarena has
transformed traditional
Valencian cuisine with his
creative cooking.
🪑 50 🅿 🕐 Closed
Sun.-Mon.; holidays vary
🚭 ❄ 💳 AE, MC, V

🍴 LA SUCURSAL
$$$$$

CALLE GUILLEM DE CASTRO 118
TEL 963 746 665
restaurantelasucursal.com
In this restaurant inside
the Institute of Modern
Art (IVAM), chef Jorge
Bretón offers innovative
contemporary cuisine, such
as risotto of ribs, snails, and
wild mushrooms.
🪑 50 🅿 🕐 Closed Sun., L
Sat., Easter week, & 2 weeks
in Aug. 🚭 ❄ 💳 All major
cards

🍴 RÍAS GALLEGAS
$$$$

CALLE CIRILO AMORÓS 4
TEL 963 525 111 OR 963 512 125
riasgallegas.es
This restaurant receives
its ingredients and wines
sent from Galicia. Sample
the scallops and Galician-
style turbot.
🪑 77 🅿 🕐 Closed Sun., D
Mon., & Aug. ❄ 💳 All major
cards

🍴 LA PEPICA
$$$

PASEO NEPTUNO 2, 6, & 8,
PLAYA DE LA MALVAROSA
TEL 963 710 366
lapepica.com
La Pepica has been dishing
up exquisite seafood and
rice dishes since 1898,
either inside or out on the
breezy terrace.
🪑 450 🕐 Closed D Sun. &
2 weeks in Nov. 💳 All major
cards

🍴 MONUMENTAL
$$

AD HOC HOTEL,
CALLE DE BOIX 4
TEL 963 919 091
adhochoteles.com
The restaurant in this 1880s
house, which combines
modern and antique, serves
pan-Mediterranean cuisine.
🪑 40 🚭 ❄ 💳 All major
cards

GRANADA

🍴 RESTAURANTE CALLE REAL
$$$$$

PARADOR DE GRANADA, REAL
DE LA ALHAMBRA S/N
TEL 958 221 440
parador.es/es/paradores/
parador-de-granada
Even if you are not staying
in this famous *parador*—a
15th-century convent in
the Alhambra gardens con-

verted to a posh hotel—it is
well worth treating yourself
to an upscale meal in the
Calle Real restaurant, which
focuses on traditional,
regional cuisine.
🪑 100 🅿 ❄ 💳 All major
cards

🍴 RUTA DEL AZAFRÁN
$$$

PASEO DE LOS TRISTES 1
TEL 958 226 882
rutadelazafran.es
This friendly, relaxed spot
along the Darro River offers
modern twists on Andalu-
sian classics.
🪑 71 ❄ 💳 All major cards

🍴 CUNINI
$$-$$$

PLAZA DE LA PESCADERÍA
14-BAJO
TEL 958 267 587 OR 958 250 777
marisqueriacunini.es
A popular place near the
cathedral. Try the superb
seafood spread at the tapas
bar. Reservations required.
🪑 45 🕐 Closed D Sun. & all
Mon. ❄ 💳 All major cards

MÁLAGA

🍴 GORKI
$$

CALLE STRACHAN 6
TEL 952 221 466
grupogorki.com
A good place for gourmet
tapas a few blocks from the
waterfront; it also has a fine
range of wines by the glass.
🪑 50 ❄ 💳 All major cards

BALEARIC ISLANDS

MALLORCA (MAJORCA)
🍴 ES RACO DES TEIX
$$$$$

CALLE DE SA VINYA VELLA
6, DEIÀ
TEL 971 639 501

🚭 Nonsmoking   ❄ Air-conditioning   💳 Credit Cards

esracodesteix.es
In this beautiful old house at the foot of Teix Mountain chef Josef Sauerschell has won a Michelin star for his fresh and inventive Mediterranean cuisine. Try dishes such as Mallorcan lamb with tomato, fennel, and olives, or hake and lobster in shellfish sauce.
⬛ 30-35 🅿 🕐 Closed Mon.-Tues. & mid-Nov.-early Feb. 🔘 AE, MC, V

🍴 CAN CERA
$$$$
CALLE SAN FRANCISCO 8, PALMA DE MALLORCA
TEL 971 715 012
cancerahotel.com
The restaurant of this spacious 13th-century mansion in Palma's old quarter—now a boutique hotel—serves tapas and creative Mediterranean-Asian fusion cuisine.
⬛ 40 🔘 🔘 All major cards

🍴 SIMPLY FOSH
$$$$
CONVENT DE LA MISSIÓ, CARRER DE LA MISSIÓ 7A, PALMA DE MALLORCA
TEL 971 720 114
conventdelamissio.com
Come to admire this stunningly converted 17th-century monastery in the heart of the old town and sample the seasonal cuisine in the sleek, contemporary dining room of the hotel's Simply Fosh restaurant.
⬛ 65 🅿 🔘 🔘 🕐 Closed Sun. 🔘 All major cards

🍴 CELLER SA PREMSA
$$
PLAÇA OBISPO BERENGUER DE PALOU 8, PALMA DE MALLORCA

TEL 971 723 529
cellersapremsa.com
A tavern full of old-wood wine barrels and walls covered in faded *feria* posters. Basic food in a great setting.
⬛ 200 🔘 All major cards

EIVISSA (IBIZA)
🍴 EL CORSARIO
$$$
EL CORSARIO HOTEL, CALLE PONIENTE 5
TEL 971 301 248
elcorsario-ibiza.com
Housed in a hotel at the highest point inside the city walls, in a 17th-century corsair's palace, this restaurant offers only a short and expensive menu, but the food is superb.
⬛ 45 🔘 All major cards

MENORCA (MINORCA)

🍴 JÁGARO
$$$$
MOLL DE LLEVANT 334, MAÓ
TEL 971 362 390
Jágaro is located on the port shore (and easily missed) and serves excellent seafood. Menorcan lobster is famed: Try the *caldereta* (stew) or *fritada de pescado* (a fry-up of assorted fresh fish).
⬛ 200 🕐 Closed month before Easter 🔘 🔘 All major cards

🍴 LA CARABA
$$$
CAMÍ D'ES BALIACS 1, S'UESTRÀ, SANT LLUÍS
TEL 971 150 682
restaurantelacaraba.com
This restaurant in a lovely old Menorcan house offers inventive Mediterranean cooking and a friendly local atmosphere.

Fine terrace and garden. Reserve in high summer.
⬛ 60 🕐 Closed L & Nov.-May

■ FRENCH RIVIERA & PROVENCE
Wherever you go in southern France, you will find a variety of restaurants, from humble auberges to the great classics. Lunch usually starts around midday and continues until 2 p.m. Dinner is eaten around 8 p.m. but may start at 7 p.m.; in smaller places or in the countryside, you may be too late after 9 p.m.

At the height of the season, or if you have a particular place in mind, make a reservation.

Restaurants often have outdoor tables for good weather, and even in towns and cities you may find yourself sitting on the sidewalk or in a courtyard.

Menus must be displayed outside any establishment serving food, and studying and comparing these before making your choice is part of the pleasure. Most restaurants offer one or more prix fixe menus—set meals at a fixed price, sometimes including wine. Otherwise (and usually more expensively), you order individual items à la carte—from the menu.

The French usually eat a salad after the main course and sometimes with the cheese course, which comes before dessert. Bread and water are supplied free. (French tap water is safe to drink.)

Local wines usually dominate wine lists, and all restaurants offer a *vin du pays* by the carafe or demi carafe. Smoking is forbidden in all public places in France, but some restaurants have smoking terraces.

Cafés remain a French institution, good for morning coffee, leisurely drinks, or modest meals. In small towns and villages, they are very much the center of local life. Note that drinking at the bar is cheaper than sitting at a table.

A service charge is usually included in the bill. Add more only if the service has been particularly good.

MARSEILLE

SOMETHING SPECIAL

🍴 MIRAMAR
$$$$$
QUAI DU PORT 12
TEL 04 9191 1040
lemiramar.fr
The Minguella family has been simmering pots of authentic bouillabaisse here for 40 years now. A classy, not-to-be-missed way of experiencing Marseille at its best.
🕐 Closed Mon. 🕙 All major cards

🍴 UNE TABLE, AU SUD
$$$-$$$$$
2 QUAI DU PORT
TEL 04 9190 6353
unetableausud.com
A gem tucked between the portside cafés, with the type of refined eating experience that you'd expect

in Paris—with a southern twist, of course.
🪑 50 🕐 Closed D Sun. & all Mon. 🕙 AE, MC, V

AIX-EN-PROVENCE

🍴 LE FORMAL
$$$-$$$$$
RUE ESPARIAT 32
TEL 04 4227 0831
restaurant-leformal.com
Hidden away on a quiet street beneath overhanging arches, this reconverted cellar promises romantic dining. Foie gras of duck accompanied with stewed apples and walnuts is the appetizer par excellence.
🪑 35 🕐 Closed L Sat., Sun.-Mon., 1 week in Jan., & 2 weeks in late Aug.-early Sept.
🕙 MC, V

🍴 LE PASSAGE
$$$-$$$$$
RUE VILLARS 10
TEL 04 4237 0900
le-passage.fr
Reine Sammut's hip restaurant cum culinary center (with cooking classes, wine cellar, and tearoom) offers a rare combination: It's stylish, delicious, and affordable.
🕙 All major cards

🍴 BASTIDE DU COURS
$$$-$$$$$
COURS MIRABEAU 43-47
TEL 04 4226 1006 OR
04 4291 5756
bastideducours.com
Set in a gorgeous bed-and-breakfast in a historic mansion along the Cours Mirabeau, this renowned eponymous restaurant serves deceivingly simple creations, such as the delicious roast duck with pumpkin chutney.
🕙 All major cards

🍴 LES DEUX GARÇONS
$$-$$$
COURS MIRABEAU 53
TEL 04 4226 0051
les2garcons.fr
A classic terrace café on the Cours Mirabeau, a favorite with artists and intellectuals since the 18th century.
🕙 All major cards

ARLES

🍴 LE MAS DE PEINT
$$$$-$$$$$
LE SAMBUC
TEL 04 9097 2062
masdepeint.com
Converted stables attached to an old Camargue farmhouse hold exquisite rooms and a pretty, wood-beamed restaurant.
🪑 35 🕐 Closed Thurs. & early Jan.-March 🕙 All major cards

🍴 LA GUEULE DE LOUP
$$$-$$$$
RUE DES ARÈNES 39
TEL 04 9096 9669
A wood-beamed restaurant above the kitchen serves Midi classics with an original twist, like the *charlotte d'agneau* with eggplant and red pepper coulis, or *tarte tatin* of turnips with foie gras and guinea fowl with pears. It is popular, so reserve.
🪑 30 🕐 Closed Sun.-Mon. & 4 weeks in Jan.-Feb.
🕙 MC, V

AVIGNON

🍴 LA MIRANDE
$$$$$
LA MIRANDE HOTEL,
PLACE DE L'AMIRANDE 4
TEL 04 9085 9393
la-mirande.fr
This elegant restaurant of an 18th-century hotel close to the Palais des Papes offers Provençal

specialties at a price.
🔲 🔲 All major cards

🍴 LA VIEILLE FONTAINE
$$$-$$$$$
HÔTEL D'EUROPE,
PLACE CRILLON 12
TEL 04 9014 7676
heurope.com
Hôtel d'Europe is Avignon's
top hotel—even Napoleon
stayed here. The restau-
rant, La Vieille Fontaine,
lives up to the splendor of
the establishment.
🕐 Closed Sun.-Mon. & 4
weeks in Aug. 🔲 🔲 All
major cards

🍴 RESTAURANT
ST.-LOUIS
$$$-$$$$
CLOÎTRE ST.-LOUIS,
RUE DU PORTAIL BOQUIER 20
TEL 04 9027 5555
cloitre-saint-louis.com
This formal restaurant
of the beautiful Cloître
St.-Louis hotel occupies
part of a 16th-century
Jesuit cloister, with views
of the cloister courtyard.
Seasonal menu.
🕐 Closed L Sat. Nov.-March
🔲 🔲 All major cards

🍴 CHEZ BRUNEL (LE 46)
$$-$$$
RUE DE LA BALANCE 46
TEL 04 9085 2483
le46avignon.com
This established Avignon
favorite is also known
as Le 46. The vegetarian
dishes are especially well
prepared; try the wild
mushroom ravioli.
🕐 Closed Sun.-Mon.
🔲 MC, V

🍴 L'ÉPICERIE
$$-$$$
PLACE ST.-PIERRE 10
TEL 04 9082 7422
restaurantlepicerie.fr
Located opposite the

16th-century Église
St.-Pierre, this tiny café
offers local dishes such
as lamb in apricot sauce
and a tempting selection
of cheeses.
🕐 Closed Jan.-Feb. & 1 week
in mid-Dec. 🔲 DC, MC, V

CANNES

🍴 LA MÈRE BESSON
$$$-$$$$
RUE DES FRÈRES PRADIGNAC 13
TEL 04 9339 5924
A Cannes institution,
this popular little bistro
serves a different fish dish
every day.
🔲 45/30 🕐 Closed Sun.-
Mon. Dec.-Jan. 🔲 🔲 🔲 AE,
MC, V

🍴 LA BROUETTE DE
GRAND' MÈRE
$$$
RUE D'ORAN 9 BIS
TEL 04 9339 1210
La Brouette dishes up
traditional French cooking
as good as grand-mère
(grandmother) used to
make. A convivial atmo-
sphere, helped along by
plenty of wine.
🔲 50/50 🕐 Closed L, Sun.,
& 3 weeks in Jan. 🔲
🔲 MC, V

🍴 L'ECHIQUIER
$$$
RUE ST.-ANTOINE 14
TEL 04 9339 7779
An intimate, candlelit
place in Suquet that caters
to stars and locals alike.
The traditional standards
include foie gras, bouilla-
baisse, sea bass, and magret
de canard (duck breast).
🔲 40/18 🕐 Closed L & 2
weeks in Jan.-Feb. 🔲 🔲 All
major cards

ST.-TROPEZ

🍴 LA TABLE DU MARCHÉ
$$$-$$$$
RUE DES COMMERÇANTS 11
TEL 04 94 97 0125
christophe-leroy.com
Chef Christophe Leroy has
added a gourmet note to
many French standards:
lobster and macaroni au
gratin, shepherd's pie with
duck and foie gras.
🕐 Closed 2 weeks in Jan.
🔲 AE, MC, V

🍴 LE CAFÉ
$$-$$$
PLACE DES LICES
TEL 04 9497 4469
lecafe.fr
The former star-studded
Café des Arts, whose
adjoining restaurant in the
back is reputedly still fre-
quented by the occasional
celebrity. The most regular
patrons, however, are the
boules players from the
square out front.
🔲 AE, MC, V

🍴 CAFÉ SÉNÉQUIER
$$
PLACE AUX HERBES 4/
QUAI JEAN JAURÈS
TEL 04 94 97 2020
senequier.com
A favorite café on the port.
It's pricey, but it's good for
evening aperitifs and for
watching celebrities on
yachts drink theirs.
🔲 No credit cards

NICE

🍴 LA RÉSERVE DE NICE
$$$-$$$$$
BOULEVARD FRANCK PILATTE 60
TEL 04 9708 1480
lareservedenice.fr
La Réserve has a fine
waterfront overlooking the
Baie des Anges. It features

🍴 Restaurant 🔲 No. of Seats 🅿 Parking 🕐 Closed 🛗 Elevator

light, creative cooking that cuts down on the Côte's usual decadence. Reserve.
🍴 83 🚭 AE, MC, V

🍴 LE SAFARI
$$$-$$$$
COURS SALEYA 1
TEL 04 9380 1844
restaurantsafari.fr
A big café with Mediterranean blue shutters, close to the market on Cours Saleya. Great for alfresco dining. Try the deep rich calamari, daube, or *bagna cauda,* a hot anchovy dip with raw vegetables.
🍴 35 🚭 All major cards

🍴 LA MERENDA
$$$
RUE RAOUL BOSIO 4
lamerenda.net
This tiny bistro is famous for its traditional Niçois dishes: stockfish, beignets, stuffed sardines, beef daube. No phone. Get there early to find a table.
🍴 26 🕐 Closed Sat.–Sun.
🚭 🚭 No credit cards

🍴 TERRES DE TRUFFES
$$-$$$$
RUE ST.-FRANÇOIS-DE-PAULE 11
TEL 04 9362 0768
terresdetruffes.com
Chef Bruno Clément's boutique sells truffle-related products. The elegant truffle-tasting bar inside has appetizers in addition to full course meals—look for tortellini soup with truffles and the popular truffle ice cream.
🕐 Closed Sun. 🚭 All major cards

🍴 LE COMPTOIR DU MARCHÉ
$$-$$$
RUE DU MARCHÉ 8
TEL 04 9313 4501

A small, relaxed spot on the edge of the Old Town, with pleasant service and classic French food.
🕐 Closed Sun.–Mon.
🚭 MC, V

VILLEFRANCHE-SUR-MER
🍴 LA MÈRE GERMAINE
$$$$
QUAI COURBET 9
TEL 04 9301 7139 OR
0800 673 496
meregermaine.com
A Vieux Port restaurant with a new take on southern classics. Inventive dishes, good local wine list, and an attractive waterfront setting.
🍴 120 🕐 Closed mid-Nov.–Dec. 25 🚭 AE, MC, V

BEAULIEU-SUR-MER
🍴 LE RESTAURANT DES ROIS
$$$$$
LA RÉSERVE DE BEAULIEU HOTEL, BOULEVARD DU MARÉCHAL LECLERC 5
TEL 04 9301 0001
reservebeaulieu.com
The fabulous Réserve de Beaulieu hotel grew out of a seafood restaurant founded in 1880. A century and a quarter later, the Michelin-starred restaurant continues to specialize in fish and spectacular views of the sea.
🍴 65/65 🕐 Closed mid-Oct.–mid-Dec. 🚭 All major cards

ANTIBES
🍴 LE CÉSAR
$$$-$$$$
CHEMIN DE LA GAROUPE 1040
TEL 04 9361 3374
restaurant-plage-cesar-antibes.fr
Dishes might include fish cooked in salt crust, pasta flambé, and artichoke ravioli. Waterfront setting just

up a small staircase above Keller Beach.
🍴 160/250 🕐 Closed Oct.–March 🚭 AE, MC, V

🍴 OSCAR'S
$$-$$$$$
RUE DU DOCTEUR ROSTAN 8
TEL 04 9334 9014
Stone walls, copper cookware, and Roman-style sculptures set the tone for this cheery Italian seafood eatery in the old town. Scampi tortellini, scallop raviolis, and sea perch and lemongrass lasagna are some of the many seasonal delicacies.
🕐 Closed Sun.–Mon., 2 weeks in June, & 2 weeks in Dec.–early Jan. 🚭 MC, V

MONACO

🍴 HERMITAGE
$$$$$
SQUARE BEAUMARCHAIS, MONTE-CARLO
TEL 377 9806 4000
hotelhermitagemontecarlo.com
A luxurious belle epoque palace with a huge, glass-domed winter garden, opulent restaurant, and terrace of cool marble.
🅿 🚭 🚭 All major cards

🍴 LOUIS XV
$$$$$
HÔTEL DE PARIS, PLACE DU CASINO, MONTE-CARLO
TEL 377 9806 8864
hoteldeparismontecarlo.com
Monaco's most famous restaurant, a three-Michelin-star establishment that is presided over by the celebrated chef Alain Ducasse. If you need to look at the prices, don't go. Typical dishes might be Provençal vegetables with black truffles, or pigeon with *foie gras de canard*

(duck foie gras).
🍴 40/20 🕐 Closed Tues., Wed. (except D late June–late Aug.), 3 weeks in late Feb.–mid-March, & 4 weeks in late Nov.–late Dec. 🚫 All major cards

🍴 LE CAFÉ DE PARIS
$$$$
PLACE DU CASINO, MONTE-CARLO
TEL 377 98 06 7623 OR 377 98 06 7624
Monte-Carlo's front-and-center brasserie with an enormous terrace and extravagant fin de siècle interior.
🍴 70 🚫 All major cards

■ ITALIAN RIVIERA & TUSCANY

Once an *osteria* was a simple inn, a *trattoria* was a basic neighborhood eatery, and a *ristorante* was upscale. Now *osterie* are often revamped as informal restaurants with innovative cooking; *trattorie* are, sadly, fast disappearing; and ristorante is a term now applied to just about any eating place. A *pizzeria* remains a simple, usually modern place that often serves basic pasta, main courses, and desserts as well as pizzas.

As a rule, Italians dress well but informally to eat out, especially in better restaurants. A relaxed casual style is a good rule of thumb. Jacket and tie for men are rarely necessary.

The check (*il conto*) must be presented by law as a formal receipt. You are within your rights to demand an itemized *ricevuta*. Bills may include a cover charge (*pane e coperto*), a practice the authorities are trying to outlaw.

In restaurants where a service charge (*servizio*) is not levied, tip 10–15 percent; even where it is, you may wish to leave 5–10 percent. In bars, tip a few cents for drinks consumed standing at bars, and 50 cents to 1 euro for waiter service.

Bars and cafés often provide snacks such as filled rolls (*panini*) or sandwiches (*tramezzini*) throughout the day. A few may offer a light meal at lunch. Stands or small stores selling slices of pizza (*pizza al taglio*) with different toppings are common.

In cafés it costs less to stand at the bar. Specify what you want and pay at the separate cash desk (*la cassa*), then take your receipt (*lo scontrino*) to the bar and repeat your order. A small coin slapped on the bar often helps secure prompt service. Where a bar has tables, especially outside tables, you pay more to sit and place your order with a waiter. Only in small rural bars can you pay at the bar and then sit down.

Smoking in bars, cafés, restaurants, and other public places is prohibited.

GENOA

🍴 GRAN GOTTO
$$$$
VIALE BRIGATE BISAGNO 69/R
TEL 010 564 344
grangotto.com
This venerable, slightly dated restaurant has been in the same family since 1937 and serves classic Ligurian food with a creative twist. The emphasis is on fish, but meat dishes and pasta are also available.
🍴 60 🕐 Closed L Sat. & all Sun. 🅿 🚫 AE, MC, V

🍴 MAXELA
$$$
VICO INFERIORE DEL FERRO 9/R
TEL 010 247 4209

maxela.it
Meat dominates Maxela's menu: Choose from the cuts displayed—fillet with pesto is recommended. Attractive brick-vaulted ceilings, a cordial atmosphere, wood benches, marble tables, and a central location just off Via Garibaldi three blocks east of Palazzo Rosso, make this a good bet.
🍴 60 🕐 Closed L Sat. & all Sun. (except Dec. & Easter); holidays vary 🅿 🚫 All major cards

🍴 ANTICA OSTERIA DI VICO PALLA
$$–$$$
VICOLO PALLA 15R
TEL 010 246 6575
anticaosteriavicopalla.com
This venerable inn in the old port area (convenient for the Acquario) has been in business since the 17th century, serving the freshest fish and seafood.
🍴 95 🕐 Closed Mon. & 1 week in Aug. 🚫 All major cards

PORTOFINO

🍴 DA PUNY
$$$$$
PIAZZA MARTIRI DELL' OLIVETTA 5
TEL 0185 269 037
A Portofino institution, this long-established restaurant is set on the chic square overlooking the harbor, with

two comfortable salons and tables set under trees on a terrace. A predominantly fish and seafood menu.

🍴 40/70 🕐 Closed Thurs. & Dec.-Feb. 💳 AE, MC, V

🍴 LA GRITTA
$$$$$

CALATA MARCONI 20
TEL 0185 269 126
One of Portofino's oldest bars. Rex Harrison once shared cocktails here with the Duke of Windsor, just two among many illustrious past habitués.

🕐 Closed Thurs. & Oct.-March 💳 DC, MC, V

CINQUE TERRE
🍴 GAMBERO ROSSO
$$$$

PIAZZA MARCONI 7, VERNAZZA
TEL 0187 812265
www.ristorantegambero rosso.net
One of several small and welcoming restaurants around the square on Vernazza's tiny beach and harbor. Delightful outdoor dining (mainly fish and seafood, but be sure to try the pesto) and a cozy interior for colder days.

🍴 40/40 🕐 Closed Thurs. & Jan.-Feb. 💳 AE, MC, V

FLORENCE

SOMETHING SPECIAL
🍴 ENOTECA PINCHIORRI
$$$$$

VIA GHIBELLINA 87
TEL 055 242 757 or 055 242 777
enotecapinchiorri.it
Florence's most expensive restaurant has three Michelin stars and—with more than 80,000 bottles—one of Europe's finest wine cellars. The setting—a Renaissance palazzo with frescoed ceilings—and

Tuscan-international cuisine are predictably chic, although the formality and ceremony may not be to all tastes. Jacket and tie recommended for men.

🍴 60 🕐 Closed Sun.-Mon. & 2-3 weeks in Aug. 💳 AE, MC, V

🍴 CIBREO
$$$$

VIA DEL VERROCCHIO 8R
TEL 055 234 1100
cibreo.com
The first choice of most Florentine gastronomes and the city's best place to enjoy creative interpretations of traditional Tuscan dishes such as *trippa in insalata* (cold tripe salad) and the celebrated *fegato brasato* (braised liver). The dining room is plain—simple wooden tables and painted walls—and the service and atmosphere relaxed. Prices are set for each course—leave room for the desserts. A reservation several days in advance is essential, but you might be luckier with the less expensive trattoria offshoot, **Cibrèino**, at nearby Via de' Macci 122r.

🍴 70 🅿 🕐 Closed Mon., Aug., & 1 week in Feb. 💳 All major cards

🍴 ORA D'ARIA
$$$$

VIA DE' GEORGOFILI 11-13R
TEL 055 200 1699
www.oradariaristorante.com
Young chef Marco Stabile has caused a stir at this location just south of Piazza della Signoria. The modern Tuscan and Italian cooking is light, imaginative, and beautifully presented.

🍴 40 🕐 Closed Sun., L Mon., last week Jan., first week Feb., & Aug. 💳 All major cards

🍴 BACCAROSSA
$$$-$$$$

VIA GHIBELLINA 46R
TEL 055 240 620
baccarossa.it
Tasty pan-Mediterranean fish and meat dishes and homemade pastas are served in this informal bistro-style restaurant two blocks north of Santa Croce. The restaurant's eclectic but attractive decor includes old wooden tables and vivid furnishings.

🍴 35 🕐 D only; L by appt. 💳 AE, MC, V

🍴 IL FRANCESCANO
$$$

VIA SAN GIUSEPPE 22R
TEL 055 241 773
ilfrancescano.com
This bustling, innovative, and pleasantly chic restaurant, just behind Santa Croce, offers pizzas baked in traditional Neapolitan style in wood-fired ovens or a choice of Tuscan pasta and meat dishes.

🍴 130 🕐 Closed Mon. Nov.-Feb. 💳 All major cards

🍴 CAFFÈ ITALIANO
$$-$$$

VIA ISOLE DELLE STINCHE 11-13R
TEL 055 289 368
caffeitaliano.it
osteriacaffeitaliano.com
This restaurant is split into three areas: a formal restaurant (osteria); a simple pizzeria for lunches, pizza, and less formal dining—both the osteria and pizzeria serve good-value Tuscan food; and the SUD, a restaurant with the fragrances, colors, and hospitality typical of southern Italy. All the areas have a fine medieval setting, with vast beams, brick vaults, and terra-cotta floors.

🍴 50/120 🕐 Closed Mon. Nov.-March 💳 MC, V

🔲 Nonsmoking   🔲 Air-conditioning   💳 Credit Cards

🍴 OSTERIA DE' BENCI

$$-$$$

VIA DE' BENCI 13R

TEL 055 234 4923

osteriadeibenci.it

A busy dining room painted in tasteful pastel colors that lend it a fresh modern air. Staff is young, energetic, and informal, and the food offers light, well-cooked takes on Tuscan staples such as *zuppa di verdura* (vegetable soup) and *agnello scottadito* (grilled lamb chops).

🔲 50/80 🚫 All major cards

🍴 PAOLI

$$-$$$

VIA DEI TAVOLINI 12R

TEL 055 216 215

casatrattoria.com/
restaurant/ristorante-paoli

A tempting place to eat at the very heart of the city (just off Via dei Calzaiuoli), although the temptation lies not so much in the food—Tuscan-style grilled meats, pastas, and soups—as in the beautiful frescoed dining room.

🔲 80 🕐 Closed Jan. 1
🔲 🚫 All major cards

🍴 IL SANTO BEVITORE

$$-$$$

VIA SANTO SPIRITO 66R

TEL 055 211 264

ilsantobevitore.com

The informal Saintly Drinker is just across the Carraia bridge, in the Oltrarno district. The atmosphere is young and welcoming, and the Tuscan food has a creative edge.

🔲 60 🕐 Closed L Sun.
🔲 🚫 MC, V

🍴 DEL FAGIOLI

$$

CORSO TINTORI 47R

TEL 055 244 285

The same family has run this trattoria close to Santa Croce for more than 40 years, perfecting both traditional Florentine standards such as *ribollita* (vegetable soup) and house specialties like *involtini alla Gigi* (rolled and filled meat).

🔲 50 🕐 Closed Sat.-Sun. & Aug. 🔲 🚫 No credit cards

🍴 ZÀ-ZÀ

$$

PIAZZA DEL MERCATO CENTRALE 26R

TEL 055 215 411

trattoriazaza.it

This former market-traders' retreat has gone from strength to strength, increasing in size and popularity without sacrificing its reasonable prices and reliable Florentine food. Forgo the outside tables on a forgettable square for the cheerful, informal, and pleasing old-style trattoria atmosphere inside.

🔲 90/30 🕐 Closed Dec. 25 🔲 🚫 All major cards

🍴 CAFFÈ GILLI

$

PIAZZA DELLA REPUBBLICA 39R/ VIA ROMA 1R

TEL 055 213 896

gilli.it

The vast characterless Piazza della Repubblica square is distinguished only by its four historic cafés, of which Gilli is the best. Founded in 1733, it moved to its present corner site in 1910, the date of its magnificent belle epoque interior. Food and service can be shaky, but the large terrace is a fine place for an aperitif.

🚫 All major cards

🍴 CANTINETTA DEI VERRAZZANO

$

VIA DEI TAVOLINI 18R

TEL 055 268 590

verrazzano.com/il-locale

A tempting retreat for take-out snacks, cakes, or slices of pizza, or a more leisurely lunch and glass of wine at the tables to the rear. Choose from the array of food under the huge glass-fronted display. Owned by a notable Chianti vineyard, so the wines are as good as the food.

🚫 All major cards

🍴 I DUE FRATELLINI

$

PIAZZA DEI CIMATORI 38R

TEL 055 239 6096

iduefratellini.it
anticotrippaio.com

A wonderful, central spot minutes from the Duomo that's been in business since 1875 selling fresh sandwiches and panini with the odd glass of wine. Moments away is **L'Antico Trippaio** (*Via Dante Alighieri at Piazza dei Cimatori 9, tel 339 742 5692*), one of the few remaining tripe kiosks, selling classic Florentine street food as well as conventional panini.

🚫 No credit cards

🍴 MERCATO CENTRALE

$

PIAZZA DEL MERCATO CENTRALE

Not a restaurant, but a large covered market crammed with superb food stalls—**Perini Gastronomia** (*Via dell'Ariento entrance, tel 055 239 8306, perinigastronomia.it, closed Sun.*) is one of the most famous—for putting together a picnic or sitting down at one of the venerable lunch spots, such as **Nerbone** (*Piazza del*

Mercato Centrale 12r, tel 055
219 949), for a cheap and
simple hot dish or sand-
wiches all day. Nearby **Casa
del Vino** (Via dell'Ariento
16r, tel 055 215 609, casadel
vino.it, closed Sun., Aug., &
Sat. Jun.–Sept.) is an old
wine bar offering panini
and wine by the glass.
🕐 Closed Sun. 🚫 No credit
cards

🍴 LE VOLPI E L'UVA
$
PIAZZA DE' ROSSI 1R
TEL 055 239 8132
levolpieluva.com
A discreet wine bar tucked
away off Piazza di Santa
Felicita south of Ponte Vecchio. It offers a well-chosen
selection of regularly
changing wines and a first-
rate selection of cheese
and snacks.
🕐 Closed Sun. 🚫 AE, MC, V

PISA

🍴 OSTERIA DEI CAVAL-
IERI
$$$
VIA SAN FREDIANO 16
TEL 050 580 858
osteriacavalieri.pisa.it
A welcoming trattoria at
the heart of the old city.
The well-priced Tuscan
dishes include cinghiale
(wild boar) and a sprinkling
of more adventurous meat
and fish dishes.
🔢 60 🕐 Closed L Sat.,
all Sun., & 3 weeks in Aug.
🔲 🚫 All major cards

LUCCA

🍴 BUCA DI
SANT'ANTONIO
$$$–$$$$
VIA DELLA CERVIA 3

TEL 0583 55881 OR 339 154 0668
bucadisantantonio.it
A restaurant established
in 1787, the Buca di
Sant'Antonio relies on old
Lucchese cooking tradi-
tions, but it does not shy
from innovation. Try the
celebrated buccellato semi-
freddo, the house dessert,
a mix of chilled cream and
wild berries.
🔢 90 🕐 Closed D Sun., all
Mon., & some of Jan. & July
🔲 🚫 All major cards

🍴 OSTERIA DEL NENI
$$
VIA PESCHERIA (OFF VIA
VITTORIO VENETO)
TEL 0583 492 681
Classic trattoria on a small
street one block south of
Piazza San Michele. It can
be slow at busy times, but
it offers reliable and inexpensive food, with some
local specialties.
🔢 35/20 🕐 Closed Mon.
🔲 🚫 No credit cards

🍴 PIZZERIA DA FELICE
$
VIA BUIA 12
TEL 0583 494 986
A tiny, family-run place for
inexpensive pizza and other
freshly baked snacks to go.
Do not confuse it with the
pricier, larger, and modern
Felice Ristorante Pizzeria
across town (Via Casgruccio
Buonamici 352, tel 0583 587
412, pizzeriafelice.it, closed
Mon. & 2 weeks in July, all
major cards), which also has
a self-serve lunch buffet.
🕐 Closed Sun. (except in
Sept. & Dec.) 🔲 🚫 All major
cards

SIENA

🍴 OSTERIA LE LOGGE
$$–$$$
VIA DEL PORRIONE 33

TEL 0577 48 013
giannibrunelli.it
No Sienese restaurant is
prettier than this former
medieval pharmacy just
off the Campo. Innovative
but occasionally hit-or-miss
Sienese cuisine. Avoid the
bland upstairs dining room.
🔢 40/80 🕐 Closed Sun. &
some of Jan. 🔲 🚫 All major
cards

🍴 OSTERIA IL CARROCCIO
$$
VIA DEL CASATO DI SOTTO 32
TEL 0577 41165
A tiny and discreet one-
room trattoria barely two
minutes from the Campo.
Simple Sienese dishes
(excellent antipasti) plus
pleasant, easygoing service.
🔢 35/20 🕐 Closed Wed. &
periods in Feb. & Nov. 🚫 No
credit cards

SAN GIMIGNANO

🍴 DORANDÒ
$$$$–$$$$$
VICOLO DELL'ORO 2
TEL 0577 941 862
ristorantedorando.it
A small, welcoming,
intimate restaurant in a
medieval setting but with
a modern ambience. It
re-creates ancient recipes
from Etruscan, Medici, and
early medieval periods.
🔢 50 🕐 Closed early Dec.–
Dec. 25, Jan. 7–early Feb.,
& Mon. (winter) 🔲 🚫 All
major cards

🍴 LE VECCHIE MURA
$$$
VIA PIANDORNELLA 15
TEL 0577 940 270
vecchiemura.it
Reliable Tuscan food
from an unpretentious and
long-established restaurant
with fine stone-vaulted
dining rooms by the city
walls and great views from

the terrace. Reservations are essential.
🪑 60/30 🕐 Closed Tues., mid-Nov.–mid-Dec., & Feb. 💳 🅿 AE, MC, V

🍴 OSTERIA DEL CARCERE
$$
VIA DEL CASTELLO 13
TEL 0577 941 905
More a wine bar than an osteria, with snack plates of cold cuts, cheeses, crostini, and terrines, plus soups and a handful of hot dishes daily.
🪑 30 🕐 Closed mid-Jan.–mid-March, Wed., & L Thur. 💳 🅿 MC, V

■ ROME & NAPLES

ROME

🍴 ANTONELLO COLONNA
$$$$$
VIA MILANO 9A
TEL 06 4782 2641
antonellocolonna.it/roma
Antonello Colonna won Michelin stars from 2010 through 2013 for his cooking in this striking contemporary restaurant in the renovated Palazzo delle Esposizioni.
🪑 35 🕐 Closed D both Sun. & Mon.; holidays vary 💳 🅿 AE, MC, V

🍴 GLASS HOSTARIA
$$$$$
VICOLO DEL CINQUE 58
TEL 06 5833 5903
glass-restaurant.it
The bold, contemporary styling of this Trastevere restaurant breaks the mold of the more traditional Roman trattoria. The creative Italian cooking earned a Michelin star in 2011.
🪑 50 🕐 Closed Mon., L, & parts of Jan. & July 💳 🅿 All major cards

🍴 LA ROSETTA
$$$$–$$$$$
VIA DELLA ROSETTA 8-9
TEL 06 686 1002
larosetta.com
A small, formal restaurant of long-standing repute on a small street immediately north of the Pantheon. Patrons usually include politicians from the nearby parliament building. Fish and seafood only.
🪑 50 🕐 Closed 2 weeks in Aug. 💳 🅿 All major cards

🍴 SORA LELLA
$$$$
VIA DI PONTE QUATTRO CAPI 16, ISOLA TIBERINA
TEL 06 686 1601
soralella.com
The two cozy dining rooms and their wood-paneled walls and rows of bottles still bear witness to the simple trattoria origins of this restaurant on Tiber Island, but the food has increased in sophistication.
🪑 45 💳 🅿 All major cards

🍴 GRANO
$$$–$$$$
PIAZZA RONDANINI 53
TEL 06 6819 2096
ristorantegrano.it
The virtually all-white decor of this rustic-styled bar and restaurant east of San Luigi dei Francesi will not be to all tastes, but the pastas and creative, mostly southern Italian cooking, are first-rate.
🪑 60/30 🕐 Closed 1 week in Aug. & Dec. 24-25 🅿 AE, MC, V

🍴 PARIS
$$$–$$$$
PIAZZA SAN CALISTO 7/A
TEL 06 581 5378
ristoranteparis.it
An understated and elegant restaurant just off Piazza

Santa Maria in Trastevere. The fish and pasta dishes are good, and outdoor dining is available in summer.
🪑 90/70 🕐 Closed L Mon. April–Oct. & all Mon. Nov.–March 💳 🅿 All major cards

🍴 PIPERNO
$$$–$$$$
VIA MONTE DE' CENCI 9
TEL 06 6880 6629
ristorantepiperno.it
Rome has a strong tradition of Jewish culture and cooking, and this old-fashioned and rustic restaurant in the former Ghetto is the best place to sample specialties such as *carciofi alla giudìa* (deep-fried artichoke) and *fiori di zucca ripieni* (deep-fried zucchini flowers filled with mozzarella).
🪑 100/30 🕐 Closed D Sun., all Mon., & Aug. 💳 🅿 All major cards

🍴 VECCHIA ROMA
$$$–$$$$
PIAZZA CAMPITELLI 18
TEL 06 686 4604
ristorantevecchiaroma.com
One of the city's prettiest restaurants, situated on a charming piazza at the heart of the old Ghetto—reserve a table outside. The food is merely notable, though salads are excellent, pastas are innovative—*stringhelli con basilico e pecorino* combines

basil, cheese, and chewy noodles—while the main courses tend toward fish and seafood.

100/120 Closed Wed. All major cards

HOSTARIA DA NERONE
$$-$$$
VIA DELLE TERME DI TITO 96
TEL 06 481 7952
This friendly, old-fashioned trattoria very convenient to the Colosseo is noted for its buffet of cold antipasti (appetizers) and robust Abruzzese and Roman cooking. In summer there is a handful of tables outdoors.

30/50 Closed Sun. & Aug. All major cards

MACCHERONI
$$-$$$
PIAZZA DELLE COPPELLE 44
TEL 06 6830 7895
ristorantemaccheroni.com
Popular and informal, with attractive, rustic dining rooms (and outdoor tables on a pretty piazza), but avoid the basement room. It serves good-value and quality traditional Italian dishes; convenient for the Pantheon.

120/60 All major cards

MATRICIANELLA
$$-$$$
TEL 06 683 2100
VIA DEL LEONE 4
matricianella.it
In business since 1957, the Matricianella is close to Via del Corso and the parliament building and offers classic Roman cooking in understated, traditional-looking dining rooms. Outdoor seating available.

45/25 Closed Sun., 3 weeks in Aug., Dec. 24–26,

& Dec. 31–Jan. 1 All major cards

L'ORSO 80
$$-$$$
VIA DELL'ORSO 33
TEL 06 686 4904 OR C€ 686 1710
orso80.it
Invariably filled with vacationers—but none the worse for that—this big restaurant close to Piazza Navona is a reliable standby for basic meat and fish dishes at a moderate price.

170 Closed Mon. & 3 weeks in Aug. All major cards

IL PICCOLO
$$
VIA DEL GOVERNO VECCHIO 74–75
TEL 06 6880 1746
This small wine bar just a few steps west of Piazza Navona is perfect for a quiet glass of wine by candlelight. Nearby **Cul de Sac** (Piazza Pasquino 73, tel 06 6880 1094, enotecaculdesacroma.it, $$-$$$) is a little less romantic, but equally good for wine and snacks.

20 All major cards

IVO
$-$$
VIA DI SAN FRANCESCO A RIPA 158
TEL 06 581 7082
This is one of the biggest and most popular of Trastevere's many pizzerias. You may have to wait in line, but turnover is quick and the atmosphere lively.

200 Closed Tues. DC, MC, V

ANTICO CAFFÈ DELLA PACE
$
VIA DELLA PACE 3–7 (OFF PIAZZA NAVONA)

TEL 06 686 1216
caffedellapace.it
By night, this pretty ivy-covered café is one of Rome's trendiest places, but by day it is quieter, its enchanting old mirror-and-wood interior providing a perfect place for a coffee or a predinner drink.

Closed Mon. a.m. & 3 days in Aug. All major cards

CAVOUR 313
$
VIA CAVOUR 313
TEL 06 678 5496
cavour313.it
Perfect for a snack or glass of wine after visiting the Forum.

Closed Sun. July–mid-Sept. All major cards

ENOTECA CORSI
$
VIA DEL GESÙ 87–88
TEL 06 679 0821
enotecacorsi.com
Little has changed at this simple wine bar–trattoria a few minutes south of the Pantheon in more than 30 years. The food is simple Roman cooking at its best—you can eat a full meal or simply have a glass of wine and a snack.

Closed Sun., D Sat. & Mon.–Wed., & 3 weeks in Aug. All major cards

GELATERIA DELLA PALMA
$
VIA DELLA MADDALENA 19–23
TEL 06 6880 6752
dellapalma.it
This big, bright, and modern empor um just north of the Pantheon sells more than a 150 flavors of ice cream, cakes, chocolates, and other calorie-filled treats.

Closed Wed. No credit cards

NAPLES

🍴 PALAZZO PETRUCCI
$$$$-$$$$$
PIAZZA SAN DOMENICO
MAGGIORE 4
TEL 081 552 4068
palazzopetrucci.it
Refined cooking in an un-Italian minimalist dining room in a period palace on one of the historic center's most attractive squares.
🔲 55 🕐 Closed D Sun., L Mon., L Sun. July & Aug., & 3 weeks in Aug. 🔵 🔷 All major cards

🍴 LA BERSAGLIERA
$$$$
BORGO MARINARI 10-11
TEL 081 764 6016
labersagliera.it
This waterfront restaurant can be busy with vacationers, but its atmosphere and long history make it a fun, if pricey place to visit at least once.
🔲 200 🕐 Closed Tues. & some of Jan. 🔵 🔷 All major cards

🍴 CIRO A SANTA BRIGIDA
$$$-$$$$$
VIA SANTA BRIGIDA 71-73A-74
TEL 081 552 4072
ciroasantabrigida.it
Ciro is considered a touchstone for refined Neapolitan cuisine. Fish and seafood are generally better bets than meat-based dishes (there is also a pizzeria). Service is charming, and while the interiors are rather bland, the setting below the Castel dell'Ovo is lovely.
🔲 130 🕐 Closed Sun. (except Dec.) 🔵 🔷 All major cards

🍴 DA ETTORE
$$$
VIA SANTA LUCIA 56
TEL 081 764 0498
An unpretentious neighborhood restaurant since 1914, Da Ettore specializes in fish and seafood, but many come here for the pizzas and *pagnotielli* (pizza-dough wraps with fillings). House wine is poor—go for a bottle. Make reservations or arrive early.
🔲 180 🕐 Closed Sun., Easter, 3 weeks in Aug., & Dec. 24-26 🔵 🔷 DC, MC, V

🍴 MIMÌ ALLA FERROVIA
$$$
VIA ALFONSO D'ARAGONA 21
TEL 081 553 8525
Mimì has been drawing visitors and wealthier and celebrity locals alike for decades. Lively, cordial atmosphere, an elegant interior, though the Neapolitan dishes can be uneven.
🔲 180 🕐 Closed Sun. & 1 week in Aug. 🔵 🔷 All major cards

🍴 OSTERIA LA CHITARRA
$$$
RAMPE SAN GIOVANNI
MAGGIORE 1/B
TEL 081 552 9103
osterialachitarra.it
A simple trattoria run by two courteous brothers.
🔲 32 🕐 Closed L Mon.-Sat., L Sun. July-Easter, & last 2 weeks in Aug. 🔵 🔷 All major cards

🍴 HOSTERIA TOLEDO
$$-$$$
VICO GIARDINETTO A TOLEDO
78/A (OFF VIA TOLEDO)
TEL 081 421 257
hosteriatoledo.it
This restaurant, founded in 1951, in a Quartieri Spagnoli tenement from the 17th century, serves simple but perfect Neapolitan food such as *pasta alle cozze e vongole* (pasta with clams and mussels). Ask for a table on the upper floor.
🔲 70 🕐 Closed D Tues. & 2 weeks in Aug. 🔵 🔷 All major cards

🍴 LA VECCHIA CANTINA
$$-$$$
VICO SAN NICOLA ALLA
CARITÀ 13-14
TEL 081 552 0226 OR
348 44 93 803
Proximity to the Pignasecca market ensures the freshest produce at this tiny restaurant on the northern fringes of the Quartieri Spagnoli. This is the sort of Old World trattoria that is fast disappearing in northern and central Italy.
🔲 50 🕐 Closed D Sun. 🔵 🔷 DC, MC, V

🍴 ANTICA OSTERIA PISANO
$$
PIAZZETTA CROCELLE AI
MANNESI 1
TEL 081 554 8325
A location with lots of passing trade on the corner of Via del Duomo and Spaccanapoli plus inexpensive Neapolitan food make this tiny trattoria a popular place for lunch.
🔲 35 🕐 Closed Sun. Jan.-Oct. & 3 weeks in Aug. 🔵 🔷 No credit cards

🍴 BRANDI
$-$$
SALITA SANT'ANNA DI PALAZZO
1-2 (OFF VIA CHIAIA)
TEL 081 416 928
brandi.it
Naples's most famous pizzeria and birthplace of the Margherita (tomato, basil, and mozzarella cheese). It is often full of vacationers, but the atmosphere, pizzas, and pasta dishes are good. Other famous historic

pizzerias in Naples: **Da Michele** (*Via Cescre Sersale 1–3, tel 081 553 9204, damichele.net, closed Sun. Jan.–Nov., $–$$*) and **Di Matteo** (*Via dei Tribunali 94, tel 081 455 262, pizzeriadimatteo .com, closed Sun., $–$$*).

🍴 100 🕐 Closed Mon. & D Sun. 🚭 🏧 All major cards

🍴 GRAN CAFFÈ GAMBRINUS

$

VIA CHIAIA 1–2 (OFF PIAZZA TRIESTE E TRENTO)

TEL 081 417 582

grancaffegambrinus.com

Dating from 1860, this is the city's most famous and most opulent café. Wonderful coffees and celebrated cakes and pastries.

🍴 170 🏧 All major cards

HERCULANEUM

🍴 VIVA LO RE

$$$

CORSO RESINA 261

TEL 081 739 0207

vivalore.it

Good dining options are rare near the archaeological site. Take a cab to this restaurant on the outskirts of the town. Pleasantly rustic in style, it offers simple, well-prepared Campanian dishes such as *zuppa di verdure* (vegetable soup).

🍴 55 🕐 Closed D Sun., Mon., & 3 weeks in Aug. 🚭 🏧 All major cards

POMPEII

🍴 PRESIDENT

$$$$$

PIAZZA SCHETTINI 12–13

TEL 081 850 7245

www.ristorantepresident.it

An elegant but expensive restaurant, popular with locals, that offers creative Campanian meat and fish dishes.

🍴 55/25 🕐 Closed D Sun.–Mon. & 2 weeks in Jan. 🚭 🏧 All major cards

CAPRI

CAPRI TOWN

🍴 LA CAPANNINA

$$$$$

VIA LE BOTTEGHE 12B-S/14

TEL 081 837 0732

capanninacapri.com

A glamorous but unstuffy and consistently good restaurant just off the Piazzetta. Mostly classic fish creations with some meat dishes.

🍴 120 🕐 Closed mid-Nov.–mid-March 🚭 🏧 All major cards

🍴 DA TONINO

$$$$$

VIA DENTECALE 12–14

TEL 081 837 6718

Tonino Aprea runs this charming restaurant away from the town's visitor-filled streets. Innovative meat and fish dishes, and in summer you can dine alfresco. The 800-strong wine list is stellar.

🍴 45 🕐 Closed Mon. & mid-Jan.–Easter 🚭 🏧 DC, MC, V

🍴 RENDEZ-VOUS

$$$$$

GRAND HOTEL, VIA CAMERELLE 2

TEL 081 837 0788

quisisana.com

This restaurant in the famous Grand Hotel is the island's best. Come for a drink in one of the stylish bars, even if you do not have time for a full meal.

🍴 30 🕐 Closed Nov.–March 🚭 🚭 🏧 All major cards

ANACAPRI

🍴 L'OLIVO

$$$$$

CAPRI PALACE HOTEL VIA CAPODIMONTE 14

TEL 081 978 0111

capripalace.com

Even if you are not staying at the Capri Palace Hotel, L'Olivo restaurant is outstanding in its own right for a big treat, and the roof terrace views stretch as far as Vesuvius.

🍴 50 🕐 Closed Nov.–mid-April 🚭 🚭 🏧 All major cards

🍴 GELSOMINA ALLA MIGLIARA

$$$–$$$$

VIA MIGLIARA 72

TEL 081 837 1499

dagelsomina.com

The Gelsomina alla Migliara serves up sweeping sea views from its glorious hilltop location in the countryside a short drive from the village. The restaurant offers local meat and fish classics.

🍴 90/110 🕐 Closed Jan.–Feb. & Tues. Oct.–Dec. & March–April 🚭 🏧 All major cards

AMALFI COAST

AMALFI

🍴 LA CARAVELLA

$$$$$

VIA MATTEO CAMERA 12

TEL 089 871 029 OR 333 453 7633

ristorantelacaravella.it

The location near the main road into town may not be the best, but the food here has won a Michelin star as recently as 2013.

🍴 30 🕐 Closed Tues., Jan.–mid-Feb., & part of Nov. & Dec. 🚭 🏧 AE, MC, V

🍴 DA GEMMA
$$$-$$$$

VIA FRÀ GERARDO SASSO 11

TEL 089 871 345

trattoriadagemma.com

Charming old-fashioned trattoria with the odd modern decorative and culinary flourish. Fair prices, first-rate food, and a warm welcome.

🪑 30 🕐 Closed Wed. Nov.-Feb., holidays mid-Nov.- mid-Dec., & Jan. 7-mid-Feb. 🅿 🛗 All major cards

RAVELLO
🍴 ROSSELLINIS
$$$$$

PALAZZO AVINO, VIA SAN GIOVANNI DEL TORO 28

TEL 089 818 181

palazzoavino.com

The Rossellinis restaurant at the Palazzo Avino hotel is exceptional—it has a Michelin star (2013)—but rather formal. If possible, dine outside on the terrace.

🪑 70 🕐 Closed L & Nov.- March 🅿 🛗 All major cards

🍴 CUMPÀ COSIMO
$$$$

VIA ROMA 48

TEL 089 857 156

A simple pizzeria/restaurant in the middle of the village that has been run by the same family for more than 70 years.

🪑 50 🕐 Closed some Mon. 🅿 🛗 All major cards

🍴 DA SALVATORE
$$$$

VIA DELLA REPUBBLICA 2

TEL 089 857 227

salvatoreravello.com

A modest-looking and relaxed restaurant with delicious food and stupendous views from both the dining room and summer terrace.

🪑 90/50 🕐 Closed Nov.-

March & Mon. April-Oct. (except Aug.) 🅿 🛗 All major cards

POSITANO
🍴 LA CAMBUSA
$$$$

PIAZZA AMERIGO VESPUCCI 4

TEL 089 812 051

lacambusapositano.com

La Cambusa, close to the beach, has been a fixture of Positano since 1970, serving a large variety of fish and seafood prepared every which way, from pastas and carpaccios to soups and salads.

🪑 60 🕐 Closed Nov.-Dec. & usually Tues. Jan.-Feb. 🅿 🛗 All major cards

🍴 IL CAPITANO
$$$-$$$$

HOTEL MONTEMARE, VIA PASITEA 119

TEL 089 811 351

hotelmontemare.it

Virtually everything here, from bread sticks to pasta, is homemade. Fish and seafood are excellent, especially the seafood antipasti. In summer, book a table on the terrace, overlooking the sea.

🪑 35 🕐 Closed Nov.-March 🛗 All major cards

🍴 IL RITROVO
$$$

VIA MONTEPERTUSO 77

TEL 089 812 005 OR 089 875 453

ilritrovo.com/en/main _en.html

Escape Positano's summer heat, high prices, and summer crowds in a rustic ambience high above the village. Il Ritrovo offers old Amalfitan dishes such as spaghetti con pomodorini (spaghetti with cherry tomatoes) and simple chicken and rabbit stews.

🪑 65 🕐 Closed Jan.-early Feb. & Wed. except Easter- Oct. 🅿 🛗 All major cards

---

PRICES

RESTAURANTS

For a three-course meal without drinks:

$$$$$	Over $80
$$$$	$50-$80
$$$	$35-$50
$$	$20-$35
$	Under $20

SORRENTO
🍴 L'ANTICA TRATTORIA
$$$$$

VIA PADRE REGINALDO GIULIANI 33

TEL 081 807 1082

lanticatrattoria.com

A restaurant with a pergola and tables arranged around six small dining salons. It has been in business since 1930, offering local specialities such as pezzogna (fish baked in salt) and fish all'acqua pazza (fish with cherry tomato sauce or in a spicy tomato and shellfish sauce).

🪑 50 🕐 Closed Feb. & Mon. Nov.-Dec. 🅿 🛗 All major cards

SOMETHING SPECIAL

🍴 DON ALFONSO 1890
$$$$$

CORSO SANT'AGATA 11, SANT'AGATA SUI DUE GOLFI

TEL 081 878 0026

donalfonso1890.com

Many claim that Don Alfonso 1890 is the best restaurant in southern Italy (Michelin has awarded it two stars). The setting, with views over two gulfs, is superb, and the dining rooms and service are elegant without being too formal. Most of the produce comes from the owners' organic farm. In the same village but at the

---

🍴 Restaurant 🪑 No. of Seats 🅿 Parking 🕐 Closed 🛗 Elevator

other extreme, the rustic **Fattoria Terranova** *(Via Pontone 10, tel 081 533 0234, fattoriaterranova.it, closed Nov.–early March)* offers good, simple local cooking. 🏠 50 🕐 Closed Nov.–March, Mon. & L Tues. mid-June–mid-Sept., & Mon.–Tues. April–mid-June 🚭 💳 All major cards

■ SICILY, MALTA, & PUGLIA

SICILY

TAORMINA

🍴 LA GIARA
$$$$$
VICO LA FLORESTA 1
TEL 0942 23 360 OR
0942 625 083
lagiarataormina.it
Expensive, large, and decidedly upscale, with elaborate food and service. In addition, the draws here are the panoramic terrace and the restaurant's historical associations: Ava Gardner and other stars dined and partied here in the 1950s. 🏠 200/80 🕐 Closed L & Nov.–March 🚭 💳 All major cards

🍴 SANTANERA RISTORANTE SLOWDRINK
$$$$$
VIA SANTA MARIA DE' GRECI
TEL 0942 21 208
This fine-dining restaurant occupies a lovely historic building, and offers a sophisticated menu of revisited classic Sicilian dishes. In addition to the intimate dining room, there is an outdoor terrace. Reservations are recommended

in summer. 🏠 35/15 🕐 Closed L, Sun. & early Jan.–early March 🚭 💳 All major cards

🍴 'A ZAMMÀRA
$$$$
VIA FRATELLI BANDIERA 15
TEL 0942 24 408
zammara.it
The attraction here is the chance to dine (in summer) in a lovely garden of orange and mandarin trees. Regional Sicilian cuisine and a particularly good wine list. Other central, reliable, lower-cost options include the family-run **La Piazzetta** *(Vico Francesco Paladini 5, tel 0942 626 317, ristorantelapiazzettataor mina.it)*, and **Vecchia Taormina** *(Vico Ebrei 3, tel 0942 625 589)* is the place for pizza. 🏠 90/60 🕐 Closed Jan. 7–March 20 & Wed. Oct.–April 🚭 💳 All major cards

🍴 AL DUOMO
$$$$
VICO EBREI 11
TEL 0942 625 656
ristorantealduomo.it
Al Duomo is an excellent, lively restaurant in a small alley just off the cathedral square (with good outdoor dining options in summer). Marble tables and homey atmosphere, good service, and well-prepared local meats, fish, and seafood. 🏠 40/35 🕐 Closed Mon. Nov.–March; winter holidays vary 🚭 💳 All major cards

PALERMO

🍴 SANTANDREA
$$$$
PIAZZA SANT'ANDREA 4
TEL 091 334 999 OR 328 131 4595
Close to the Vucciria markets and San Domenico,

Santandrea is a delightful, well-located restaurant with a good reputation, but the food can be occasionally uneven. The food features many creative twists but never strays far from its Palermitan roots. Good wine list. 🏠 80/80 🕐 Closed L, Sun., & parts of Aug. 🚭 💳 AE, MC, V

🍴 IL MAESTRO DEL BRODO
$$$
VIA PANNIERI 7
TEL 091 329 523
Fresh ingredients from Palermo's Vucciria markets go into traditional dishes such as *pasta con le sarde* (pasta with sardines) and *pesce spada e menta* (swordfish with mint) at this welcoming, family-run trattoria conveniently situated near the corner of Via Roma and Corso Vittorio Emanuele II. 🏠 60 🕐 Closed Mon. Sept.–June, Sun. June–Aug., 2 weeks in Aug., & D (except Fri.–Sat. Sept.–May) 🚭 💳 AE, MC, V

🍴 CASA DEL BRODO
$$–$$$
CORSO VITTORIO EMANUELE II 175
TEL 091 321 655
casadelbrodo.it
This Palermitan favorite, founded in 1890, offers good value for the money, especially if you go for the *brodo* (broth or soup), several different choices of which are available each day. Or choose from the antipasti buffet laid out between the two dining rooms. 🏠 60 🕐 Closed Tues. Oct.–May, Sun. June–Sept., & 2 weeks in July 💳 All major cards

---

🍴 PICCOLO NAPOLI
$$-$$$
PIAZZETTA MULINO A VENTO 4
TEL 091 320 431
The lively and perennially popular Piccolo Napoli has been a touchstone for the freshest fish and seafood at the heart of the Borgo Vecchio market district since 1951. Start with a buffet of seafood and try local specialties such as pasta with *ricci* (sea urchin) or stick to simply grilled or roasted fish.
🪑 52 🕐 Closed Sun., D Mon., & some of Aug. 💳 🏧 All major cards

🍴 TRATTORIA PRIMAVERA
$$
PIAZZA BOLOGNI 4
TEL 091 329 408
Antonella Saviano has run this homey and traditional trattoria in the historic center of the city for almost four decades, offering fair prices and a nice mix of comforting Palermitan classics such as *polpette di sarde al sugo* (sardine "meatballs" with sauce). You can eat à la carte or try the set menu, which starts with a selection of antipasti (appetizers) that is a meal in itself.
🪑 50/35 🕐 Closed Mon. 💳 🏧 DC, MC, V

🍴 ANTICA FOCACCERIA
$
VIA ALESSANDRO PATERNOSTRO 59
TEL 091 320 264
afsf.it
An atmospheric, family-run tavern founded in 1834, with marble tables, old mirrors, wrought iron, and wood paneling. It offers a handful of hot dishes and snacks such as *panelle*

(chickpea fritters) and *purpa* (boiled octopus). More conventional snacks and sandwiches are also available.
🪑 200/100 🏧 All major cards

MALTA

VALLETTA

🍴 MALATA
$$$
PALACE SQUARE
TEL 21 223 967 OR 79 207 521
malatamalta.com
This restaurant on Valletta's main square has a fine period setting, with a venerable stone-vaulted cellar adorned with caricatures of Maltese politicians, though you can also dine at tables outside on the square. The cooking combines Maltese, French, and modern Mediterranean dishes.
🪑 60/40 🕐 Closed Sun. 💳 🏧 All major cards

🍴 RAMPILA
$$$
ST. JOHN'S CAVALIER ST.
TEL 21 226 625 OR 99 441 120
rampila.com
A fine historic setting in the city's bastion walls, including a tunnel once cut through the defenses. Modern Mediterranean food, which you can eat inside or out on the pretty terrace.
🪑 60/40 💳 🏧 All major cards

🍴 LEGLIGIN
$$-$$$
117-119 ST. LUCY ST.
TEL 21 221 699 OR 79 932 985
A cozy, candlelit cellar popular with locals: Try the Legligin Meze, nine different dishes, all from traditional Maltese recipes. Reservation advised on weekends; or just drop

by for a glass of wine. **Rubino** (*53 Old Bakery St., tel 21 224 656, rubinomalta .com, closed Sun., D Mon., & 1 week in Aug., $$*) is another small, relaxed local favorite.
🪑 50 🕐 Closed Tues. & L 💳 🏧 All major cards

🍴 CAFFÈ CORDINA
$$
244 REPUBLIC ST.
TEL 21 234 385 OR 21 241 359
caffecordina.com
Valletta's grandest and oldest café, founded in 1837, occupies part of the former treasury of the Knights of Malta at the heart of the old city. Be sure to sample the homemade pastries and pay slightly over the odds to sit on the terrace with a drink, snack, or light lunch for Valletta's best people-watching.
🪑 110/200 💳 🏧 All major cards

PUGLIA

BARI

🍴 LA PIGNATA
$$$$
CORSO VITTORIO EMANUELE II 173-175
TEL 080 523 2481
ristorantelapignatabari.com
La Pignata is the best and most expensive of Bari's many fish and seafood restaurants. On one of the modern city's busiest main streets, its single dining room provides a calm and elegant retreat.
🪑 90 🕐 Closed Mon. & Aug. 💳 🏧 All major cards

🍴 AL SORSO PREFERITO
$$$
VIA VITO NICOLA DE NICOLÒ 46
TEL 080 523 5747
sorso-preferito.com

🍴 Restaurant   🪑 No. of Seats   🅿 Parking   🕐 Closed   ⬍ Elevator

A popular and busy fish and seafood restaurant in the modern town with reasonable prices.
🍴 130 🕐 Closed D Sun. & 2-3 weeks in Aug. 🚭 🅰 All major cards

🍴 OSTERIA DELLE TRAVI
$-$$
LARGO IGNAZIO CHIURLIA 12
TEL 339 157 8848
A family-run trattoria with a warm welcome, low prices, and old-fashioned Puglian home cooking, including a wonderful buffet of antipasti.
🍴 95 🕐 Closed D Sun., all Mon., & 1 week in Aug. 🚭 🅰 No credit cards

TRANI

🍴 TORRENTE ANTICO
$$$$$
VIA EDOARDO FUSCO 3
TEL 088 348 7911
Traditional dishes are given a modern edge at this intimate restaurant in Trani's old quarter. Dishes might include *risotto con zucchine e gamberi* (risotto with zucchini and shrimp) or *rum babà* with a Chantilly cream.
🍴 30 🕐 Closed D Sun., all Mon., 1 week in Jan., & 2 weeks in July 🚭 🅰 All major cards

TRULLI COUNTRY

🍴 IL POETA CONTADINO
$$$$$
VIA INDIPENDENZA 21, ALBEROBELLO
TEL 080 432 1917
ilpoetacontadino.it
An elegant, central restaurant, with one of Italy's best wine cellars and delightful cooking, including a *budino* (pudding) of wild *cardoncelli* mushrooms with smoked

scamorza and walnuts, served as an appetizer.
🍴 50 🕐 Closed 3 weeks in Jan. & Mon. Oct.–June 🚭 🅰 All major cards

🍴 OSTERIA CANTONE
$$$$
CONTRADA FANTESE, CISTERNINO
TEL 080 444 6902
masseriacantone.it
A stately *masseria*—fortified country house—and its attractive garden. The dining room resembles a private home, and the Puglian cuisine uses many local ingredients.
🍴 60 🕐 By reservation only 🚭 🅰 No credit cards

🍴 OSTERIA DEL TEMPO PERSO
$$$$
VIA G. TANZARELLA VITALE 47, OSTUNI
TEL 083 130 4819 OR
339 185 1652
osteriadeltempoperso.com
A traditional trattoria at the heart of the old quarter, the Osteria del Tempo Perso has been a reliable source of typical Puglian cooking
🍴 70 🕐 Closed Mon. (except Aug.) & L Mon.-Sat July-Aug. 🚭 🅰 All major cards

🍴 LA CANTINA
$$$
VICO LIPPOLIS 8/CORSO VITTORIO EMANUELE ALBEROBELLO
TEL 080 432 3473 OR
347 740 1588
ilristorantelacantina.it
Four small steps take you from the crowded streets of central Alberobello into a tiny restaurant that has been run by the Lippolis family since 1958. The traditional food includes Puglian classics.

🍴 32 🕐 Closed Tues., 1 week in Feb., & 2 weeks in July 🚭 🅰 All major cards

MATERA

🍴 BACCANTI
$$$$
VIA SANT'ANGELO 58-61
TEL 083 533 3704
baccantiristorante.com
Located in the heart of the *sassi* district, with dining rooms partly excavated from the rock. Traditional dishes with a modern twist.
🍴 90/110 🕐 Closed D both Sun. & Mon. 🚭 🅰 All major cards

🍴 LE BOTTEGHE
$$$
PIAZZETTA SAN PIETRO BARISANO 22
TEL 083 534 4072 OR
338 303 8421
lebotteghematera.it
The four striking dining rooms here were used for centuries as workshops (*botteghe*). The food served is honest regional fare—*fave* (broad beans), *tagliatelle e ceci* (noodles and chickpeas), *agnello alla brace* (grilled lamb).
🍴 60 🕐 Closed L Tues.-Fri. Oct.-March 🚭 🅰 DC, MC, V

■ VENICE & THE ADRIATIC

VENICE

🍴 ANTICO MARTINI
$$$$$
CAMPO SAN FANTIN, SAN MARCO 1983
TEL 041 522 4121
anticomartini.com
The refined Venetian cuisine is almost overshadowed by the decor, a grand ensemble of chandeliers,

paneled walls, and precious paintings. The restaurant, in the shadow of the Teatro La Fenice opera house, is almost three centuries old. Its 350-label wine list is outstanding.
🪑 50/40 🕐 Closed 3 weeks in Jan. 🅿 💳 All major cards

🍴 BANCOGIRO
$$$$
SOTOPORTEGO DEL BANCO GIRO/CAMPO SAN GIACOM-ETTO, SAN POLO 122
TEL 041 523 2061
osteriabancogiro.it
This refined, successful *osteria* near the waterfront close to the Rialto markets offers the option of a glass of wine in the bar downstairs, with a view of the Canal Grande, or a meal of creative Venetian dishes in the dining room upstairs. It stays open late.
🪑 35 🕐 Closed Mon. & 3 weeks in Jan. 💳 V

🍴 CORTE SCONTA
$$$$
CALLE DEL PRESTIN (ARSENALE), CASTELLO 3886
TEL 041 522 7024
It is increasingly difficult to secure a table in this simple, trattoria-style restaurant, a favorite of locals and foreigners in the know. The atmosphere is lively, at times almost chaotic, and there is no real menu: The waitstaff brings a selection of appetizers and a limited choice of main and pasta dishes. Quality is good, but perhaps not reflective of the price and reputation.
🪑 50/70 🕐 Closed Sun.-Mon., 3 weeks in Jan., & 3 weeks in late July-Aug.
🅿 💳 MC, V

🍴 AL COVO
$$$$
CAMPIELLO DE LA PESCARIA, CASTELLO 3968
TEL 041 522 3812
ristorantealcovo.com
A wonderful little two-room restaurant that produces exquisite and often innovative takes on Venetian classics such as *fritto misto* (mixed fish and seafood grill).
🪑 60/100 🕐 Closed Wed.-Thurs. & 2 weeks in both Jan. & Aug. 🅿 💳 DC, MC, V

🍴 FIASCHETTERIA TOSCANA
$$$$
SALIZADA SAN GIOVANNI CRISOSTOMO, CANNAREGIO 5719
TEL 041 528 5281
fiaschetteriatoscana.it
This stylish restaurant close to the Rialto Bridge has been a safe bet for good Venetian fish dishes—despite its Tuscan name—since 1956. Tables are close together, and the atmosphere can be busy. The wine list is intriguingly eclectic.
🪑 80/110 🕐 Closed Tues., L Wed., 2 weeks in Jan., & 2 weeks in both July & Aug. 🅿 💳 DC, MC, V

🍴 TRATTORIA ALLA MADONNA
$$$$
CALLE DELLA MADONNA, SAN POLO 594
TEL 041 522 3824
ristoranteallamadonna.com
A trattoria of the old school: The Trattoria alla Madonna is big, busy, and low on frills. The mainly fish-oriented cooking is unexceptional, but as a dining experience it is far more genuine and earthy than the tourist-filled

haunts on the nearby Rialto waterfront.
🪑 220 🕐 Closed Wed. & 3 weeks in Jan. 🅿 💳 All major cards

🍴 VINI DA GIGIO
$$$$
FONDAMENTA DELLA CHIESA DI SAN FELICE, CANNAREGIO 3628/A
TEL 041 528 5140
vinidagigio.com
A perfect little canalside restaurant for a quiet lunch or romantic dinner. Simple but elegantly cooked and presented Venetian cooking, friendly service, and two plain dining rooms with bar, beamed ceilings, and pretty wooden cabinets around the walls. Try the *carpaccio di spada* (thin slices of swordfish).
🪑 40 🕐 Closed Mon.-Tues., 2 weeks in Jan., & 3 weeks in Aug. 🅿 💳 MC, V

🍴 ANTICA LOCANDA MONTIN
$$$-$$$$
FONDAMENTA DI BORGO, DORSODURO 1147
TEL 041 522 7151
locandamontin.com
Artists, writers, and the rich and famous have patronized the Montin for decades. Food may not be exceptional, but the rear garden is one of the

loveliest places in Venice to eat alfresco, and the main dining rooms are equally cozy and appealing. They have an old-fashioned atmosphere and painting-covered walls.

🍴 125 🕐 Closed Tues. year-round & Wed. Nov –March 💳 MC, V

🍴 LA BITTA
$$$
CALLE LUNGA DE SAN BARNABA, DORSODURO 2753/A
TEL 041 523 0531

The tiny La Bitta *osteria* and bar is ideal for an *ombra* (aperitif), wine by the glass, or *cicheti* (snacks), as well as light meals of often creative, mostly meat-based regional dishes (with vegetarian options).

🍴 28/12 🕐 Closed L, Sun., & some of July 💳 No credit cards

🍴 DONA ONESTA
$$$
PONTE DE LA DONA ONESTA, DORSODURO 3922
TEL 041 710 586
donaonesta.com

The "Honest Woman" is true to her name: This simple trattoria charges fair prices for good, basic Venetian fish and meat dishes in a plain, one-room restaurant near San Rocco and the Frari.

🍴 45 🕐 💳 All major cards

🍴 NARANZARIA
$$$
SOTOPORTEGO DEL BANCO GIRO, SAN POLO 130
TEL 041 724 1035
naranzaria.it

One of the new breed of bars and restaurants near the Rialto markets (see also Bancogiro, p. 294), this small establishment on two levels (there is a bar on the lower level) offers an

unusual but popular hybrid of Venetian and Japanese food in an attractive brick-vaulted dining room, plus a few tables outside over-looking the Canal Grande.

🍴 30 🕐 Closed Mon. Nov – March & 4 weeks in Jan.-Feb. 💳 MC, V

🍴 ANTICO DOLO
$$
RUGA VECCHIA SAN GIOVANNI, SAN POLO 778
TEL 041 522 6546
anticodolo.it

A café not quite as old as nearby Do Mori (see below), but an almost equally authentic and atmospheric source of wines and snacks (*cicheti* in Venetian dialect). Limited seating.

💳 All major cards

🍴 ACIUGHETA
$-$$
CAMPO SS. FILIPPO E GIACOMO, CASTELLO 4357
TEL 041 522 4292

Revamped in a sleek contemporary style, this pizzeria-trattoria just west of the Basilica di San Marco is one of the more reasonably priced places in this busy quarter for a simple meal.

🍴 70/70 🕐 Closed some Wed. in Jan. 💳 MC, V

🍴 IL CAFFÈ ROSSO
$
CAMPO SANTA MARGHERITA, DORSODURO 2963
TEL 041 528 7998
cafferosso.it

A tiny red-fronted café with a spread of busy outdoor tables on a lovely and lively square a few minutes' walk from the Frari church.

🕐 Closed Sun., some holidays, & Dec. 25-26 💳 No credit cards

🍴 DO MORI
$
CALLE DO MORI (OFF RUGA VECCHIA SAN GIOVANNI), SAN POLO 429
TEL 041 522 5401

Venetians and market traders have been crowding this dark, cramped *bacaro*, or wine bar, since 1462. No chairs or tables, but tasty snacks and more than 350 different wines. An essential Venetian experience.

🕐 Closed Sun. & D Wed. Jan.-March & June-Aug.

CROATIA

Croatian restaurants come in several guises: *restoran* (restaurant), *konoba* (a slightly more homey place, though this is absolutely no indication of a drop in quality), and *gostionica* (a simpler version of a *konoba*). The larger hotels generally have their own restaurants (often more than one), and even many of the smaller *pansions* (pensions) have their own terrace restaurant or pizzeria. A handy resource for basic details on Croatian restaurants is *gastronaut.hr*.

Where prices are concerned, the cost of a main course in the same establishment often ranges dramatically from a cheap pasta dish to premium seafood charged per kilo, so these price categories should be taken only as a rule of thumb.

Tipping in restaurants and cafés (in the vast majority of which a service charge is not added to the bill) for good service is always appreciated, with 5 or 10 percent of the bill, or a few kuna, being sufficient.

🚭 Nonsmoking   ❄ Air-conditioning   💳 Credit Cards

SPLIT

🍴 NOŠTROMO
$$$
KRAJ SV. MARIJE 10
TEL 091 405 6666
restoran-nostromo.hr
Excellent seafood restaurant right next to the fish market, serving top-notch fresh, grilled fish as well as less common dishes such as fish kebabs and traditional pan-fried sea anemones. The interior is hung with paintings by various Croatian artists. Reservations advised.
🔳 40 🚫 🚫 No credit cards

🍴 KONOBA HVARANIN
$$
BAN MLADENOVA 9
TEL 091 767 5891
Small, busy family-run place that may not look smart but has good traditional homemade fare.
🔳 30 🚫 🚫 No credit cards

🍴 KONOBA KOD JOŽE
$$
SREDMANUŠKA 4
TEL 021 347 397
This establishment is a good-value konoba, located across the park behind the palace. It dishes up great food and has a nice terrace.
🔳 100 🚫 🚫 All major cards

🍴 MAKROVEGA
$$
LEŠTINA 2
TEL 021 394 440
makrovega.hr
Vegetarian, vegan, and macrobiotic restaurant off Ban Jelačićeva, with good-value daily combination menus but a stark, modern interior. If you're a vegetarian, this is the place for you.
🕐 Closed D Sat. & all Sun.
🚫 🚫 No credit cards

🍴 PIZZERIA PORTAS
$
KOD ZLATNIH VRATA 1
TEL 021 482 888
Hidden away down an alley near the Golden Gate, Portas has good, well-priced pizzas, pasta, and Dalmatian dishes, and a decent terrace. Also try **Pizzeria Galija** (Tončićeva 12, tel 021 347 932, $), popular with locals, and with a wood-fired oven and a central, busy, and informal setting.
🔳 32 🕐 Closed Nov.–March
🚫 🚫 AE, DC, V

HVAR

🍴 LUNA
$$$$
PETRA HEKTOROVIĆA
TEL 021 741 400
Good, if relatively expensive, seafood restaurant (with meat options) serving wonderful dishes, with a delightful open-roof terrace.
🔳 84 🕐 Closed Oct.–April
🚫 🚫 All major cards

🍴 ZLATNA ŠKOLJKA
$$$
PETRA HEKTOROVIĆA 8
TEL 098 168 8797
zlatna.skoljka.com
Set in a 13th-century house with a nice terrace, the excellent Zlatna Školjka ("golden shell") has typical seafood dishes alongside more inventive fare, some tasty gnocchi entrees, and opulent lamb and rabbit dishes, all prepared with an emphasis on "slow food." There are also four- and six-course "challenge" menus. Reservations recommended.
🔳 25 🕐 Closed L Sat., all Sun., Nov.–April, & holidays
🚫 🚫 All major cards

KORČULA

🍴 KONOBA GAJETA
$$
ŠETALIŠTE PETRA KANAVELIĆA,
TEL 020 716 359 OR 091 503 2829
Nice, unpretentious restaurant serving up a good range of reasonably priced dishes, with tables along both sides of the pleasant waterfront promenade on the east side of the old town. The tables overlooking the water tend to fill up fast.
🔳 100 🚫 🚫 No credit cards

🍴 PIZZERIA CAENAZZO
$
TRG SV. MARKA
TEL 098 244 012
Excellent, well-priced pizzeria in a wonderful setting, with tables spilling out across the square in front of the cathedral. Come in the evening when the light from the setting sun hits the cathedral facade and swallows swoop through the sky above.
🔳 60 🕐 Closed Oct.–April
🚫 No credit cards

DUBROVNIK

🍴 PROTO
$$$$
ŠIROKA 1
TEL 020 323 234
esculaprestaurants.com
One of Dubrovnik's most famous restaurants, just off Stradun. The upscale Proto has been serving up premium fare since 1886, its list of customers including such dignitaries as Edward VIII. Excellent seafood and other dishes, and a lovely terrace upstairs. Reservations recommended.
🔳 200 🚫 🚫 All major cards

🍴 KLARISA
$$$
PASKA MILEČEVIĆA 1
TEL 020 413 100

klarisa-dubrovnik.com
Worth going to for the
setting alone—located in
the 13th-century cloisters
of the former Convent of
St. Clare. Good food.
🔲 330/350 🚭 🗞 All major
cards

🍴 KAMENICE
$$
GUNDULIĆEVA POLJANA 8
TEL 020 323 685
Kamenice (which means
"oysters" in Croatian)
serves up excellent, good-
value shellfish, and other
seafood. Big and always
busy, it remains a favorite
with locals as well as
foreign visitors.
🔲 60 🕐 Closed D Nov.–
March 🚭 🗞 All major cards

🍴 LOKANDA PESKARIJA
$$
NA PONTI BB
TEL 020 324 750
mea-culpa.hr
Tiny local favorite right on
the old port, with tables
spread out across the
waterfront, serving well-
priced seafood and other
dishes from a succinct
menu. Extremely popular
and packed to overflowing
in the summer, and perhaps
at its best out of season.
🔲 60/100 🕐 Closed Jan.
🗞 All major cards

🍴 NISHTA
$$
PRIJEKO BB 30
TEL 020 322 088
nishtarestaurant.com
Nice, if boldly decorated
old-town vegetarian res-
taurant, with a variety of
soups, snacks, and main
dishes, and vegan as well
as gluten-free options in
colorful surroundings.
🔲 14/12 🕐 Closed Sun. &
Nov.–Feb. 🚭 🗞 DC, MC, V

🍴 TAJ MAHAL
$$
NIKOLE GUČETIĆA 2
TEL 020 323 221
Not, as you might expect
an Indian restaurant, but a
great place serving Bosnian
dishes. Just the place to
go for a plate of succulent
ćevapčići (minced meat
served on a flat bread)
and lashings of kajmak (a
creamy dairy product), with
several vegetarian options.
🔲 50/20 🚭 🗞 No credit
cards

⬛ ATHENS & THE ISLANDS
Greece has several types of
eating establishments. An
estiatorio (restaurant) is classier
and a taverna more casual. In a
taverna you may well have a
paper tablecloth, and in more
out-of-the-way places the waiter might even use it to write the
bill on at the end of the meal.
An ouzerie is an old-fashioned
bar serving ouzo as well as
other drinks and snacks. There
are also psarotavernes, which
specialize in fish, and psistaries,
which specialize in food cooked
on a grill or spit roasted.
There is no rating system
for restaurants, and ordinary-
looking places can be wonderful, while classy-looking ones
can be dreadful. It is best to
avoid anywhere that employs
someone to stand outside and
tempt you in, a ploy used only
to inveigle overseas visitors
who will probably never return,
not Greek customers. Be
cautious, although the rule is
not infallible.
Many restaurants in tourist
areas do not take reservations,
so in some cases you will find
no telephone number in the
listings below. Most places are

expandable; another table will
be brought out unless they are
absolutely at their maximum
capacity, in which case you will
be told how long you have to
wait for a table. For this reason,
the number of restaurant seats
is not listed as, for the vast
majority of establishments, it
simply does not apply.
Greeks tend to eat late, like
other Mediterranean people.
Lunch is not normally served
before about 2 p.m., and dinner
may begin as late as 9 p.m.
or 10 p.m. Most restaurants
catering to overseas customers
open much earlier to suit their
different dining habits.
Many restaurants, especially
in Athens, close for August
and sometimes longer in the
summer. This is often to escape
the summer heat, at a time
when many of their Athenian
customers leave the city for a
break on the islands. Set dates
cannot be given here, as they
vary year by year according
to the whim of the owner, but
where possible a rough indication of major closings is given in
the listings.
In Old Athens, the Plaka
is a popular eating area. It
has a number of poor places
aimed purely at the passing
tourist trade as well as some
excellent and authentic Greek
establishments. Nearby, the
Psirri district has a wide choice
of truly Greek dining places,
although you will almost certainly need your phrase book
and menu reader.

ATHENS

🍴 BYZANTINO
$$$$$
HILTON HOTEL,
VASILISSIS SOFIAS 46
TEL 210 728 1000 OR
210 333 0265

🚭 Nonsmoking　🅰 Air-conditioning　🗞 Credit Cards

hilton.com
Byzantino is a fine upscale restaurant in the landmark Hilton Hotel. Convenient for Syntagma, Benaki Museum, and National Gallery, but not the Plaka.
⊟ 🅢 🅐 All major cards

🍴 TOP FLOOR
$$$$$
ST. GEORGE LYCABETTUS LYKAVITTOS HOTEL, KLEOMENOUS 2
TEL 210 729 0711
sglycabettus.gr
Living up to its name, the Top Floor restaurant is located on the roof of a very convenient and comfortable luxury hotel. The restaurant is highly recommended for both its great views of the city, especially at night, and its menu.
⊟ 🅢 🅐 All major cards

🍴 TUDOR HALL
$$$$$
KING GEORGE PALACE HOTEL, VAS. GEORGIOU A' 3, SYNTAGMA SQUARE
TEL 210 322 2210
tudorhall.gr
Come to the sumptuous King George Palace Hotel for the elegant Tudor Hall restaurant, whose seventh-floor Acropolis view is matched only by its superb food.
⊟ 🅢 🅐 All major cards

🍴 PIL POUL
$$$$
APOSTOLOU PAVLOU 51/ POULOPOULOU
TEL 210 342 3665
The Thissio and Psirri districts are the places to head for good modern Greek cooking, and this fashionable place also offers views of the Acropolis.
🕐 Closed L & Sun. 🅢 🅐 All major cards

🍴 L'ABREUVOIR
$$$-$$$$
XENOKRATOUS 51
TEL 210 722 9106 OR
210 722 9061
abreuvoir.gr
The Abreuvois is an upscale French restaurant in Kolonaki, where Pavarotti and other celebrities have dined. Elegant decor and equally elegant food: steaks a specialty. Extensive and expensive wine list.
🅢 🅐 All major cards

🍴 BABY GRAND RESTAURANT
$$$
CLASSICAL BABY GRAND HOTEL, ATHINAS 65
TEL 281 030 0330 OR
281 022 0088
lux-hotels.com/Baby_Grand_Hotel
Traditional taverna food but with a 21st-century atmosphere and style is served at this contemporary, fun, and inexpensive restaurant at the boutique Classical Baby Grand Hotel.
🅢 🅐 All major cards

🍴 GB CORNER
$$$
GRANDE BRETAGNE HOTEL, SYNTAGMA SQUARE
TEL 210 333 0750
gbcorner.gr
Part of the Grande Bretagne Hotel, the GB Corner restaurant serves a variety of good Mediterranean cuisine and has a mouth-watering grill section.
🅢 🅐 All major cards

🍴 HERMION
$$$
PANDROSOU 7-15
TEL 210 324 6725 OR
210 324 7148
hermion.gr
The Hermion is a long-established restaurant

PRICES

RESTAURANTS

For a three-course meal without drinks:

$$$$$	Over $80
$$$$	$50-$80
$$$	$35-$50
$$	$20-$35
$	Under $20

---

just off the flea market, with both indoor seating and an attractive courtyard dining area. It features excellent service and good-quality, moderately priced Greek favorites.
🅢 🅐 All major cards

🍴 KONA KAI
$$$
LEDRA MARRIOTT HOTEL, SYNGROU 115
TEL 210 930 0000 OR
210 930 0074
marriott.com
This restaurant in the Ledra Marriott Hotel specializes in Polynesian food (with decor as exotic as the dishes) but also has a Japanese menu. It is very popular, so reservations are advised.
🕐 Closed L Sun. & period of time mid-Aug. 🅢 🅐 All major cards

🍴 TO KAFENEIO
$$-$$$
LOUKIANOU 26
TEL 210 722 9056 OR
210 723 7757
tokafeneio.gr
To Kafeneio is a chic but relaxed restaurant in Kolonaki that serves excellent Greek specialties such as spinach pie, baked eggplant with cheese, chicken in lemon sauce, and other dishes to an international clientele.
🅢 🅐 All major cards

🍴 Restaurant 🪑 No. of Seats 🅿 Parking 🕐 Closed ⊟ Elevator

🍴 PRUNIER
$$-$$$

IPSILANTOU 63
TEL 210 722 7379

This French bistro near the Hilton Hotel offers a romantic setting with typical bistro dishes, such as coq au vin and escargots. Some more exotic choices, too, like quail in oregano and lemon sauce.

🕐 Closed L & Sun. 🚭 🆂 All major cards

🍴 XINOS
$$-$$$

ANGELOU GERONTA 4
TEL 210 322 1065

On a Plaka backstreet that few tourists find, this place is very popular with Athenians. Superior food, music late in the evening, and charming outdoor garden seating.

🕐 Closed L, Sat.-Sun., & winter 🚭 🆂 All major cards

🍴 IDEAL
$$

PANEPISTIMIOU 46
TEL 210 330 3000

This 90-plus-year-old restaurant has attentive service and an extensive menu, along with an historic art nouveau interior.

🕐 Closed Sun. 🚭 🆂 All major cards

🍴 BAKALIARAKIA TOU DAMIGOU
$

KYDATHINEON 41
TEL 210 322 5084
mpakaliarakia.gr

Simple Greek food in what claims to be the oldest taverna in Athens, established in 1865. Salt cod in garlic is the specialty that gives this basement place its name.

🕐 Closed L midsummer
🚭 🆂 No credit cards

🍴 BARBA YANNIS
$

EMMANUEL BENAKI 94
TEL 210 330 0185

This great favorite frequently has lines outside the door. Brisk service and a limited menu of good hearty Greek dishes There is often impromptu music.

🕐 Closed D Sun. & Aug.
🚭 🆂 No credit cards

🍴 O PLATANOS
$

DIOGENOUS 4
TEL 210 322 0666

An Athenian favorite, with few concessions to tourism, that offers reliable, inexpensive, and standard Greek dishes. It has one of the best locations in the Plaka, with tables outside in the summer under the plane tree that gives it its name.

🕐 Closed Sun. June–Aug. & D Sun. March–May & Sept.–Oct. 🚭 🆂 No credit cards

SOMETHING SPECIAL

🍴 SHOLARHIO TO GERANI (OUZERI KOUKLIS)
$

TRIPODON 14
TEL 210 324 7605
sholarhio.gr

This *ouzerie* is a well-established popular watering hole, concentrating on hearty mezes such as *saganaki* (deep-fried cheese), *taramosalata*, fried fish, and sausages cooked in ouzo. Pleasant dining terrace, too.

🚭 🆂 MC, V

🍴 SIGALAS
$

PLATEIA MONASTIRAKI 2
TEL 210 321 3036

For an authentic Athenian dining experience, Sigalas cannot be beaten. It is right on busy Monastiraki Square, with the bustle extending into the warren of the restaurant itself. Waiters in red sweaters rush about, some looking as if they have been there since the restaurant opened at the end of the 19th century. It is a casual place where arguments and laughter rage, old photos plaster every wall, and the food comprises good, inexpensive examples of standard Greek taverna fare. On weekends, arrive early.

🚭 🆂 No credit cards

THE PELOPONNESUS

NAFPLIO

🍴 MEZEDOPOLEIO O NOULIS
$

MOUTZOURIDOU 22
TEL 275 202 5541

Most Greek eating places serve meze, but places like family-run Noulis that specialize in them are surprisingly rare. Order small dishes until you are full, or leave the decisions to others and go for the house's ten-dish special.

🕐 Closed D Oct.–Apr. & Sun.
🆂 No credit cards

MYCENAE

🍴 OREA ELENI-TOU MENELAOU (LA BELLE HELENE)
$$

HR. TSOUNTA 15
TEL 275 107 6225 or
275 107 6434

Visit this old hotel and eat in the dining room for the history and character as much as the food, which is better than most of the tourist-trap places locally: It was here that archaeologist Heinrich Schliemann stayed while excavating Mycenae nearby.

🖪 All major cards

THE ISLANDS

CORFU
🍽 LA CUCINA
$$$
GUILDFORD 15, CORFU TOWN
TEL 266 104 5029
An elegant restaurant offering Greek, Italian, and international cuisine and a large wine list. Expect to pay more than in most other places in Corfu town, but the options are worth it. If it is available, try the Exotica salad—a mix of avocado, mango, and shrimp—or the pizzas, king crab legs, or juicy steaks.

🕐 Closed midwinter
🖪 All major cards

🍽 REX
$$
KAPODISTRIOU 66, CORFU TOWN
TEL 266 103 9649
rexrestaurant.gr
For real Greek food try Rex, which has been in business since 1932. The restaurant is decorated with local paintings, and the service is friendly. Choose from a wide variety of tasty dishes.
🖪 All major cards

SANTORINI
🍽 KATINA
$
AMMOUDI PORT, OIA
TEL 228 607 1280
If you can face the trek down to the harbor at Oia—or rather face the climb back up again (though you can always phone for a taxi)—then Katina's is a great place for seafood, right by the sea. Or up in town, with views, try **Floga** (tel 22860 71152) right on the main street for Greek food with a twist; or the nearby inexpensive **Flora Café** for snacks and light meals.
🖪 No credit cards

RHODES
🍽 ALEXIS 4 SEASONS
$$$
ARISTOTELOUS 33, RHODES OLD TOWN
TEL 224 107 0522
alexis4seasons.com
One of the best fish restaurants in the Dodecanese. You will encounter seafood here not commonly seen on other menus (sea urchins, for example) and the best of the catch from the harbor. All vegetables are also organically grown by the owners.
🖪 All major cards

🍽 TA KIOUPIA
$$
MENEKLEOUS 22, TRIS VILLAGE
TEL 224 109 1824
Make sure you come here with an appetite. After a choice of soups you will be faced with a table full of tempting meze dishes and hearty main courses. Remember, too, that there is a big and mouthwatering dessert menu.
🕐 Closed L Mon.-Sat. & D Sun. 🖪 All major cards

CRETE
🍽 KYRIAKOS
$$-$$$
DIMOKRATIAS 53, IRAKLIO
TEL 281 022 2464
kiriakos-restaurant.com
Some of the best food in Iraklio, with traditional Cretan dishes served with great style and attention to detail. Formal dress preferred, although it's a remarkably friendly place. Try the octopus with onions or the house specialty: snails.
🕐 Closed Sun. sometimes in summer 🖪 All major cards

◼ TURKEY
Although Turks generally lunch at set hours and dine late, most restaurants serve from around midday to 4 p.m., and from 7 p.m. until midnight, with a good percentage also offering nonstop service. Almost all the establishments listed open daily, barring religious holidays.

Menus in most restaurants are in English as well as Turkish, and restaurant staff can usually shed light on any hard-to-translate dishes. Many locals, however, forgo the official menu and banter with the waiter about what fish, meat, or vegetable has just been landed, picked, and purchased—although a menu will almost always exist if you require one. Only the smartest restaurants in European Istanbul require a reservation.

Locals start their meal with a selection of cold meze, such as stuffed vine leaves or eggplant salad, selected from a waiter's trolley. These tasty appetizers are never more than a few dollars each. Next come any hot appetizers (grilled squid and stuffed peppers among them), followed by the main course. Most meals are washed down with beer, local wine, or *rakı*, Turkey's aniseed-flavored spirit, although a few restaurants recommended in this guide are alcohol free. Credit cards are universally accepted in medium to large restaurants, although cash is still very useful for tips and the occasional network problem.

Most restaurants have serviceable restrooms. Tiny cafés will point you to the nearest public toilets if they lack facilities themselves. Finally, some restaurants in this book may be tricky to find. If in doubt, point out the place you'd like to go to a local shopkeeper or businessperson, and you'll be swiftly guided in the right direction.

Istanbul restaurants below are in the Old City (Sultanahmet), unless stated.

ISTANBUL

🍴 SEASONS RESTAURANT
$$$$$

FOUR SEASONS HOTEL ISTANBUL AT SULTANAHMET, TEVKIFHANE SOKAK 1
TEL 0212 402 3000 OR 0212 402 3150
fourseasons.com/istanbul
The refined Seasons at this luxury hotel boasts modern world cuisine such as tiger-prawn-and-pineapple terrine and almond-crusted lamb with sweet shallots, and is home to a famed Sunday brunch.
🔲 115 🅿 🔃 🔳 🔳 🔳 All major cards

🍴 KONYALI
$$$$

TOPKAPI PALACE
TEL 0212 513 9696
konyalilokantasi.com
Patrons pay a premium to dine in these regal surroundings with Bosporus views. Foreign and domestic tourists alike lap up the traditional Ottoman

cuisine, much of it slow-cooked in a *tandır* oven. Dishes include baked baby lamb and eggplant caviar. Former patrons include Britain's Queen Elizabeth I and American boxer Muhammad Ali.
🔲 110 🔳 🔳 🔳 Closed Tues. 🔳 AE, MC, V

🍴 PANDELI
$$$$

MISIR ÇARŞISI 1
TEL 0212 527 3909
pandeli.com
Pandeli has been rated one of the best restaurants in Istanbul for more than a century. Little of Pandeli's decor (marble counters, turquoise Ottoman tiles) has changed since the turn of the 20th century, but its traditional menu is positively 1950s. There are no help-yourself shared platters here, only classic plates of eggplant kebab and thyme-roasted lamb shank, served by deferential waiters in white jackets.
🔲 70 🔳 🔳 🔳 MC, √

🍴 ALBURA KATHISMA
$$$

CANKURTARAN MAHALLESI, AKBIYIK CADDESI 36-38
TEL 0212 517 9031
alburakathisma.com
This utterly congenial restaurant and café is located in the string of tourist-friendly places to eat just south of the Blue Mosque. Sample Turkish cuisine, from yogurt-laden *İskender kebab* to earthenware-baked *testi kebab*, or opt for international favorites, such as saffron chicken and Gorgonzola steak.
🔲 100 🔳 🔳 🔳 All major cards

🍴 ASITANE
$$$

KARIYE CAMII SOKAK 6
TEL 0212 635 7997
asitanerestaurant.com
Asitane boasts over 200 authentic Ottoman recipes discovered in the Dolmabahçe and Topkapı Palace kitchen libraries. Uniquely, its menu often cites the recipe's archived date, such as almond soup (1539), or vine leaves stuffed with sour cherries (1844). Pair your meal with a visit to the nearby Chora Museum (formerly both a church and a mosque), famed for its stunning mosaics.
🔲 70 🔳 🔳 All major cards

🍴 BALIKÇI SABAHATTIN
$$$

SEYIT HASAN KUYU SOKAK 1
TEL 0212 458 18 24
balikcisabahattin.com
Long an insider secret, word's now out on this rustic, atmospheric seafood restaurant located half inside a crumbling 1920s villa, half on a vine-covered outdoor terrace. Authentic home-cooked cuisine—try anchovy kebabs, local turbot, or octopus salad. Early booking is essential.
🔲 120 🔳 🔳 🔳 All major cards

🍴 CAFÉ TURING
$$$

SOĞUKÇEŞME SOKAK 38
TEL 0212 513 3660
ayasofyakonaklari.com
The prices for drinks, salads, and light snacks at this bourgeois wooden mansion may be expensive, but what a location. Seconds from the Hagia Sophia, it also possesses an opulent outdoor terrace.
🔲 110 🔳 🔳 🔳 All major cards

🔳 Nonsmoking   🔳 Air-conditioning   🔳 Credit Cards

🍴 DÂRÜZZIYAFE
$$$
ŞIFAHANE SOKAK 6
TEL 0212 511 8414 OR
0212 511 8415
daruzziyafe.com.tr
A tranquil-by-day, often raucous-by-night, classic Ottoman restaurant, set in the expansive former kitchens of the Süleymaniye Mosque. More than 50 traditional Turkish dishes are served daily, from chicken and walnut stew to pistachio-stuffed lamb and Noah's pudding. The drink menu includes sherbet, rose hip juice, and grenadine *pressé* (no alcohol).
🪑 720 🚇 🌐 All major cards

🍴 DUBB INDIAN RESTAURANT
$$$
ALEMDAR MAHALLESI,
INCILI ÇAVUŞ SOKAK 10
TEL 0212 513 7308
dubbindian.com
Widely regarded as the best Indian restaurant in town, Dubb serves world-beating Asian cuisine on its Parisian-style outdoor terrace and in its subtle southeast Asian interior. Try *raita* (cool cucumber yoghurt), *chana chat* (chickpea curry), or tandoori-oven baked Peshwari kebabs. The Indian desserts are a dream.
🪑 80 🌐 🚇 All major cards

🍴 HAMDI
$$$
TAHMIS CADDESI,
KALÇIN SOKAK 17
TEL 0212 528 0390 OR
0533 658 8011
hamdi.com.tr
Decades-old kebab specialist Hamdi is set over various intimate dining rooms on three vast floors, one of which is open to the stars. Well-presented classics include *testi kebabı* (a ceramic-baked meaty meal from Cappadocia), *İskender kebab* (a heart-stoppingly heavy dish from Bursa), and *fıstıklı kebab* (with chewy pistachios).
🪑 320 🚇 🌐 All major cards

🍴 NEYZADE
$$$
SIRKECI MANSION,
TAYA HATUN SOKAK 5
TEL 0212 528 4344
sirkecimansion.com
The rooftop Neyzade at the Sirkeci Mansion hotel is the place to go for classic Anatolian cuisine.
🪑 120 🚇 🌐 All major cards

🍴 AKDENIZ HATAY SOFRASI
$$
ISKENDERPASA MAHALLESI,
AHMEDIYE CADDESI 44/A
TEL 0212 444 7247 OR
0533 777 9300
akdenizhataysofrasi.com.tr
By day, the manifold dishes at Akdeniz Hatay Sofrasi, such as hummus, *mumbar dolması* (intestine and rice rolls), *muamara* (walnut and garlic dip)—almost all hailing from Turkey's Hatay region near Syria—are worth the tram ride to the Aksaray neighborhood. On Sunday mornings a gastronomically intense 100-plus dishes are laid out for brunch, a meal that qualifies as perhaps the best value in Istanbul.
🪑 120 🌐 🚇 All major cards

🍴 CAFERAĞA MEDRESESI
$$
CAFERIYE SOKAK,
SOĞUKKUYU ÇIKMAZI 1
TEL 0212 259 3101

PRICES

RESTAURANTS
For a three-course meal without drinks:

$$$$$	Over $80
$$$$	$50–$80
$$$	$35–$50
$$	$20–$35
$	Under $20

A hidden gem surrounded by the porticoes of an old religious school, just steps from the Hagia Sophia. Simple dishes such as stuffed *mantı* pasta and *köfte* meatball sandwiches are served on wooden stools in the courtyard.
🪑 20 🌐 🚇 All major cards

🍴 HAVUZLU
$$
GANI ÇELEBI SOKAK,
KAPALIÇARSI CADDEŞI 3,
GRAND BAZAAR
TEL 0212 527 3346
havuzlurestaurant.com
A fabulously atmospheric Grand Bazaar favorite. Fading wallpaper is dotted with yellowing newspaper clippings; the dining room is covered with ceiling fans and twinkling chandeliers. The menu is of the look-and-point variety. Steaming platters include *köfte* meatballs, lamb chops, and artichokes under oil, plus a solid range of syrupy Turkish desserts.
🪑 60 🌐 🕐 Closed Sun. 🚇 All major cards

🍴 SULTANAHMET FISH HOUSE
$$
ALEMDAR MAHALLESI,
PROFESSOR KAZIM ISMAIL
GÜRKAN CADDESI 14
TEL 0212 527 4441 OR
0212 527 4445

---

sultanahmetfishhouse.com
Istanbul's European shores
may be famed for their
raucous seafood restaurants, but this simple Old
City fish house offers fried
squid, fish soup, and grilled
sea bass in slightly more
sanitized conditions. The
handmade lamps that light
up the dining room are all
for sale.
🔲 70 ⬛ ⬛ ⬛ A l major
cards

EUROPEAN ISTANBUL

SOMETHING SPECIAL

🍴 BEBEK BALIKÇI
$$$$
CEVDET PAŞA CADDESI 26,
BEBEK
TEL 0212 263 3447 OR
0212 263 3669
bebekbalikci.net
Bebek Balıkçı's seafood is
served with aplomb either
in its maritime-themed
dining room or on a terrace
built on stilts over the Bosporus. It's a classic feast of
cold meze (fish dumplings,
shrimp, seaweed) followed
by larger hors d'oeuvres
(salted tuna, marinated
sea bass, and tarama like
you've never tasted), then
harbor-fresh fish by the
kilo. Excellent.
🔲 80 ⬛ ⬛ ⬛ All major
cards

🍴 THE GALATA HOUSE
$$$
GALATA KULESI SOKAK 15,
BEYOĞLU, GALATA
TEL 0212 245 1861
thegalatahouse.com
Experimental diners and
lovers of Eastern European cuisine might try this
Russo-Georgian restaurant,
housed in Galata's old
British prison. Sweet
Georgian wine accompanies courses of spicy warm

cheeses, borscht, and other
beetroot-heavy appetizers
or stewed plums with lamb.
🔲 40 ⬛ 🕐 Closed Mon.
⬛ All major cards

🍴 KIVA HAN
$$$
GALATA KULESI MEYDANI 4,
BEYOĞLU, GALATA
TEL 0212 292 9898
galatakivahan.com
A light, refreshingly modern
restaurant in the shadow
of Galata Tower. Provides
lip-smackingly good
breakfasts and specialist
dishes from eastern Turkey.
Smartly presented bites
include imambayıd (stuffed
eggplant) and corn soup
with yogurt from the Black
Sea region.
🔲 110 ⬛ ⬛ ⬛ All major
cards

🍴 FÜRREYYA GALATA BALIKÇISI
$$
SERDARI EKREM SOKAK 2,
BEYOĞLU
TEL 0212 252 48 53
Of the ring of restaurants
around Galata Tower, this
low-key fish house is an
eminently affordable treat.
Seafood snacks include
balık durum (a sea bass and
salad wrap) and fish cakes
with tangy garlic sauce. No
alcohol.
🔲 10 ⬛ All major cards

SOMETHING SPECIAL

🍴 VAN KAHVALTI EVI
$$
KILIÇ ALI PAŞA MAHALLESI,
DEFTERDAR YOKUŞU 52,
CIHANGIR
TEL 0212 293 6437
The Van Breakfast Club
brings together wholesome dishes from Turkey's
breakfast capital: Lake
Van in the country's

distant east. Bites include
village cheese with herbs,
menemen scrambled eggs,
grape molasses, tahini, and
kaymak clotted cream with
honey. Stupendous.
🔲 60 ⬛ ⬛ ⬛ All major
cards

EPHESUS

SELÇUK

🍴 ARTEMIS RESTAURANT & ŞARAPEVI
$$–$$$
ŞIRINCE KÖYÜ, ESKI OKUL
BINASI, SELÇUK
TEL 0232 898 3240 OR
0232 898 3241
artemisrestaurant.com
Built 150 years ago to
house the village primary
school, today Artemis is
the village of Şirince's best
restaurant and wine bar.
Stop to sip local fruit wines
in their manicured gardens,
or during winter, sample
heartier fare alongside the
roaring fire.
🔲 70 ⬛ ⬛ All major cards

SOMETHING SPECIAL

🍴 HOTEL BELLA
$$
ATATURK MAHALLESI,
ST. JOHN ST. 7, SELÇUK
TEL 0232 892 3944
hotelbella.com
Gregarious childhood pals
Erdal and Nazmi own and
operate this charming
hotel, but for nonresidents
the draw is the congenial
rooftop restaurant.
🔲 50 🅿 ⬛ ⬛ ⬛ All major
cards

Shopping

Opportunities, hours, and prices vary as much as the locations themselves. If you're fortunate enough to be in port on market day, by all means take advantage of it. Markets usually start early in the morning and last until around 2 p.m. For the pick of the produce go early. Other places to get high-quality and original souvenirs are the sales shops at local museums.

Here are a few suggestions for items and locales throughout the Mediterranean.

■ COASTAL SPAIN

A number of goods are particularly associated with Spain, such as leather, ceramics, embroidery, fans, and foods like olives, almonds, hams, honey, marzipan, chocolates wines, and sherry. Try to shop for these items in their place of origin, where often prices are lower and the quality is higher. Spain is still full of fantastic old-fashioned shops, with service to match, where everything from cheese to apple liquor to dish detergent is beautifully laid out.

BARCELONA

Barcelona thinks of itself as the style capital of Spain, much in the way Milan is the fashion capital of Italy. You'll find just about every conceivable kind of store, ranging from local junk markets to cutting-edge design, from traditional foods to African crafts, from local lace to candles made by traditions left over from the 18th century.

Apart from the bakeries (panaderías) that open at 8 a.m., shops here tend to open later, and many places take a two- or three-hour break beginning at 1:30 p.m. or 2 p.m. Some shops close on Mondays, and bakers are open on Sunday mornings.

Markets
Often there will be a stand where you can buy freshly made churros (fritters) accompanied by coffee for breakfast. Buy things such as almonds, straw-berries, avocados, and wonder-ful red and green tomatoes. Look also for local delicacies like cheeses, honey, olives, dried peppers and tomatoes, hams, and herbs.

Feria Nova Artesanía, Rambla Santa Mónica; Metro Drassanes; Sat. p.m. & all day Sun. (arts & crafts)
Mercat dels Encants, Plaça de les Glories Catalanes; Metro Glories; Mon., Wed., Fri., & Sat. (miscellaneous items—furniture to fabrics)
Mercat Gòtic, Plaça de la Sèu; Metro Jaume I; Thurs., closed Aug. (antiques)
Mercat de Sant Antoni, Comte d´Urgell; Metro Sant Antoni; Mon.-Sat., & Sun. a.m. (old-style market)
Mercat de Sant Josep (de la Boqueria), Rambla de Sant Josep; Metro Liceu; Mon.-Sat. all day (food market)

MÁLAGA & GRANADA

Markets & Specialty Stores
Alcaicería, Plaza Alonso Cano, Granada; daily (Old Arab Market)
Atarazanas, Málaga; Sat.-Sun. (flea market)
Cerámica Fajalauza, Carretera de Murcia 15, Granada; closed Sun. (Granada pottery factory)
Mercado San Augustín, Plaza de San Augustín, Granada; Mon.-Sat. (general market)

BALEARIC ISLANDS

S'Alambic, Andén de Poniente 33–36, Maó (local pottery & clothes)
Colmado la Montaña, Jaime II 27, Palma de Mallorca (local food products)

■ FRENCH RIVIERA & PROVENCE

Among the items to shop for along the French Riviera are brightly printed indiennes fabrics; terra-cotta Provençal figurines known as santons, soaps, creams, chocolates, herbs, olive oils, and lavender-related products such as honey.

Flea Markets
Aix-en-Provence: Place du Verdun; Tues., Thurs., & Sat.
Cannes: Rue Forville; Mon.
Marseille: Ave. du Cap Pinède; Sun.
Nice: Cours Saleya; Mon.

■ ITALIAN RIVIERA & TUSCANY

Italy has a cornucopia of exquisite gifts and treats. Food delicacies are obvious purchases, but check import restrictions on meat and produce into North America. Lingerie, silks, lace, linens, soaps, shoes, bags, wallets, marbled paper products, and jewelry are all easily transportable items, as well as wine, clothes, and design objects.

Most neighborhoods have their own baker (panificio), fruit

seller (fruttivendolo), butcher (macellaio), and food shop (alimentari). Pastry and home-made candy stores (pasticceria) are particular features of southern towns.

All towns and cities have at least one street market (mercato). In cities, these usually run daily except Sunday, starting at dawn and closing early afternoon; in smaller towns, such provincial markets are generally held just once a week.

Many southern Italian stores are small, family-run affairs.

GENOA

Genoa's Via Soziglia is a good place to pick up Ligurian handicrafts such as lace, ceramics, marble, gold, and silverware. Jewelers line Via dei Orefici, and luxury shops cluster on Via XX Settembre and Via Luccoli.

FLORENCE

Florence is a great shopping city for luxury goods. Leather, clothes, jewelry, and antiques are top buys, thanks to a long tradition of outstanding artisanal work. Less expensive gift possibilities include marbled paper and goods from the city's thriving markets. Most clothes and other luxury goods stores are found on and around Via de' Tornabuoni. Antiques stores group together south of the Arno River on and around Via Maggio. Jewelers congregate on the Ponte Vecchio.

Markets
Mercato Centrale, Piazza del Mercato Centrale; Mon.-Sat. (Europe's largest indoor food market)
San Lorenzo, Piazza San Lorenzo; daily (clothes & other goods)

■ ROME & NAPLES

ROME

The key shopping streets cluster around **Via dei Condotti,** home to most of the big names in designer clothes and shoes. Less expensive stores line **Via del Corso, Via Nazionale,** and **Via del Tritone.** Antiques and art stores are found on **Via del Babuino, Via Margutta, Via Giulia, Via Monserrato,** and **Via dei Coronari.** The best food stores are on **Via Santa Croce** and **Via Cola di Rienzo.**

NAPLES

Even if you aren't buying anything, it is still great fun to wander the many markets, window-shop along **Via Toledo,** or marvel at the bald-faced cheek of the many street vendors selling counterfeit goods.

There are some good buys to be found, however. Naples is filled with antiques and jewelry shops; its food is tremendous; shoes and leather goods are inexpensive; and there are items here—such as the city's famous Christmas crèche (presepio) figures—that you won't find anywhere else.

As a rough guide, the most upscale shopping area is on and around **Via Chiaia,** plus **Piazza Vanvitelli** and **Via Scarlatti,** while for shopping on a budget, head to **Via Toledo, Corso Umberto I,** or the streets in the centro storico (historic center).

CAPRI & THE AMALFI COAST

Capri is famous for its chic sandals and for the much sought-after perfumes of Carthusia. **Positano,** while famous for its indigenous fashions in

the 1960s, today mostly sells mass-produced items. Ceramics, though, are good buys up and down the coast. So, too, are food and drink, whether the fine local cheeses of Agerola and other mountain villages or the ubiquitous limoncello (a lemon-based liqueur).

Traditional paper can be found in **Amalfi,** and the olive oil from around Sorrento is prized. Sorrento also offers lace, wood, and embroidery handicrafts, but sadly all three traditions are dying out.

■ SICILY, MALTA, & PUGLIA

SICILY

Sicily has some of the best new wines in Italy, with Planeta one of the outstanding producers. Food, again, is another good buy, especially cheeses, oils, capers, candied fruits, and the almond-paste "fruit" (frutta alla Martorana) of Palermo. Coral jewelry is common, but of widely varying quality, and traditional lace and embroidery can still be found in some rural centers.

In Palermo itself, **Via Bara all'Olivella** is the street for arts and crafts, along with **Via Calderai.** Designer and other fashionable names line **Via della Libertà** and nearby streets such as **Via Enrico Parisi. Via Roma, Via Maqueda, Via Ruggero Settimo,** and the pedestrian-only **Via Principe di Belmonte** are also major shopping streets.

MALTA

Malta is a haven for hand embroidery and lace, as well as wrought iron and brass pieces.

Markets
Valleta Sunday Market, Floriana; Sun. a.m.
Merchant Street Market, Valleta; daily a.m.

■ VENICE & THE ADRIATIC

VENICE

Venice's most famous products are glass, lace, fabrics, and marbled paper. Many glass shops are on the **Fondamenta dei Vetrai** on the island of Murano, but there are also numerous stores around **San Marco.** Lace can be found on the island of **Burano,** and paper and fabric stores are dotted across the city.

The key shopping streets are around **Calle dei Fabbri,** the **Frezzeria,** and **Le Mercerie—** between San Marco and the Rialto Bridge—and on and around **Calle Largo XXII Marzo** west of Piazza San Marco.

Market
Rialto, north of the Rialto Bridge; Mon.-Sat. a.m. (general goods & food markets, the Erberia, or the fish market, the Pescheria)

CROATIA

There is a huge range of attractive souvenirs available in Croatia, including foodstuffs such as local olive oil, wine, *rakija* (a distilled spirit), truffles, cheeses, *pršut* (home-cured ham), olives, and anchovies, as well as handmade soaps and natural cosmetics. Textiles include the exquisite lace (*čipka*) from Pag and the beautiful Konavle embroidery from the region south of Dubrovnik. Artwork by local Croatian

artists can be found in street stalls and galleries.

Market
Gunduliieva Poljana Market, Gunduliieva Poljana, Dubrovnik (local foods & crafts)

■ ATHENS & THE ISLANDS

Many shops sell ceramics (especially on Rhodes), a range of knickknacks such as handmade puppets, leather (on Crete), and gold and silver jewelry. Generally Greek food and wine do not travel well, although some brand-name spirits are good bargains and so is the virgin olive oil. Also look for delicate embroidery and handwoven items, such as lace, cotton skirts, and blouses.

ATHENS

Central Market, south of Omonia Square on Athinas; weekdays & Sat. a.m. (herbs, spices, nuts, olives, & cheeses)
Monastiraki Flea Market, Avissynias Square; Sun. a.m.
Greek Women's Institution, Ypatias 6 (embroidery)

RHODES

Ministry of Culture Museum Reproduction Shop, Ippitou, Rhodes Old Town (reproductions of statuary)

■ TURKEY

Leave plenty of space in your suitcase: Istanbul is nothing short of a shopper's paradise. It is home to what is arguably the world's first shopping mall—the **Grand Bazaar.** The covered market is a cornucopia of delights, from hammam towels to pashmina scarves, from glass

items to ceramics.

Fanning out from the Grand Bazaar, **Sultanahmet**'s streets are similarly littered with hand-knotted carpets and kilims. European Istanbul is the city's best spot for one-off boutiques. The nearby neighborhood of **Nişantaşı** houses unique Turkish designers and their high-end ateliers. And of course, **Beyoğlu**'s main pedestrian thoroughfare, **İstiklal Caddesi,** can satisfy any whim, from chocolates to discount T-shirts to contemporary art.

Cruise Lines

Numerous cruise ship companies service the Mediterranean, so there are ships and itineraries to suit everyone's fancy. You'll find boats ranging from small cruisers to large ships equivalent to a floating city, each providing a smorgasbord of shipboard amenities and a selection of onboard and onshore activities. And the voyages can be as short as a few days to as long as several weeks.

Azamara Cruises
Midsize ships; deluxe treatment, part of Royal Caribbean Brand. azamaraclubcruises.com

Carnival Cruise Lines
Ultracasual, family friendly; teen and young adults organized fun carnival.com

Celebrity Cruises
Premium service, known for its service and food. celebritycruises.com

Compagnie du Ponant
Smaller yachts; mainly French passengers. en.ponant.com

Costa Cruises
Italian cruise line, multiple Mediterranean sailings with extended season. costacruise.com

Crystal Cruises
Upscale fine food and service. crystalcruises.com

Cunard Line
Vintage cruise line, part of Carnival family. cunard.com

Disney Cruise Line
Family focused, with Barcelona and Venice serving as home ports. disneycruise.disneygo.com

Hapag-Lloyd Cruise Line
German cruise line catering to luxury and upmarket clientele. hl-cruises.com

Holland America Line
Traditional decor and ambience appropriate for multigenerational groups. hollandamerica.com

Lindblad Expeditions
Partners with National Geographic for sailing voyages. expeditions.com

MSC Cruises
Family oriented; 12 ships travel the Mediterranean, some year-round; multilingual. msccruisesusa.com

Norwegian Cruise Line
Resort-cruise experience, with limited Mediterranean departures. ncl.com

Oceania Cruises
Midsize ships offering long (up to 24 days) Mediterranean cruises. oceaniacruises.com

P&O Cruises
British-owned company providing longer at-sea time; supervised child-centered activities. pocruises.com

Princess Cruises
Mid-price line; activity filled. princess.com

Regent Seven Seas Cruises
Midsize ships with laid-back style. rssc.com

Royal Caribbean International
Family and young couple oriented; variety of destinations. royalcaribbean.com

Seabourn
Luxury cruising on midsize ships. seabourn.com

SeaDream Yacht Club
Smaller ships that dock at non-touristy ports. seadream.com

Silversea
Luxury line for the active and involved traveler. silversea.com

Star Clippers
Tall ships; many European passengers. starclippers.com

Windstar Cruises
Tall ships that dock at less visited ports; mostly American passengers. windstarcruises.com

Language Guide

General

Breakfast
S: desayuno
F: petit déjeuner
I: colazione
C: dorucak
G: proino
T: vkahvalti

Lunch
S: almuerzo
F: déjeuner
I: prazno
C: rucak
G: mesimerianó
T: öğle yemeği

Dinner
S: cena
F: dîner
I: cena
C: vecera
G: deípno
T: akşam yemegi

Entrée
S: entrada
F: entrée
I: entrata
C: predjelo
G: eísodos
T: mezeler

Main course
S: plato principal
F: plat principal
I: secondo
C: glavno jelo
G: kýrio piáto
T: ana yemek

Dessert
S: postre
F: dessert
I: dolci
C: desert
G: epidórpio
T: tatlı

Grilled
S: a la parrilla
F: grillé
I: alla griglia
C: na žaru
G: scharas
T: ızgara

Boiled
S: hervido
F: bouilli
I: bollito
C: kuhano
G: vrastó
T: haşlanmiş

Fried
S: frito
F: frit
I: fritto
C: prženo
G: tiganito
T: kızarmiş

Pasta
S: pasta
F: pâtes
I: pasta
C: tjestenina
G: zymariká
T: makarna

Eggs
S: huevos
F: œufs
I: uova
C: jaje
G: auýa
T: yumurta

Bread
S: pan
F: pain
I: pane
C: kruh
G: psomi
T: ekmek

Vegetarian (food)
S: comida vegetariana
F: nourriture végétari-
enne
I: vegetariano
C: vegetarijanska
(hrana)
G: khortofagos
T: etsiz yemekleri

Entrée

Soup
S: sopa
F: soupe
I: zuppa
C: juha
G: soupa
T: çorba

Fish
S: pescado
F: poisson
I: pesce
C: riba
G: psári
T: balık

Shellfish
S: mariscos
F: fruits de mer
I: mollusco
C: školjke
G: ostrakódermo
T: kabuklu deniz
hayvanı

Shrimp
S: camarón
F: crevette
I: gamberi
C: škamp
G: garides
T: karides

Meat
S: carne
F: viande
I: carne
C: meso
G: kreas
T: et

Beef
S: ternera
F: bœuf
I: manzo
C: govedina
G: vódino kreas
T: sığır eti

Pork
S: cerdo
F: porc
I: maiale
C: svinjetina
G: khirino
T: domuz

Chicken
S: pollo
F: poulet
I: pollo
C: piletina
G: kotopoulo
T: tavuk

Vegetables
S: verduras
F: légumes
I: verdure
C: povrie
G: lakhanika
T: sebze

Potatoes
S: patatas
F: pommes de terre
I: patate
C: krumpir
G: patates
T: patates

French fries
S: patatas fritas
F: pommes frites
I: patate fritte
C: pomfrit
G: patates tighanites
T: patates kızartması

Lettuce
S: lechuga
F: laitue
I: lattuga
C: zelena salata
G: marouli
T: marul

Tomato
S: tomate
F: tomate
I: pomodoro
C: rajčica
G: domates
T: domates

Salad
S: ensalada
F: salade
I: insalata
C: salata
G: salata
T: salata

Green salad
S: ensalada verde
F: salade verte
I: insalata verde
C: zelena salata

G: prasinos salata
T: yeşil salata

Tomato salad
S: ensalada de tomate
F: salade de tomates
I: insalata di pomodoro
C: salata od rajčica
G: tomatosalata
T: domates salatası

Fruit
S: fruta
F: fruit
I: frutta
C: voie
G: karpós
T: meyve

Orange
S: naranja
F: orange
I: arance
C: naranca
G: portokalia
T: portakal

Apple
S: manzana
F: pomme
I: mele
C: jabuka
G: mila
T: elma

Strawberry
S: fresa
F: fraise
I: fragole
C: jagoda
G: fraoules
T: çilek

Pear
S: pera
F: poire
I: pere
C: kruška
G: akladia/krystalia
T: armut

Lemon
S: limón
F: citron
I: limone
C: limun
G: lemoni
T: limon

Dessert
Ice cream
S: helado
F: crème glacée
I: gelato
C: sladoled
G: pagoto
T: dondurma

Cake
S: torta
F: gâteau
I: torta
C: kolac
G: kéik
T: kek

Pie
S: pastel
F: tarte
I: torta
C: pita
G: píta
T: turta

Beverages
Water
S: agua
F: eau
I: acqua
C: voda
G: nero
T: su

Mineral water
S: agua mineral
F: eau minérale
I: acqua minerale
C: mineralna voda
G: metaliko nero
T: maden suyu

Wine
S: vino
F: vin
I: vino
C: vino
G: krasi
T: şarap

Beer
S: cerveza
F: bière
I: birra
C: pivo
G: bira
T: bira

Tea
S: té
F: thé
I: te
C: caj
G: tsai
T: çay

Coffee
S: café
F: café
I: caffè
C: kava
G: kafes
T: kanve

Milk
S: leche
F: lait
I: latte
C: mlijeko
G: gala
T: süt

Greetings
Hello
S: hola
F: bonjour
I: ciao / salve
C: dobar dan
G: geia sou
T: merhaba

Goodbye
S: adiós
F: au revoir
I: arrivederci
C: bok
G: antio
T: Hoşça kalır

Good morning
S: buenos dias
F: bonjour
I: buon giorno
C: dobro jutro
G: kaljnéra
T: günaydın

Good evening
S: buenas tardes
F: bonsoir
I: buona sera
C: dobra vecer
G: kaljspéra
T: Iyi akşamlar

Good night
S: buenas noches
F: bonsoir
I: buona notte
C: laku noi
G: kaljnýchta
T: Iyi geceler

Yes
S: sí
F: oui
I: sì
C: da
G: nai
T: evet

No
S: no
F: non
I: no
C: ne
G: óchi
T: hayır / yok

Okay
S: bueno
F: d'accord
I: OK
C: u redu
G: endáxi
T: tamam

Please
S: por favor
F: s'il vous plait
I: per favore
C: molim
G: parakaló
T: lütfen

Thank you
S: gracias
F: merci
I: grazie
C: hvala
G: efcharistó
T: teşekkür ederim / sagol / mersi

Sorry!
S: ilo siento!
F: désolé!
I: mi dispiace!
C: oprostite! / pardon!
G: sighnómi!
T: özür dilerim!

Excuse me

S: perdón
F: excusez-moi
I: mi scusi (for attention) / permesso (to get past)
C: oprostite
G: me sinchoríte
T: affedersiniz

Do you speak English?

S: ¿Habla ingles?
F: Parlez-vous anglais?
I: Parla inglese?
C: Govorite li engleski?
G: Miláte angliká?
T: İngilizce biliyor musunuz?

Shopping

How much does it cost?

S: ¿Cúanto es?
F: C'est combien?
I: quanto costa?
C: Koliko košta?
G: Póso káni?
T: Ne kadar?

Can I pay by credit card?

S: ¿Se aceptan tarjetas de crédito?
F: Est-ce que vous acceptez les cartes de crédit?
I: Posso pagare con la carta di credito?
C: Mogu li platiti s kredit nom karticom?
G: Boró na pilróso me pistotikí kárta?
T: Kredi kartleri geçerlimi?

Restaurants

Do you have a table for two?

S: ¿Tiene una mesa para dos?
F: Avez-vous une table pour deux?
I: Avete un tavolo per due?
C: Imate li stol za dvoje?
G: Échete éna trapézi gia dýo?
T: İki kişilik bir masa, lütfen?

Can I have an English menu, please?

S: ¿Puedo tener un menú Inglés, por favor?
F: Puis-je avoir un menu en anglais, s'il vous plaît?
I: Avete un menù in inglese?
C: Mogu li dobiti meni na engleskom molim?
G: Éhete éna katálogho sta angliká?
T: İngilizce menü var mı?

Can I have the bill, please?

S: ¿Puedo tener la cuenta, por favor?
F: L'addition, s'il vous plaît
I: Il conto, per favore
C: Molim vas racun?
G: To loghariazmó, ç?
T: Hesap lütfen

It was very good

S: Fue muy bueno
F: Il était très bon
I: Era squisito!
C: Bilo je vrlo dobro
G: Ítan polý kaló
T: Çok iyi

Travel & Directions

Excuse me, where is the bus station?

S: Perdón, ¿dónde está la estación de autobuses?
F: Excusez-moi, où est la gare d'autobus?
I: Dov'è la stazione degli autobus?
C: Oprostite, gdje je autobusni kolodvor?
G: Me sinchoríte, poú einai j stásj tou leoforíou?
T: Affedersiniz, nerede otogar?

Train

S: tren
F: métro
I: treno
C: vlak
G: tréno
T: tren

Bus

S: autobús
F: autobus
I: autobus
C: autobus
G: leoforío
T: otobüs

Ferry

S: transbordador
F: bac
I: traghetto
C: trajekt
G: porthmeío
T: feribot / vapur

Money

Money

S: dinero
F: argent
I: soldi
C: novac
G: chrímata
T: para

Bank

S: banca
F: banque
I: banca
C: banka
G: trápeza
T: banka

Credit card

S: carta di credito
F: carte de crédit
I: carta de credito
C: kreditna kartica
G: pistotiki kárta
T: kredi kartı

INDEX

Bold page numbers
indicate illustrations.
CAPS indicates
thematic categories.

A

Acquario, Genoa, Italy 92
Acropolis, Athens, Greece **221, 222,**
222-228, **224-225**
Acropolis Museum, Athens, Greece
226, **226**
Adriatic Sea *see* Venice & the Adriatic
Agora, Athens, Greece 226-227
Aix-en-Provence, France 70-73, **71,
72,** 279
Akronafplia, Nafplio, Greece 236
Alberobello, Puglia, Italy **174,** 175
Alhambra, Granada, Spain 50-54,
52-53, 54
Amalfi, Italy 157, 289-290
Amalfi Coast, Italy **14-15,** 123, **156,**
156-157, 289-291, 305
Anacapri, Italy **154,** 154-155, 289
Anafiotika, Athens, Greece 226
Ancient Rome, Rome, Italy ˉ25-132
   Arco di Costantino 131
   Capitolino 125-126
   Colosseo ˉ29-131, **130**
   Fori Imperiali 127
   Fori Romano 127-129, **129,** 137
   Musei Capitolini 125
   Palatino 125
   Palazzo Altemps 133
   San Clemente 131-132
   Santa Maria in Aracoeli 126, ˉ37
   see also Roman Empire
Antibes, France 82-83, 281
Archaeological Museum, Iraklio.
   Greece 245
Archaeological Museum, Nafplio,
   Greece 236
Archaeological Museum, Rhodes,
   Greece 243
Archaeological Museum of Olympia,
   Greece 239
Archaeology Museum, Istanbul, Turkey
   255-256, **256**
Arco di Costantino, Rome, Italy ˉ31
Arènes d'Arles, France 71
Argos, Greece 237-238
Arles, France 71, 74, 279
Arts & culture 24-27
   dance 34, 217
   frescoes 27
   Gaudí & *modernisme* 46-47, **47**
   Atelier Cézanne, Aix-en-Provence,
      France 70
Athens, Greece 222-235
   Acropolis **221, 222,** 222-228,
      224-225
   Acropolis Museum 226, **226**
   Agora 226-227
   Anafiotika 226
   Benaki Museum 231
   Benaki Museum of Islamic Art 229
   Byzantine Museum 232
   Cathedral Square 228-229
   Central Market 234, 306
   Elgin Marbles 225
   Erechtheion **222, 224,** 224-225
   Gazi 229

Hadrian's Library 227-228
Herodes Atticus Theater **221,** 225
introduction 221
Kanellopoulos Museum 229-230
Kerameikos cemetery 228
Kolonaki 232-233
Lykavittos 232-233, **233**
map 223
Metro Galleries 232
Monastiraki Square **228,** 228-229
Mosque of Fethiye Tzami 227
Museum of Cycladic Art 232-233
Museum of Greek Folk Art 230
Museum of Greek Musical
   Instruments 229
National Archaeological Museum
   234-235
National Gallery of Greece 231-232
National Gardens 230
Numismatic Museum 235
Omonia Square 233-235
Parthenon **221,** 223-225, **224**
Plaka 229-230
Pnyka 226
port logistics 235
Psirri 229
restaurants **23,** 297-299
Roman Forum 227
shopping 234, 306
Stoa of Attalos 227
Syntagma Square 230-232
Technopolis 229
Temple of Hephaistos 226-227
Theater of Dionysos 225
Tomb of the Unknown Soldier 230
Tower of the Winds 227
transportation 235
War Museum 231, **231**
Athens & the islands 218-247
   arts & culture 25
   Athens **23, 221, 222,** 222-235,
      224-225, 226, 228, 231, 233,
      297-299, 306
   Crete **244,** 244-247, **246,** 300
   islands **11, 240,** 240-243, **242,** 300
   maps 220-221, 223
   Peloponnesus **236,** 236-239, **238,**
      299-300
   port logistics 235, 239, 243 247
   restaurants **23,** 297-300
   shopping 306
   transportation 235
   see also Athens, Greece; Crete,
      Greece; Greek islands;
      Peloponnesus, Greece
Avignon, France 74-75, 279-280

B

Balearic Islands, Spain 59-63
   Eivissa (Ibiza) 62-63, 278
   introduction 31, 59
   Mallorca (Majorca) **28, 59, 60,**
      60-61, 63, 277-278
   Menorca (Minorca) 62, 63, 278
   port logistics 63
   restaurants 277-278
   shopping 304
Barcelona, Spain 32-48
   Barri Gòtic (Gothic Quarter) **4,**
      32-34, 36-37
   Casa Milà 45, 46, **47**
   Catedral (La Seu) 32-34, 36 **36**
   Eixample 43-45
   El Born 34-35, 38

Fundació Joan Miró 42
Gaudí & *modernisme* 46-47, **47**
highlights 48
introduction 30
La Barceloneta 39, 42
La Rambla 38, **40,** 40-41
La Ribera 34-35, **35,** 38
La Sagrada Família **44,** 44-45
maps 32-33, 37, 41
Monestir de Santa Maria de
   Pedralbes 45
Montjuïc **42,** 42-43
Museu d'Art Contemporani de
   Barcelona 40
Museu d'Història de Barcelona 37
Museu d'Història de Catalunya 39
Museu Frederic Marès 37
Museu Marítim 39
Museu Nacional d'Art de Catalunya
   42-43
Museu Picasso 35, **35**
Palau Reial de Pedralbes 45, 48
Parc de la Ciutadella 48
port logistics 48
Port Olímpic 39, 42
restaurants 274-277
Santa Maria del Mar 35, 38
Santa Maria del Pi 36
shopping 304
skyline (W Hotel) **30**
transportation 43, 48
walks 36-37, **40,** 40-41
waterfront 38-39, **39,** 42
Bari, Puglia, Italy 161, 174-175, 177, 292-293
Barri Gòtic (Gothic Quarter), Barcelona,
   Spain **4,** 32-34, 36-37
Basilica Cistern, Istanbul, Turkey
   258-259
Basilica di San Marco, Venice, Italy
   185-189, **186-187, 188**
Basilica di San Nicola, Bari, Italy 174
Basilica di San Pietro, Rome Italy
   139-140, **141**
Basilique Notre-Dame-de-la-Garde,
   Marseille, France 69
Battistero di San Giovanni, Florence, Italy
   94, 96-97
Bay of Naples, Italy 144-151
   Herculaneum 148-149, 151, 289
   map 145
   Naples **17,** 122, **144,** 144-148, **147,**
      151, 288-289, 305
   Pompeii **148-149,** 149-151, **150,** 289
   port logistics 151
   transportation 151
   see also Naples, Italy
Beaulieu-sur-Mer, France 82, 281
Benaki Museum, Athens, Greece 231
Benaki Museum of Islamic Art, Athens,
   Greece 229
Blue Grotto, Capri, Italy 153
Blue Mosque, Istanbul, Turkey 259-260,
   260
Borgo Medioevale, Taormina, Italy 164
Bouillabaisse 70
Bourtzi, Nafplio, Greece **236,** 236-237
Brunelleschi, Filippo 98-99
Byzantine Museum, Athens, Greece 232

C

Ca' d'Oro, Venice, Italy 202, **203**
Ca' Rezzonico, Venice, Italy 193, **193**
CAC (Centro de Arte Contemporáneo),
   Málaga, Spain 50

Caffè Florian, Venice, Italy 189
Campanile, Florence, Italy 97, 100
Campanile, Venice, Italy 185
Il Campo, Siena, Italy 116–117
Campo de' Fiori, Rome, Italy 133
Campo dei Miracoli, Pisa, Italy 112–113
Campo Marzio, Rome, Italy 132–133
Canal Grande, Venice, Italy **182,** 182–184, **203**
Cannaregio, Venice, Italy 202–203
Cannes, France **76,** 76–77, 280
Cap d'Antibes, France 83
Cap Ferrat peninsula, France 82
Capitolino, Rome, Italy 125–126
Cappella Brancacci, Florence, Italy 109
Cappella dei Pazzi, Florence, Italy 104
Cappella Sistina, Rome, Italy 27, 142–143
Cappelle Medicee, Florence, Italy 106–107
Capri (island), Italy 123, **152,** 152–155, **154,** 289, 305
Capri Town, Italy 152–154, 289
Casa Milà, Barcelona, Spain 45, 46, **47**
Casa Rocca Piccola, Valletta, Malta 173
Casino de Monte-Carlo, Monaco 85
Castel del Monte, Puglia, Italy 177
Castellana Grotte, Puglia, Italy 176
Castello, Venice, Italy 203–205
Castelmola, Sicily, Italy 164
Catacombe dei Cappuccini, Palermo, Italy 168
Catedral, Granada, Spain 54–55
Catedral, Valencia, Spain 57
Catedral (La Seu), Barcelona, Spain 32–34, 36, **36**
Cathedral, Málaga, Spain 49
Cathedral of St. Dominus, Split, Croatia **206,** 207
Cathedral Square, Athens, Greece 228–229
Cathédrale St.-Sauveur, Aix-en-Provence, France 70, **72**
Cathédrale Ste.-Réparate, Nice, France 78, 80
Catherine de' Medici 97
Cattedrale di San Lorenzo, Genoa **90,** 90–91
Cave churches, Matera, Italy 176–177
Central Market, Athens, Greece 234, 306
Centro de Arte Contemporáneo (CAC), Málaga, Spain 50
Cézanne, Paul 70
Chagall, Marc 79
Château Grimaldi, Antibes, France 82–83
Church of St. Blaise, Dubrovnik, Croatia 213
Church of St. Roch, Dubrovnik, Croatia 209, 212
CHURCHES
  Basilica di San Marco, Venice, Italy 185–189, **186–187, 188**
  Basilica di San Nicola, Bari, Italy 174
  Basilica di San Pietro, Rome, Italy 139–140, **141**
  Basilique Notre-Dame-de-la-Garde, Marseille, France 69
  Battistero di San Giovanni, Florence, Italy **94,** 96–97
  Cappella Brancacci, Florence, Italy 109
  Cappella dei Pazzi, Florence, Italy 104
  Cappella Sistina, Rome, Italy 27, 142–143
  Cappelle Medicee, Florence, Italy 106–107
  Catedral, Granada, Spain 54–55
  Catedral, Valencia, Spain 57

Catedral (La Seu), Barcelona, Spain 32–34, 36, **36**
cathedral, Málaga, Spain 49
Cathedral of St. Dominus, Split, Croatia **206,** 207
Cathedral Square, Athens, Greece 228–229
Cathédrale St.-Sauveur, Aix-en-Provence, France 70, **72**
Cathédrale Ste.-Réparate, Nice, France 78, 80
Cattedrale di San Lorenzo, Genoa **90,** 90–91
cave churches, Matera, Italy 176–177
Church of St. Blaise, Dubrovnik, Croatia 213
Church of St. Roch, Dubrovnik, Croatia 209, 212
Collegiata di Santa Maria Assunta, San Gimignano, Italy 118–119
Dominican Church & Monastery, Dubrovnik, Croatia 211, 215
Dubrovnik Cathedral, Dubrovnik, Croatia 213
Duomo, Pisa, Italy 113
Duomo, Siena, Italy **116,** 117
Duomo di Monreale, Sicily, Italy **168,** 169
Duomo di San Martino, Lucca, Italy 114–115
Église Notre-Dame de l'Annonciation, Nice, France 80
Église St.-Jacques, Nice, France 80
Église St.-Trophime, Arles, France 71
Franciscan Church & Monastery, Dubrovnik, Croatia 211, 212
Hagia Sophia, Istanbul, Turkey **12, 26, 248,** 256–258, **259**
La Sagrada Família, Barcelona, Spain **44,** 44–45
Madonna dell'Orto, Venice, Italy 202–203
Naples, Italy **144,** 146–147
Orsanmichele, Florence, Italy 100–101
Palermo, Italy 166–167, **167**
Pantheon, Rome, Italy 133–135, **134,** 136
San Clemente, Rome, Italy 131–132
San Donato, Genoa, Italy 91
San Frediano, Lucca, Italy 115
San Lorenzo, Florence, Italy 105–107
San Michele in Foro, Lucca, Italy 114
San Miniato al Monte, Florence, Italy 110–111
San Sabino, Bari, Italy 175
San Zaccaria, Venice, Italy 205
Santa Croce, Florence, Italy 104–105, **105**
Santa Maria dei Miracoli, Venice, Italy 203
Santa Maria del Fiore (Duomo), Florence, Italy **94,** 96, **98,** 98–99, **99**
Santa Maria del Mar, Barcelona, Spain 35, 38
Santa Maria del Pi, Barcelona, Spain 36
Santa Maria del Popolo, Rome, Italy 138
Santa Maria della Salute, Venice, Italy 197, 198
Santa Maria di Castello, Genoa, Italy 91
Santa Maria Draperis Church, Istanbul, Turkey 264
Santa Maria Gloriosa dei Frari, Venice, Italy 199, 201
Santa Maria in Aracoeli, Rome, Italy 126, 137

Santa Maria Novella, Florence, Italy 108
Santa Maria sopra Minerva, Rome, Italy 134–135, 137
Sant'Agostino, Genoa, Italy 91
Santi Giovanni e Paolo, Venice, Italy 203–205
St. John's Co-Cathedral, Valletta, Malta 171
St. Paul's Shipwreck, Valletta, Malta 172
Cimiez, France 79
Cinque Terre, Italy **86,** 89, 93, 283
Ciudad de las Artes y las Ciencias, Valencia, Spain **57,** 58
Civitavecchia, Rome, Italy 143
Climate 9, 272
Coastal Spain 28–63
  Balearic Islands **28,** 31, **59,** 59–63, **60,** 277–278, 304
  Barcelona **4,** 30, **30,** 32–48, **35, 36, 39, 40, 42, 44, 47,** 274–277, 304
  Gibraltar 56, **56**
  Málaga & Granada 30–31, **49,** 49–55, **52–53, 54,** 277, 304
  map 30–31
  restaurants 274–278
  shopping 304
  Valencia 31, **57,** 57–58, 277
  see also Balearic Islands, Spain; Barcelona, Spain; Granada, Spain; Málaga, Spain
Collegiata di Santa Maria Assunta, San Gimignano, Italy 118–119
Collezione Peggy Guggenheim, Venice, Italy 195, 197, 198, **198**
Colline du Château, Nice, France 78
Colosseo, Rome, Italy 129–131, **130**
Conversions (measurement) 273
Corfu (island), Greece 221, **240,** 240–242, **242,** 243, 300
Côte d'Azur *see* French Riviera
Crete (island), Greece 244–247
  Archaeological Museum, Iraklio 245
  Historical Museum of Crete, Iraklio 245–246
  introduction 221
  Iraklio **244,** 244–246, 247
  Knossos **246,** 246–247
  Museum of Religious Art, Iraklio 246
  port logistics 247
  restaurants 300
Croatia
  money matters 273
  restaurants 295–297
  shopping 306
  see also Dubrovnik, Croatia; Hvar, Croatia; Korcula, Croatia; Split, Croatia
Cruises 9–11, 307
Currency 273
Cyclades islands, Greece **218**

D
Dance 34, 217
Diocletian's Palace, Split, Croatia **206,** 206–207
Dogana di Mare, Venice, Italy 199
Dominican Church & Monastery, Dubrovnik, Croatia 211, 215
Dominican Monastery Museum, Dubrovnik, Croatia 215
Donatello 100, 101, 104, 106
Dorsoduro, Venice, Italy 193–198
Dubrovnik, Croatia 208–215
  Church of St. Blaise 213
  Church of St. Roch 209, 212

city walls **208,** 209, 210–211
Dominican Church & Monastery
  211, 215
Dominican Monastery Museum 215
Dubrovnik Cathedral 213
Franciscan Church & Monastery
  211, 212
Gundulić Square 214, **214**
  introduction 180, 208
Luža Square 212–213
  map 211
Mount Srđ **2–3,** 212
  port logistics 215
Prijeko 214–215
Pustjerna 214
Rector's Palace **210,** 211, 213
  restaurants 296–297
Sponza Palace 212–213
Stradun area 209, 211, 212–213, **213**
  walking tour **210,** 210–211
War Photo Limited 214–215
Dubrovnik Cathedral, Dubrovnik,
  Croatia 213
Duomo, Florence, Italy see Santa Maria
  del Fiore, Florence, Italy
Duomo, Naples, Italy **144,** 146–147
Duomo, Pisa, Italy 113
Duomo, Siena, Italy **116,** 117
Duomo di Monreale, Sicily, Italy
  168, 169
Duomo di San Martino, Lucca, Italy
  114–115

E
Église Notre-Dame de l'Annonciation,
  Nice, France 80
Église St.-Jacques, Nice, France 80
Église St.-Trophime, Arles, France 71
Eivissa (Ibiza), Balearic Islands, Spain
  62–63, 278
Eixample, Barcelona, Spain 43–45
El Born, Barcelona, Spain 34–35, 38
Elgin Marbles 225
Embassies 273
Emergencies 273
Eminönü, Istanbul, Turkey 262–263
Ephesus, Turkey **24,** 251, **268,**
  268–271, 303
Epidavros, Greece 237
Erechtheion, Athens, Greece **222, 224,**
  224–225
Etna (volcano), Sicily, Italy 165, **165,** 169
European Union 16–17, 21
Eyüp Sultan Mosque Complex,
  Istanbul, Turkey 266

F
Ferragamo, Salvatore 97
Florence, Italy 94–111, **108**
  Battistero di San Giovanni **94,** 96–97
  Campanile 97, 100
  Cappella Brancacci 109
  Cappella dei Pazzi 104
  Cappelle Medicee 106–107
  Galleria degli Uffizi 102–103, 111
  Galleria dell'Accademia 107
  highlights 111
  history 20
  introduction 89, 94, 96
  Loggia della Signoria 102
  map 95
  Museo Nazionale del Bargello 103–104
  Museo Salvatore Ferragamo 97
  Museo Storico dell'Opera del
    Duomo 100, **100**

Orsanmiche e 100–101
Palazzo Medici-Riccardi 107
Palazzo Pitti 110
Palazzo Vecchio 101
Piazza del Duomo 96–97, 100
Piazza della Signoria 101–102
Ponte Vecchio & the Oltrarno
  108–111, **110**
  restaurants 283–285
San Lorenzo & around 105–107, **106**
San Miniato al Monte 110–111
Santa Croce 104–105, **105**
Santa Maria del Fiore (Duomo) **94,**
  96, **98,** 98–99, **99**
Santa Maria Novella 108
  shopping 305
  transportation 111
Fondation Vasarely, Aix-en-Provence,
  France 70–71
Fontana dei Quattro Fiumi, Rome,
  Italy **122**
Fontana di Trevi, Rome, Italy **135,** 136,
  138, **138**
Food & drink **8, 22,** 22–23, **23**
  bouillabaisse 70
  lokum (Turkish delight) 266
  Roman coffee & gelato 139
Fori Imperiali, Rome, Italy 127
Fori Romano, Rome, Italy 127–129,
  129, 137
France see French Riviera & Provence
Franciscan Church & Monastery,
  Dubrovnik, Croatia 211, 212
French Riviera & Provence 64–85
  Cannes & St.-Tropez **76,** 76–77, 280
  map 66–67
  Marseille & Provence **66,** 63–75, **68,**
    71, 72, 279
  Monaco **84,** 84–85, 281–282
  Nice **64, 78,** 78–83, 280–281
    restaurants 278–282
    shopping 304
  see also Marseille & Provence
France; Nice & around, France
Frescoes 27
Fundació Joan Miró, Barcelona,
  Spain 42

G
Galata Bridge, Istanbul, Turkey **250,** 267
Galata Tower, Istanbul, Turkey 267
Galatasaray Square, Istanbul, Turkey
  265
Galileo's tomb, Florence, Italy 105, **105**
Galleria Borghese, Rome, Italy 139
Galleria degli Uffizi, Florence, Italy
  102–103, 111
Galleria dell'Accademia, Florence,
  Italy 107
Galleria Regionale di Sicilia, Palermo,
  Italy 167
Gallerie dell'Accademia, Venice, Italy
  193–195, 197
GARDENS
  Giardini di Augusto, Capri, Italy 153
  Jardin Exotique, Monaco 85
  National Gardens, Athens, Greece 230
Gaudí, Antoni 44–47
Gazi, Athens, Greece 229
Generalife, Granada, Spain 53
Genoa & the coast, Italy 90–93
  Cinque Terre **86,** 89, 93, 283
  Genoa **90,** 90–92
  introduction 88–89
  port logistics 93

Portofino **92,** 92–93
  restaurants 282
  shopping 305
George Cross 171
Giardini di Augusto, Capri, Italy 153
Gibraltar 56, **56**
Giotto 105
The Godfather (film) 163
Gondolas **178,** 200, **200,** 201
Gothic Quarter, Barcelona, Spain see
  Barri Gòtic, Barcelona, Spain
Granada, Spain 50–55
  Alhambra 50–54, **52–53, 54**
  Catedral 54–55
  downtown Granada 54–55
  Generalife 53
  introduction 30–31
  La Cartuja 55
  map 51
  Monasterio de San Jerónimo 55
  restaurants 277
  shopping 304
Grand Bazaar, Istanbul, Turkey 261–262,
  262, 306
Grand Master's Palace, Valletta, Malta
  171
Greece see Athens & the islands
Greek islands **11,** 240–243
  Corfu 221, **240,** 240–242, **242,** 243
    300
  port logistics 243
  restaurants 300
  Rhodes 242–243, 300, 306
  Santorini **218,** 242, 243, 300
Gülhane Park, Istanbul, Turkey 257
Gundulić Square, Dubrovnik, Croatia
  214, **214**

H
Hadrian's Library, Athens, Greece
  227–228
Hagia Sophia, Istanbul, Turkey **12, 26,**
  248, 256–258, **259**
Hal Saflieni Hypogeum, Malta 173
Herculaneum, Italy 148–149, 151, 289
Herodes Atticus Theater, Athens, Greece
  221, 225
Hippodrome, Istanbul, Turkey 260
Historical Museum of Crete, Iraklio,
  Greece 245–246
History **18–19,** 18–21, **21**
Hvar, Croatia 216, 296

I
Ibiza, Balearic Islands, Spain see Eivissa,
  Balearic Islands, Spain
Iraklio, Greece **244,** 244–245, 247
Istanbul, Turkey 252–267
  Archaeology Museum 255–256, **256**
  Basilica Cistern 258–259
  Blue Mosque 259–260, **260**
  Eminönü 262–263
  European Istanbul 266–267
  Eyüp Sultan Mosque Complex 266
  Galata Bridge **250,** 267
  Galata Tower 267
  Galatasaray Square 265
  Grand Bazaar 261–262, **262,** 306
  Gülhane Park 257
  Hagia Sophia **12, 26, 248,** 256–258, **259**
  highlights 267
  Hippodrome 260
  introduction 250–251
  İstiklal Caddesi walk **264,** 264–265
  lokum (Turkish delight) 265

Maiden's Tower **252**
maps 253, 265
Museum of Turkish & Islamic Arts
    260–261
New Mosque 262
port logistics 267
restaurants 23, 301–303
Santa Maria Draperis Church 264
Southern Golden Horn 263, 266
Spice Market 263
Süleymaniye Mosque 262–263
Topkapı Palace 252–256, **255**
walks **264,** 264–265
İstiklal Caddesi, Istanbul, Turkey **264,**
    264–265
Italian Riviera & Tuscany 86–119
Florence 20, 89, **94,** 94–111, **98,**
    99, 100, 105, 106, 108, 110,
    283–285, 305
Genoa & the coast **86,** 88–93, **90,**
    92, 282, 305
Lucca 89, **114,** 114–115, 285
maps 88–89, 95
Pisa 89, **112,** 112–113, 285
restaurants 282–286
San Gimignano 89, **118,** 118–119,
    285–286
shopping 304–305
Siena 89, **116,** 116–117, 285
see also Florence, Italy; Genoa & the
    coast, Italy
Italy see Italian Riviera & Tuscany;
    Puglia, Italy; Rome & Naples; Sicily,
    Italy; Venice, Italy

J
Jardin Exotique, Monaco 85

K
Kanellopoulos Museum, Athens,
    Greece 229–230
Katakolon, Greece 239
Kazantzakis, Nikos 245
Kerameikos cemetery, Athens, Greece
    228
Knossos, Greece **246,** 246–247
Kolonaki, Athens, Greece 232–233
Koper, Slovenia 216–217
Korčula, Croatia **216,** 217, 296
Kotor, Montenegro 217
Kuşadası, Turkey 271

L
La Barceloneta, Barcelona, Spain 39, 42
La Cartuja, Granada, Spain 55
La Rambla, Barcelona, Spain 38, **40,**
    40–41
La Ribera, Barcelona, Spain 34–35, **35,** 38
La Sagrada Família, Barcelona, Spain
    44, 44–45
La Seu, Barcelona, Spain see Catedral,
    Barcelona, Spain
Language
language guide 308–310
Venetian vocabulary 195
Leaning Tower, Pisa, Italy **112,** 112–113
Lecce, Puglia, Italy **176,** 177
Leonardo da Vinci 103
Ligurian coast, Italy **86**
Livorno, Italy
    introduction 89
    port logistics 111
    transportation 111, 113, 115, 117, 119
Locorotondo, Italy 175
Loggia della Signoria, Florence, Italy 102

Lokum (Turkish delight) 266
Lucca, Italy 89, **114,** 114–115, 285
Luža Square, Dubrovnik, Croatia 212–213
Lykavittos, Athens, Greece 232–233,
    233

M
Machiavelli, Niccolò 105
Madonna dell'Orto, Venice, Italy
    202–203
Maiden's Tower, Istanbul, Turkey **252**
Majorca, Balearic Islands, Spain see
    Mallorca, Balearic Islands, Spain
Málaga, Spain **49,** 49–50
CAC (Centro de Arte
    Contemporáneo) 50
cathedral 49
introduction 30–31
Museo Carmen Thyssen 50
Museo Picasso 49
port logistics 55
restaurants 277
shopping 304
Mallorca (Majorca), Balearic Islands,
    Spain **28, 59, 60,** 60–61, 63,
    277–278
Malta 170–173, **172**
George Cross 171
introduction 161, 170
port logistics 173
restaurants 292
scuba diving **159**
shopping 305–306
Valletta **21,** 161, **170,** 171–173, 292
Manarola, Italy **86,** 93
Maó, Menorca, Spain 63
Maps
Aix-en-Provence, France 73
Athens, Greece 223
Athens & the Greek islands 220–221
Barcelona, Spain 32–33, 37, 41
Coastal Spain 30–31
Dubrovnik, Croatia 211
Florence, Italy 95
French Riviera & Provence 66–67
Granada, Spain 51
Istanbul, Turkey 253, 265
Italian Riviera & Tuscany 88–89, 95
Marseille, France 69
Naples, Italy 145
Nice, France 81
Rome, Italy 126–127, 137
Rome & Naples 123, 126–127, 137, 145
Sicily, Malta, & Puglia 160–161
Turkey 251, 253, 265
Venice, Italy 183, 196–197
Venice & the Adriatic 180–181, 211
Marsaxlokk, Malta **172,** 173
Marseille, France **68,** 68–69, **71, 72,**
    75, 279
Marseille & Provence, France 66–75
Aix-en-Provence 70–73, **71, 72,** 279
Arles 71, 74, 279
Avignon 74–75, 279–280
introduction 66–67
maps 69, 73
Marseille **68,** 68–69, **71, 72,** 75, 279
port logistics 75
Provence village **66**
sightseeing tours 75
transportation 75
walks **72,** 72–73
Matera, Italy 176–177, 293
Matisse, Henri 79
Medici family 97, 102, 106–107

Menorca (Minorca), Balearic Islands,
    Spain 62, 63, 278
Meryemana, Turkey 271, **271**
Metro Galleries, Athens, Greece 232
Milos (island), Greece 241
Minorca, Balearic Islands, Spain see
    Menorca, Balearic Islands, Spain
Modernisme 46–47, **47**
Monaco **84,** 84–85, 281–282
Monasterio de San Jerónimo, Granada,
    Spain 55
Monastiraki Square, Athens, Greece
    228, 228–229
Monestir de Santa Maria de Pedralbes,
    Barcelona, Spain 45
Money matters 273
Monte-Carlo, Monaco 85
Monte Solaro, Capri, Italy 155
Montenegro 217, **272**
Montjuïc, Barcelona, Spain **42,** 42–43
Moreška (dance) 217
Mosque of Fethiye Tzami, Athens,
    Greece 227
MOSQUES
Blue Mosque, Istanbul, Turkey
    259–260, **260**
Eyüp Sultan Mosque Complex,
    Istanbul, Turkey 266
Hagia Sophia, Istanbul, Turkey **12, 26,**
    248, 256–258, **259**
Mosque of Fethiye Tzami, Athens,
    Greece 227
New Mosque, Istanbul, Turkey 262
Süleymaniye Mosque, Istanbul,
    Turkey 262–263
Mount Srđ, Dubrovnik, Croatia **2–3,** 212
MuCEM (Museum of the Civilizations
    of Europe and the Mediterranean),
    Marseille, France 68
Musée d'Archéologie, Antibes, France 83
Musée d'Archéologie Mediterranéenne,
    Marseille, France 68
Musée d'Art et d'Histoire, Nice, France 79
Musée d'Art Moderne et d'Art
    Contemporain, Nice, France 78
Musée de l'Annonciade, St.-Tropez,
    France 77
Musée des Beaux-Arts, Nice, France 79
Musée Granet, Aix-en-Provence,
    France 70
Musée International d'Art Naïf, Nice,
    France 79
Musée Matisse, Cimiez, France 79
Musée National Marc Chagall, Cimiez,
    France 79
Musée Océanographique, Monaco
    84–85
Musée Picasso, Antibes, France 82–83
Musei Capitolini, Rome, Italy 125
Musei Vaticani, Rome, Italy 141, **142**
Museo Archeologico Nazionale, Naples,
    Italy 145–146
Museo Carmen Thyssen, Málaga,
    Spain 50
Museo Civico, San Gimignano, Italy 119
Museo Civico, Siena, Italy 116–117
Museo dell'Opera del Duomo, Pisa,
    Italy 113
Museo e Parco di Capodimonte, Naples,
    Italy 147–148
Museo Internazionale delle Marionette
    Antonio Pasqualino, Palermo, Italy 168
Museo Nazionale del Bargello, Florence,
    Italy 103–104

Museo Nazionale di Villa Guinigi, Lucca, Italy 115
Museo Nazionale Romano, Rome, Italy 133
Museo Picasso, Málaga, Spain 49
Museo Pio-Clementino, Rome, Italy 141
Museo Salvatore Ferragamo, Florence, Italy 97
Museo Storico dell'Opera del Duomo, Florence, Italy 100, **100**
Museu d'Art Contemporani de Barcelona, Spain 40
Museu d'Història de Barcelona, Spain 37
Museu d'Història de Catalunya, Barcelona, Spain 39
Museu Frederic Marès, Barcelona, Spain 37
Museu Marítim, Barcelona, Spain 39
Museu Nacional d'Art de Catalunya, Barcelona, Spain 42-43
Museu Picasso, Barcelona, Spain 35, **35**
Museum of Asian Art, Corfu, Greece 241
Museum of Cycladic Art, Athens, Greece 232-233
Museum of Greek Folk Art, Athens, Greece 230
Museum of Greek Musical Instruments, Athens, Greece 229
Museum of Religious Art, Iraklio, Greece 246
Museum of the Civilizations of Europe and the Mediterranean (MuCEM), Marseille, France 68
Museum of Turkish & Islamic Arts, Istanbul, Turkey 260-261
MUSEUMS
Acropolis Museum, Athens, Greece 226, **226**
Archaeological Museum, Iraklio, Greece 245
Archaeological Museum, Nafplio, Greece 236
Archaeological Museum, Rhodes, Greece 243
Archaeological Museum of Olympia, Greece 239
Archaeology Museum, Istanbul, Turkey 255-256, **256**
Arles, France 74
Atelier Cézanne, Aix-en-Provence, France 70
Benaki Museum, Athens, Greece 231
Benaki Museum of Islamic Art, Athens, Greece 229
Byzantine Museum, Athens, Greece 232
Ca' d'Oro, Venice, Italy 202, **203**
Ca' Rezzonico, Venice, Italy 193, **193**
CAC (Centro de Arte Contemporáneo), Málaga, Spain 50
Collezione Peggy Guggenheim, Venice, Italy 195, 197, 198, **198**
Dogana di Mare, Venice, Italy 199
Dominican Monastery Museum, Dubrovnik, Croatia 215
Fondation Vasarely, Aix-en-Provence, France 70-71
Fundació Joan Miró 42
Fundació Pilar i Joan Miró, Mallorca, Spain 60
Galleria Borghese, Rome, Italy 139

Galleria degli Uffizi, Florence, Italy 102-103, 111
Galleria dell'Accademia, Florence, Italy 107
Galleria Regionale di Sicilia, Palermo, Italy 167
Gallerie dell'Accademia, Venice, Italy 193-195, 197
Hagia Sophia, Istanbul, Turkey **12, 26, 248,** 256-258, **259**
Historical Museum of Crete, Iraklio, Greece 245-246
Kanellopoulos Museum, Athens, Greece 229-230
Loggia della Signoria, Florence, Italy 102
Metro Galleries, Athens, Greece 232
MuCEM (Museum of the Civilizations of Europe and the Mediterranean), Marseille, France 68
Musée d'Archéologie, Antibes, France 83
Musée d'Archéologie Mediterranéenne, Marseille, France 68
Musée d'Art et d'Histoire, Nice, France 79
Musée d'Art Moderne et d'Art Contemporain, Nice, France 78
Musée de l'Annonciade, St.-Tropez, France 77
Musée des Beaux-Arts, Nice, France 79
Musée Granet, Aix-en-Provence, France 70
Musée International d'Art Naïf, Nice, France 79
Musée Matisse, Cimiez, France 79
Musée National Marc Chagall, Cimiez, France 79
Musée Océanographique, Monaco 84-85
Musée Picasso, Antibes, France 82-83
Musei Capitolini, Rome, Italy 125
Musei Vaticani, Rome, Italy 141, **142**
Museo Archeologico Nazionale, Naples, Italy 145-146
Museo Carmen Thyssen, Málaga, Spain 50
Museo Civico, San Gimignano, Italy 119
Museo Civico, Siena, Italy 116-117
Museo dell'Opera del Duomo, Pisa, Italy 113
Museo e Parco di Capodimonte, Naples, Italy 147-148
Museo Internazionale delle Marionette Antonio Pasqualino, Palermo, Italy 168
Museo Nazionale del Bargello, Florence, Italy 103-104
Museo Nazionale di Villa Guinigi, Lucca, Italy 115
Museo Nazionale Romano, Rome, Italy 133
Museo Picasso, Málaga, Spain 49
Museo Pio-Clementino, Rome, Italy 141
Museo Salvatore Ferragamo, Florence, Italy 97
Museo Storico dell'Opera del Duomo, Florence, Italy 100, **100**

Museu d'Art Contemporani de Barcelona, Spain 40
Museu d'Història de Barcelona, Spain 37
Museu d'Història de Catalunya, Barcelona, Spain 39
Museu Frederic Marès, Barcelona, Spain 37
Museu Fundación Juan March, Mallorca, Spain 60
Museu Marítim, Barcelona, Spain 39
Museu Nacional d'Art de Catalunya, Barcelona, Spain 42-43
Museu Picasso, Barcelona, Spain 35, **35**
Museum of Asian Art, Corfu, Greece 241
Museum of Cycladic Art, Athens, Greece 232-233
Museum of Greek Folk Art, Athens, Greece 230
Museum of Greek Musical Instruments, Athens, Greece 229
Museum of Religious Art, Iraklio, Greece 246
Museum of Turkish & Islamic Arts, Istanbul, Turkey 260-261
National Archaeological Museum, Athens, Greece 234-235
National Gallery of Greece, Athens, Greece 231-232
National Museum of Archaeology, Valletta, Malta 171
Numismatic Museum, Athens, Greece 235
Palazzo Doria Pamphilj, Rome, Italy 135
Palazzo Pitti, Florence, Italy 110
Palazzo Spinola, Genoa, Italy 92
Palazzo Vecchio, Florence, Italy 101
Pinacoteca Provinciale, Bari, Italy 175
Scuola di San Giorgio deg Schiavoni, Venice, Italy 204
Scuola Grande di San Rocco, Venice, Italy 201-202
Sponza Palace, Dubrovnik, Croatia 212-213
Technopolis, Athens, Greece 229
War Museum, Athens, Greece 231, **231**
War Photo Limited, Dubrovnik, Croatia 214-215
Music 27
Mycenae, Greece 238, 299-300

N
Nafplio, Greece **236,** 236-238, 239, 299
Naples, Italy **17,** 144-148, **147**
Duomo & other churches **144,** 146-147
introduction 122, 144-146
map 145
Museo Archeologico Nazionale 145-146
Museo e Parco di Capodimonte 147-148
port logistics 151
restaurants 288-289
shopping 305
south & north of Naples's center 147-148
subterranean Naples 146
National Archaeological Museum, Athens, Greece 234-235

National Gallery of Greece, Athens, Greece 231–232
National Gardens, Athens, Greece 230
National Museum of Archaeology, Valletta, Malta 171
New Mosque, Istanbul, Turkey 262
Nice & around, France 78–83
  Antibes 82–83, 281
  beaches **64**
  Cathédrale Ste.-Réparate 78, 80
  Cimiez 79
  city center 79
  Colline du Château 78
  Église Notre-Dame de l'Annonciation 80
  Église St.-Jacques 80
  map 81
  Musée d'Art et d'Histoire 79
  Musée d'Art Moderne et d'Art Contemporain 78
  Musée des Beaux-Arts 79
  Musée International d'Art Naïf 79
  Nice **78,** 78–81
  port logistics 83
  restaurants 280–281
  transportation 83
  Vieux Nice 78, 80–81
  Villefranche-sur-Mer 79, 82, 83, 281
Numismatic Museum, Athens, Greece 235

O

Oltrarno, Florence, Italy see Ponte Vecchio & the Oltrarno, Florence, Italy
Olympia, Greece **238,** 238–239
Omonia Square, Athens, Greece 233–235
Online information 10
Opéra, Monte-Carlo, Monaco 85
Orsanmichele, Florence, Italy 100–101
Ostuni, Italy 176
Ottoman Empire 20

P

Palace of the Grand Masters, Rhodes, Greece 243
Palacio del Marqués de Dos Aguas 57–58
Palais des Papes, Avignon, France 74
Palamidi Fortress, Nafplio, Greece 236
Palatino, Rome, Italy 125
Palau Reial de Pedralbes, Barcelona, Spain 45, 48
Palazzo Altemps, Rome, Italy 133
Palazzo Bianco, Genoa, Italy 91
Palazzo dei Normanni, Palermo, Italy 166
Palazzo Doria Pamphilj, Rome, Italy 135
Palazzo Doria-Tursi, Genoa, Italy 91
Palazzo Ducale, Venice, Italy 189, 192–193, 196
Palazzo Medici-Riccardi, Florence, Italy 107
Palazzo Pitti, Florence, Italy 110
Palazzo Rosso, Genoa, Italy 91
Palazzo Spinola, Genoa, Italy 92
Palazzo Vecchio, Florence, Italy 101
Palermo, Italy 161, 165–169, **167, 168,** 291–292
Palma de Mallorca, Balearic Islands, Spain 60, **60**
Pantheon, Rome, Italy 133–135, **134,** 136
Parc de la Ciutadella, Barcelona, Spain 48
PARKS
  Gülhane Park, Istanbul, Turkey 257

Parc de la Ciutadella, Barcelona, Spain 48
Pnyka, Athens, Greece 226
Parthenon, Athens, Greece **221,** 223–225, **224**
Passports & visas 273
Peiraiás (Pireas), Greece 235
Peloponnesus, Greece 236–239
  Argos 237–238
  Epidavros 237
  introduction 221
  Katakolon 239
  Mycenae 238, 299–300
  Nafplio **236,** 236–238, 239, 299
  Olympia **238,** 238–239
  port logistics 239
  restaurants 299–300
  Tiryns 237
Petit Palais, Avignon, France 74
Piazza del Campidoglio, Rome, Italy 125–126, **136,** 137
Piazza del Duomo, Florence, Italy 96–97, 100
Piazza del Duomo, Siena, Italy 117
Piazza della Signoria, Florence, Italy 101–102
Piazza di Spagna, Rome, Italy 136, 138
Piazza Navona, Rome, Italy **122,** 132, 137
Piazza San Marco, Venice, Italy **184,** 184–189, 192–193, 196–197
Piazza San Pietro, Rome, Italy **124,** 140
Picasso, Pablo 35, **35,** 49, 82–83
Pinacoteca Provinciale, Bari, Italy 175
Pisa, Italy 89, **112,** 112–113, 285
Plaka, Athens, Greece 229–230
Pnyka, Athens, Greece 226
Pompeii, Italy **148–149,** 149–151, **150,** 289
Ponte Vecchio & the Oltrarno, Florence, Italy 108–111, **110**
Port logistics
  Amalfi Coast, Italy 157
  Athens, Greece 235
  Athens & the islands 235, 239, 243, 247
  Balearic Islands, Spain 63
  Barcelona, Spain 48
  Bari, Italy 177
  Cannes, France 77
  Capri, Italy 155
  Corfu (island), Greece 243
  Crete (island), Greece 247
  Dubrovnik, Croatia 215
  Genoa, Italy 93
  Greek islands 243
  Iraklio, Greece 247
  Istanbul, Turkey 267
  Kuşadası, Turkey 271
  Livorno, Italy 111
  Málaga, Spain 55
  Marseille & Provence, France 75
  Monaco 85
  Naples, Italy 151
  Nice, France 83
  Peloponnesus, Greece 239
  Puglia, Italy 177
  Rhodes (island), Greece 243
  Rome, Italy 143
  Rome & Naples 143, 151, 155, 157
  Santorini (island), Greece 243
  Sicily, Italy 169
  Split, Croatia 207
  Valencia, Spain 58
  Valletta, Malta 173

Venice, Italy 205
  Venice & the Adriatic 205, 207, 215
Port Olímpic, Barcelona, Spain 39, 42
Portofino, Italy 89, **92,** 92–93, 282–283
Positano, Italy 156, 290
Prijeko, Dubrovnik, Croatia 214–215
Provence, France see Marseille & Provence, France
Psirri, Athens, Greece 229
Puglia, Italy 174–177
  Bari 161, 174–175, 177, 292–293
  introduction 161
  Lecce **176,** 177
  Matera 176–177, 293
  port logistics 177
  restaurants 292–293
  trulli **174,** 175–176, 293
Pustjerna, Dubrovnik, Croatia 214

R

Raphael 103, 141–142
Ravello, Italy 157, 290
Rector's Palace, Dubrovnik, Croatia **210,** 211, 213
Restaurants 274–303
  Athens & the islands **23,** 297–300
  Coastal Spain 274–278
  French Riviera & Provence 278–282
  Italian Riviera & Tuscany 282–286
  Rome & Naples 286–293
  Turkey 23, 300–303
  Venice & the Adriatic 189, 293–297
Restrooms 273
Rhodes (island), Greece 242–243, 300, 306
Riomaggiore, Italy 93
Roman Empire
  Arles, France 71
  arts & culture 25–26
  Athens, Greece 227
  Ephesus, Turkey **24,** 251, **268,** 268–271
  Herculaneum, Italy 148–149, 151, 289
  Istanbul, Turkey 260
  Pompeii, Italy **148–149,** 149–151, **150,** 289
  Rome, Italy 125–132, **129, 130**
  Split, Croatia **206,** 206–207
Roman Forum, Athens, Greece 227
Rome, Italy 124–143, **133**
  ancient Rome 125–132, **129, 130**
  Arco di Costantino 131
  Basilica di San Pietro 139–140, **141**
  Campo de' Fiori 133
  Campo Marzio & around 132–133
  Capitolino 125–126
  Cappella Sistina 27, 142–143
  Civitavecchia 143
  Colosseo 129–131, **130**
  Fontana dei Quattro Fiumi **122**
  Fontana di Trevi 135, 136, 138, **138**
  Fori Imperiali 127
  Fori Romano 127–129, **129,** 137
  Galleria Borghese 139
  highlights 143
  introduction 122, 124–125
  maps 126–127, 137
  Musei Capitolini 125
  Musei Vaticani 141, **142**
  Museo Nazionale Romano 133
  Museo Pio-Clementino 141
  Palatino 125
  Palazzo Altemps 133
  Palazzo Doria Pamphilj 135
  Pantheon 133–135, **134,** 136
  Piazza del Campidoglio 125–126, **136,** 137

Piazza di Spagna 136, 138
Piazza Navona **122,** 132, 137
Piazza San Pietro **124,** 140
port logistics 143
restaurants 286-287
Roman coffee & gelato 139
San Clemente 131-132
Santa Maria del Popolo 138
Santa Maria in Aracoeli 126, 137
Santa Maria sopra Minerva 134-135, 137
shopping 305
Spanish Steps **120,** 135, 136, 138
Stanze di Raffaello 141-142
transportation 143
Il Vaticano 139-143, **141, 142**
Vestal Virgins 132
Villa Borghese 139
walk around central Rome **136,** 136-137
Rome & Naples 120-157
Amalfi Coast, Italy **14-15,** 123, **156,**
156-157, 289-291, 305
Bay of Naples **144,** 144-151, **147,**
148-149, 150, 288-289, 305
Capri 123, **152,** 152-155, **154,** 289, 305
maps 123, 126-127, 137, 145
Naples & points south **17,** 122-123,
144, 144-148, **147,** 151, 288-239, 305
port logistics 143, 151, 155, 157
restaurants 286-293
Rome 27, **120,** 122, **122, 124,** 124-143,
129, 130, 133, 134, 136, 138, 141,
142, 286-287, 305
shopping 305
walks **136,** 136-137
see also Bay of Naples, Italy, Naples,
Italy; Rome, Italy

S
Sacra Infermeria, Valletta, Malta 172-173
San Clemente, Rome, Italy 131-132
San Donato, Genoa, Italy 91
San Frediano, Lucca, Italy 115
San Gimignano. Italy 89, **118,** 118-119,
285-286
San Lorenzo & around, Florence, Italy
105-107, **106**
San Michele in Foro, Lucca, Italy 114
San Miniato al Monte, Florence, Italy
110-111
San Polo, Venice, Italy 198-199, 201-202
San Sabino, Bari, Italy 175
San Zaccaria, Venice, Italy 205
Santa Croce, Florence, Italy 104-105, **105**
Santa Maria dei Miracoli, Venice,
Italy 203
Santa Maria del Fiore (Duomo), Florence,
Italy **94,** 96
Campanile 97, 100
Duomo **98,** 98-99, **99**
Museo Storico dell'Opera del
Duomo 100, **100**
Santa Maria del Mar, Barcelona, Spain
35, 38
Santa Maria del Pi, Barcelona, Spain 36
Santa Maria del Popolo, Rome, Italy 138
Santa Maria della Salute, Venice, Italy
197, 198
Santa Maria di Castello, Genoa. Italy 91
Santa Maria Draperis Church, Istanbul,
Turkey 264
Santa Maria Gloriosa dei Frari, Venice,
Italy 199, 201
Santa Maria in Aracoeli, Rome, Italy
126, 137
Santa Maria Novella, Florence, Italy 108

Santa Maria sopra Minerva, Rome, Italy
134-135, 137
Sant'Agostino, Genoa, Italy 91
Santi Giovanni e Paolo, Venice, Italy
203-205
Santorini (island), Greece **218-** 242,
243, 300
Sardana (dance) 34
Savoca, Sicily, Italy 163
Scuola di San Giorgio degli Schiavoni,
Venice, Italy 204
Scuola Grande di San Rocco, Venice,
Italy 201-202
Selçuk, Turkey 270-271
SHOPPING 304-306
Central Market, Athens, Greece
234, 306
Grand Bazaar, Istanbul, Turkey
261-262, **262,** 306
Spice Market, Istanbul, Turkey 263
Shore excursions 10
Sicily, Italy 162-169
Etna 165, **165,** 169
food & drink **22,** 23
introduction 160-161
Palermo 161, 165-169, **167, 168,**
291-292
port logistics 169
restaurants 291
shopping 305
Taormina 160-164, **162,** 169, 291
Sicily, Malta, & Puglia 158-177
Malta **21, 159,** 161, **170,** 170-173, **172,**
292, 305-306
map 160-161
port logistics 169, 177
Puglia 161, **174,** 174-177, **176,**
292-293
restaurants 291-293
shopping 305-306
Sicily **22,** 23, 160-169, **162, 165, 167,**
168, 291-292, 305
see also Malta; Puglia, Italy; Sicily, Italy
Siena, Italy 89, **116,** 116-117, 285
Sistine Chapel, Rome, Italy see Cappella
Sistina, Rome, Italy
Site Memorial Les Milles, Aix-en-
Provence, France 71
Slovenia see Koper, Slovenia
Sorrento, Italy **14-15,** 123, **156,** 290-291
Southern Golden Horn, Istanbul, Turkey
263, 266
Spain see Coastal Spain
Spanish Steps, Rome, Italy **120,** 135,
136, 138
Spice Market, Istanbul, Turkey 263
Split, Croatia 180, **206,** 206-207, 296
Sponza Palace, Dubrovnik, Croatia
212-213
St. Jean Bazilikası, Selçuk, Turkey 271
St. John's Co-Cathedral, Valletta,
Malta 171
St. Paul's Shipwreck, Valletta, Malta 172
St. Peter's Basilica, Rome, Italy see
Basilica di San Pietro, Rome, Italy
St.-Tropez, France 76, 77, 280
Stanze di Raffaello, Rome, Italy 141-142
Stoa of Attalos, Athens, Greece 227
Stradun area, Dubrovnik, Croatia 209,
211, 212-213, **213**
Süleymaniye Mosque, Istanbul, Turkey
262-263
Syntagma Square. Athens, Greece
230-232

T
Taormina, Sicily, Italy 160-164, **162,**
169, 291
Teatro Greco, Taormina, Sicily, Italy 164
Technopolis, Athens, Greece 229
Temple of Hephaistos, Athens, Greece
226-227
Theater of Dionysos, Athens. Greece 225
Tipping 273
Tiryns, Greece 237
Tomb of the Unknown Soldier, Athens,
Greece 230
Topkapı Palace, Istanbul. Turkey
252-256, **255**
Torre Pendente (Leaning Tower), Pisa
Italy **112,** 112-113
Tower of the Winds, Athens, Greece 227
Transportation
Athens, Greece 235
Barcelona, Spain 43, 48
Bay of Naples, Italy 151
Capri, Italy 155
Florence, Italy 111
Herculaneum & Pompeii, Italy 151
Livorno, Italy 111, 113, 115, 117, 119
Lucca, Italy 115
Marseille & Provence, France 75
Naples, Italy 151
Nice, France 83
Pisa, Italy 113
Rome, Italy 143
San Gimignano, Italy 119
Siena, Italy 117
Trulli (conical dwellings), Puglia, Italy
174, 175-176, 293
Turkey 248-271
Ephesus **24,** 251, **268,** 263-271, 303
introduction 250-251
Istanbul **12,** 23, **26, 248, 250, 252,**
252-267, **255, 256, 259, 260,**
262, 264, 306
maps 251, 253, 265
Meryemana 271, **271**
money matters 273
port logistics 267, 271
restaurants 23, 300-303
Selçuk 270-271
shopping 306
walks **264,** 264-265
Tuscany, Italy see Italian Riviera & Tuscany

V
Valencia, Spain 31, **57,** 57-58, 277
Valletta, Malta **21,** 161, **170,** 171-173, 292
Van Gogh, Vincent 74
Il Vaticano (Vatican) 139-143, **141, 142**
Venice, Italy 180-205, **181**
Basilica di San Marco 185-189,
186-187, 188
building Venice 190-191, **190-191**
Ca' d'Oro 202, **203**
Ca' Rezzonico 193, **193**
Caffè Florian 189
Campanile 189
Canal Grande **182,** 182-184, **203**
Cannaregio 202-203
Castello 203-205
Collezione Peggy Guggenheim 195,
197, 198, **198**
Dogana di Mare 199
Dorsoduro 193-199
Gallerie dell'Accademia 193-195, 197
gondolas **178,** 200, **200, 201**
highlights 205

history 20
introduction 180-181
Madonna dell'Orto 202-203
maps 183, 196-197
Palazzo Ducale 189, 192-193, 196
Piazza San Marco **184,** 184-189,
192-193, 196-197
port logistics 205
restaurants 189, 293-295
San Marco & Dorsoduro walk 196-197
San Polo 198-199, 201-202
San Zaccaria 205
Santa Maria dei Miracoli 203
Santa Maria della Salute 197, 198
Santa Maria Gloriosa dei Frari 199,
201
Santi Giovanni e Paolo 203-205
Scuola di San Giorgio degli Schiavoni
204
Scuola Grande di San Rocco 201-202
shopping 306
vocabulary 195
Venice & the Adriatic 178-217
Dubrovnik, Croatia **2-3,** 180, **208,**
208-215, **210, 213, 214,** 296-297

Hvar, Croatia 216, 296
introduction 180-181
Koper, Slovenia 216-217
Korčula, Croatia **216,** 217, 296
Kotor, Montenegro 217
maps 180-181, 183, 196-197, 211
port logistics 205, 207, 215
restaurants 189, 293-297
shopping 306
Split, Croatia 180, **206,** 206-207, 296
Venice, Italy 20, **178,** 180-205, **182,**
184, 186-187, 188, 190-191, 193,
198, 200, 203, 293-295, 306
walks 196-197, 210-211
see also Dubrovnik, Croatia; Venice,
Italy
Venus de Milo 241
Vernazza, Italy 93
Vestal Virgins 132
Vieux Nice, France 78, 80-81
Villa Borghese, Rome, Italy 139
Villa Ephrussi de Rothschild, Cap Ferrat,
France 82
Villa Grecque Kérylos, Beaulieu-sur-Mer,
France 82

Villa San Michele, Anacapri, Italy
154-155
Villefranche-sur-Mer, France 79, 82,
83, 281
Visas & passports 273
Vittoriosa, Malta 173

W
WALKS
Aix-en-Provence, France **72,** 72-73
Barcelona, Spain 36-37, **40,** 40-41
Dubrovnik, Croatia **210,** 210-211
Istanbul, Turkey **264,** 264-265
Nice, France 80-81
Rome, Italy **136,** 136-137
Venice, Italy 196-197
Walled cities **208,** 209, 210-211
War Museum, Athens, Greece 231,
231
War Photo Limited, Dubrovnik, Croatia
214-215
Waterfront, Barcelona, Spain 38-39,
39, 42
Weather 9, 272
World War II 21, **21,** 71

ACKNOWLEDGMENTS

Some of the material in this publication is based on previous guides published by National Geographic and written by Tim Jepson, Fiona Dunlop, Damien Simonis, Barbara A. Noe, Sari Gilbert, Michael Brouse, Erla Zwingle, Rudolf Abraham, Mike Gerrard, Joanna Kakissis, Tristan Rutherford, and Kathryn Tomasetti.

ILLUSTRATIONS CREDITS

Cover, imagIN.gr Photography/Shutterstock; Spine, Miguel Garcia Saavedra/Shutterstock; 2-3, Alan Copson/JAI/Corbis; 4, fotoVoyager/iStockphoto.com; 8, 5ugarless/iStockphoto; 11, letty17/iStockphoto.com; 12, Jean-Pierre Lescourret/Imagebroker/Photolibrary/Getty Images; 14-5, Tino Soriano; 17, Tino Soriano; 18-9, Tino Soriano; 21, Hulton-Deutsch Collection/Corbis; 22, Tino Soriano; 23, Silwen Randebrook/Imagebroker/photolibrary/Getty Images; 24, tunart/iStockphoto; 26, anilakduygu/iStockphoto; 28, Madrugada Verde/Shutterstock; 30, mauro grigollo/iStockphoto.com; 35, Tino Soriano; 36, Tino Soriano; 39, Philip Lange/Shutterstock; 40, Tino Soriano; 42, Tino Soriano; 44, prognone/iStockphoto; 47, Tino Soriano; 49, Tino Soriano; 52-3, Maltings Partnership, Derby, England; 54, Tino Soriano; 56, fauk74/iStockphoto; 57, Tino Soriano; 59, Slow Images/Getty Images; 60, Tino Soriano; 64, hallphoto/Shutterstock; 66, Konstantin/Shutterstock; 68, VIEW Pictures Ltd/Alamy; 71, Itinerant Lens/Shutterstock; 72, Gerard Sioen/Anzenberger; 76, johnbraid/Shutterstock.com; 80, Malgorzata Drewniak/Shutterstock; 82, Derek Gordon/Shutterstock; 84, photovideostock/iStockphoto; 86, Estremo/Shutterstock; 90, fotofojanini/iStockphoto; 92, maudanros/Shutterstock; 94, Matt Propert/National Geographic Creative; 98, Scala/Art Resource, NY; 99 (UP), Maltings Partnership, Derby, England; 99 (LO), Maltings Partnership, Derby, England; 100, Tino Soriano; 105, Tino Soriano; 106, Matt Propert/National Geographic Creative; 108, Tino Soriano; 110-118, Matt Propert/National Geographic Creative; 120, FrankvandenBergh/iStockphoto.com; 122-130, Matt Propert/National Geographic Creative; 133, Bob Krist; 134-142, Matt Propert/National Geographic Creative; 136, Matt Propert/National Geographic Creative; 144, Tino Soriano; 146-7,

Maltings Partnership, Derby, England; 148, Alfio Ferlito/Shutterstock; 150, Tino Soriano; 152, Mikadun/Shutterstock; 154, Tino Soriano; 156, Tino Soriano; 158, szgogh/iStockphoto; 162, Tino Soriano; 164, Erik Kruthoff/National Geographic Your Shot; 166, Tino Soriano; 168, duchy/Shutterstock; 170, Valeria73/Shutterstock; 172, Tino Soriano; 174, Cassianus12/iStockphoto; 176, cenix/iStockphoto; 178, fotoVoyager/iStockphoto; 181-184, Matt Propert/National Geographic Creative; 186-7, Maltings Partnership, Derby, England; 188, Matt Propert/National Geographic Creative; 190, borsheim/iStockphoto; 190-1, Maltings Partnership, Derby, England; 193-203, Matt Propert/National Geographic Creative; 206, Mrak.hr/Shutterstock; 208, Frederic49/Shutterstock; 210, villorejo/Shutterstock; 213, Brian Bumby/National Geographic Your Shot; 214, Erica Schroeder/Dreamstime.com; 216, Przemyslaw Skibinski/Shutterstock; 218, Pixachi/Shutterstock; 221, Lambros Kazan/Shutterstock; 222, Anastasios71/Shutterstock; 224-5, Maltings Partnership, Derby, England; 226, Grigorios Moraitis/iStockphoto.com; 228, Travel Pictures/Alamy; 231, War Museum Internet Creative Commons © Konstantinos Stampoulis; 233, Alfonso de Tomas/Shutterstock; 236, jvoisey/iStockphoto; 238, oversnap/iStockphoto; 240, Ljupco Smokovski/Shutterstock; 242, Michael Good/Photolibrary/Getty Images; 244, majaiva/iStockphoto; 246, Anterovium/iStockphoto; 248, tunart/iStockphoto; 250, Juergen Stampe/Look-foto/photolibrary/Getty Images; 252, tunart/iStockphoto; 255, ARSELA/iStockphoto.com; 256, Prometheus72/Shutterstock; 259, Hebert Spichtinger/photolibrary/Getty Images; 260, tanhi36/iStockphoto.com; 262, onfilm/iStockphoto; 264, Julia161/Dreamstime.com; 268, Tomasetti & Rutherford; 270, volmart/iStockphoto; 272, Kushch Dmitry/Shutterstock.

National Geographic
TRAVELER
the mediterranean

Published by the National Geographic Society
Gary E. Knell, *President and Chief Executive Officer*
John M. Fahey, *Chairman of the Board*
Declan Moore, *Chief Media Officer*
Chris Johns, *Chief Content Officer*
Keith Bellows, *Senior Vice President and Editor in Chief, National Geographic Travel Media*

Prepared by the Book Division
Hector Sierra, *Senior Vice President and General Manager*
Janet Goldstein, *Senior Vice President and Editorial Director*
Jonathan Halling, *Creative Director*
Marianne R. Koszorus, *Design Director*
Barbara A. Noe, *Senior Editor, National Geographic Travel Books*
R. Gary Colbert, *Production Director*
Jennifer A. Thornton, *Director of Managing Editorial*
Susan S. Blair, *Director of Photography*
Meredith C. Wilcox, *Director, Administration and Rights Clearance*

Staff for This Book
Caroline Hickey, *Project Manager*
Jane Sunderland, *Text Editor*
Kay Kobor Hankins, *Art Director and Photo Editor*
Federica Romagnoli, *Researcher*
Carl Mehler, *Director of Maps*
Mike McNey & Mapping Specialists, *Map Production*
Nicholas Rosenbach, *Map Researcher*
Marshall Kiker, *Associate Managing Editor*
Mike O'Connor, *Production Editor*
Galen Young, *Rights Clearance Specialist*
Katie Olsen, *Design Production Specialist*
Nicole Miller, *Design Production Assistant*
Marlena Serviss, *Contributor*
Robert L. Barr, *Manager, Production Services*

The information in this book has been carefully checked and to the best of our knowledge is accurate. However, details are subject to change, and the National Geographic Society cannot be responsible for such changes, or for errors or omissions. Assessments of sites, hotels, and restaurants are based on the author's subjective opinions, which do not necessarily reflect the publisher's opinion.

The National Geographic Society is one of the world's largest nonprofit scientific and educational organizations. Founded in 1888 to "increase and diffuse geographic knowledge," the member-supported Society works to inspire people to care about the planet. Through its online community, members can get closer to explorers and photographers, connect with other members around the world, and help make a difference. National Geographic reflects the world through its magazines, television programs, films, music and radio, books, DVDs, maps, exhibitions, live events, school publishing programs, interactive media, and merchandise. *National Geographic* magazine, the Society's official journal, published in English and 38 local-language editions, is read by more than 60 million people each month. The National Geographic Channel reaches 440 million households in 171 countries in 38 languages. National Geographic Digital Media receives more than 25 million visitors a month. National Geographic has funded more than 10,000 scientific research, conservation, and exploration projects and supports an education program promoting geography literacy. For more information, visit www.nationalgeographic.com.

For more information, please call 1-800-NGS LINE (647-5463) or write to the following address:

National Geographic Society
1145 17th Street N.W.
Washington, D.C. 20036-4688 U.S.A.

For information about special discounts for bulk purchases, please contact National Geographic Books Special Sales: ngspecsales@ngs.org

For rights or permissions inquiries, please contact National Geographic Books Subsidiary Rights: ngbookrights@ngs.org

National Geographic Traveler: The Mediterranean
ISBN: 978-1-4262-1463-9

Printed in Hong Kong
14/THK/1

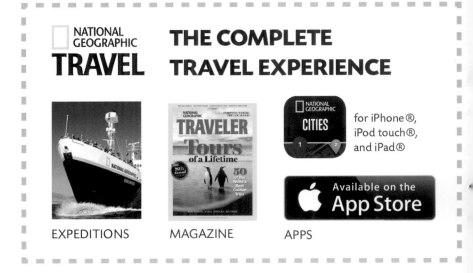